WITHDRAWN

£25.99

Fundamentals of Computer Architecture

An accompanying
CD is enclosed
inside this book

Fundamentals of Computer Architecture

Mark Burrell

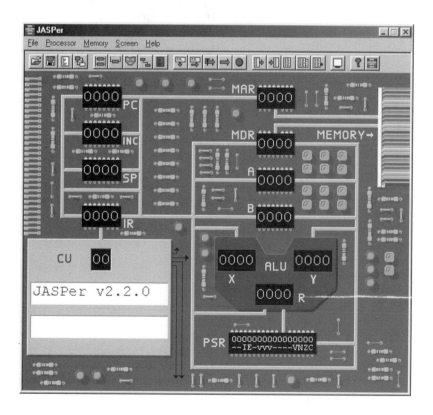

First published 2004 by
PALGRAVE MACMILLAN
Houndmills, Basingstoke, Hampshire RG21 6XS and
175 Fifth Avenue, New York, N.Y. 10010
Companies and representatives throughout the world

PALGRAVE MACMILLAN is the global academic imprint of the Palgrave
Macmillan division of St. Martin's Press, LLC and of Palgrave Macmillan Ltd.
Macmillan© is a registered trademark in the United States, United Kingdom
and other countries. Palgrave is a registered trademark in the European Union
and other countries.

ISBN 0-333-99866-9

This book is printed on paper suitable for recycling and made from fully
managed and sustained forest sources.

A catalogue record for this book is available from the British Library.

10   9   8   7   6   5   4   3   2   1
13 12 11 10 09 08 07 06 05 04

Printed and bound in China

Contents

Contents

Preface

What Is This Book About?

This book teaches the reader how the key components of any computer - the processor and memory - actually work. This core topic of computing is known as computer architecture and organization.

► *Computer architecture* describes the properties of the computer as viewed from the perspective of the programmer;
► *Computer organization* describes the internal properties of the computer as viewed from the perspective of the hardware engineer.

The book is aimed at all first-year undergraduates taking a computer architecture and organization module. Such a course is normally compulsory on computing degrees, software engineering degrees and HN computing courses. Additionally, many electronic engineering undergraduate courses have similar modules in their first year. It will also be useful to those studying a taught conversion Masters in computing, as well as further reading for 'A' level computing students.

Many undergraduates find the topic of computer architecture immensely challenging - this book, through many examples throughout the text and the use of simulation software, leads the student to a successful completion of their first computer architecture course.

To meet this essential aim the text is based around a software simulation of a simple processor. By using a simplified processor the student gains an understanding of the fundamental concepts of computer systems architecture and organization, upon which he or she can subsequently build to understand the more advanced facilities and techniques employed by modern day processors.

Note For Lecturers

This book is intended to be the primary text for a first computer architecture course - PDF slides for each chapter are available from the book website (details are within this preface).

The book can be used in a number of ways, to suit the wide range of computer architecture syllabi.

► It can be used as sole material for a 24 lecture course;
► It can be used in conjunction with other materials in order to best fulfil your own unique syllabus, in order to give flexibility for either a 12 or a 24 lecture course. Each syllabus for a computer architecture course is slightly different, so it is expected that you will select the particular chapters that your syllabus concentrates on, using further material to expand your appropriate areas of interest.

The exercises at the end of chapters can be used as either seminar or homework materials as required. All solutions are available to lecturers from the website listed later.

It is worth noting that the student is expected to have little or no programming knowledge prior to studying this text. However, although programming concepts are introduced, it is expected that the student will at least be undertaking a programming course concurrently while studying this material.

How Is The Book Organized?

This book consists of four key parts, together with a number of appendices. The main parts are: -

The building blocks - which contains chapters on designing a simple processor, fundamental concepts, registers, buses, memory, the ALU, and how our processor runs stored programs;

Using the processor - which contains chapters on writing structured programs, stacks and writing subroutines, addressing modes, memory-mapped I/O, interrupts and systems software;

Under the bonnet - which contains chapters on micro-instructions, building an instruction set, and the control unit;

The real world - which closes with chapters on advanced features found in microprocessors in the wild.

Each section consists of a number of chapters - the largest sections being the first two. Each chapter consists of the same sub-divisions. These are:

▶ An overview;

▶ The main body of the chapter (using practical examples, either programs for a simulated processor called JASP or circuit designs for a circuit simulation tool called Digital Works);

▶ A summary;

▶ Where appropriate, a set of self test questions - answers are in appendix G;

▶ Where appropriate, a set of further exercises to aid the learning process.

The contents of each section and the chapters within it are given below.

Part 1 - The Building Blocks

We look at the processor from the viewpoint of the hardware engineer. This part establishes the key concepts and introduces a simple processor, focusing on how it can be built from relatively basic elements (registers, an ALU, a control unit, and buses to interconnect them). We then discuss how these elements, in conjunction with a memory, form a basic computer system.

Part 2 - Using The Processor

We look at the processor from the point of view of the programmer. This part establishes the practical usability of such a processor, starting with simple programs and building up to using memory-mapped I/O and interrupts. Additionally, tools that can be used to aid program development are discussed.

Part 3 - Under The Bonnet

After looking at the processor from the programmer's perspective it is now time to return to the viewpoint of the hardware engineer to examine the fetch-execute cycle in more depth. We discuss how we can extend our instruction set to provide further functionality and then finally, we look at how we could extend the hardware of our processor to give yet more functionality.

Part 4 - The Real World

In this final part we take a look at the features of real processors and point out the similarities they share with our simple processor - and hence come full circle by showing the relevance, simplicity and practicality of our simple processor as a basis for understanding modern processors.

Appendices

The appendices contain reference material for the JASP processor and its instruction sets as well as a brief introduction to the Digital Works package.

Software

The software packages distributed with this text are the JASP toolkit and Digital Works. Each is detailed below.

The JASP Toolkit

The JASP toolkit is based around the design of a simple processor named JASP - *Just Another Simulated Processor*.

The main tool is JASPer (*Just Another Simulated Processor emulator*) - a simulated processor used throughout this text.

The set of tools include:

- ► *JASPer* - the simulated processor;
- ► *Aspen* - a command-line version of JASPer that can be used with DOS or Linux;
- ► *The JASP C−− Cross-compiler* - a cross-compiler for the JASP architecture;
- ► *The JASP Cross-assembler* - a cross-assembler, written in Perl, that assembles programs for the JASP architecture;
- ► The basic and advanced JASP instruction sets;
- ► Two software libraries, for use with each instruction set.

Most screen shots of JASPer within this text make use of a simple graphic display to better show the functionality of the processor.

All the tools within the JASP toolkit are copyright Mark Burrell, except for the C−− cross-compiler which is copyright David Harrison.

Digital Works

The Digital Works package is copyright *Mechanique* and is distributed by Matrix Multimedia Ltd.

Their website is http://www.matrixmultimedia.co.uk

What Is On The Accompanying CD?

On the accompanying CD you will find:

▶ The JASP toolkit;
▶ The Digital Works package (30 day license);
▶ All example programs;
▶ All example circuit diagrams;

Is There A Website?

Yes. It's here:

`http://www.palgrave.com/science/computing/burrell/`

On the site you'll find such useful materials as:

▶ The latest copy of the JASP toolkit;
▶ A link to the Digital Works website;
▶ Further exercises;
▶ Lecturers' materials including answers to exercises and PDF slides for each chapter;
▶ Errata for this text.

About The Author

Mark is a Principal Lecturer within the School of Informatics at Northumbria University located in the North-East of England. He has taught computing fundamentals for many years and his package JASPer has been used as a teaching aid in this area since 1995.

Mark has held a UK Private Pilot's License since 1995, although he doesn't get time to use it these days - instead he currently get his kicks by riding fast motorcycles.

Acknowledgements

I would like to thank the many friends and colleagues who helped me, in so many ways, to write this text. They include Jago Boardman, Michael Brockway, Ian Chilton, Jonathan Edwards, Mark Elsom-Cook, David Harrison, William Henderson, Dan Hodgson, Adrian Jones, Alun Moon, Tony Morrell, John Morton, Adrian Robson, Gregor Schwake and Iain Wallace. Apologies to all those I have inadvertently missed out, my thanks and appreciation go to you all.

I must also thank Dave Hatter and Rebecca Mashayekh of Palgrave and John Dobson of Matrix Multimedia for their great support of this text.

Additionally, I must thank the couple of thousand students who have helped field test JASPer for the last eight years or so. Special mention goes to those students who took time out to find errors, query particular sections, and generally help improve this text, notably Merle Cavagin, Sam Stevens, Lee Charlton and Wai-Ching Leung. This text is better for their input.

Lastly, as is traditional, I must of course point out that any remaining errors within this text are entirely my own.

Part I

The Building Blocks

In this section we look at the processor from the viewpoint of the hardware engineer.

Introducing The Processor

CHAPTER OVERVIEW

In this chapter we describe the fundamental features of a computer system and focus on the use of the processor.

This chapter includes:

▶ The key aspects of a computer;

▶ A brief history of the computer and its place within our modern society;

▶ The typical components within a computer system, focusing on the processor;

▶ The simulated processor, *JASPer* - the primary tool with which we are going to study the fundamental concepts of modern computers.

1.1 Computers Are Everywhere

You've seen a computer before - they are in almost every office, every shop, every school classroom and many private homes - if you closed your eyes right now you could picture a computer. When many people think of a computer they think of the typical desktop PC, or laptop, or even the PDA (all shown in figure 1.1). Within this chapter I'll show you that computers come in more guises than these, and yet they all contain the same fundamental components.

Before we open up a computer and take a peek inside, the first thing we should do is throw away all our current conceptions (and misconceptions) of what we

3

think a computer is, and try to answer the question - *what is a computer?* It isn't as simple as you might first think - in fact, before you read any further, try writing down five points that you think describe what a computer is, I'll give you my five points shortly.

Figure 1.1   *The more visible computers - a PC, a laptop and a PDA*

A hundred years ago a *computer* was a *human being*, either a mathematician or someone who worked for a mathematician. A computer was someone who performed calculations to find the answer to a complex mathematical equation. They might not have even understood the calculations they were performing (in fact, it was often found that those individuals who *didn't* understand the complex calculations actually performed better. Why? Because they wouldn't be tempted to perform short cuts on their set of operations, which could actually introduce errors into the calculations). A good computer simply followed very stringent rules. Often, a calculation might be performed by a set of computers (people) in a room - in that case a particular set of rules for one individual computer in the room might have been something like:

▶ Take the card from the person on your left;
▶ Multiply the last number on the card by three;
▶ Write the result on the card;
▶ Hand the card to the person on your right;
▶ Repeat all operations again.

Human computers like this were used as late as the 1940s. Richard Feynman (a physicist who would later win a Nobel prize) used his team of people in this way to perform key calculations for the American atomic bomb programme.

It wasn't until the early 1940s that electrical devices were first referred to (most probably by an American called Atanasoff) as computers, and over the years the rough definition of a computer has evolved to this:

► It must take *input* of some sort;
► It must produce *output* of some sort;
► It must *process* the information somehow;
► It must have some sort of *information store*;
► It must have some way of *controlling* what it does.

I bet my set of points differ from yours.

So, a computer is a device that meets the above five constraints - and even though we don't yet fully know what these points mean (we'll cover each point in more detail soon) - please note that being able to run a word processor, or a spreadsheet, or play MP3 sound files are most definitely not in our definition!

At the heart of any computer you will find a component called a *processor*, more formally described as a *Central Processing Unit*, or *CPU*. A processor that is constructed completely as a very large electrical circuit - called an *integrated circuit* - on one single chip of silicon (colloquially called a *computer chip*) is called a *microprocessor*. What we term a computer these days is more accurately called a *microprocessor based computer system* or *micro-computer*.

Here, at the beginning of the twenty-first century, microprocessors pervade our society. Every day you may use anything up to a couple of hundred microprocessors, and most of the time you aren't even aware of them. They are in everything from your mobile phone to your microwave. They are in most modern cars, controlling everything from the windscreen wipers and electric windows to the engine management system that ensures the optimal performance of the engine. In our modern world most microprocessors no longer come in large rectangular boxes - the conventional guise of a modern personal computer.

It used to be said that any electronic device worth over 100 Euros had a microprocessor in it - but microprocessors can now be built so cheaply that the cost of an electronic device no longer gives an indication as to whether the device contains a microprocessor or not.

It is these microprocessors used within *embedded systems* (contained in some greater device, like a car or a mobile phone - such that the microprocessor is part of the greater device) that are becoming the largest market within computing. Never has there been a better time to gain a fundamental knowledge of how microprocessors work, as this knowledge is increasingly in demand now that microprocessors are truly everywhere.

1.2 A Very Brief History Of The Computer

1.2.1 Babbage And His Difference Engine

Let's take a step back and move on to a further question - *who invented the computer?* This depends on which history books you read and indeed, which court judgements you believe (this question has even been ruled on by a judge before now, as I will mention shortly). The truth is that key elements of the computer were invented by a number of people, some of these people have since been given credit, while others have gone relatively unsung.

The birth of computers can be traced back to the mid nineteenth century when an Englishman called Charles Babbage invented mechanical machines, using features of earlier mechanical machines, called the *Difference Engine* and the *Analytical Engine*. The latter was never completed as Babbage's main investor (the British government) eventually withdrew his funding - he was not to be the last hardware engineer to overstep his budget! Many features of a modern computer are based on ideas first formulated by Babbage - he is considered by many to have been a century ahead of his time.

1.2.2 Turing And His Machine

It took many decades before others would carry on the work started by Babbage. Alan Turing, a leading mathematician in the twentieth century, wrote a defining paper in 1936 called '*On Computable Numbers, With An Application To The Entscheidungsproblem*'[Tur36] where he solved a famous mathematical problem by defining a concept he called a *Turing Machine* - the practical grounding for computing machines. Turing would make a major impact in computing during World War II when he developed electronic machines to break the German Enigma codes. Wartime generated massive development of the early computing devices, mostly by the Allies in the United Kingdom and in the United States.

NOTES

Andrew Hodges wrote an excellent biography of Alan Turing [Hod92].

In the United Kingdom, electronic devices of increasing complexity were used at Bletchley Park (home to the UK's Code and Cipher School - later to become famous as 'Station X') to attempt to break the German wartime codes, of which the most complex were the codes produced by the Enigma machine - a part mechanical, part electronic, cipher machine. The Enigma machine was used throughout the German military, and so cracking the Enigma could provide the Allies with information to change the course of the war. Turing, using the

NOTES

[Aga01] describes the early developments of the computer.

ideas he first developed in the 1930s, designed machines to decipher Enigma encryption.

Station X was also the birthplace of a machine called *Colossus*. Colossus was effectively the first programmable logic calculator.

In the United States too, many organizations were attempting to build the first electronic computers, to aid the war effort. These included Howard Aiken's Harvard Mark 1, and ENIAC, built by John Mauchly and J. Presper Eckert. ENIAC arrived too late to help in the war effort but was later used to test key calculations for the atomic bomb programme. It was Mauchly and Eckert who later attempted to use the courts to claim the patent for the digital computer as their own; after many years their claim was thrown out.

NOTES

The life of John von Neumann is described in [Pou92]. von Neumann compares the computer with the brain in [vN00].

1.2.3 The Birth Of The Von Neumann Architecture

After the war many organizations around the World joined in the efforts to produce electronic computers. One worthy of note was known as the Manchester 'Baby', built at Manchester University - it was the first computer that stored its programs and its data in the same memory - an idea that is used by almost all modern computers today; it's referred to now as a *von Neumann architecture*, named after the famous Hungarian born mathematician John von Neumann. John von Neumann was the author of a key report produced in 1945 that laid down the structure of a stored program computer that used binary arithmetic.

DEFINITION

Transistor *: A transistor is an electronic device that can be thought of as an electronic switch. They can be combined to build special circuits called* logic gates*, and we will examine these in chapter 3.*

DEFINITION

Integrated Circuit *: A circuit formed completely on a single piece of silicon - colloquially known as a* chip.

1.2.4 The Pace Of Development

Rather than mention every key development since the 1940s, let's just look at some key moments in computing history since then. The invention of the *transistor* in 1947 is one of those moments, it signalled the start of much more reliable hardware, as earlier vacuum tube technology was very unreliable.

In 1958 the invention of the *integrated circuit* changed the world - it meant that it was now much easier to build more complex devices. As the 1960s went by, more and more electronics could be packed into integrated circuits and in 1971 a young company called *Intel* produced the very first microprocessor. It was called the *Intel 4004* and contained around 2300 transistors on a single chip - this was the chip that dawned the microcomputer revolution. The grandchild of this chip would be at the heart of the first IBM PCs that began shipping in 1981. The technology to build integrated circuits is now so advanced that we are close to having one billion transistors on a single chip.

Developments in computing have been divided retrospectively into separate ages based on the key technologies used; these boundaries can also be shown to have a relationship with the developments in programming. No one quite agrees on the boundaries of these ages, as in reality they have over-lapped quite significantly. Table 1.1 shows the most often quoted dates for each age. Some people argue that we are now in the fifth age of computing, but this is disputed by others as the fourth age technology (VLSI) is still being used, albeit at an extremely high level of integration.

Throughout this book we will focus on the usage of computing devices, individual technologies won't be discussed any further.

Age	Time Period	Technology Used
0th.	pre 1943-5	Mechanical devices
1st.	1943-5 — 1955-9	Vacuum tubes
2nd.	1955-9 — 1964-5	The use of transistors and printed circuits
3rd.	1964-5 — 1972-80	The rise of the integrated circuit
4th.	1972-80 — present	LSI and VLSI

Table 1.1   *The ages of computing - based on technology used*

1.3 Inside A Computer

Now it's time for us to take a peek inside a modern computer to see what's inside. In figure 1.2 I've taken the case off a typical PC, and as you can see, even with many of the internal cables removed, it looks complicated and it's pretty hard to see exactly what is in there, but the main parts have been labelled.

▶ The most important component is the processor. Throughout this book we will focus on the processor - it runs a series of instructions (called a *program*), and controls the activity of all other components within the computer;

▶ Next we have the *memory* chips. These are used to store our data and instructions - there are different types of memory chips, and they are discussed in more detail in chapter 7;

▶ The other labelled components include the hard disk, the graphics card, network card and the power supply. All are used by modern computer systems, but are actually quite minor in the scale of things - we don't need to refer to them to learn how a computer works.

What does the processor do? Essentially it is the core of the computer - everything else just helps it to do its job. Its job is to take information and follow strict rules (the program) to produce output. What does that mean? Let us look at an example - when you use an ATM to get money out of your bank account you are using a computer with a processor at its centre. You give the ATM information, both from your bank card (which contains your bank details on a magnetic strip) and by hand (as you type in your secret key number and also enter how much money you want to withdraw).

Hard Disk

Memory

Processor

Power Supply

Graphics Card

Sound Card

Network Card

Figure 1.2   *The innards of a typical personal computer today*

The ATM uses that information to talk to other computers (which contain your current bank balance) to find out if you can have the money or not. Once the ATM has done that it presents information (using a display screen) about your account and dispenses your money. An ATM fulfills all the rules we saw before that described a computer.

DEFINITION

PC : *Personal Computer - a desktop machine usually used by one person at a time. Although other companies produced personal computers before them, it was IBM that cornered the market. IBM first produced their PCs in 1981.*

▶ *It must take input of some sort* - the ATM takes your bank details from your bank card and information from the keypad detailing how much money you require;

▶ *It must produce output of some sort* - the ATM drives a screen display and also controls a set of motors that are used to dispense cash;

▶ *It must process the information somehow* - the ATM uses information in its information store, together with the details you have given it and - following precise rules - it figures out if you can have the cash you require or not;

▶ *It must have some sort of information store* - the ATM gathers information on your bank details from another computer and stores this locally - it is this information it uses to process your requirements;

> ▶ *It must have some way of controlling what it does* - the ATM can change what it does - if your account is in credit, you can have money; if it's in debit, you can't.

It is the processor that takes the information given to it, processes that information and produces some form of output.

NOTES

[Lev94] gives an interesting look into the world of the computing industry in the 1970s and 1980s.

1.4 The Minimalist Approach

As we saw when looking into the case of a typical PC, a computer can look pretty complicated. So instead, we will spend our time looking at something simpler - something that has all the key features of a modern computer, but without all the complexities of the system we can see in figure 1.2. Once we manage to understand our simpler computer, we can scale back up to the complex computer systems that we see around us everyday.

What are the smallest number of components we need to build a computer? We need:

- ▶ A processor - to process information, and to control the system;
- ▶ Memory - for data and instruction storage;
- ▶ Some form of input device; we'll use a keyboard to enter data into the system;
- ▶ Some form of output device; we'll use a monitor screen so we can see what our computer is doing.

Using just these components we can build a computer that meets our five constraints and can show us all the concepts we need to understand to allow us to understand how most modern computers work.

Additionally, both the input device and the output device can be integrated into the memory - we will see how in chapter 12. We connect the processor and the memory together using special sets of wires called *buses* - buses allow us to send data from one component to another.

Our minimalist system is shown in figure 1.3.

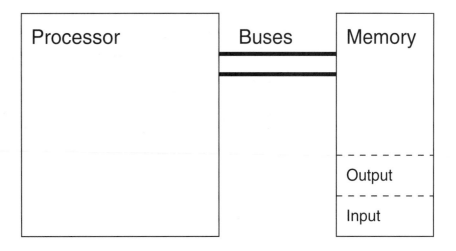

Figure 1.3   *Our minimalist computer system*

1.4.1   Inside The Processor

It is now time to look inside the processor of our minimalist computer system. Using the same philosophy as before, this processor needs only the bare minimum in order to work - we are not concerning ourselves with all the additional complexities used by modern processors.

To build our simple processor we need the following components:

▶ Some *Registers* - a register is a store where we can place one piece of data;

▶ An *Arithmetic Logic Unit*, or *ALU* - a very basic calculator for our processor. The ALU will have some registers inside it, as we will see later;

▶ A *Control Unit*, or *CU* - to run the processor;

▶ Some buses - to allow us to move data from one component to another.

These components can be seen in figure 1.4.

You can see that our processor uses 12 registers, a bus to connect them, an ALU and a CU. Even with so few components, our processor can actually do quite complex tasks, as we will see shortly.

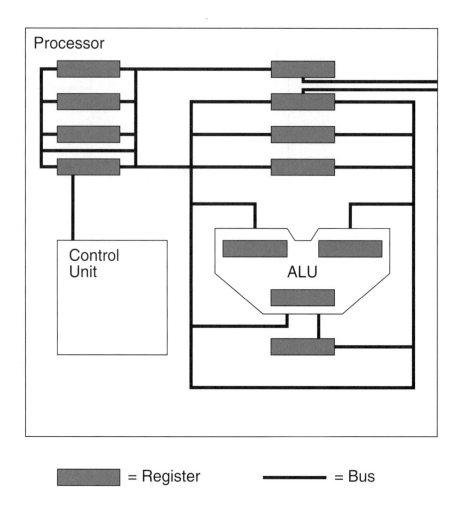

= Register ──────── = Bus

Figure 1.4 *Our minimalist processor*

1.4.2 Here's One We Prepared Earlier

In future chapters we will look at the different components that make up our simple processor, but in the meanwhile it is time to introduce a software package that we will make use of throughout this text. The package is called *JASPer*, short for *Just Another Simulated Processor emulator*, and it simulates the simple processor design from figure 1.4. When we first start up JASPer we see a more detailed view of our processor, as shown in figure 1.5.

JASPer shows a stylized view of the processor as a set of components placed on a *motherboard*, a circuit board that connects all the key components of a computer. This view of JASPer is called the *white-box* mode - you can see inside the processor itself. Later we will introduce the *black-box* mode where instead of seeing inside the processor we see a display screen that shows the textual output of programs - we'll see this in a moment.

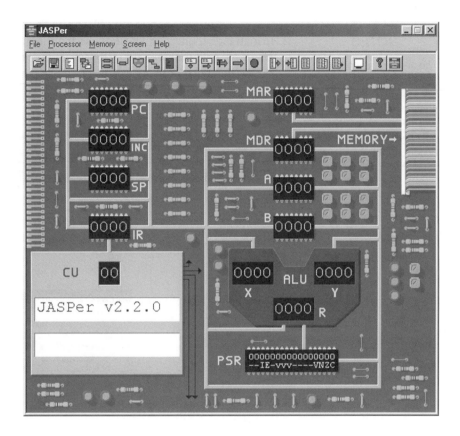

Figure 1.5   *Introducing JASPer - our simple processor*

1.4.3 Our First Program - 'Hello World'

Without needing to look at details as to what it is doing, we can demonstrate this simple processor by running our first program on it.

Normally, when learning any new programming language, it is traditional that the very first program attempted is the 'Hello World' program. This is usually one of the simplest programs you could write in your new language - this statement is not true when writing our first program for JASPer! However, it is important that we attempt to run our first program to see the sort of things that our simple processor design can do.

Here is what to do:

DEFINITION

Black-box : *We treat our processor as a component.*

NOTES

The JASPer button bar : you can tell what a button does by holding the mouse pointer over each button in turn - a pop-up text box describes the use of the button.

1   The program we want to run is stored on the CD that accompanies this book. On the CD, the 'Hello World' program is stored in the location:

    `\examples\chapter01\hello.jas`

2   To load the program into JASPer use the 'file/open' menu option, or use the 'file open' button. If you are unsure what is meant by this then browse the JASP reference in Appendix A before continuing;

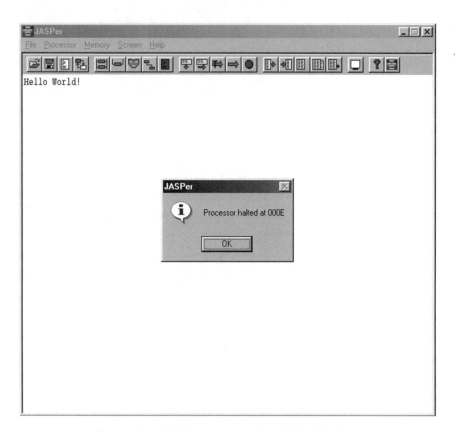

Figure 1.6   *JASPer - after running 'Hello World'*

3   To see the output from the program we will go into 'black-box' mode, which is done by the menu option 'file/switch state' (there is a button that does this too). Using this option twice will set the view back into 'white-box' mode - you want the view to appear completely white (which perversely shows that we are back in 'black-box' mode). Once we are in 'black-box mode, think of the white screen as the screen of a monitor attached to our computer system;

4   Run the program with 'processor/go' (again, there is a button);

5 Once you've done this, two things should happen. Firstly, you see the words 'Hello World!' appear on the screen. Secondly, a box appears that says 'Processor halted at 000E' - this is a message that tells us that the processor has stopped running. We will find out what 000E means later.

If you have followed the instructions above to the letter than you see the JASPer display as it is shown in figure 1.6. Well done, you've run your first program!

It is important to remember that our simple processor, consisting of only 12 registers, an ALU, a CU and joined by buses, has produced this output. Our minimal processor is actually very capable!

Our processor has read the instructions in the program, and it has blindly followed these instructions. Later we will learn how to understand these instructions ourselves, but first we will look at the concepts of number representation and simple electronics. Once we have done that we can start to examine our simple processor in much more detail.

CHAPTER SUMMARY

The key aspects of a computer

▶ Any processor based system has five key aspects - it takes input, it produces output, it processes data, it has an information store and it controls what it does;

▶ Most modern computers use a von Neumann architecture.

A brief history

▶ A computer was originally a person - someone who processed data;

▶ The key aspects of the computer were developed during, and just after, World War II;

▶ Hardware developments, notably the invention of the transistor in 1947, and the development of integrated circuits during the 1970s, lead to the introduction of the personal computer. Although other companies produced PCs before IBM, it is IBM that cornered the PC market.

The typical components within a computer

▶ A rudimentary computer requires a processor and a memory, as well as some simple I/O devices;

▶ Modern computers have many I/O devices that we do not need to examine in order to understand the fundamentals of a computer system.

▶ A processor consists of registers, an ALU and a CU all connected by buses.

The simulated processor, JASPer

▶ JASPer models our simple processor, and can be used to execute programs.

SELF TEST QUESTIONS

1 Computers require very precise instructions in order to complete a task. Write down the program required to teach someone how to make toast.

2 Write down the program required to give someone enough information to be able to travel from your home to the centre of the nearest town.

EXERCISES

1 Think of a device that you suspect is controlled by a processor, for example, a mobile phone. Using this device as a reference, explain the five fundamental aspects of a computer.

2 Name as many input devices and as many output devices as you can.

3 Attempt to count the number of processors that you may have used so far today.

Fundamental Concepts I - Data Representation

In this chapter we cover the key aspects of number representation and arithmetic and logical operations used within digital computers.

This chapter includes:

▶ Number representation - decimal, binary, octal, hexadecimal and Binary Coded Decimal (BCD);
▶ Conversion between different bases;
▶ Binary arithmetic;
▶ Signed representations - sign and modulus, 1's complement, 2's complement and floating point;
▶ Logic operations - AND, OR and NOT;
▶ Data representation - ASCII and Unicode.

2.1 Introducing Number Representation

To understand the actions of our simple processor we first need to look at the concepts of number representation. We will examine a selection of useful number representations, and then look at how we can perform arithmetic using these representations.

Throughout this book we'll make extensive use of base 16, which is called *hexadecimal*, as well as using numbers in base 2 (called *binary*). We'll also briefly look at numbers represented in base 8, which is called *octal*. It is important to remember, that whatever base we use to look at a number, *we are looking at different representations of the same number - the number has not changed.*

Going back to the 'Hello World' example that we ran in the last chapter, after running the program in JASPer (in 'black-box' mode as we discussed) try flipping back to 'white-box' mode. It is in this mode that we see the contents of all the registers.

Look at the register labelled *IR* (this is the *Instruction Register*, and we'll find out what it is used for later) - it contains F000. This is not some bizarre word for 'stop', but a hexadecimal value. The contents of each register in JASPer are displayed in hexadecimal, apart from one. This is the register labelled 'PSR', the contents of this register is displayed in binary.

We tend to use the particular base that helps us understand what is happening. We use binary most when we want to perform arithmetic or understand logical operations - but we tend to use hexadecimal when we want to describe the contents of registers, or indeed when we want to write our programs in machine code, ready to be executed by JASPer. Why? Because we humans are very poor at dealing with long strings of digits. Could you tell if 45678987396 is larger than 145671876893 without counting the individual digits?

So when dealing with numbers, whether in hexadecimal or in binary, we are just concerned with the number we are representing, and in how many bits.

2.2 Representing Numbers

DEFINITION

Decimal : *A number system that uses base 10.*

2.2.1 Base 10 - Decimal

Let us start with a rethink about decimal. Decimal is base 10 and we learned in very early childhood that we can use the digits:

▶ '0', '1', '2', '3', '4', '5', '6', '7', '8' and '9'.

With those digits we can represent very large numbers (like 5672 or 679100000) as well as very small numbers (using a decimal point as in 0.000000005), because when we build up larger (or smaller) numbers we also use the position of each digit to mean something as well as its value.

Let's take a number, say 453, in decimal. What are we actually saying here? Back in infants' school we learned that we are saying 4 hundreds, 5 tens and 3 units, or $400 + 50 + 3$. *The position as well as the size of each digit is*

NOTES

When we write numbers, we use the subscript to indicate the base used. So 111_2 uses base 2, if we converted it to a decimal representation it would be 7_{10}. The normal convention is to not show the subscript of numbers in a decimal representation.

important, because as we can see here, working from the right of the number, each position to the left is ten times larger than before, in fact it's ten times larger because we are using base 10 (decimal).

So, 453 can be written as

$$(4 \times 10^2) + (5 \times 10^1) + (3 \times 10^0)$$

This is shown in table 2.1.

Value	100 (10^2)	10 (10^1)	1 (10^0)
Decimal number	4	5	3

Table 2.1 *Base 10*

Now we've remembered base 10 let's move on to the bases we need to know in order to understand our processor.

DEFINITION

Binary : *A number system that uses base 2.*

2.2.2 Base 2 - Binary

Base 2 is similar to decimal, apart from the fact that we can only use the digits '0' and '1'.

If we look at a number, like 101011_2, every bit has a value and a position, as shown in table 2.2. Once again the position is important, because as we move leftwards through our number each bit position represents a value twice as large as its rightmost counterpart.

101011_2 can therefore be written as

$$(1 \times 2^5) + (0 \times 2^4) + (1 \times 2^3) + (0 \times 2^2) + (1 \times 2^1) + (1 \times 2^0)$$

DEFINITION

Bit : *Binary digit. The digit can be 1 or 0. A sequence of bits is often called a* bit pattern.

As any number multiplied by zero equals zero, this can be shortened to

$$(1 \times 2^5) + (1 \times 2^3) + (1 \times 2^1) + (1 \times 2^0)$$

Each bit is twice the size as it would be if it were one place further right because we are using base 2. For example, 10100_2 is twice as large as 1010_2.

In fact, we can now see that even though we are using binary, the same rules as we had when we were using decimal numbers still apply. Now however we can see that there is a generic rule of position that we hadn't considered before, that *whatever the base, in any number a digit is larger than a similar digit one place to the right by a factor of the base.*

Value	32	16	8	4	2	1
	(2^5)	(2^4)	(2^3)	(2^2)	(2^1)	(2^0)
Binary number	1	0	1	0	1	1

Table 2.2   *Base 2*

All the registers in JASPer are 16-bit registers. This means that they can store bit patterns that are sixteen bits long . These values in binary then are from 0000000000000000_2 to 1111111111111111_2. This can be quite a mouthful, and is the reason that we generally refer to the contents of registers using hexadecimal, as we will see later.

A group of 8 bits is known as a *byte* , so we can also say that the JASPer registers are 2 bytes wide.

Another term widely used for bit patterns of a certain width is a *word*. A word is considered to be the size of the bit pattern that can be transferred between different registers in one go. Within JASPer the word size is 16 bits, so we can also say that our registers can contain 1 word. Different processors have different word sizes, whereas a byte is always 8 bits (it didn't used to be however, but it is the convention today).

Within a 16-bit word, the most significant 8 bits is often termed the *high-byte* (sometimes *hi-byte*), whereas the least significant 8 bits is termed the *low-byte* (sometimes *lo-byte*).

2.2.3 Base 16 - Hexadecimal

Hexadecimal use the same rules as before, only we have a wider range of digits which are:

▶ '0', '1', '2', '3', '4', '5', '6', '7', '8', '9', 'A', 'B', 'C', 'D', 'E' and 'F'.

'A' represents 10, 'B' represents 11, 'C' represents 12, 'D' represents 13, 'E' represents 14 and 'F' represents 15.

So in *hex* (which we will start to use as an abbreviation of hexadecimal) we can have numbers like 3419_{16}, $FFFF_{16}$, $163D_{16}$ and $F00D_{16}$. It takes practice before you can start dealing with hex numbers, but it comes with time.

For example, the hexadecimal value $53F_{16}$ can be written as

$$(5 \times 16^2) + (3 \times 16^1) + (15 \times 16^0).$$

Value	256 (16^2)	16 (16^1)	1 (16^0)
Hex number	5	3	F

Table 2.3 *Base 16*

As mentioned previously, we usually display the contents of the 16-bit registers in JASPer using hexadecimal. Using hexadecimal, the contents of the registers can range from 0000_{16} to $FFFF_{16}$.

2.2.4 Base 8 - Octal

The last base we will look at is base 8, otherwise known as octal. The digits we can make use of are:

▶ '0', '1', '2', '3', '4', '5', '6' and '7'.

Once again, now we know the general rule, we know that if we take a typical octal number like 563_8 that each position is eight times larger than the previous.

For example, the octal value 375_8 can be written as

$$(3 \times 8^2) + (7 \times 8^1) + (5 \times 8^0).$$

Value	64 (8^2)	8 (8^1)	1 (8^0)
Octal number	3	7	5

Table 2.4 *Base 8*

Octal is not used very often these days, binary and hexadecimal are far more common bases used within computing. The most common use of octal still around today is in the file system attributes of a UNIX operating system. We won't use octal anymore in this book.

2.2.5 BCD - Binary Coded Decimal

This is a format whereby decimal representations are stored in a binary format. Patterns of four bits can be used to represent the decimal values of 0 through to 9. These are shown in table 2.5.

Decimal	BCD
0	0000
1	0001
2	0010
3	0011
4	0100
5	0101
6	0110
7	0111
8	1000
9	1001

Table 2.5 *BCD representation*

For example, if we wished to represent the decimal number 14 in BCD we would look up the representations of the individual digits and then place them together.

▶ $1 = 0001_2$
▶ $4 = 0100_2$
▶ Therefore 14 in a BCD representation is 00010100_2.

BCD is less common than it used to be. It has two key drawbacks, these are:

▶ It is an inefficient representation - as the binary values 1010_2 to 1111_2 are unused in BCD (some BCD representations use two of the unused codes to represent '+' and '-'), and 4 bits for a single digit takes up space.
▶ Some processors have support in the ALU to perform BCD arithmetic, but it requires additional circuitry. JASPer doesn't support BCD arithmetic in the ALU. If the processor doesn't have support for BCD then it takes a lot of work by the programmer to perform BCD arithmetic.

We won't use BCD anymore in this book.

2.2.6 Converting Between Bases

Converting between the most common bases is made easy by following a few simple rules - the most common conversions are included below.

Decimal $\Leftrightarrow$ Binary

▶ **Binary to Decimal Conversions**
Let's start off by converting a number in a binary representation into decimal. We'll choose the 8-bit binary number 00100111_2 and see how we go about converting it. Firstly, let's lay it out in a table showing the positional value of each bit.

Value	128 (2^7)	64 (2^6)	32 (2^5)	16 (2^4)	8 (2^3)	4 (2^2)	2 (2^1)	1 (2^0)
Binary number	0	0	1	0	0	1	1	1

Table 2.6 *Binary to decimal conversion*

So, we can state

$$(0\times2^7)+(0\times2^6)+(1\times2^5)+(0\times2^4)+(0\times2^3)+(1\times2^2)+(1\times2^1)+(1\times2^0) = 39$$

Or more simply,

$$(1 \times 2^5) + (1 \times 2^2) + (1 \times 2^1) + (1 \times 2^0) = 39$$

$00100111_2 = 39.$

▶ **Decimal to Binary Conversions**
We can use the reverse process of the above. Let's imagine that we want to convert the decimal value 28 to an 8-bit binary value. To do this we can fill in a table like before. For each column, starting with 128, it's a simple case of division and remainder.

▶ So, if we start off, obviously 128 doesn't go into 28, and neither does 64 or 32 (place a 0 in each of these columns);

▶ 16 does go into 28 so we put a 1 in the 16's column. We now have 12 to convert (28 - 16);

▶ 8 goes into 12 (1 in the 8's column) with a remainder of 4;

▶ 4 goes into 4 (place a 1 in the 4's column) - there isn't any remainder, so fill the other columns with 0.

As you can see, we end up with a value of 00011100_2, the binary equivalent of the decimal value 28.

Value	128 (2^7)	64 (2^6)	32 (2^5)	16 (2^4)	8 (2^3)	4 (2^2)	2 (2^1)	1 (2^0)
Binary number	0	0	0	1	1	1	0	0

Table 2.7 *Decimal to binary conversion - converting 28*

Hexadecimal $\Leftrightarrow$ Binary

Converting between hex and binary is very simple indeed - as four binary digits can be grouped together and represented as one hex digit. Table 2.8 shows you how.

Binary	Hex
0000	0
0001	1
0010	2
0011	3
0100	4
0101	5
0110	6
0111	7
1000	8
1001	9
1010	A
1011	B
1100	C
1101	D
1110	E
1111	F

Table 2.8 *Binary to hex conversion*

▶ **Hexadecimal to Binary Conversions**

Let's imagine that we want to convert the hex value $ABCD_{16}$ into binary. Nothing could be easier! For each hex digit, look up the binary equivalent in table 2.8 and write down the 4 bits that represent that hex digit. You get 1010 1011 1100 1101, which when we write these all together we get the value 1010101111001101_2 which is the binary equivalent of $ABCD_{16}$.

▶ **Binary to Hexadecimal Conversions**
Again, this is easy. Let's convert 1010001001000100_2 into hex. Firstly, we group the bits starting from the right into fours to get $1010\ 0010\ 0100\ 0100$ and then convert each group to get $A\ 2\ 4\ 4$, so the hex equivalent we were looking for is $A244_{16}$. All bit groups must start from the right, if you have an incomplete group of four bits on the left then write zeroes to the left of the number until the left most group consists of four bits.

Decimal $\Leftrightarrow$ Hexadecimal

For converting between decimal and hexadecimal, I could show you yet another conversion method. Or we could cheat by using what we already know.

▶ **Decimal to Hexadecimal Conversions** - convert the decimal number to binary, and then convert that to hexadecimal.

▶ **Hexadecimal to Decimal Conversions** - convert the hexadecimal number to binary, and then convert that to decimal.

2.3 Introducing Binary Arithmetic

Now we have covered the representations we need, it is time to begin studying binary arithmetic, so let us attempt to add two binary numbers together. We will add 5 to 7.

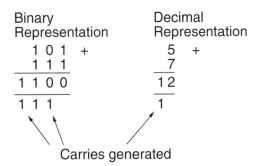

We perform the addition in binary using the same process that we have always used for decimal; we may have changed the base we are using but the rules of arithmetic have not changed! So, right to left, we first add 1 to 1, which of course gives us 2 in decimal, and in binary the result 10, or 0 carry 1. Next, we add 1 to 0, plus the previously generated carry to get 0 carry 1, etc. The result is 1100_2, which when converted to decimal is 12.

This process is the same whether we are adding two 4-bit numbers together or two 64-bit numbers together.

2.4 Signed Numbers

So far we have only discussed unsigned numbers, and we need to figure out how to represent negative numbers too before we can start to think about arithmetic further.

The first method we'll discuss is *sign and modulus*, but it turns out that this method of representing signed values gives us a few problems. So we then look at *1's complement* which solves some of the problems associated with a sign and modulus representation but gives us some more problems of its own. Finally, within this section we introduce *2's complement*, which solves the problems of the 1's complement representation. It does have one minor issue of its own, but as it solves all our other issues it is our accepted method of choice.

For illustrative purposes, we will use 8-bit representations within this section, only moving to 16-bit representations when we perform arithmetic using our simple processor.

2.4.1 Sign And Modulus

The first issue to solve, when looking at how to represent signed numbers, is how to store the sign information - whether a number is positive or negative. A possible solution is to use the leftmost bit to represent the sign of the number represented.

> **DEFINITION**
>
> **MSB** : *The leftmost bit of a number is known as the* **M**ost **S**ignificant **B**it, or **MSB**.

> **DEFINITION**
>
> **LSB** : *The rightmost bit of a number is known as the* **L**east **S**ignificant **B**it, or **LSB**.

If the left most bit contains a '0' we'll say the bit pattern represents a positive number, and if it contains a '1' we'll say the bit pattern represents a negative number. So the leftmost bit of an 8-bit sign and modulus value indicates the value of the sign, therfore we can represent the number $+7$ as 00000111_2. Obviously it means in our 8-bit representation that we can't store as many positive numbers, because we are using half of the possible bit patterns to indicate negative numbers, but on the plus side we now have a representation that we can use to indicate both positive and negative numbers.

Sign	Modulus
0	0000111

Table 2.9 *Sign and Modulus positive numbers*

We can represent -7 as 10000111_2.

Sign	Modulus
1	0000111

Table 2.10 *Sign and Modulus negative numbers*

This looks like we've solved all our problems, because we can now represent both positive and negative numbers. All we have to be able to do now is perform arithmetic on these numbers, and we have the basis for our ALU, the basic calculator in our processor.

So, let's just prove that sign and modulus solves our arithmetic problem. We'll add $+5$ to -5, and, all things considered, we would expect the result 0. Let's see what happens.

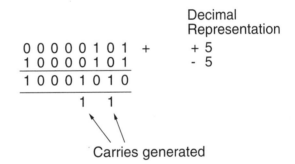

Decimal
Representation

```
0 0 0 0 0 1 0 1  +      + 5
1 0 0 0 0 1 0 1         - 5
─────────────────
1 0 0 0 1 0 1 0
      1   1
```

Carries generated

We can see this answer is a negative number, and when we convert into decimal we have -10. This isn't what we expected; in fact it means that if we were to use sign and modulus representations in our processor then we would have to design quite a complicated circuit within our ALU to actually add these numbers together and get the right answer - actually we would have to deal with the number representation and the sign representation separately. In fact, this issue is so major, that it's time for us to throw away this number representation and try another: 1's complement.

2.4.2 1's Complement

We were happy before with our representation for positive numbers, but we seemed to have problems with our negative representation. This time we will alter our way of representing negative numbers. With 1's complement, if we want to represent a negative number, we start with the positive representation of that number and then flip all the bits, which means that where we encounter a '1' in the bit pattern we change it to a '0', and vice versa.

$$+5_{10} = 0\ 0\ 0\ 0\ 0\ 1\ 0\ 1_2$$

$$-\ 5_{10} = 1\ 1\ 1\ 1\ 1\ 0\ 1\ 0_2$$

We can still use the MSB to indicate the sign as you can see that it was flipped along with the other bits in the representation. However, now we've flipped the bits it's not so obvious to actually see the value of the number represented - 11111010_2 isn't obviously a representation of -5, but that doesn't matter because we can just set the rule that, when we see that the MSB is set to 1, we flip all the bits to find out the value of the negative number represented.

Now let's see if we can perform arithmetic on this representation.

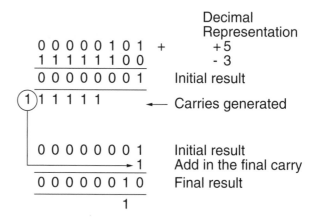

When we perform this calculation we have to stick to the range of our bit patterns. The above example uses 8-bit bit patterns, and so the result must also be represented in 8 bits - this is why we don't add in the final carry, as this would give us a 9-bit result. However, we don't forget about this as we add in this final carry to our initial result to achieve the final result.

We do get the correct answer, but only when we have the extra rule to always add in any left over carry into our final result - that way we will always arrive at the correct answer.

Let's try another simple sum.

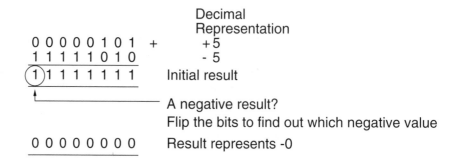

How can we have -0? Unfortunately, we have just hit on the second and most important issue with 1's complement - we have two separate representations for 0, these being $+0$ and -0. This will have a major impact on our processor, because it means that, when we test to see if the result of an arithmetic operation was zero, then we have to check the result for two distinct values.

So, apart from the problems of multiple representations of zero and the issue of always having to remember to add in the final carry (which doubles the time to do an add), we have a representation that not only allows us to represent positive and negative numbers - but we can also successfully perform arithmetic on them. Next, we'll turn to 2's complement, an improvement on 1's complement that removes the two issues we discussed.

2.4.3 2's Complement

2's complement is very similar to 1's complement. Positive numbers are again represented exactly as we have seen before, but negative numbers are represented slightly differently. For example let's take the 2's complement representation of 7 in 8 bits.

	Decimal Representation
0 0 0 0 0 1 1 1	+7
1 1 1 1 1 0 0 0	Flip the bits
1	Add 1
1 1 1 1 1 0 0 1	Result represents -7

The simple rule for obtaining the 2's complement representation of the negative of a number is

► Flip the bits
► Add 1

and that's it. This also simplifies the type of operations we need to perform, since any subtraction operation can be termed instead as an addition with the 2's complement representation of one of the values. For example, instead of performing:

$7 - 5$

We can perform:

$7 + (-5)$

Now we know how to figure out the representation of a negative number, let's try our arithmetic from before.

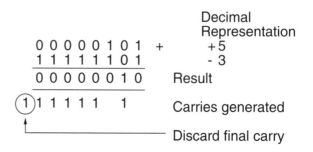

So, we generated a final carry, do we care? No, we throw it away (actually in our ALU it will be used as something called a *flag*, but more on that much later) ensuring that we have a result with the correct number of bits. In one arithmetic operation we were able to produce the correct answer, without any additional operations required. All we have to figure out now is when the result of the operation is to be zero - let's see what happens.

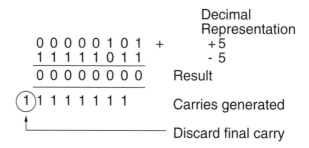

A carry is generated as before, but again we throw it away. The final result is 0. Unlike with the 1's complement representation, we no longer have two representations of zero, as 11111111_2 in 1's complement is a valid negative number (if we flip the bits and add one we find out that it's the 2's complement representation of -1).

There is one oddity left with 2's complement, and we are willing to put up with it because it solves so many of the issues that we had with other representations. If we take the 2's complement of the largest negative number, 10000000_2, let's see what we end up with.

```
  1 0 0 0 0 0 0 0
  ─────────────────
  0 1 1 1 1 1 1 1      Flip the bits
                1      Add 1
  ─────────────────
  1 0 0 0 0 0 0 0      Result : Back where we started!
  ─────────────────
  1 1 1 1 1 1 1        Carries generated
```

That's right, the 2's complement of the largest negative number is itself - this is because of the fact that we have one less positive number than we do negative numbers (the extra negative number is because zero is non-negative).

2.4.4 The Overflow Problem

There is one major issue that we have yet to discuss on the subject of 2's complement arithmetic, and that is the concept of *overflow*.

Overflow occurs when we limit ourselves to representations that use a restricted number of bits. For example, let us add the numbers 88 and 41 using a 2's complement 8-bit representation.

```
                                         Decimal
                                         Representation
  0 1 0 1 1 0 0 0  +                        +88
  0 0 1 0 1 0 0 1                           +41
  ─────────────────
  1 0 0 0 0 0 0 1                        Initial result
  ─────────────────
  1 1 1 1           ◄─────────           Carries generated


  1 0 0 0 0 0 0 1                        Initial result is negative
  ─────────────────

  0 1 1 1 1 1 1 0                        Flip the bits
                1                        Add 1
  ─────────────────
  0 1 1 1 1 1 1 1                        Result is therefore -127 ????
```

What has happened here? We do not have enough bits to represent the correct positive result, and the sign bit of the result has been changed. Overflow has occurred.

We define overflow as:

▶ When the signs of both initial values are the same, and the sign of the result is different.

31

Therefore it is only possible for overflow to occur when we add two positive numbers together, or add two negative numbers together. It is impossible to have overflow when we add a positive and a negative number together.

Overflow is something that we need to check for when we later come to write programs that use signed binary arithmetic. It is so important that our processor gives us a way to detect it, and we'll see this in chapter 5.

2.4.5 2's Complement In JASPer

JASPer performs 2's complement arithmetic in its ALU. Try the following:

▶ Using the 'Update Registers' dialog box, enter these values into the ALU (these are hexadecimal values - but shown without a subscript so you can see exactly what to enter into the ALU registers, and what is displayed): ALUx = 000F, ALUy = 0008;

▶ Use the 'ALU operation' dialog box (as shown in figure 2.1) to perform an add operation. To do this you need to click on 'add' and then 'OK' to remove the dialog box;

▶ The result in the ALUr should now be 0017 which is 17_{16}. If you convert each of these values into decimal you will find that you have just performed $15 + 8 = 23$.

Figure 2.1 *The JASPer ALU dialog box*

We can also do a subtraction. Try the following:

▶ Enter these values into the ALU: ALUx = 0008, ALUy = 000F;

▶ Perform a sub (for subtract) operation;

▶ We can see that the result is FFF9, and because the MSB is set to 1 (in binary we have 1111111111111001_2) we know that this result represents a negative number. However, it is not immediately obvious to us what particular negative number this result represents, so we can actually use JASPer to take the 2's complement of this result. To do this, set the ALUx value to FFF9 and then run the neg operation - this performs a 2's complement operation;

▶ The result now in the ALUr is 0007, in other words we have shown that $8 - 15 = -7$.

Remember that a subtraction is actually a complement and an add.

The ALU will be covered in much greater depth in chapter 5.

2.5 Floating Point Numbers

So far we have only discussed integer values. For real numbers we need a *floating point* representation to represent real numbers like 3.14 or 1.563×10^{28}.

Early processors could not perform floating point operations, instead the programmer had to write subroutines to perform floating point operations in software. Later, some processor systems included an extra processor called a *floating point co-processor* (*FPC*). The processor would communicate with the FPC whenever a floating point operation was required. Nowadays modern processors tend to have a *floating point unit* (*FPU*) as part of the processor itself.

Initially, those machines that could perform floating point operations tended to use proprietary methods which made transferral of programs from one machine type to another very difficult. Eventually a standard was introduced known as IEEE 754. All modern processors refer to this standard to perform floating point operations.

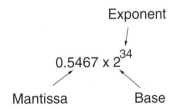

Figure 2.2 *Parts of a floating point number*

Essentially, floating point numbers can be defined in terms of the mantissa, the exponent, and the base - as shown in figure 2.2. The base for binary floating point values is always 2.

IEEE 754 defines both 32-bit and 64-bit floating point number representations. These are shown in figure 2.3.

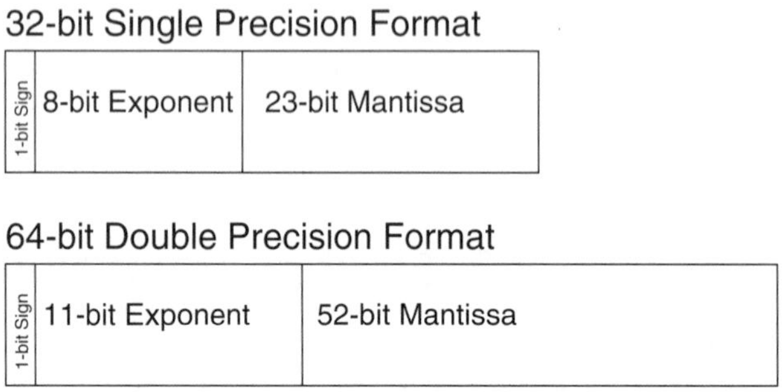

32-bit Single Precision Format

1-bit Sign	8-bit Exponent	23-bit Mantissa

64-bit Double Precision Format

1-bit Sign	11-bit Exponent	52-bit Mantissa

Figure 2.3 *Floating point number formats*

JASPer cannot perform floating point operations, and as a knowledge of floating point is not necessary to understand the fundamental aspects of processors, we won't consider floating point any further.

If you want to read more on the subject of floating point, I recommend [Sta03] or [MH00].

2.6 Logical Operations

Now we have looked at arithmetic operations on bit patterns it is time to look at logical operations. The most common logical operations that we can apply to bit patterns are AND, OR and NOT. They are each described here in turn.

2.6.1 AND

With an AND operation, the result is set to 1 only when both initial values are 1, otherwise the result is 0.

X	Y	R
0	0	0
0	1	0
1	0	0
1	1	1

Figure 2.4 *The Logical AND operation*

A table containing the possible initial values and the result for each is shown in figure 2.4. This sort of table is known as a *truth table*.

If we wanted to perform a logical AND operation on two 8-bit bit patterns we would perform this process on each bit position of both bit patterns. For example, if we were to AND the values 00100111_2 and 00101110 we would first perform the AND operation on the LSB of each, followed by the next pair, and so on. This operation, as all logical operations, works for any number of bits.

```
0 0 1 0 0 1 1 1     X
0 0 1 0 1 1 1 0     Y
─────────────────
0 0 1 0 0 1 1 0     X AND Y
```

2.6.2 OR

With an OR operation, the result is set to 1 when either (or both) of its initial values are 1, otherwise the result is 0.

X	Y	R
0	0	0
0	1	1
1	0	1
1	1	1

Figure 2.5 *The Logical OR operation*

Applying an OR operation to two values is a similar process to the AND process we saw before, except that we apply the OR process as displayed in figure 2.5.

For example, if we were to OR the values 00100111_2 and 00101110 we would first perform the OR operation on the LSB of each, followed by the next pair, and so on.

```
0 0 1 0 0 1 1 1     X
0 0 1 0 1 1 1 0     Y
0 0 1 0 1 1 1 1     X OR Y
```

2.6.3 NOT

Finally, the NOT operation negates the individual bits of a single bit pattern as shown in figure 2.6.

X	R
0	1
1	0

Figure 2.6 *The Logical NOT operation*

We apply this process to all bits in the bit pattern, as shown here.

```
0 0 1 0 0 1 1 1     X
1 1 0 1 1 0 0 0     NOT X
```

2.7 Dealing With Text

So far we have only looked at ways to represent numbers, but what about when we need to represent text? Without a text representation we couldn't have had our 'Hello World' program in chapter 1. To deal with text we need to associate each character with a numeric value. The most common text representation used in computers these days is *ASCII*, which is a text representation that uses 7 bits, so it can only represent up to 128 separate character codes. ASCII

DEFINITION

ASCII : *A set of special codes for text characters. (pronounced as* ass-key*), it stands for American Standards Code for Information Interchange.*

isn't the only character encoding available to us - some older IBM machines make use of a system called *EBCDIC*, but you are unlikely to ever find it used with microprocessor based systems.

The ASCII character set is displayed in table 2.11. To calculate the hex value of any character just take the column heading ('0' through to '7') and place after it the row heading (from '0' to 'F') and you end up with the correct code.

For example, the ASCII code for the letter 'R' is found as follows:

- The column that 'R' is in is labelled with the hexadecimal digit 5;
- The row that 'R' is in is labelled with the hexadecimal digit 2;
- This produces the hexadecimal value 52_{16}.

Sometimes we will also see this written as $52 or 0x52 which means the same thing. From now on in this text I will use the form $52 to indicate the hex value 52_{16}, etc.

Low Hexadecimal Digit \ High Hexadecimal Digit	0	1	2	3	4	5	6	7
0	NUL	DCL		0	@	P	‘	p
1	SOH	DC1	!	1	A	Q	a	q
2	STX	DC2	"	2	B	R	b	r
3	ETX	DC3	#	3	C	S	c	s
4	EOT	DC4	$	4	D	T	d	t
5	ENQ	NAK	%	5	E	U	e	u
6	ACK	SYN	&	6	F	V	f	v
7	BEL	ETB	’	7	G	W	g	w
8	BS	CAN	(	8	H	X	h	x
9	HT	EM	)	9	I	Y	i	y
A	LF	SUB	*	:	J	Z	j	z
B	VT	ESC	+	;	K	[	k	{
C	FF	FS	,	<	L	\	l	|
D	CR	GS	-	=	M	]	m	}
E	SO	RS	.	>	N	^	n	~
F	SI	US	/	?	O	_	o	DEL

Table 2.11 ***The ASCII Codes***

Two points are worth noting from the table:

1 Characters below $20 are non-printing characters. They are mostly used to send particular messages between computers and usually we don't need to ever worry about them. Some are still useful to us in JASPer, for example the codes $0A and $0D are the characters for line-feed and carriage return respectively - we can use them to drive the cursor location when printing to our simple monitor. They were used by the 'Hello World' program.

2 If we know the ASCII code for a capital letter, simply by adding $20 we can obtain the code for the respective lowercase letter. This feature can often prove useful when writing programs that use I/O, as we'll see in chapter 12.

However, even ASCII is slowly being replaced. In modern computer systems it is being replaced by *Unicode* which is designed to cope with many more character sets. ASCII is a 7-bit, and hence a limited character code system, while Unicode is a 16-bit system. Unicode can deal with the requirements of modern multi-lingual graphical user interface (*GUI*) based systems.

The processor sends the required code to the computer's monitor (we'll talk about how this happens in chapter 12), and the required character is displayed.

CHAPTER SUMMARY

Representing numbers

▶ Any representation is just that - a representation. We've looked at a number of different data representations for both numbers and text. *If we change the representation of a number from one base to another, we have not changed the value of the number - it's still the same number*;

▶ We need to know which representation is being used before we figure out what value a bit pattern represents;

▶ We need to remember the number of bits we are working with in a representation;

▶ At all times we should remember which particular representation we are using and be consistent;

▶ We examined binary, octal, decimal, hexadecimal and BCD representations;

▶ We introduced methods to convert between representations.

A quick reference for the representations covered is at the end of this section.

Binary arithmetic

▶ The process for binary arithmetic is identical to that for decimal arithmetic - only the base has changed.

Signed numbers

▶ Three methods for representing signed numbers were introduced - sign and modulus, 1's complement and 2's complement;

▶ 1's complement has two representations of zero;

▶ 2's complement has one representation of zero;

▶ To take the 2's complement of any value you flip the bits and add 1;

▶ Using a 2's complement representation we need never perform subtraction - instead we take the 2's complement of one of the values and perform an add operation instead;

▶ The majority of modern computers perform binary arithmetic using 2's complement. JASPer uses 2's complement arithmetic in its ALU.

Logical operations

▶ AND - the result is set to 1 only when both initial values are 1, otherwise the result is 0;

▶ OR - the result is set to 1 when either (or both) of its initial values are 1, otherwise the result is 0;

▶ NOT - negates the individual bits of a value.

Floating point

▶ A floating point number is defined in terms of its mantissa, exponent and base;

▶ The floating point standard used by most modern processors is IEEE 754.

Text representation

▶ Text can be represented with a code system such as Unicode or ASCII. JASPer makes use of the ASCII character set;

▶ ASCII is a 7-bit character set;

▶ Unicode is a 16-bit character set.

Some examples for the meanings of particular bit patterns are shown here:

Representation	Meaning of 00100011_2	Meaning of 11111110_2
Unsigned number	35	254
Sign and Modulus	35	-126
1's Complement	35	-1
2's Complement	35	-2
BCD	23	Not meaningful
ASCII	#	Not meaningful

Number representation quick reference

This table shows the representations of 0 to 15 in binary, octal, decimal, hexadecimal and binary coded decimal.

Binary	Octal	Decimal	Hex	BCD
0000	0	0	0	0
0001	1	1	1	1
0010	2	2	2	2
0011	3	3	3	3
0100	4	4	4	4
0101	5	5	5	5
0110	6	6	6	6
0111	7	7	7	7
1000	10	8	8	8
1001	11	9	9	9
1010	12	10	A	+
1011	13	11	B	-
1100	14	12	C	
1101	15	13	D	
1110	16	14	E	
1111	17	15	F	

SELF TEST QUESTIONS

1 Convert 42 to an 8-bit binary value.

2 Convert the 8-bit binary value 00001011_2 to decimal.

3 Convert the 8-bit binary value 01001101_2 to hexadecimal.

4 Convert the 16-bit hexadecimal value $BEEF_{16}$ to binary.

5 Convert the 16-bit hexadecimal value $BEEF_{16}$ to decimal.

6 Convert 28 to a 16-bit hexadecimal value.

7 Perform a logical AND on 00000111_2 and 00100100_2.

8 Perform a logical OR on 00000111_2 and 00100100_2.

9 Add 01100011_2 and 01100001_2 together using an 8-bit 2's complement representation. What is wrong with the result?

10 Add 00100011_2 and 01100101_2 together using an 8-bit unsigned representation. Convert the result into hexadecimal.

11 Figure out the representation of -12 in both a 16-bit and an 8-bit 2's complement representation.

12 What is the ASCII representation for 'F' in hexadecimal?

13 What is the ASCII representation for 'f' in hexadecimal?

14 What is the ASCII representation for '5' in hexadecimal?

EXERCISES

1 Convert the decimal value 12 to an 8-bit binary value.

2 Convert the 8-bit binary value 00101111_2 to decimal.

3 Convert the 8-bit binary value 00101111_2 to hexadecimal.

4 Convert the 16-bit hexadecimal value $F00D_{16}$ to binary.

5 Convert the 16-bit hexadecimal value $F00D_{16}$ to decimal.

6 Convert the decimal value 142 to a 16-bit hexadecimal value.

7 Perform a logical AND on 00111100_2 and 00110101_2.

8 Perform a logical OR on 00111100_2 and 00110101_2.

9 Add 00101100_2 and 00010001_2 together. Convert the result into hexadecimal.

10 Convert the decimal values 45 and -34 to binary using a 2's complement representation. Add them together and convert the result into hexadecimal.

11 My name ('Mark') in ASCII is '$4D $61 $72 $6B'. What is your name converted into ASCII?

12 Using the ALU in JASPer, add $00FE and $40DA together.

13 Using the ALU in JASPer, add $7012 and $103D together.

Fundamental Concepts II - Digital Electronic Circuits

CHAPTER OVERVIEW

This chapter focuses on the fundamental aspects of digital circuitry that can be used to build the components of a computer system.

This chapter includes:

▶ Gate logic - AND, OR and NOT;
▶ How to build circuits with gates;
▶ Modelling circuits with truth tables;
▶ Boolean algebra, including De Morgan's laws;
▶ The package 'Digital Works', used to simulate logic circuits.

3.1 Introducing Digital Electronics

All digital computers today are built up from *electronic circuitry*. We can examine the use of circuit elements called *logic gates* (or *gates* for short) without worrying how they are created - in fact their usage can be entirely separated from what they are built from. In the past, gates were built from vacuum tubes, and later from transistors. Today they are all generally built from integrated circuits (many transistors created on one single silicon chip). It is not important what we build our circuits from, provided that we are only interested in what they do, rather than how fast they do it.

All logic circuits can be built using the most simple of logic gates. There are three elementary gates called AND, OR and NOT (after the logical operations they can perform), and using these we can build more useful gates called NAND, NOR and XOR gates. All gates are binary - they take one or more binary input values, and produce a binary output value; each of these gates can be described using truth tables. This shows all the inputs to the gate, and the output it produces dependant on the values of the inputs.

3.1.1 AND

Figure 3.1 contains the truth table and the symbol for the AND gate - the truth table shows all possible input values for the gate, and lists the output for each set of inputs. If we look at the symbol for the gate first, we can see that it has two inputs (labelled X and Y), and one output labelled R. The truth table shows us, for each possible set of input values, what the output would be.

With the AND gate, the output is set to 1 only when both inputs are 1, other-wise the output is 0 - this is identical to the AND operation in binary arithmetic that we discussed in chapter 2.

Sometimes we refer to the value 1 in a truth table as *true* and a 0 as *false*. We can also sometimes refer to the value 1 as *high* and the value 0 as *low*.

It is possible to have AND gates with more than two inputs but their output follows these same rules.

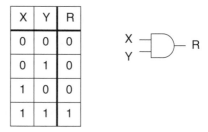

X	Y	R
0	0	0
0	1	0
1	0	0
1	1	1

Figure 3.1 *The AND gate*

Compare this figure to figure 2.4 in chapter 2.

3.1.2 OR

Figure 3.2 shows the truth table and the symbol for an OR gate. With the OR gate, the output is set to 1 when either (or both) of its inputs are 1, otherwise the output is 0.

X	Y	R
0	0	0
0	1	1
1	0	1
1	1	1

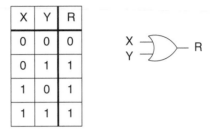

Figure 3.2 *The OR gate*

Compare this figure to figure 2.5 in chapter 2.

It is possible to have OR gates with more than two inputs but their output follows these same rules.

3.1.3 NOT

Figure 3.3 shows the truth table and the symbol for a NOT gate. A NOT gate, sometimes referred to as an *inverter*, is simpler than the other two gates that we've seen so far as it has only a single input - it simply inverts whatever its single input is.

X	R
0	1
1	0

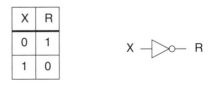

Figure 3.3 *The NOT gate*

Compare this figure to figure 2.6 in chapter 2.

3.1.4 NAND

Now we can move on to some useful gates that can be built from AND, OR and NOT. The first of these is the NAND gate. NAND is short for NOT AND.

Figure 3.4 shows the truth table and symbol for the NAND gate, as well as how the gate can be built from an AND and a NOT gate - the output from the AND gate is the input to the NOT gate. As you can see, the NAND gate produces the exact opposite output of the AND gate

X	Y	R
0	0	1
0	1	1
1	0	1
1	1	0

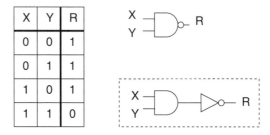

Figure 3.4 *The NAND gate*

3.1.5 NOR

Figure 3.5 shows the truth table and symbol for the NOR gate, as well as how the gate can be built from an OR and a NOT gate. The NOR gate produces the exact opposite output of the OR gate. NOR is short for NOT OR.

X	Y	R
0	0	1
0	1	0
1	0	0
1	1	0

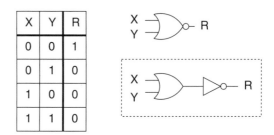

Figure 3.5 *The NOR gate*

3.1.6 XOR

Figure 3.6 shows the truth table and symbol for an XOR gate (sometimes referred to in some texts as an EOR gate). You can see that it is very similar to the OR gate - apart from the fact that it's an *exclusive or* which means that the output is 1 only when either input is 1. If both inputs are set to 1 then the output is 0 - compare this with the OR gate in figure 3.2.

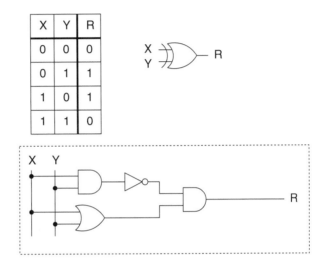

X	Y	R
0	0	0
0	1	1
1	0	1
1	1	0

Figure 3.6   *The XOR gate*

Figure 3.6 also shows how the XOR gate can be built from basic OR, AND and NOT gates too:

▶ Reading the diagram from left to right, X and Y are the inputs to the first AND gate and the OR gate;

▶ The output from the first AND gate is the input to the NOT gate;

▶ The outputs from the OR gate and the NOT gate are inputs to the second AND gate;

▶ The output of the second AND gate is the output R.

3.2 Building Circuits With Gate Logic

All logic circuits can be built from the gates we've just described - in fact we can describe our entire processor in this fashion - but let's start with more simple circuits.

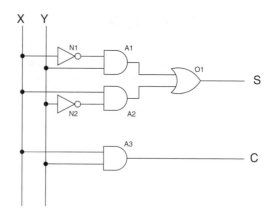

Figure 3.7 *Building circuits*

We can connect gates together as in figure 3.7. We can see from this circuit all of the key features found in much more complicated circuits. This particular circuit has two inputs (X and Y), and two outputs (labelled S and C).

We can see that the output from one logic element can be used as an input to another logic element, and we can see that the same input can be used as inputs to multiple logic elements. To understand how we can connect the parts of a circuit you need to understand the following points:

▶ When we draw circuits, where two wires cross over each other they are not logically joined;

▶ Two wires are logically joined only when a dot is shown over the intersection of the two wires. Look at the diagram in figure 3.7 to understand which logic gates are connected to others.

Any circuit like this can be described in a truth table, almost treating the circuit itself as a single element - the circuit has inputs and can have one or more outputs, and our truth table can describe the outputs for all possible inputs to our circuit. The truth table for the circuit displayed in figure 3.7 is shown in figure 3.8. Later on, at the end of this chapter, we will use the package *Digital Works* to test this circuit, so we can prove that the truth table is correct.

X	Y	S	C
0	0	0	0
0	1	1	0
1	0	1	0
1	1	0	1

Figure 3.8 *Building circuits - the truth table*

One thing worth noting before we move on to a more complicated example, is the use of specific wires as a connection to NOT X, which we write as $\bar{X}$. This is shown in figure 3.9, where the inputs for the gates are taken from the wires for X, Y, $\bar{X}$ and $\bar{Y}$.

In figure 3.7 we used individual NOT gates to obtain the inputs $\bar{X}$ and $\bar{Y}$ as required by the AND gates A1 and A2. Larger circuits often need to reference $\bar{X}$ and $\bar{Y}$ quite often, and so we draw our circuit as shown in figure 3.9.

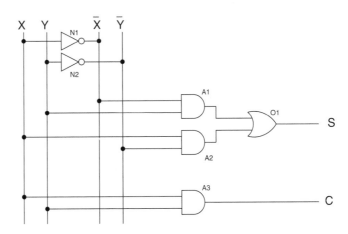

Figure 3.9 *A way of dealing with $\bar{X}$ and $\bar{Y}$*

3.3 Building A Circuit From A Truth Table

In a moment I'll show you how it is possible to build any circuit from a truth table - but it's worth noting a very important point. We will not be building *efficient* circuits. There are many rules we could follow in order to minimize the number of gates that we use (or more accurately to minimize the number of underlying transistors), but these rules only complicate matters, so we aren't going to use them. For our purposes we don't care about creating efficient circuits - we want them to work; we aren't trying to get a job as a chip designer for Intel!

Let's take a complicated truth table, like the one shown in figure 3.10. This particular table has three inputs and two outputs. The circuit it describes has an interesting function, but we don't want to be bothered with that at the moment, we just want to draw the corresponding circuit diagram that this truth table models.

We will take this in two stages, firstly we will model the output labelled as S, and then we will model the output labelled as C_{out}. Once we've done that, using some very simple rules, we will draw the complete circuit.

X	Y	C_{in}	S	C_{out}
0	0	0	0	0
0	0	1	1	0
0	1	0	1	0
0	1	1	0	1
1	0	0	1	0
1	0	1	0	1
1	1	0	0	1
1	1	1	1	1

Figure 3.10   *Building a circuit from the truth table*

Here are the rules for drawing the circuit with the inputs, X, Y and C_{in}:

► Identify all lines in the truth table where the required output is set to 1;
► For each identified line, connect the inputs to an AND gate such that the output from the AND gate is a 1;
► Feed all of the outputs from the set of AND gates into an OR gate.

Let's go through that in stages for the first part of our truth table for output S. There are four lines in the truth table that result in the value of S being set to 1. These are shown in figure 3.11. Have a look back at figure 3.10 to see where these values have come from. These lines of the truth table with outputs of 1 are known as *minterms*.

X	Y	C_{in}	S
0	0	1	1
0	1	0	1
1	0	0	1
1	1	1	1

Figure 3.11   *The truth table for output S*

Now, for each line in figure 3.11 we connect an AND gate into our circuit. For example the first line has $X = 0$, $Y = 0$ and $C_{in} = 1$. We wire up our first AND gate such that it takes three inputs related to this first line in the truth table - we need all inputs to the gate to be 1. Currently this isn't so as both X and Y are set to 0. We can modify these inputs by the use of two NOT gates, as we showed before, or we can connect our AND gate to the lines that represent $\bar{X}$ and $\bar{Y}$ respectively. Now, when $X = 0$, $Y = 0$ and $C_{in} = 1$, all inputs to the AND gate A1 are 1, therefore the output from this gate is 1. Success! If you don't believe me, check out figure 3.12 that shows the inputs to our first AND gate - calculate the values of X, Y and C_{in} required to make the AND gate output the value 1.

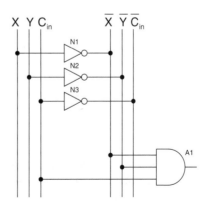

Figure 3.12   *Building the circuit for output S - the first AND gate*

We now follow this process for each of the four lines in the truth table from figure 3.11 until we have the four AND gates correctly wired up to the input lines.

The next task is to feed all outputs from the four AND gates into an OR gate to get a single output. This circuit, shown in figure 3.13, correctly models the truth table from figure 3.11. We won't win any prizes with our implementation, but it *works*!

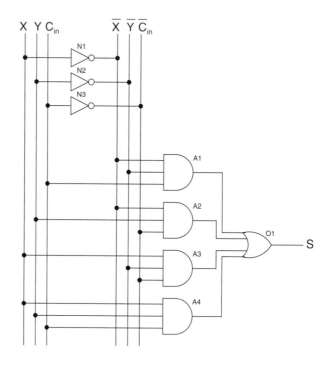

Figure 3.13 *Building the circuit for output S*

We are not finished yet, we need to follow the same procedure again to model the truth table in figure 3.14 - which contains the parts of the whole truth table from figure 3.10 that we are interested in in order to model the output C_{out}. Check back to make sure you understand how the truth table in figure 3.14 was derived.

X	Y	C_{in}	C_{out}
0	1	1	1
1	0	1	1
1	1	0	1
1	1	1	1

Figure 3.14 *The truth table for output C_{out}*

Once we've created our circuit using the same rules as before, to model the output C_{out}, we end up with a diagram like figure 3.15.

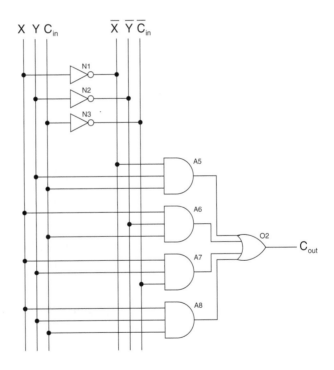

Figure 3.15 *Building the circuit for output C_{out}*

Finally, to implement the complete circuit we can put the figures 3.13 and 3.15 together to get figure 3.16 - our finished circuit.

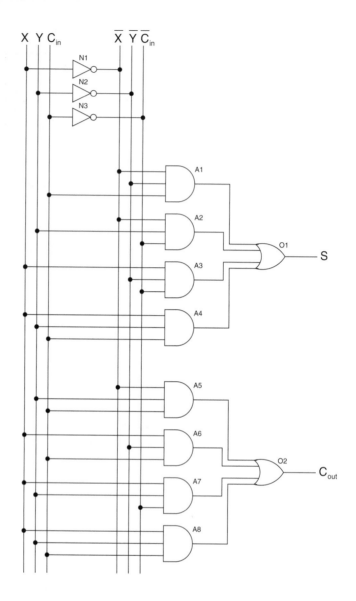

Figure 3.16 *Our finished circuit*

3.4 Boolean Algebra

Our circuits follow the laws of boolean algebra, first discovered by (and named after) George Boole in the nineteenth century. It wasn't until the 1930s that these laws were used to help design efficient electronic circuits.

Boole's algebra uses values than can either be true or false (or 1 or 0 as we have been using in our truth tables) - in fact nowadays within the field of computing a boolean variable is a variable that can be set only to either boolean value, 1 or 0.

The rules of boolean algebra, for our needs, are actually very simple - they contain only three different functions, AND, OR and NOT. Does this sound familiar?

How we write these functions is shown in table 3.1.

Function	Example	Description
AND	$A \cdot B$	Read this as A AND B. Sometimes it's written as AB
OR	$A + B$	Read this as A OR B
NOT	$\bar{A}$	Read this as NOT A

Table 3.1 *The Functions of boolean algebra*

Boolean algebra is perfect for describing our circuits, in fact we will shortly return to the circuit in figure 3.7 to see how it can be described using boolean algebra.

The set of rules that we can make use of are known as the identities of boolean algebra. All the identities are shown in table 3.2. Each identity (apart from the absorbtion and double complement) has two forms, one for the AND form, and the other for the OR form.

We can draw a circuit for any of these identities to show that they are correct. In fact, figure 3.17 shows a circuit to display the OR form of the associative law.

From the diagram we can describe the outputs R1 and R2 as follows:

▶ $R1 = x + (y + z)$;
▶ $R2 = (x + y) + z$.

Law	Identity
Absorbtion	$x \cdot (x + y) = x$
Associative	$x + (y + z) = (x + y) + z$
	$x \cdot (y \cdot z) = (x \cdot y) \cdot z$
Complement	$x + \bar{x} = 1$
	$x \cdot \bar{x} = 0$
Commutative	$x + y = y + x$
	$x \cdot y = y \cdot x$
De Morgan's Laws	$\overline{(x \cdot y)} = \bar{x} + \bar{y}$
	$\overline{(x + y)} = \bar{x} \cdot \bar{y}$
Distributive	$x + (y \cdot z) = (x + y) \cdot (x + z)$
	$x \cdot (y + z) = (x \cdot y) + (x \cdot z)$
Dominance	$x + 1 = 1$
	$x \cdot 0 = 0$
Double Complement	$\overline{(\bar{x})} = x$
Idempotent	$x + x = x$
	$x \cdot x = x$
Identity	$x + 0 = x$
	$x \cdot 1 = x$

Table 3.2 **The Identities of boolean algebra**

If we produced the truth table for both R1 and R2, we would find that both outputs are identical for each set of inputs.

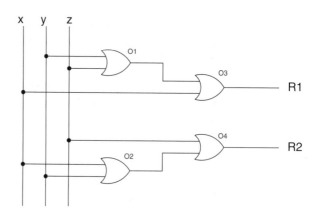

Figure 3.17 **A circuit showing the associative law**

Let's see boolean algebra in action, by describing the circuit in figure 3.7. Let's look at output S first.

- The output of AND gate A1 can be described as $\bar{X} \cdot Y$;
- The output of AND gate A2 can be described as $X \cdot \bar{Y}$;
- The output of OR gate O1 can be described as $(\bar{X} \cdot Y) + (X \cdot \bar{Y})$;
- Therefore the output $S = (\bar{X} \cdot Y) + (X \cdot \bar{Y})$;
- This form of expression is known as a *sum of products*.

Output C is easier to write down.

- The output of AND gate A3 can be described as $X \cdot Y$;
- Therefore the output $C = X \cdot Y$.

There is another way to describe our circuits using the functions of boolean algebra - in fact we've already seen this other method - it's the use of truth tables.

3.4.1 De Morgan's Laws

I won't dwell on all the identities shown in table 3.2, apart from one in particular that we can make use of in the creation of *efficient* digital circuits. These particular identities are De Morgan's Laws. Let's look at the two identities for this law again.

- $\overline{(x \cdot y)} = \bar{x} + \bar{y}$
- $\overline{(x + y)} = \bar{x} \cdot \bar{y}$

You can see that, for each identity, we can convert from using OR gates to using AND gates. Why would we want to do this? The answer lies in table 3.3 - by converting our circuits to make use of NAND and NOR gates, we can significantly reduce the number of transistors to build the circuit. So what? Well, reducing the number of transistors required in a circuit lowers its cost by a tiny amount (and could also cause a speed improvement), but when this circuit is used a couple of million times in, say, the automotive industry, we can make enormous cost reductions.

Gate	Number of transistors
AND	3
OR	3
NOT	1
NAND	2
NOR	2

Table 3.3 *How many transistors to build a gate?*

It is worth mentioning that an AND gate takes three transistors because it is actually built of a NAND gate followed by a NOT gate - reducing our circuits to sets of NAND gates can significantly reduce the amount of transistors we need to use.

NOTES

An explanation of the use of Karnough maps can be found in [Cle00] and [Gib84].

NOTES

The Quine/McCluskie method is described in [MH00].

Reducing a sum of products expression describing a circuit to its most efficient form can be done using a technique that makes use of *Karnough maps*. A Karnough map can be used to reduce a sum of products expression with up to four separate inputs by way of a pictorial description of the inputs. More complicated techniques, such as the *Quine/McCluskie method* can be used for greater numbers of inputs.

3.5 Introducing Digital Works

Throughout this text, we'll make use of a package called Digital Works. This package not only lets us draw circuits, but also to 'run' them so we can see what they do. The full description of how to use Digital Works is in Appendix F, all we'll do here is have a look at some example circuits that we've already looked at - but this time we'll be able to test them to see if they do what we think they do.

3.5.1 Running Our First Circuit

First of all, we will run the first circuit we built - the circuit from figure 3.7. You'll find this circuit in a Digital Works file called `halfadder.dwm` on the CD in the location

```
\examples\chapter03\halfadder.dwm
```

When you load this file into Digital Works, you'll see something like figure 3.18.

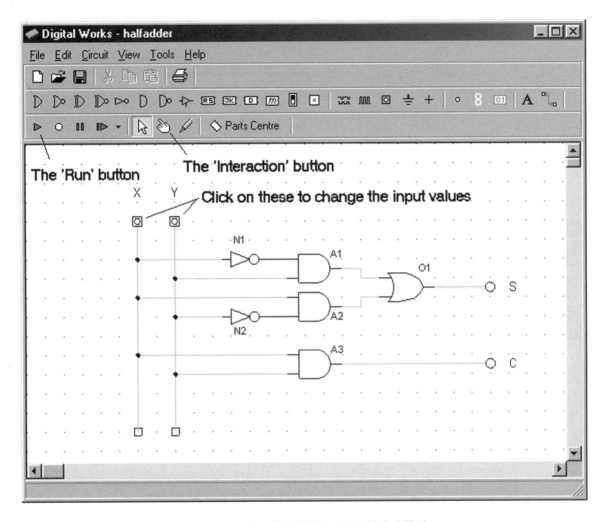

Figure 3.18 *Our finished circuit in Digital Works*

To run our circuit you need to:

▶ Click on the 'Run' button (labelled in figure 3.18) - this will enable us to run this particular circuit;

▶ Click on the 'Interaction' button - when the mouse pointer is over the circuit it should change into a hand with a pointing finger. This will allow us to interact with our circuit;

▶ Click on input X, or more properly the interactive input button below the X symbol (as shown in figure 3.19) - you should find that the output S (shown connected to a simulated *light emitting diode*, or *LED*) should light up. When the LED is lit, the output S is set to 1, and when it is clear, output S is set to 0 - in fact we can see the truth levels of all the wiring too as a wire carrying a logical 1 is shown in black while a wire carrying a logical 0 is shown in grey.

Try changing the inputs and see what the outputs change to - this should match completely the definition for this circuit in the truth table in figure 3.8. And that's it!

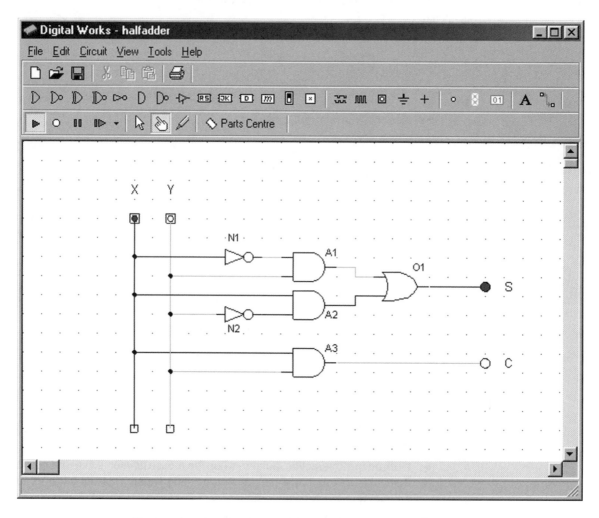

Figure 3.19 *Our finished circuit in Digital Works, showing X = 1*

CHAPTER SUMMARY

Gate logic

▶ The fundamental gates are AND, OR and NOT. All other gates and circuits can be constructed from these;

▶ These gates model the logical operations AND, OR and NOT as we described in the previous chapter;

▶ Truth tables describe, given a set of inputs, the outputs for a given gate or circuit;

▶ Circuits can be built that model truth tables, by modelling the minterms with AND gates and feeding their outputs into an OR gate.

Boolean algebra

▶ Named after George Boole, boolean algebra can be used to describe circuits. The set of rules are known as the identities of boolean algebra, and most laws have two forms - an AND and an OR form;

▶ De Morgan's laws can be used to make circuits more efficient by reducing the number of transistors used within a circuit.

Using Digital Works

▶ Digital Works can be used to draw and then simulate logic circuits.

SELF TEST QUESTIONS

1 Draw a circuit, using the methods described above, to meet the following truth table.

X	Y	R
0	0	1
0	1	0
1	0	0
1	1	1

2 Run the circuit in \examples\chapter03\assoc.dwm. This circuit demonstrates the associative law - prove to yourself that the outputs match as expected.

3 Run the circuit in \examples\chapter03\st3-3.dwm and write down the truth table for this circuit. What task does this circuit do?

4 Draw a circuit within Digital Works to demonstrate the $\overline{(x \cdot y)} = \bar{x} + \bar{y}$ identity of De Morgan's law.

EXERCISES

1 Draw a circuit within Digital Works to demonstrate the $x \cdot (x + y) = x$ identity.

2 Draw a circuit within Digital Works to demonstrate the $\overline{(x + y)} = \bar{x} \cdot \bar{y}$ identity of De Morgan's law.

3 Draw circuits within Digital Works to demonstrate the absorbtion and idempotent identities.

Registers

This chapter examines the use of registers and describes how they can be built using gate logic.

This chapter includes:

▶ Bistables - the RS latch, the D latch and the D flip-flop;

▶ How to build a register;

▶ Tri-state logic;

▶ The concept of a clock and a clock cycle;

▶ Using registers in JASPer.

4.1 Introducing An Electronic Memory

So far we've looked at how to build up circuits to match truth tables, but we haven't looked at circuits to meet particular tasks. In this chapter we will look at how we can build circuits to store bit patterns - these can then be used to create larger storage elements such as registers (I'll explain how to build these soon) and whole computer memories (which I'll describe in chapter 7).

To store a value we need a special circuit called a *bistable*, which means that the output of such a circuit can be stable in one of two distinct states. The first bistable we'll look at (one that is at the heart of the other bistables that we'll make use of) is called the *RS latch*. It's shown in figure 4.1 - and you can see that it's called the RS latch after its two inputs, imaginatively labelled R and S.

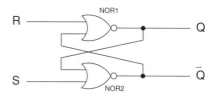

Figure 4.1 *The RS latch*

We can see that the circuit has two outputs, Q and $\bar{Q}$ - where $\bar{Q}$ is the opposite of Q, with one notable exception, so we are only really concerned with the output Q.

Let us look at the use of the RS latch. The R stands for *Reset*, and when we set R to 1, Q is set to 0; when S (which stands for *Set*) is set to 1, then Q is set to 1. If both S and R are set to 0, then the value of Q will be left at whatever it was last set to. This is important - effectively the circuit *remembers* whether the last operation was 'Set' or 'Reset'. In other words, the RS latch will successfully store 1 bit of information as long as it is powered. Don't take my word for it, try running the file:

```
\examples\chapter04\rslatch.dwm
```

in Digital Works to see the operation of an RS latch first hand. The operation of the RS latch is described in table 4.1.

R	S	Description
0	0	Q is left at what it was previously set to
0	1	$Q = 1$
1	0	$Q = 0$
1	1	$Q = \bar{Q} = 0$

Table 4.1 *The Truth table for the RS latch*

However, the RS latch isn't perfect - in fact it has a particular failing that could cause us problems - what happens when both R and S are set to 1? We can see that within the truth table we can see that when both inputs are set to 1, then *both* Q and $\bar{Q}$ are set to 0. Apart from indicating that for this case the traditional labels are incorrect (some texts treat the outputs as Qa and Qb), if both inputs are simultaneously set to 0 the outputs are then undefined. Q

will jump to either 0 or 1 (with $\bar{Q}$ now correctly being the opposite of Q). It is impossible to predict which state Q will take after both inputs have been 1, as it depends so much on the speed of the individual gates. This circumstance is something we need to guard against, so we need to add a few new gates to our RS latch to produce a new circuit called the *D latch*.

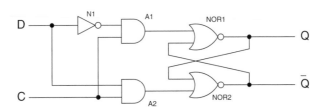

Figure 4.2   *The D latch*

The D latch is shown in figure 4.2. It's called a D latch because the key input is now D (which stands for *Data*) You can see that it still has an RS latch at its heart, but we've added two features:

▶ The D input now goes (via AND gates that we'll talk about in a moment) to both NOR gates - with one input being inverted with a NOT gate. Effectively, D takes the place of both the R and S inputs to the RS latch, so now the condition R = S = 1 of the RS latch cannot occur.

▶ We have added an extra input called the C input (the C stands for *Clock* - we'll discuss what we mean by a clock later). We can see that for the input value D to reach the NOR gates the C input has to be set to 1 (because of the AND gates).

You can check out the use of a D latch in the example:

```
\examples\chapter04\dlatch.dwm
```

Try updating the output Q by changing the inputs to the D latch with this example:

▶ Set D to 0;
▶ Set C to 1;
▶ Set C back to 0;
▶ Q should now be set to 0;
▶ Set D to 1;

► Q is still set to 0;

► Set C to 1;

► Set C back to 0;

► Q should now be set to 1.

The truth table for the D latch is shown in table 4.2.

D	C	Description
0	0	Q is left at what it was previously set to.
0	1	Q = 0
1	0	Q is left at what it was previously set to.
1	1	Q = 1

Table 4.2 *The truth table for the D latch*

Finally, we are getting to a circuit that we can make use of to build storage devices for our processor, there is only one minor change that we want to make - and that's to do with how we make use of the C input. So far, when we set the C input to 1, any changes we make to D will be reflected in the output Q - so what we want to do is limit the time that the C input is set to 1 (we will see why later), and we can do that with one more minor update to our D latch - to create a circuit called a *D flip-flop*. The D flip-flop is shown in figure 4.3.

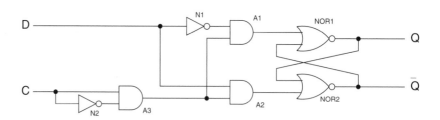

Figure 4.3 *The D flip-flop*

The only change we've made is to add an extra NOT gate to the C input line, that routes C and $\bar{C}$ into the AND gate A3. At first glance you would think that such a circuit wouldn't work - as passing 0 and 1 into an AND gate will always result in a 0 - hence it looks like the C input to the rest of the circuit will always be 0, which as we've seen in table 4.2 should mean that the output Q could never change. However, the circuit in figure 4.3 *does* work - due to a property of real logic gates called *latency*.

Latency is essentially how long it takes for an input signal to a gate to *propagate*, or transmit energy, through the gate and to set the output. The electronic signal from C reaches the gate A3 at something like half the speed of light, whereas the signal passing through the NOT gate N2 takes longer (only very slightly longer!) due to the latency of that gate - so, for a very brief time period, the output of the AND gate A3 will be set to 1 before it is set to 0 (as the signal has passed through the NOT gate such that the inputs to the AND gate are now 1 and 0).

As D flip-flops are so common, we have a special way of drawing them in a circuit, shown in figure 4.4. The triangle at the C input indicates that the clock is a *positive edge trigger* - more on what is meant by edge triggering later.

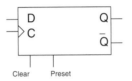

Figure 4.4 *The symbol for a D flip-flop*

Figure 4.4 indicates the practical addition of two further connections to the D flip-flop. The *Clear* and *Preset* connections to the D flip-flop can be used to set the output Q to either 1 or 0. Setting the Clear line high will set the output Q to 0, while setting the Preset line high will set the output Q to 1.

4.2 Building A Register

Now we have our memory elements in the form of D flip-flops, we can build registers. A register is a finite storage element in a processor. We'll start off by building a 4-bit register, and then show how we can build a 16-bit register for use in our processor.

A 4-bit register consists of four D flip-flops wired as you can see in figure 4.5. The inputs consist of four data values labelled from D0 to D3 and the C input for the clock. The C input is wired to all the C inputs on the flip-flops, so that they can all be triggered at the same time. Getting back to the data inputs, D0 will be the least significant bit (LSB, the rightmost bit in the number) moving up to the most significant bit (MSB, the leftmost bit in the number) in D3. If we wanted to store the value 12_{10} (1100_2) we would store the bits as in table 4.3. The outputs to the circuit, R0 through to R3 are the outputs from our register - these outputs show the value we have stored in our register.

Input	Value
D0	0
D1	0
D2	1
D3	1

Table 4.3   *Storing a 4-bit number in our register*

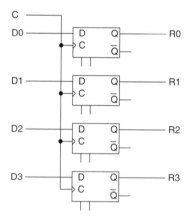

Figure 4.5   *A 4-bit register*

So, assuming that the bit pattern to be placed inside the register is on the data lines (inputs D0 to D3), all we have to do is clock the register for it to store the bit pattern from the data lines in the register.

Creating a 16-bit register is a simple matter of scaling up the 4-bit register, as shown in figure 4.6. The 16-bit register has 17 inputs, the data inputs D0 to D15 and the C input (wired to all the C inputs of each D flip-flop). The outputs, R0 to R15, again show the value we have stored in our register, and if we wanted to use the value from our register (to store it in another register perhaps) it is these wires that we would connect to. From here on in, we will just use diagrams of 4-bit registers to understand their workings, as you can see that if we were to use 16-bit registers in all diagrams, the diagrams could get unnecessarily complicated!

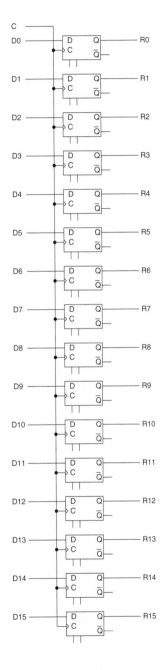

Figure 4.6 *A 16-bit register*

We still can't wire our registers together, as we'll need to in our processor to transfer values between registers, but that will be covered next.

4.3 Tri-state Logic

To wire our registers together, so that we can pass values between them, we need to introduce a new form of gate called a *tri-state gate*, the symbol of which is shown in figure 4.7.

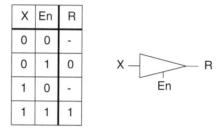

X	En	R
0	0	-
0	1	0
1	0	-
1	1	1

Figure 4.7 *A tri-state gate*

The tri-state gate has two inputs, X and En and one output called R. This type of gate has a very special purpose - to connect or disconnect the input X to the output R. It does this by using the En input, which stands for *enable*. When En = 1 the input X is directly connected to the output R, effectively we can think of the gate in this state as being exactly the same as a straight piece of wire - R has the same value as X. However, when En = 0 something totally different happens - effectively X and R are disconnected from each other, whatever value X takes, R is not affected in any way. In fact it would be wrong to attempt to measure the value of R in this state, it could be 0 or it could be 1 - this state is called *floating*.

Why would we want such a gate? We need sets of such gates to allow us to connect a number of registers to the same set of wires, so we can transfer values between the registers. We call this set of wires a *data bus* and we'll talk about the data bus itself in chapter 6. If we didn't make use of tri-state logic to connect our registers to the data bus, then we might have a situation whereby one register tries to put the bit pattern 1000_2 onto the data bus, whereas another register might put the bit pattern 0111_2 on to the data bus. What would happen? We have no way of knowing what the value on the bus will become, it could be set to 0111_2, 1000_2 or something totally different. The act of attempting to have two registers (or any other component) place different bit patterns on the data bus is called *bus contention* and it's something we avoid by using tri-state logic.

Look at figure 4.8. In this diagram we have wired up two registers to the data bus and we want to copy a bit pattern from register 1 to register 2. How do we do this? Let's assume that register 1 contains 0011_2, so the flip-flop F1 contains the bit value '1', F2 contains '1', F3 contains '0' and F4 contains '0'. Check the diagram to see if you agree with me. To move this value to register 2 we need to do the following:

▶ Set the register 1 OE line to 1. OE stands for *output enable* - in other words we have enabled the tri-state gates connected to the outputs of register 1, so that the value from register 1 is now on the data bus wires.

▶ We now set register 2 C line to 1. This is the clock line for register 2, which when set allows the flip-flops in this register to take the value from the data bus - in other words, we have transferred the value to register 2.

▶ Lastly, we set register 1 OE line back to 0, to disconnect the flip-flops of register 1 from the data bus.

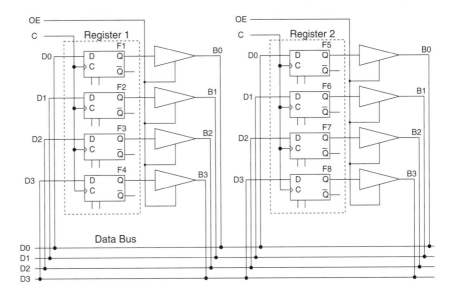

Figure 4.8 *Copying bit patterns between registers*

You can use the Digital Works example at

```
\examples\chapter04\4bitregister2.dwm
```

to try copying bit patterns between registers yourself (a screen shot of this example is in figure 4.9). Note that the Digital Works version of this circuit has two minor differences from the diagram in figure 4.8. These are that interactive buttons are connected to the set and preset inputs of the flip-flops to allow easy setting of values for the registers, and that LEDs have been connected to the flip-flop outputs to more easily see the value they store.

Try the following with this circuit:

▶ Use the interactive inputs on the flip-flops to store a value in register 1;
▶ Click on the OE of register 1 (tri-state gates now enabled);
▶ Click on the C of register 2 (bit pattern taken from the bus into register 2);
▶ Click on the C of register 2 again, to set it back to 0;
▶ Click on the OE of register 1 again, to set it back to 0;
▶ You've now successfully completed the transfer of the register 1 bit pattern to register 2.

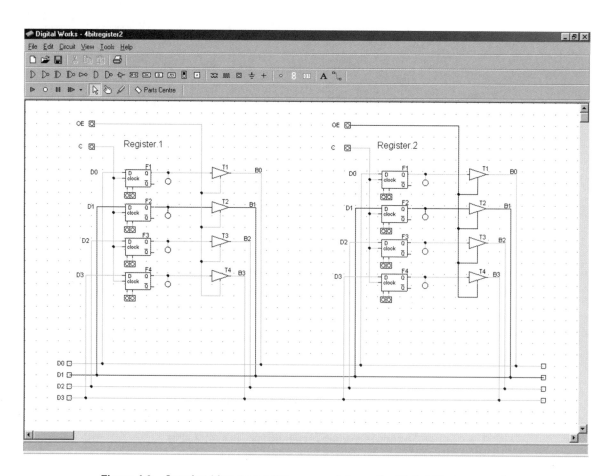

Figure 4.9 *Copying bit patterns between registers - the Digital Works example*

Try setting the OE line to 1 for both registers while running the circuit - you can see how Digital Works points out that you have a bus contention issue. A real circuit would continue running, with the value on the bus being indeterminate.

We still have some work to do. The 4-bit registers in figure 4.8 have ten connections, six of these are inputs (C, OE and D0 to D3) and four are outputs (B0 to B3). By moving the tri-state logic inside the registers, we can reduce the number of connections to six for our registers, (C, OE and D0 to D3). This refinement is shown in figure 4.10, along with an additional connection, 'Reset', making a total of seven connections. The improvements that we have made are:

1 The register only requires connection to the bus four times, using D0 to D3. We can read the values on the bus through these connections to set the register (by setting C), and we can put the value stored in this register onto the bus through these connections (by setting OE);

2 We have also added a 'Reset' line into our register and with this we can set the value of the register to 0 just by setting the Reset line to 1 (as the reset line is connected to all the reset lines of each flip-flop inside the register). Strictly speaking, we don't need this feature in our register, but it aids practical use of the register.

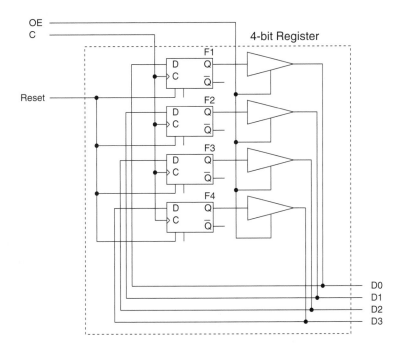

Figure 4.10 *A further refinement to our register*

73

Now that we understand fully what is going on inside our registers, it makes sense to use a symbol to represent them, to aid the clarity of our circuits. The symbols for a 4-bit and a 16-bit register are shown in figure 4.11.

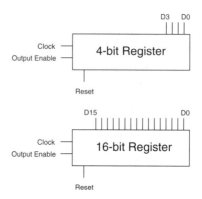

Figure 4.11 *Symbols for registers*

Using these symbols, we can now refine the earlier figure showing registers connected to a bus to that shown in figure 4.12.

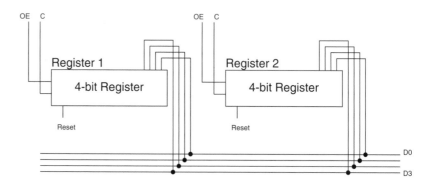

Figure 4.12 *Copying bit patterns between registers, a refinement*

To move a bit pattern from register 1 to register 2 we would do as before:

▶ Set register 1 OE to 1 (bit pattern now on the bus);
▶ Clock register 2 (for register 2 to take the bit pattern from the bus);
▶ Set register 1 OE to 0;

All transfers of bit patterns from one register to another take this form. We call the act of copying data from one register to another a *data movement*, even though the first register is left with the same contents as before the data movement.

4.4 Introducing The Clock

We've sometimes talked about a *clock* input to our circuits, and now it's time to explain what we mean by this. Also, we'll describe something related called the *clock cycle*.

We need a clock to *synchronize* all the components of our processor. It would be no good if we wanted to transfer a bit pattern from one register to another, if the second register doesn't access the data bus at the right time, to take the data put there by the first register. Our processor needs order.

We use a *clock line* in our processor that, like the ticking of a clock (actually produced by an oscillating crystal), sends out a signal that looks like that in figure 4.13. The amount of time between the clock pulse changing from 1 to 0, and that from 0 to 1 is the same. The speed of the clock is often used in advertisements for computers as a measure of how fast a computer is (it's not the only factor deciding how fast the computer is, but it's the simplest for a computer novice to recognize) - clock speeds can be anything from 1 *MHz* to 1 *GHz* and higher.

1 clock cycle is where the signal changes from 0 to 1, and then back to 0, probably best understood from figure 4.13.

> **DEFINITION**
>
> **1 MHz** : *1* megahertz - *1 million cycles per second.*

> **DEFINITION**
>
> **1 GHz** : *1* gigahertz - *1 thousand million cycles per second.*

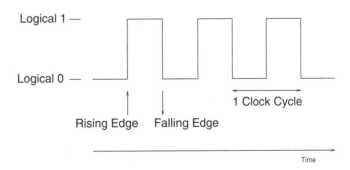

Figure 4.13   *The clock cycle*

Just because we call an input to a register the clock line, doesn't necessarily mean that it is connected to the processor clock - it just indicates that the clock line is used to *trigger* the register in some way. Clock lines for registers are actually triggered by part of the circuit that defines the control unit - we'll describe that in chapter 17, and see that the control unit needs to make use of the clock.

There are effectively four different types of trigger. These are:

▶ 1 triggered - when the clock signal becomes 1;

▶ 0 triggered - when the clock signal becomes 0;

▶ Positive edge triggered - when the clock signal changes from a 0 to a 1;

▶ Negative edge triggered - when the clock signal changes from a 1 to a 0.

A D latch is triggered (and stays active) when its C line is set to 1, whereas a standard D flip-flop triggers on a positive edge. Triggering on an edge is better than triggering on a particular value, as an *edge transition* happens for only a tiny amount of time and can be used for very accurate timing.

4.5 Using Registers

Let's have a look at the registers in JASPer. There are 12 of them, as you can see in figure 4.14. The registers in JASPer have their current contents displayed in them, and most register contents are displayed as hexadecimal - all apart from the PSR which is shown in binary. All of the JASPer registers are 16 bits wide. Don't worry just yet about the register names - we'll cover their individual usage in chapter 8.

We can easily put values in the JASPer registers and move the values from one register to another.

To put a value in a JASPer register, click on 'processor/registers' and use the dialogue box (as shown in figure 4.15) to enter the values you want to store. When you click on the 'OK' button, provided the values you entered were perfectly reasonable 16-bit values in a hexadecimal representation, you'll see the registers change in the main display. To move a bit pattern from one register to another, we can use a set of commands that the processor understands that are accessed from 'processor/microcode list/data movement'. These commands are specified in a language called *Register Transfer Language (RTL)*.

In RTL the destination is given first followed by a left pointing arrow and then the source register. Each data movement can be described using RTL, so for example, the data movement from the MDR register to the A register can be described as:

$$A \leftarrow [MDR]$$

The brackets mean *contents of*. So read this RTL instruction as 'move the contents of the MDR register to the A register'.

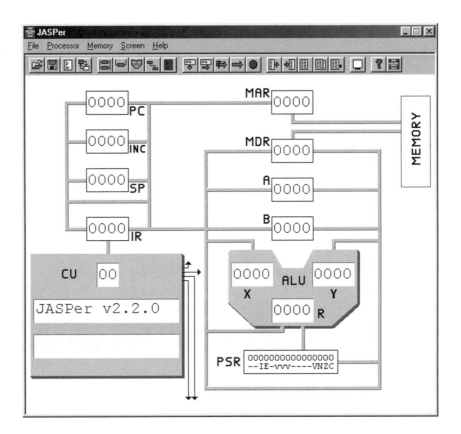

Figure 4.14 *Another look at JASPer*

Try a few data movements for yourself and see what they do - you'll see the data movement animated on the screen for you.

Now that we've looked at the view of JASPer and moved some data values between registers, we can see that if JASPer were a real processor then the electronic circuitry in the registers would match everything that we've described in this chapter - no magic required!

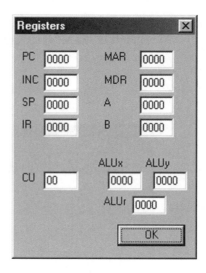

Figure 4.15 *The JASPer registers dialog box*

CHAPTER SUMMARY

Bistables

▶ The RS latch can store 1 bit of data, but it has an issue whereby if both inputs are set to 1 and then simultaneously reset, the output Q is unpredictable;

▶ The D latch is an update to the RS latch to ensure that the RS latch will never have both inputs set to 1;

▶ The D flip-flop is an advancement on the D latch that is edge triggered.

Building registers

▶ Registers can be built from sets of D flip-flops;

▶ The clock lines to each flip-flop are wired to the same clock input;

▶ To store an 8-bit value, the register must have eight flip-flops, while a 16-bit register requires 16 flip-flops, etc.

Tri-state logic

▶ A tri-state gate can be used to disconnect parts of circuits from each other;

▶ When the En line is set to 1, a tri-state gate places its input on its output. When the En line is set to 0, a tri-state gate disconnects its output from its input;

The clock cycle

▶ The clock cycle is used to synchronize components;

▶ The clock is driven by an oscillating signal;

▶ The clock can trigger components - these triggers can be 1, 0, positive edge or negative edge.

Registers in JASPer

▶ Registers in JASPer are all 16 bits wide;

▶ Data movements between registers are described with RTL.

SELF TEST QUESTIONS

1 How can we write in RTL a description of moving a data value from the PC register to the MAR register?

2 Run the circuit \examples\chapter04\dlatch.dwm. Firstly, set the output Q to 1, then set the output Q to 0.

3 Run the circuit \examples\chapter04\dflipflop.dwm. Firstly, set the output Q to 1, then set the output Q to 0.

4 Describe the key difference between using a D flip-flop and using a D latch.

5 Run the circuit \examples\chapter04\4bitregister.dwm. Store the bit pattern 1010_2 in the register.

6 Using \examples\chapter04\bitregister2.dwm, first store the bit pattern 1011_2 in register one, and then transfer the value to register two.

EXERCISES

1 Using \examples\chapter04\bitregister2.dwm, first store the value 1100_2 in register two, and then transfer the value to register one.

2 Using JASPer, place the value 1234_{16} in the MDR register. Transfer the value from the MDR register to the A register. Describe this data movement using RTL.

3 Using JASPer, place the value $F0DA_{16}$ in the B register. Transfer the value from the B register to the MAR register. Describe this data movement using RTL.

4 Using JASPer, place the number $97 into the CU, set the animation option to a very slow rate and then hit the 'execute' button. Write down the sequence of data movement operations that you see executed.

The ALU

In this chapter we discuss the uses of the ALU and show how ALU functionality can be built from gate logic.

This chapter includes:

▶ The role of the ALU and PSR within the processor;
▶ The control circuitry of the ALU;
▶ Adder circuits - the half adder and the full adder;
▶ Building circuits to demonstrate the functionality of the ALU - the ADD, SL and NEG circuits;
▶ Using the ALU in JASPer.

5.1 About The ALU

The ALU, or *Arithmetic Logic Unit*, is a processor's calculator - and without it the processor could not do many useful tasks at all. In this chapter I'll describe the sort of operations provided by an ALU, look at how to build a selected few of these operations from gate logic, and then look at the ALU in JASPer.

The typical symbol for an ALU is shown in figure 5.1. Essentially, the ALU consists of three registers, the ALUx and ALUy (which are used as inputs to the ALU), the ALUr (which contains the result when an ALU operation is executed) and some special circuitry to execute the ALU operations. Although strictly speaking not part of the ALU, the PSR (*Processor Status Register*) is also required both to aid the functionality of the ALU but also to help control the processor.

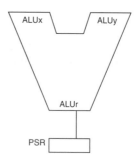

Figure 5.1 *The ALU and PSR symbols*

The ALU, as its name implies, executes arithmetic and logical operations. The sort of arithmetic operations include binary addition and subtraction (as we saw in chapter 2), and the logical operations including AND, OR and NOT as we discussed in chapters 2 and 3.

The ALU and PSR in JASPer are shown in figure 5.2.

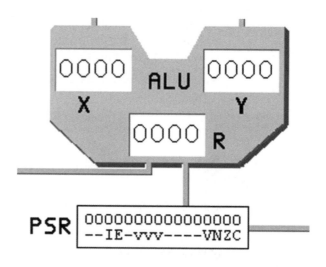

Figure 5.2 *The JASPer ALU and PSR*

Some ALUs can also cope with floating point numbers, which is how we can represent numbers such as 3.14 or 1.563×10^{28}, but many small processors don't have an ALU that can use floating point numbers. We'll not include this functionality in our processor design.

5.1.1 The Role Of The PSR

We can see the PSR included in figure 5.1. It serves the purpose of helping us keep track of what is happening inside the processor. As we've mentioned before, PSR stands for *Processor Status Register*. Although we call it a register, we don't quite use it in the same way as other registers - we tend just to use parts of the register bit pattern at a time, and it would be implemented differently from the way we built our registers in chapter 4 - largely because we use individual bits from the PSR rather than the complete bit pattern. The PSR actually contains a broad range of information, various parts of its contents are used for a whole variety of tasks - we put all of this together into the one register so we have all the processor status information in the one place.

In our discussion of the ALU, the only part of the PSR that we are interested in are the V, N, Z and C *flags* - I'll describe the meanings of each of these shortly and leave the other parts of the PSR to later chapters.

Firstly, why do we call these parts of the PSR flags? A flag tells us something about the ALU operation - in fact each of the V, N, Z and C flags tell us about the contents of the ALUr after an arithmetic or logical operation has been executed. Each of these flags is listed in table 5.1.

Flag	Name	Meaning when the bit is set to 1
V	Overflow	The last ALU operation resulted in a 2's complement overflow - in other words, the ALUr wasn't large enough to store the result. We use a 'V' to represent overflow instead of 'O' as that could be mistaken for a binary zero.
N	Negative	The last ALU operation resulted in a bit pattern that represents a negative value in the ALUr.
Z	Zero	The last ALU operation resulted in a bit pattern that represents a zero value in the ALUr.
C	Carry	The last ALU operation resulted in a carry being generated.

Table 5.1 *The PSR ALU Flags*

5.2 Inside The ALU

Let's take a first look inside our ALU in figure 5.3. You can see that it contains, as we said, the ALUx, ALUy and the ALUr, as well as the circuitry to perform the arithmetic and the logical operations. Note that in our simple processor, these registers are 16 bits wide, but the registers and buses are shown as 4 bits wide in the diagram to reduce clutter.

The ALU registers are actually connected to the data bus by a unit labelled the *ALU data bus connection circuitry* because at times we need to isolate the ALU from the other components on the data bus. This circuitry consists of some tri-state gates connecting the ALUx, ALUy and the ALUr to the data bus - it can be activated by signals on the ALU data bus lines. A 2-bit code is used to either connect the ALUx, the ALUy or the ALUr to the data bus, or to disconnect all from the data bus. We don't need to discuss the connection circuitry any further to understand the workings of the ALU.

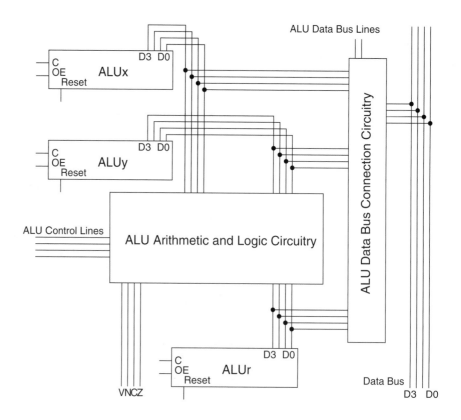

Figure 5.3 *Inside the ALU*

Code	Operation	RTL	Description
0000	ADD	ALUr=[ALUx]+[ALUy]	Perform a 2's complement ADD operation, adding the ALUx and ALUy bit patterns together and storing the result in the ALUr register
0001	ADC	ALUr=[ALUx]+[ALUy]+[PSR(c)]	Perform a 2's complement ADC operation, adding the ALUx and ALUy and C flag together and storing the result in the ALUr register
0010	SUB	ALUr=[ALUx]-[ALUy]	Perform a 2's complement SUB operation, subtracting the ALUy from the ALUx bit pattern and storing the result in the ALUr register
0011	SL	ALUr=[ALUx]<<1	Perform a logical shift left on the ALUx, storing the result in the ALUr
0100	SR	ALUr=[ALUx]>>1	Perform a logical shift right on the ALUx, storing the result in the ALUr
0101	AND	ALUr=[ALUx]&[ALUy]	Perform a logical AND operation on the ALUx and ALUy bit patterns and storing the result in the ALUr register
0110	OR	ALUr=[ALUx]|[ALUy]	Perform a logical OR operation on the ALUx and ALUy bit patterns and storing the result in the ALUr register
0111	NOT	ALUr=~[ALUx]	Perform a logical NOT operation on the ALUx and storing the result in the ALUr register
1000	NEG	ALUr=~[ALUx]+1	Perform a 2's complement negative operation on the ALUx and storing the result in the ALUr register
1001	INC	ALUr=[ALUx]+1	Add 1 to the ALUx bit pattern, storing the result in the ALUr
1010	DEC	ALUr=[ALUx]-1	Subtract 1 from the ALUx bit pattern, storing the result in the ALUr
1011	SWAP	ALUr(7:0)=[ALUx(15:8)]; ALUr(15:8)=[ALUx(7:0)]	Swap the most significant byte and the least significant byte of the ALUx, storing the result in the ALUr
1100	MUL	ALUr=[ALUx]*[ALUy]	Multiply the ALUx value by the ALUy value, storing the result in the ALUr
1101	DIV	ALUr=[ALUx]/[ALUy]	Divide the ALUx value by the ALUy value, storing the result in the ALUr
1110	MOD	ALUr=[ALUx]%[ALUy]	Divide the ALUx value by the ALUy value, storing the remainder in the ALUr

Table 5.2 *The ALU Operations*

Let's start off by defining the operations that we want our ALU to perform. We need it to perform addition and subtraction, logical operations (AND, OR and NOT), as well as multiplication and division.

It is worth noting that the logical operations work in exactly the same way as when we covered this topic in chapter 3. For example, an AND operation on two 16-bit representations would perform an AND on the LSBs of each number, then the second to right bits, etc.

Table 5.2 describes the sort of operations we want to implement - we have allocated a 4-bit binary code to each that we can use later as the control signal to the ALU to perform that operation.

As you can see, we aren't using all the possible control codes from the ALU control signal, 1111_2 is unused.

Activity in the ALU is controlled by a set of control lines, and as we aren't going to have much functionality in our ALU, four lines are enough to control it. This means that we can have a maximum of 16 distinct operations defined (because we can count from 0 to 15 in four bits). If we take a look inside the circuitry that performs the arithmetic and logical operations, we can see (in figure 5.4) that one part of the circuit is used to decode the ALU control signal, and the rest is taken up by individual units to perform each ALU operation.

Please note that if we were to look inside an ALU of a real processor - it wouldn't look like this, as there are many improvements that we could make in order to make the functionality much more efficient. However, as we said before, we aren't concerning ourselves with building the most efficient circuits, instead we want to build circuits that are more easily understood.

For clarity, figure 5.4 only shows one line for each ALUx and ALUy input and yet already we are getting the idea that most of our processor is made up of wires connecting each part of a circuit with other parts! This is actually quite a problem in creating real microprocessors - because it's very difficult to design a layout to give this connectivity that can easily be built.

5.2.1 Decoding The ALU Control Signal

To decode the control signal, we make use of a special sort of circuit called a *decoder* shown in figure 5.5. This circuit takes the 4-bit ALU control code and, using an AND gate for each possible input value, ensures that only one AND gate can produce a 1 value at a time. The output from each AND gate can then be used to activate one particular arithmetic or logic operation.

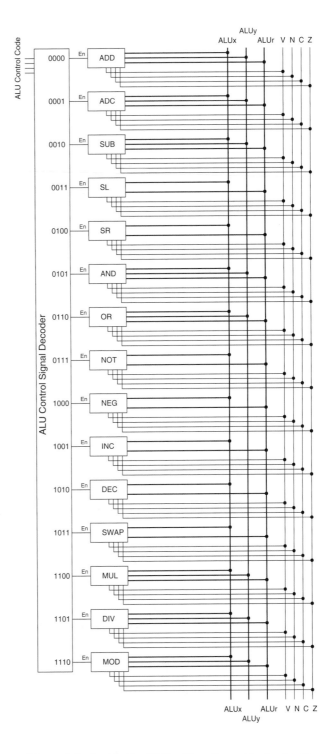

Figure 5.4 *Inside the ALU arithmetic and logic circuit*

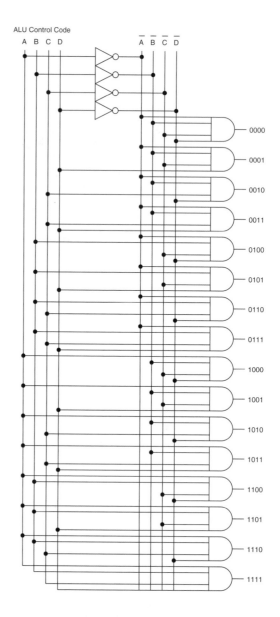

Figure 5.5 *Inside the ALU control signal decoder*

For example, the control signal 0011, would have the individual control lines set as follows:

► $A = 0$;
► $B = 0$;
► $C = 1$;
► $D = 1$;

This would result in the AND gate labelled as 0011 being the only AND gate to produce the output one, all other AND gates would produce a zero.

We are only using the first 15 codes for the functionality discussed in table 5.2, so we wouldn't connect the output for the AND gate that would be activated for the bit pattern 1111_2.

5.3 Adder Circuits

Let's start off by seeing how we would build a circuit to perform 2's complement arithmetic - to do this we will introduce two circuits that we will need to make use of. Firstly, we'll take a look at something called a *half adder*, then we'll move on to a circuit called a *full adder*, then after that we have all the building blocks we need to build the complete ADD circuit.

5.3.1 Introducing The Half Adder

Back in chapter 2 we described how we could add two binary numbers together - and we, at first glance, could use half adders to implement this form of addition. The half adder takes two inputs, X and Y, and gives two outputs, S (the sum) and C (the carry) and its truth table can be seen in figure 5.6. We can use the method that we described in chapter 3 to draw a circuit for a half adder - in fact the complete circuit is shown in figure 5.7. Does it look familiar in any way? It should, this is the first circuit we actually created back in chapter 3 in figure 3.7.

X	Y	S	C
0	0	0	0
0	1	1	0
1	0	1	0
1	1	0	1

Figure 5.6 *The truth table for the half adder*

We make use of a half adder so much when building arithmetic circuits that it even has its own symbol, shown in figure 5.8.

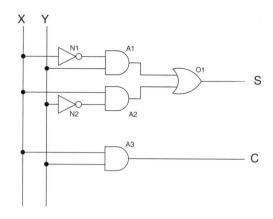

Figure 5.7 *The half adder circuit*

Check out the usage of a half adder in the Digital Works example in

\examples\chapter03\halfadder.dwm

Figure 5.8 *Symbol for a half adder*

However, the half adder does have one weakness. What happens if we want to add X and Y together with a carry input, as we needed to fully perform our binary addition in chapter 2? Quite simply, we can't as we only have two inputs to our half adder - and this is where the full adder comes in.

5.3.2 Introducing The Full Adder

We need the full adder, because as we saw in chapter 2, we need to be able to also add in a carry to perform full binary addition. The full adder takes three inputs, X, Y and the C_{in} (which means the carry in) and gives two outputs, S (the sum) and C_{out} (the carry out) and its truth table can be seen in figure 5.9. Once again, it's possible to work out the circuit from this truth table - the circuit is shown in figure 5.12 (it too should be familiar, as this is the more complicated circuit we drew in chapter 3 in figure 3.16).

X	Y	C_{in}	S	C_{out}
0	0	0	0	0
0	0	1	1	0
0	1	0	1	0
0	1	1	0	1
1	0	0	1	0
1	0	1	0	1
1	1	0	0	1
1	1	1	1	1

Figure 5.9 *The truth table for the full adder*

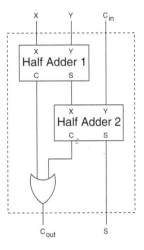

Figure 5.10 *Building a full adder from half adders*

As an aside, it's worth mentioning that it's also possible to build a full adder using two half adders - this method is shown in figure 5.10.

Check out the usage of a full adder in the Digital Works example in

`\examples\chapter03\fulladder.dwm`

We make use of a full adder so much when building arithmetic circuits that it too has its own symbol, shown in figure 5.11.

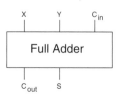

Figure 5.11 *Symbol for the full adder*

5.4 Building An ADD Circuit

Now we know how full adders work, we can actually start to build a circuit to perform binary addition. Take a look at figure 5.13 - it looks complicated at first, but I'll break it down so we can understand what it does.

Firstly, take a look at the row of full adders, there are a few points for you to take note of:

► Each full adder, looking at them from right to left, performs the addition for part of the two inputs from the ALUx and the ALUy;

► The first (from right) full adder adds bit 0 (the LSB) of the ALUx and the ALUy, together with a C_{in} of 0. We know it's 0 because the C_{in} input is connected to a symbol made up of three horizontal parallel lines - this is a symbol for 'ground', which we can interpret as indicating a logical 0 value. We could have actually used a half adder here, but often circuits are built from similar components to simplify the build process;

► The second full adder adds bit 1 of the ALUx and the ALUy, together with the carry bit generated from the first full adder, and so on;

► The S bits from each full adder are connected, by tri-state logic enabled by the En line (from the ALU control signal decoder that we saw in figure 5.5), to the output ALUr;

► The final carry, generated by the left most full adder is used to set the C flag in the PSR.

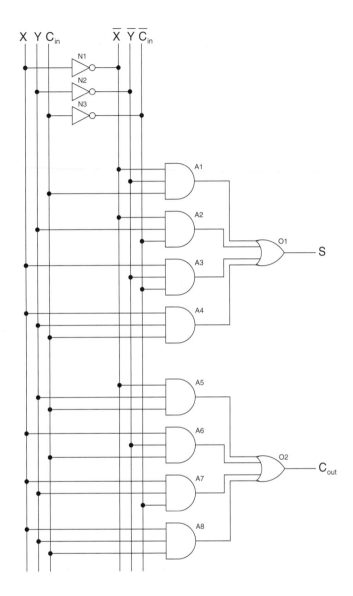

Figure 5.12 *The full adder circuit*

You can see that, not only does the circuit output the ALUr value, but it also outputs the PSR flags. For the ADD operation, the flags are set as in table 5.3.

It is worth noting that the circuitry to set the V flag looks complex, but actually it checks to see if the sign bit indicators of each bit pattern to be added are the same, and if so, if the sign indicator of the result is different (indicating overflow).

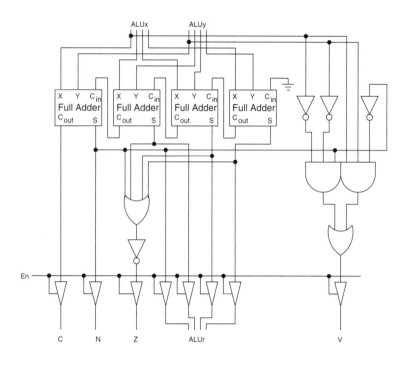

Figure 5.13 *Inside the ALU ADD circuit*

Flag	Description
Z	If (ALUr=0) then Z=1 else Z=0
N	N = MSB(ALUr)
V	If (2's complement overflow) then V = 1 else V=0
C	If (carry from MSB of addition) C=1 else C=0

Table 5.3 *The PSR flags after the ADD operation*

For the ADD circuit to update the PSR and ALUr values, you can see that the En (enable) line needs to be set to 1 - this is the input from the ALU control signal decoder. In other words, the ADD circuit is used if the code for ADD is fed into the ALU arithmetic and logic circuitry on the ALU control lines.

5.5 Building An SL Circuit

Next, we can build a circuit to perform a logical shift operation - we'll build the functionality of the SL, or shift left, circuit. This circuit, shown in figure 5.14 does two things, firstly it takes the input from the ALUx, performs a logical left shift operation, storing the result in the ALUr and secondly it also sets the PSR flags, depending on the result of the operation.

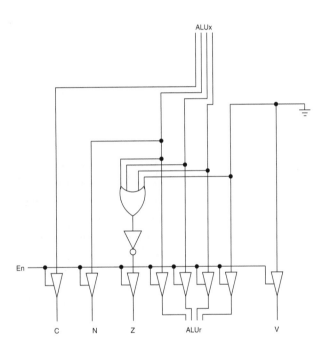

Figure 5.14 *Inside the ALU SL circuit*

The shift left operation is where each bit of the ALUx value is shifted one place to the left, bit 0 of the result is set to 0, and the MSB from the ALUx is moved into the C flag of the PSR. This functionality is shown in figure 5.15 - the top diagram shows how the result is a shifted version of the initial value, with the LSB becoming 0 and the original MSB moving to the C flag of the PSR (the bottom diagram shows the same thing but in a more concise manner - this type of diagram is popular in many processor manuals). The PSR flags for this operation are not set quite as for the ADD operation, as shown in table 5.3.

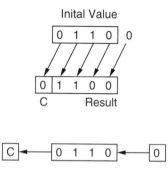

Figure 5.15 *The functionality of the SL circuit*

Once again, the En line is used to set the ALUr value and the PSR flags. The PSR flags after the SL operation would be set as in table 5.4.

Flag	Description
Z	If (ALUr=0) then Z=1 else Z=0
N	N = MSB(ALUr)
V	V=0
C	If (carry from MSB of addition) C=1 else C=0

Table 5.4 *The PSR flags after the SL operation*

It is worth noting that a shift left operation is equivalent to multiplying the contents of the ALUx by two. In early processors that couldn't perform multiplication, shift left operations were used as a poor man's multiplication. For example, if you wanted to multiply a value by nine, you would have had to write your program to perform a shift left operation three times (equivalent to multiplying by eight), followed by adding in the original value. This would have been faster than merely adding the number to itself eight times over.

5.6 Building A NEG Circuit

The last circuit we'll build is the NEG circuit - which computes the 2's complement of the value stored in the ALUx.

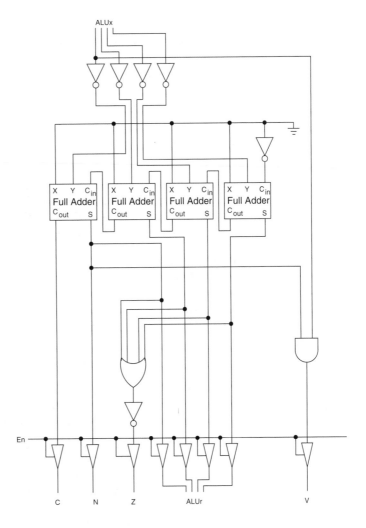

Figure 5.16 *The functionality of the NEG circuit*

The state of the flags after a NEG operation will be as shown in table 5.5.

Flag	Description
Z	If (ALUr=0) then Z=1 else Z=0
N	N = MSB(ALUr)
V	If (2's complement overflow) then V = 1 else V=0
C	If (carry from MSB of addition) C=1 else C=0

Table 5.5 *The PSR flags after the NEG operation*

The complete circuit is shown in figure 5.16 - and once again the value of ALUx is used to calculate the ALUr, and the PSR flags are set on the result.

This circuit could have used half adders instead of full adders, but full adders have been used to aid a comparison to the previous circuits.

5.7 Using The ALU In JASPer

We could carry on producing diagrams for every single ALU operation but it would get quite tedious and we wouldn't see anything greatly different to what we've seen in creating the ADD, SL and NEG circuits. Instead let's take a look at JASPer and see how we can perform these operations in the JASPer ALU.

In the standard 'black box' view of JASPer we see the ALU as an integral part of our CPU. To perform any ALU operations use the 'processor/ALU' menu option (or use the ALU menu button).

Let's perform the 2's complement addition of $00D0 and $0013.

▶ Before we execute an ALU ADD instruction we need to first put the required values into the ALUx and the ALUy. To do this we can use the 'processor/registers' menu option (or click on the registers menu button) - fill in the ALUx and ALUy values. Once you click 'OK', you can see that the ALUx and ALUy values have been updated in the main display;

▶ Now select the 'processor/ALU' menu option and then click on the 'add' button in the ALU dialog box (as shown in figure 5.17). As soon as you do, you will see the ALUr value updated, and the PSR will be updated. The ALUr will be set (if you used the correct values) to $00E3 and all the flags will have been set to 0;

▶ Finally, click the 'OK' button on the ALU dialog box to make it disappear.

Figure 5.17 *The JASPer ALU dialog box*

CHAPTER SUMMARY

The role of the ALU and PSR

▶ The ALU is the calculator of the processor - it can perform both logical operations, such as AND, as well as arithmetic operations like ADD;

▶ The V, N, C and Z flags of the PSR are updated after every ALU operation;

▶ The V flag indicates 2's complement overflow;

▶ The N flag indicates that the ALUr contains a 2's complement negative number;

▶ The C flag indicates that a carry was generated by the previous ALU operation;

▶ The Z flag indicates that the contents of the ALUr are zero.

Controlling the ALU

▶ The ALU registers are connected to the data bus by connection circuitry, as the ALU registers need to be disconnected from the data bus at certain times;

▶ A 4-bit code controls the operation of the ALU circuitry;

▶ A decoder decodes the control signal, in order to perform the given ALU operation.

Adder circuits

▶ The half adder has two inputs, X and Y and two outputs, the sum and carry;

▶ The full adder has three inputs, X, Y and the carry in. It has two outputs, the sum and carry out;

▶ A full adder can be built from two half adders and an OR gate.

ALU circuitry

▶ Individual ALU operations can be constructed from gate logic. The individual circuits can have the ALUx and ALUy as inputs, and output the ALUr and the PSR flags;

▶ Full adders are used to perform addition.

Using the ALU in JASPer

▶ The ALU in JASPer can perform operations on the contents of the ALUx and ALUy, displaying the ALUr output and setting the PSR flags accordingly.

SELF TEST QUESTIONS

1 Using JASPer, compute $0034 + $4500.

2 Using JASPer, compute $0034 - $4500. Why is the N flag of the PSR set to 1?

3 Using JASPer, compute $0005 + $FFFB. What flags are set to 1, and why?

4 Using JASPer, compute $0004<< 2, where '<<' means perform a shift left operation. What has this operation effectively done?

5 Using JASPer, compute $0004 AND $0014.

6 Using JASPer, compute $001D OR $0023.

7 Using Digital Works, build a full adder from half adders, as shown in figure 5.10. Prove that your circuit matches the truth table for a full adder.

EXERCISES

1 Using JASPer, compute $0016 + $0034.

2 Using JASPer, compute $0008>>1, where '>>' means perform a shift right operation. What has this operation effectively done?

3 Add the values $D000 and $0123 using the JASPer ALU. What is the result and what are the flags set to? Explain why the N flag has been set to 1.

4 Write down the largest positive number in a 16-bit 2's complement representation. Write down the largest negative number in a 16-bit 2's complement representation. Add these together in JASPer, what is the result, and why?

5 Using JASPer, compute $FFFF + $0001. What flags are set to 1, and why? How could the C flag be used to perform multi-word arithmetic?

Buses

This chapter examines how processor components can be linked with the use of buses.

This chapter includes:

▶ Processor buses - the data bus, the address bus and the control bus;
▶ Building a bus with gate logic;
▶ Timing diagrams;
▶ Buses in JASPer.

6.1 What is a Bus?

A bus is a collection of conductive wires that connect a number of logical elements together, to allow values to be moved from one element to another (on a silicon chip the bus is actually *etched conductive material* - but the concept is the same).

Although we don't actually need a bus, as we could create our processor with individual wire connections from each logical element to each other, the wiring requirement would end up being very convoluted. Therefore it is better to have a bus that all elements can share.

Typically, processors actually have more than one bus - JASPer for example has three, these being the data bus, the address bus, and the control bus (we'll talk about each in turn in a moment) - but still don't lose the fact that they are each effectively just the equivalent of a 'data highway'.

Back in chapter 4 we saw how to connect registers to a bus as in figure 6.1.

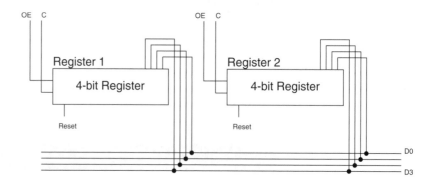

Figure 6.1 *Connecting registers with a bus*

As you remember, we have to be very careful how we transfer bit patterns - we have to ensure that we only put the contents of one register on to the bus at any one time. If we attempt to put more than one register bit pattern onto the bus at the same time we end up with a situation called *bus contention*. This would mean that our processor wouldn't work as we expected.

To connect logical units, such as registers, to the bus we use tri-state logic. In this way we can effectively disconnect the outputs from all other logical units, such that bus contention can never occur.

6.1.1 The Data Bus

The data bus is used to connect all the internal components of the processor. As its name suggests, it is used to transfer data from one logical component (a register, or perhaps the ALU) to another. The data bus is *bi-directional*, in that if we connected two registers to our bus, as in figure 6.1, it would be possible to transfer the Register 1 bit pattern to Register 2 as well as transfer the Register 2 bit pattern to Register 1.

6.1.2 The Address Bus

The address bus is different to the data bus in a number of ways. Firstly, it only connects the processor (or more precisely one particular register - the *Memory Address Register*, or *MAR*) to the external memory. We'll cover this in more detail in chapter 7. Secondly, the address bus is *uni-directional* - as we only ever need to transfer bit patterns from the MAR to memory, and never the other way around.

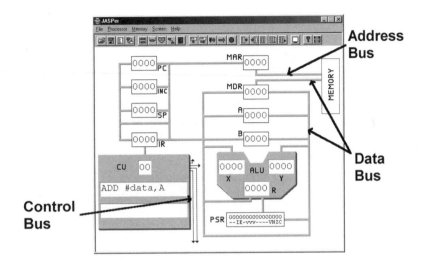

Figure 6.2   *The buses in JASPer*

6.1.3 The Control Bus

The control bus is quite different from the data and address buses. Whereas the data and address buses are generally the same width as the register size (and we tend to draw them as thick lines in a diagram rather than showing the individual wires, otherwise circuit diagrams become hugely complicated), the control bus is a conglomeration of wires for control signals connected to all parts of the processor. All the control wires of the control bus originate in the processor at a particular component known as the *Control Unit*, or *CU*. We'll describe the use of this particular component, and how it sends its control signals on the control bus, in chapter 8. Each line of the control bus is also *uni-directional* - as signals are sent from the control unit to each particular logic unit and never the other way around.

6.2 Building A Bus

Each bus itself is essentially a group of wires (or conductive etchings), and so doesn't require much design. However, the important aspect is ensuring that each logic unit (such as the registers or the ALU) is connected to the bus in such a way that it can be effectively connected or disconnected from the bus as required. This is done, as we've seen, by the use of tri-state logic gates.

Only one component should be transferring its value onto the bus at any one time.

To transfer a value from one register to another we:

▶ Enable the output of the source register, setting the value onto the bus;

▶ Clock the destination register, such that the register takes the bit pattern from the bus and stores it internally;

▶ Disable the output of the source register, ready to perform another operation on the bus.

We must always join the outputs from a logical element (like a register) to the bus using tri-state logic. We can tie all the enable pins from all the tri-state gates for a particular logic element together, so that we can have just one enable input to the logic element.

Sometimes, the use of a bus has to happen at very precise times. For example, we tend to show memory access in a *timing diagram*, like that shown in figure 6.3.

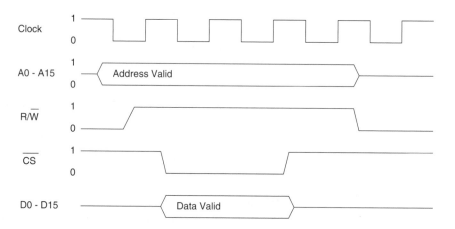

Figure 6.3   *A timing diagram*

Timing diagrams are very important to hardware engineers, they show at what point particular lines can be read from, or written to. For example, this particular timing diagram shows a memory read. We can see that the address bus initially is expected to be floating, or undefined (indicated by the address bus is initially shown as being between 0 and 1). At a certain point the address is valid on the address lines (shown as a valid block), after which it returns to a floating state. At the point when the data lines have valid content, we need to ensure that we clock the MDR to perform the data read.

6.3 Buses In JASPer

The buses in JASPer can be seen in the main 'black box' view - they are displayed as grey lines connecting the registers and the ALU. Most of the grey lines that you can see are the data bus, which is 16 bits wide, so that we can transfer bit patterns from one register to another in one operation. The address bus, which is also 16 bits wide, can be seen in the top right of the display connecting the MAR with memory while the control bus is shown in a symbolic form only - as the control lines leaving the right of the CU. When we run JASPer we can see the control lines from the CU flash briefly, signifying the control unit outputting the control line signals.

The buses in JASPer can be seen in figure 6.2.

6.3.1 Introducing Data Movement Operations

We have already seen (in chapter 4) how to to make use of the data bus to transfer a value from one register to another.

We use the bus every time we transfer a bit pattern from one register to another - this, as we saw before, is known as a data movement operation, although strictly speaking we are not moving a bit pattern but copying it from one register to another.

In JASPer we can either:

▶ Click on 'processor/data movement', and then click on our destination register followed by our source register;

▶ Use the 'processor/microcode list/data movement' menu option to select the particular data movement operation (shown in figure 6.4). Note that we select the destination first, followed by the source register.

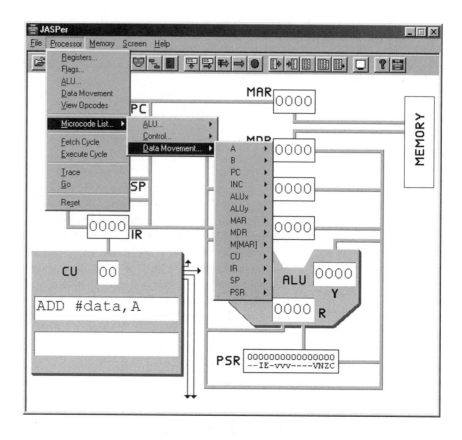

Figure 6.4 *Performing a data movement in JASPer*

Each data movement can be described using RTL, we briefly saw RTL in chapter 4. So, for example, the data movement from the MDR register to the A register can be described as:

$$A \leftarrow [MDR]$$

Where the brackets mean *contents of*. So read this RTL instruction as 'move the contents of the MDR register to the A register'.

Sometimes, it doesn't make sense to move from particular registers to another, for example it doesn't make sense to have a data movement like:

$$MAR \leftarrow [INC]$$

as this is something we would never practically need to do, as the INC register is only ever used to update the PC register, as we will find out in chapter 8. In JASPer only a required subset of data movements is allowed, reflecting the abilities of real processors.

CHAPTER SUMMARY

Processor buses

▶ Buses are required to join processor components;

▶ Our simple processor has three buses - the data bus, the address bus and the control bus;

▶ The data and address buses are used to transfer data and addresses between registers and memory;

▶ The control bus emanates from the CU - individual lines are used to control individual components.

Building a bus

▶ A bus can effectively be thought of as a set of wires;

▶ In integrated circuits the buses consist of etched conductive material;

▶ Components are joined to buses by tri-state logic;

▶ The synchronization required to make use of a bus is often shown in a timing diagram.

Buses in JASPer

▶ JASPer has three buses - the data, address and control buses. It is used to transfer values between components.

SELF TEST QUESTIONS

1 Describe the use of the data bus.

2 Describe in RTL the data movement operation where a value from the ALUr is transferred to the B register.

3 Describe in RTL the data movement operation where a value from the A register is transferred to the MDR.

4 Describe the two key differences between the control bus and the data bus.

EXERCISES

1 Using \examples\chapter04\bitregister2.dwm, cause bus contention to occur.

2 Using \examples\chapter04\bitregister2.dwm as a starting point, build a bus with three connected registers.

3 Using your circuit from exercise two, examine how you can copy the contents of register one to both register two and register three. Can you perform these data movements in parallel?

Memory

In this chapter we cover the key aspects of memory, how to build it and how to make use of it.

This chapter includes:

▶ The concepts of memory;
▶ How to build memory from gate logic;
▶ Types of memory;
▶ Address decoding strategies;
▶ Memory maps;
▶ Using memory in JASPer;

7.1 Introducing Memory

So far, we have discussed every important element of our processor; we have described the registers, the ALU, and how they all interconnect using a bus - we will look inside the control unit in chapter 17. However, even though we have almost everything we need to build our simple computer system, there is still one important element we need in order for our computer to be useful - a memory. Without a memory the processor in our computer system is effectively useless. Without a memory we don't have a von Neumann architecture (we discussed this briefly in chapter 1) - the memory is required to store our data, and (importantly for our von Neumann architecture) our program.

The first thing we need to understand is the *structure* of our memory. There are two attributes that we need to be aware of, these are *memory width* (sometimes referred to as the word size - remember that JASPer has a word size of 16 bits) and *storage size*. The first describes the width of values we wish to store in our memory (whether it is 4, 8 or 16 bits, or some totally different value), while the second describes how many values our memory can store at any one time.

If we were to examine a memory such as that in figure 7.1, we would say that it is 4 bits wide (or has a word size of 4 bits) and can store four distinct values, addressed as $00_2, 01_2, 10_2$ and 11_2. Conceptually, we can think of memory as a one dimensional array of memory locations, all locations with a unique address, and each being able to store a finite bit pattern.

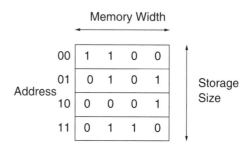

Figure 7.1 *Our initial memory*

The addresses are shown to the left of the memory store - we can see for example that memory location 01_2 contains the value 0101_2 (5). This memory consists of only four locations - hence the 2-bit address required to successfully address the entire contents of the memory.

Our memory needs the following functionality:

▶ We must be able to select a particular memory location;
▶ We need to be able to read the memory value from that location;
▶ If required we need to write a new value to that location;
▶ We need to be able to connect our memory to the data and address buses of our processor.

7.2 Building A Small Memory

Let's start off by building memory devices and connecting them to our processor, and then later we can concentrate on how to use them.

We can construct memory using similar methods to building registers, using D flip-flops. Also, we need to come up with a method by which we can read or write to particular locations.

To recap what we learnt in chapter 4, we can use a D flip-flop (as shown in figure 7.2) to store one bit of information.

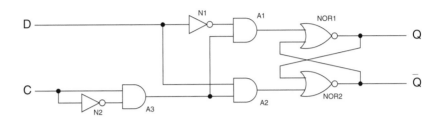

Figure 7.2 *The D flip-flop revisited*

From there we can jump to the circuit for a very small memory as shown in figure 7.3. This particular memory is very small indeed - it only contains two words, each with a word size of 4 bits; each 4-bit word is constructed using D flip-flops. Once we understand this very small memory, we understand the fundamental design aspects of all memories.

Let us examine this circuit:

▶ It connects to the data bus, an address bus (one bit only for simplicity - with one bit we can select one of two memory locations), and two control lines - CS (the *chip select* - used to activate a particular memory chip) and $R/\bar{W}$. The $R/\bar{W}$ label tells us that when this value is set to 1, we are performing a *read operation*, and when it is set to 0 we are performing a *write operation*;

▶ It has tri-state gates to separate the output of the memory from the data bus. The output of both memory words is fed to the tri-state gates through OR gates - as only one memory word at a time is selected this arrangement means that an individual word bit pattern can be placed on the data bus;

▶ The gates beneath the memory words in the diagram are used to select individual words for either read or write operations.

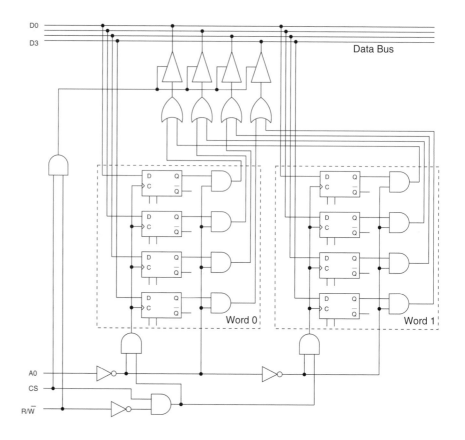

Figure 7.3 *The circuit for our small memory*

We can see that each word in memory is effectively built in the same way that the registers in chapter 4 were, but we need to examine both how to read from, and how to write to, our small memory.

7.2.1 Reading From Our Small Memory

Let's work through the steps we need to take to read from a particular memory location, and place the value stored there on the data bus. For this example we'll assume that we want to use the bit pattern stored at memory location 0, and that the pattern stored there is 1011_2.

▶ We place the address onto the address bus, setting A0 to 0 in this example;

▶ We set the $R/\bar{W}$ line to 1 to indicate that we wish this operation to be a memory read;

▶ We set the chip select line to 1, at which point data from word 0 is placed onto the data bus;

▶ At this point we would clock the destination register;

▶ Finally, we set the CS line to 0.

You can test this circuit using the Digital Works file `smallmem.dwm`. Follow this process through the logic gates to check that you understand what is happening.

7.2.2 Writing To Our Small Memory

Writing to our memory is as simple as reading.

Let us see how we would perform a memory write to this memory, to memory word 1 for example:

▶ We place the data to be transferred onto the data bus (from a register for example);

▶ We place the address onto the address bus, setting A0 to 1 in this example;

▶ We set the $R/\bar{W}$ line to 0 to indicate that we wish this operation to be a memory write;

▶ We set the chip select line to 1, at which point the clock lines of the D flip-flops making up memory word 1 will take the data from the data bus.

▶ Finally, we set the CS line to 0.

You can also test the memory write operation using `smallmem.dwm`. Follow this process through the logic gates to check that you understand what is happening.

7.3 Types of Memory

Once we have built our small memory, we can start to think of it as a functional unit in its own right. In fact, we often show memory chips in circuit diagrams using the sort of symbol shown in figure 7.4. This particular chip is known as a 4x4 (pronounced 4 by 4) *RAM* memory. A RAM chip is one that we can both read from and write to. RAM stands for *Random Access Memory*.

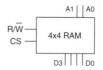

Figure 7.4   A 4x4 RAM chip

So how much data can we store in a 4x4 RAM chip? The first four indicates that this chip has four distinct memory locations (and hence will use a two bit address bus), and the second four indicates that each value stored in the memory chip is four bits wide (we could also say that this chip has a word length of four bits) - which means that we would have to attach it to a 4-bit data bus. You can see these data and address bus connections in figure 7.4, together with the CS line and the $R/\overline{W}$ line.

Memory chips can come in all sorts of word length and location sizes. Figure 7.5 shows a 4x16 RAM chip , which has four distinct memory locations each with a 16 bit word length, while figure 7.6 shows a 256x16 RAM chip which has 256 different memory locations to be used.

Figure 7.5   A 4x16 RAM chip

Figure 7.6   A 256x16 RAM chip

Incidentally, we have only looked at the sort of memory that we can either read from or write to. Not all memory has to be like this - there is also a form of memory that we can only read from. This is called ROM, or *Read Only Memory*.

A typical ROM chip is shown in figure 7.7. As you can see, it does not need a $R/\overline{W}$ line, as we can only read from it. Why would we need a memory that we can't write to? First of all, it's worth saying that we would store bit patterns in the ROM when we built it - and it could be very useful in being able to ensure that no computer program could ever overwrite these values. For example, most computer systems have a very small program called a *boot loader* in ROM, and it is this program that helps to start up the computer so that it can be used - being able to write over the boot loader program could mean that we could never start the computer again! So ROM can prove very useful.

Figure 7.7   *A 4x16 ROM chip*

7.4 Building Larger Memories

Memory chips used to be very small, holding something like 1024 values. These days it is possible to purchase much larger memory chips - 256Mx32 ($256 \times 1024 \times 1024$) 32-bit RAM chips are not uncommon. No doubt chips with greater and greater capacity will be developed over time.

However, no matter how large chips become, the chances are that we never want to construct our computer memory from just one chip, as this is very inflexible and difficult to update later. When we use multiple chips for our complete memory we need to ensure that we end up being able to make use of our memory as if it were a single entity. To make this clearer we'll introduce the concept of a *memory map* - no prizes for guessing that this is a map of all memory locations available to our processor. Programmers can use memory maps to understand which memory location is stored on which chip.

The memory map for our small memory (four unique locations) is shown in figure 7.8. The start of memory is generally shown at the bottom - so this particular memory has locations from 00_2 to 11_2 (our four locations). Normally, we would show the memory addresses in hexadecimal, but the memories we are going to use are very small and a binary representation is more appropriate for what we need to understand.

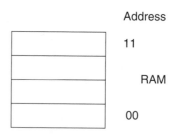

Address

11

RAM

00

Figure 7.8 *A memory map for our small memory*

If we wanted to build a memory using two chips, then it makes sense to increase our memory map to that shown in figure 7.9. We can see that the first memory chip is accessed by the lower addresses and the second memory chip is accessed by the higher addresses. We'll now look at how we can implement such an arrangement.

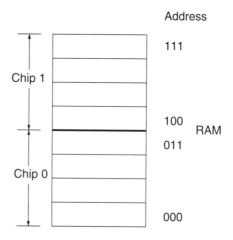

Address

111

Chip 1

100

RAM

011

Chip 0

000

Figure 7.9 *A memory map for a larger memory*

First of all, I'll show you how to connect up two memory chips to create a larger memory, and then we'll go on to create a memory that consists of four memory chips.

The key issue is that we need to ensure that when we select a particular memory location we need to ensure that we are selecting a location on one chip only.

So, our memory consisting of two chips has addresses beginning at 000_2 and ending at 111_2. If we look carefully however, we can see that the MSB is set to 0 for all locations on chip 0 and is set to 1 for all locations on chip 1 - this is our clue to a simple *access strategy*. It means that we can use the MSB of the address to select which chip we wish to make use of, and the two lower bits of the address bus can be wired to the two address pins of each memory chip - see figure 7.10 to see what I mean. Also, it's worth noticing that in figure 7.10, the chip select pin (CS) is *active low* in this diagram (shown by the $\bar{CS}$ symbol) - which is pretty common for memory chips, so we'll start to see this convention in future figures. Active low means that the chip is made use of when the CS line is set to 0. Also, the connections to the data bus are not shown as this would have unnecessarily cluttered the diagram, but remember that D0 to D15 of both chips are wired to the data bus.

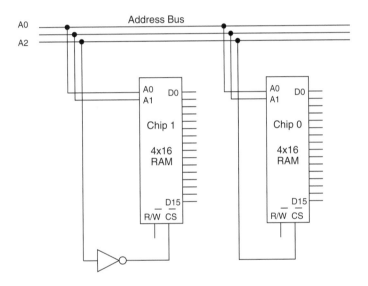

Figure 7.10 *Building a larger memory with multiple memory chips*

To use this memory, if we want to select chip 1 for example, we need an address in the format $1xx_2$ (xx indicates the address location within the chip itself). This means that address line A2 = 1 in order to select chip 1. A2 is fed through a NOT gate, so producing an output of zero - this is what we need on the CS pin of the memory chip to select it.

How can we advance on this principle to create even larger memories? Let's imagine that we want to build a memory that's twice as big again, making use of four of our memory chips. The memory map for such a memory is shown in figure 7.11. Effectively, to build our larger memory we can use the same principle as before, but instead of using the highest bit of the address to select which chip is used, we can use the top two bits of the address. Look at the memory map values to see how the top two bits of each address indicate which chip we want to use.

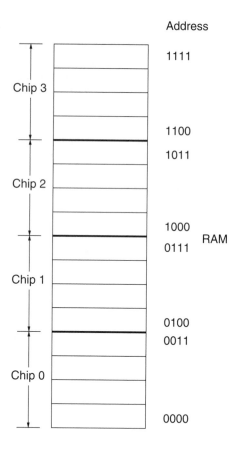

Figure 7.11 *A memory map for an even larger memory*

So, it's just a matter of using NAND gates to connect the address lines to the CS pin on each chip, as shown in figure 7.12.

For example, if we want to select chip two, we need an address in the format $10xx_2$. To get this, the address lines have to have A2 = 0 and A3 = 1, in order to select chip two. A2 is fed through a NOT gate, so that the NAND gate has inputs of one and one, so producing an output of zero - this is what we need on the CS pin of the memory chip to select it.

7.5 Building Wider Memories

We've solved the problem of building larger memories with small chips, but what if we need to use memory chips that are not wide enough? For example, can we build a memory that is eight bits wide from chips that are only four bits wide? Yes, we can.

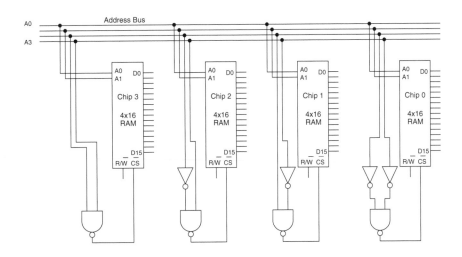

Figure 7.12 *Building an even larger memory with multiple memory chips*

We can connect up two memory chips to different lines of the data bus, and identically wire them to the address bus - see figure 7.13 to see what I mean.

Let's imagine that we want to store the value 11110000_2 at location 011_2 in our 8-bit memory (that is really built from two 4-bit chips). Here's how we can do it:

▶ Place the address on the address bus (011_2). Please note that the MSB of the address is a zero, so activating the chip selects of *both* chips.

▶ Place the value we want to store on the data bus (11110000_2).

▶ Set the $R/\bar{W}$ line (connected to the $R/\bar{W}$ pins of *both* chips) to 0, indicating that we want to write to our memory.

▶ Chip 0 will now store the value from the lower four data lines (the value 0000_2), while chip 1 will store the value from the upper 4 data lines (1111_2). Incidentally, four bits is known as a *nybble*, being half a byte (this is not a joke! Two bits in some circles used to be called a *crumb*, but this isn't really used any more).

7.6 Address Decoding Strategies

The process of figuring out how a particular chip is used within a memory map is called *address decoding*, and there are two main ways in which we can address individual memory chips. These methods are known as *partial address decoding* and *full address decoding*. We'll briefly look at each in turn.

The method we saw above in figure 7.12 was full address decoding, where we used particular address line combinations to select a particular memory chip

- this is because each address line is used to calculate the unique location on one unique memory chip.

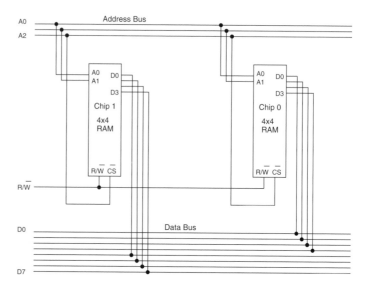

Figure 7.13 *Building a wider memory*

If the address space (the range of possible addresses) was larger than the amount of memory available, we could have used partial address decoding - in this form of decoding not all of the address lines are used, just enough to select the required memory chips. Partial address decoding is simpler (and therefore cheaper) to build. This form of addressing is used in small embedded devices, where it's very unlikely to ever want to expand the use of memory to the full address space.

Let's have a look at a particular partial address decoding example - as shown in figure 7.14. At first glance you may think that you've seen this before, in figure 7.10 - actually, it may be similar but it is different in one very important aspect - can you spot where?

The difference is with how the two memory chips are wired to the address bus. The address bus lines A0 and A1 are connected to the pins of the same name on each chip - however, the chip select line is wired only to the A3 address line. Such a layout would be fine if we were using a 4-bit bus and yet only needed to connect 2 memory chips to it. As you can imagine, we don't need any complicated logic to work out the values for the chip select line - we can just use the MSB of the address to select either chip.

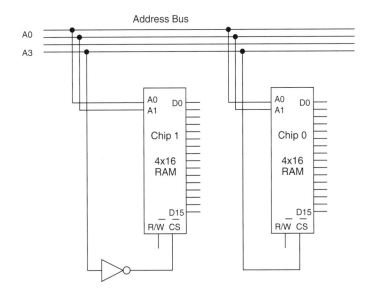

Figure 7.14 *Partial address decoding*

It does lead to a minor oddity in the memory map, as shown in figure 7.15. The address space with four bit addresses is 16 separate addresses, but effectively we are never using address line A2, so an address like 1011_2 or 1111_2 would address the *same* location in memory - we sometimes refer to such an address as $1x11_2$, as the value of address line two is immaterial. In other words, we have *duplicate* locations within our memory map.

7.7 Using Memory

The memory map is very important to the programmer of a microprocessor system - It is the memory map that defines what memory locations can be read to or written from (RAM), which areas are read-only (ROM), as well as showing any memory-mapped devices (which we will cover in depth in chapter 12) and any gaps in the memory map that the programmer cannot use.

The memory map for JASPer is shown in figure 7.16. In this we can see that individual parts of the JASPer memory have particular uses - this is fairly typical of small microcomputer devices.

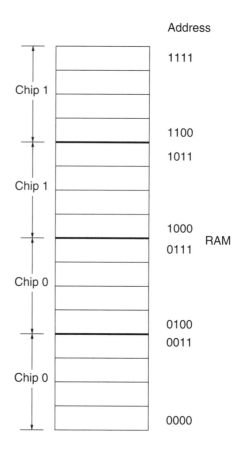

Figure 7.15 *A memory map of a system using partial address decoding*

Within the map you can see:

▶ Areas where we can write our programs and data;

▶ Three memory-mapped devices (we'll cover this in more depth in chapter 12) - one is for input/output, one is for a peripherals device and the other is a system clock (we will make use of the clock in chapter 13);

▶ Reserved areas - locations that we could use for our programs and data, but it would be unwise to use because the system designers have reserved this memory location (in order to perhaps later introduce an extra feature). If we were to use this location for our programs and data, they may not work on later versions of our processor system;

▶ An interrupt vector table - we'll describe this in chapter 13.

It's worth noting that often the memory map is not drawn showing all memory locations - the jagged lines at the side of individual memory areas indicate that the particular section has been made smaller so that the memory map can fit on a single page.

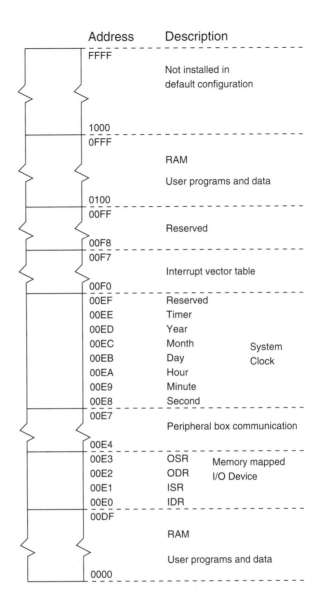

Figure 7.16 *The JASPer memory map*

Incidentally, we can 'install' extra memory in JASPer by modifying the value for memory size within the 'jumper settings' dialog box - reached by the menu option 'file/jumper settings', or by using the 'jumper settings' button on the button bar. By default, JASPer starts with memory installed from $0000 to $0FFF, which is 4Kb of 16-bit words.

7.8 Connecting Memory To JASPer

Within JASPer we can transfer bit patterns between memory and registers as simply as transferring bit patterns between registers. To do this we use two particular RTL instructions, which we'll get to in a moment, but firstly let us look at the way in which our processor is connected to our memory. This is shown in figure 7.17.

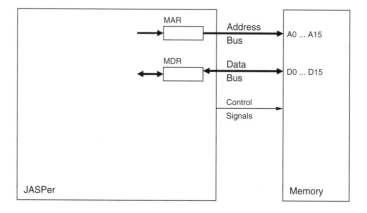

Figure 7.17 *Using memory in JASPer*

As you can see, all three buses tie the processor to the memory. These are the data bus, the address bus and the control bus.

▶ The data bus is 16 bits wide, and is bi-directional. we can use it to send data to memory or read data from memory;

▶ The address bus is 16 bits wide, and is uni-directional. We use it to select particular memory addresses;

▶ The control bus is uni-directional and sends the required signals to memory.

We effectively use two JASPer registers to communicate with our memory, these are the *Memory Address Register*, or *MAR*, and the *Memory Data Register*, or *MDR* (connectivity to the rest of the chip isn't shown in figure 7.17 - we'll look at the use of other registers in more detail in the next chapter).

We can define a memory read in RTL terms as:

$$MDR \leftarrow [M[MAR]]$$

This means transfer the contents from memory, at the location specified in the MAR, into the MDR. $[M[MAR]]$ means the contents of memory using the contents of the MAR as an index.

A memory write is the reverse of this:

$$M[MAR] \leftarrow [MDR]$$

This means transfer the contents of the MDR to memory at the location specified by the address held in the MAR.

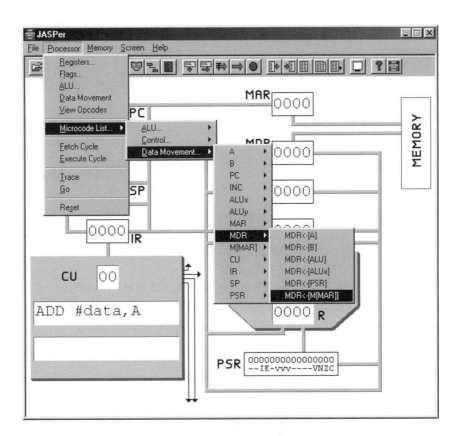

Figure 7.18 *Performing a memory read in JASPer*

7.8.1 Memory Transfers In JASPer

To perform memory transfers in JASPer we can:

▶ Use the 'processor/microcode list/data movement' menu option to select the particular data movement operation (shown in figure 7.18). This can be treated the same as any other data movement operation.

▶ Use the memory read or memory write buttons - these are shown in figure 7.19. There are five memory buttons on the JASPer button bar - we will make most use of the first three which are, left to right, memory read (which performs a memory read operation), memory write (which performs a memory write operation) and view memory (which displays the complete contents of the JASPer memory on screen).

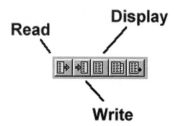

Figure 7.19 *JASPer memory buttons*

Let's perform an example. We'll put the value $00FF into memory at address $0001. How do we go about this?

▶ Place the value $00FF into the MDR;

▶ Place the address $0001 into the MAR;

▶ Perform the memory write. That's it!

CHAPTER SUMMARY

The concepts of memory

▶ Memory is the information store for our processor;

▶ A memory has width and it has size;

▶ We need to be able to access individual memory locations to both write to and read from.

How to build memory from gate logic

▶ Individual memory locations can be built in a similar way to registers;

▶ Memory has the following inputs - the address bus, a chip select line and a $R/\bar{W}$ line. The data bus can be an input or an output, depending on whether memory is being read or written to.

Types of memory

▶ Memory can be either ROM or RAM;

▶ If a chip is labelled as a '256x16 RAM' this means that it has 256 distinct memory locations and is 16 bits wide.

Address decoding strategies

▶ Larger memories can be built from small memory chips;

▶ Address decoding strategies can be either full, where all address lines are used, or partial, where not all address lines are used;

▶ Wider memories can be built with small chips - individual memory chips would be wired up to be activated at the same time, and each would hold a subsection of the bit patterns required by the larger memory.

Memory maps

▶ A memory map is used to display which chip contains which memory addresses, and to display to the programmer the areas of memory that are used for particular tasks.

Using memory in JASPer

▶ The memory display in JASPer indicates memory contents;

▶ A memory update consists of placing the address in the MAR, the data in the MDR, and then performing a memory write;

▶ A memory read consists of placing the address in the MAR and then performing a memory read, the data can then be copied from the MDR.

SELF TEST QUESTIONS

1 Write down the RTL instructions required to move a value from the B register to memory location 0001_{16}.

2 Write down the RTL instructions required to read a value from memory location $00E0_{16}$ and place it in the A register.

3 Within JASPer, place the value $00FF_{16}$ into memory location 0003_{16}.

EXERCISES

1 Within JASPer, place the value $001F_{16}$ into memory location 0002_{16}.

2 Within JASPer, place the value $02CD_{16}$ into memory location 0001_{16}.

3 Within JASPer, read the value held at memory location 0002_{16}.

4 Write down the RTL instructions required to move a value from the A register to memory location 0003_{16}

5 A 1024x16 memory is to be built using two 512x16 memory chips. Sketch out the address decoding strategy to build this memory.

Bringing It All Together - The Hardware Engineer's Perspective

CHAPTER OVERVIEW

In this chapter we show how a set of registers, a control unit, a memory, buses and an ALU can be combined to form a rudimentary computer system.

This chapter includes:

▶ Assigning tasks to individual processor components;
▶ Micro-instructions;
▶ Instruction sets;
▶ The format of a program;
▶ The fetch-execute cycle;
▶ Executing programs in JASPer.

8.1 Recap

Is it really this easy to build components to make up a processor? Well, actually, no it isn't. We've really only skimmed the surface of hardware issues - but we now have an understanding of how the individual components within the processor will work, at the hardware level at least.

However, we now have to join these components together to form a processor, one that is typical of all processors that are von Neumann architectures.

8.2 Assigning Tasks To Registers

Our rudimentary processor can be seen in figure 8.1. We can see all the elements that we have built connected together to form the processor.

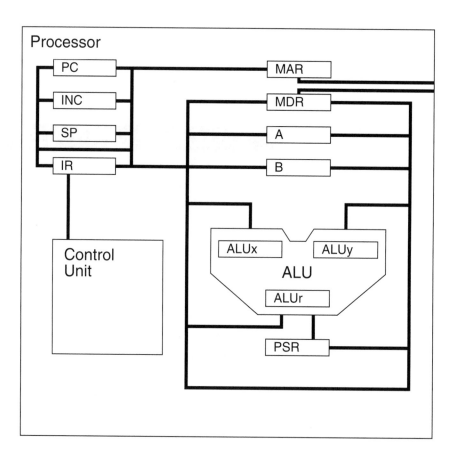

Figure 8.1 *Our rudimentary processor*

We can now assign tasks to each register to enable the device to run a program. So what sort of tasks does the processor have to do?

▶ It needs to be able to read bit patterns from, and write bit patterns to, memory. We saw how it could do this in the previous chapter;

▶ It needs to keep track of where we are within a program, so it knows what to do next. We will see why shortly;

▶ It needs to know what to do for a particular instruction;

▶ It needs to be able to perform arithmetic and logical operations;

▶ It needs some general purpose storage areas.

Let us now assign these tasks to individual registers:

▶ We can use the Memory Address Register (MAR) and the Memory Data Register (MDR) to read from, and write bit patterns to, memory;

▶ To keep track of where we are within our program, we use the *Program Counter* (*PC*) which can be thought of as a bookmark so that we know which instruction from memory we are to execute next - and we can use the *Incrementer* (*INC*) to update the PC to store the next sequential program address. This is because the INC is specially wired to always have 1 added to its input, for example, moving $0001 into the INC will result in it storing $0002. We will discuss the usefulness of this shortly;

▶ To know what to do for a particular instruction we can firstly store it in the *Instruction Register* (*IR*), and the *Control Unit* (*CU*) can decode each instruction in turn - we won't look inside the CU until chapter 17;

▶ To perform arithmetic and logical operations we can use the ALU, as we saw in chapter 5. It has three registers - the ALUx , ALUy and ALUr . The PSR stores information about the processor, including status of the last ALU operation;

▶ To store bit patterns locally for the program we need some general purpose registers - our simple processor has two of these, the *A* register and the *B* register;

▶ If you check figure 8.1 you will find that we've mentioned all the registers with the exception of the *Stack Pointer* (*SP*). We don't need to cover that until chapter 10 when we discuss subroutines.

All of these components are wired to the data bus, and their control lines are wired to the outputs of the control unit. Additionally, the MAR is wired to the address bus, so that addresses can be passed to memory. The processor and the memory together form our rudimentary computer system.

We will shortly run a program using this system - so we will see each of these components in action.

8.3 Introducing Micro-Instructions

We still have a number of concepts to examine before we can actually look at our first program in any detail.

So far we have looked at operations defined in RTL as the way in which we effect changes in our processor. These sort of operations can be termed *micro-instructions*, or *microcodes*. The micro-instruction defined in RTL as

$$A \leftarrow [MDR]$$

can be thought of as short hand for enabling the MDR and clocking the A register, as we saw in chapter 4, to put its bit pattern into the A register - in other words a data movement operation. In fact, there are four distinct types of micro-instructions that can be used by our processor. These are:

▶ *Data movement micro-instructions*, for example $MAR \leftarrow [A]$;
▶ *ALU micro-instructions*, like $ALUr = [ALUx] + [ALUy]$ which means add the ALUx and ALUy values together, storing the result in the ALUr and set the PSR on the result;
▶ *Test micro-instructions*, like $if(PSR(z) == 1)$, which checks to see if the Z flag of the PSR has been set to one;
▶ *Processor control micro-instructions* , like $halt$ which stops the processor, or nop (which is short for *no operation* - this means run a micro-instruction but don't actually change the contents of any register).

So, effectively, a micro-instruction is a way to directly control the hardware of the processor. All of the micro-instructions used by our simple processor are listed in appendix A.

8.4 Introducing The Instruction Set

If we think of some of the tasks that we want to do, like ANDing two bit patterns (performing a logical AND operation), using micro-instructions can be a lengthy process.

Let's see what I mean by way of an example. We will assume that we have a representation of a number in the A register, and another representation of a number in the B register. How can we go about obtaining the logical AND of these bit patterns?

Using the micro-instructions available to us we have:

▶ $ALUx \leftarrow [A]$, Transfer one of the number representations to the ALUx;
▶ $ALUy \leftarrow [B]$, Transfer the other number representation to the ALUy;

▶ $ALUr \leftarrow [ALUx]\&[ALUy]$, Perform a logical AND operation, storing the result in the ALUr, and setting the PSR flags on the result;

▶ $A \leftarrow [ALUr]$, Store the result of the AND operation in the A register.

So, as we can see, it took four micro-instructions to AND the two bit patterns and store the result (and this is by no means a difficult task). If we were to write programs using micro-instructions, they would be extraordinarily long and very difficult to check that we haven't introduced any mistakes. Therefore, we don't.

Instead, we group sets of micro-instructions together to form higher level instructions, known as *assembly language* instructions. For example, we can describe our previous example as the assembly language instruction

```
AND B,A
```

We read this as ANDing the bit patterns contained in the A and B registers, and placing the result in the A register (we can tell this because A is the last location named). This instruction is then encoded for the processor as a code value, or number, to represent this task.

DEFINITION

Opcode : *Sometimes referred to as the operation code, this is the code for the operation to be performed.*

The bit pattern used to code the assembly language instruction is called the *operation code* or *opcode*. The more readable form of the instruction (AND) is known as the *mnemonic* (pronounced 'nem-onnic') and is just purely for we humans - our processor does not make use of mnemonics.

The set of different assembly instructions understood by the processor is known as the *instruction set*. There are a finite number of instructions that any processor can have in an instruction set, and this is limited by the width of the opcode. In our simple processor the width of an opcode is eight bits, which means that we can define a maximum of 256 different instructions in the instruction set. In practice we don't need an instruction set as large as this - we can actually write quite complex programs with very few different assembly language instructions. You can examine the instructions available to us within the instruction set for our processor in appendix B. In appendix C you can see the individual micro-instructions that make up each assembly language instruction.

DEFINITION

Mnemonic : *A more easily remembered alphabetic code for an opcode.*

When used in a program, any instruction will be coded with the opcode together with any *operands*, or parameters to the instruction. For example, if we wanted to write the value 5 into the A register we could use an instruction like

```
MOVE #$5,A
```

The operands to this instruction are #$5, which means the number 5, and A, which refers to the A register. Our particular processor expects to be given only one operand with any opcode and so some operands are implicit to the opcode and some are explicit.

The A register is an implicit operand to this opcode, the opcode to write 5 to register B is actually a different instruction. The one explicit operand in this example is the value #$5. We write the opcode and the explicit operand together as a 16-bit *machine code* - it is these machine codes that our simple processor decodes and executes.

We will discuss how to encode instructions in the next chapter, for now we will concentrate on the structure of a program that we can later load into JASPer to see if it works as expected.

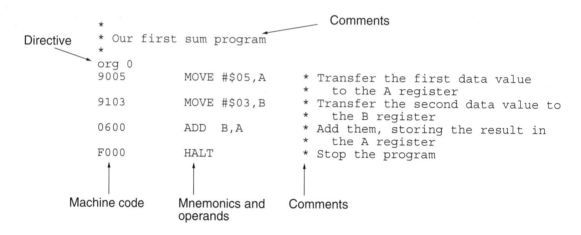

Figure 8.2 *The sum program*

Figure 8.2 displays a small program that will work on our simple processor, and we need to understand what this program is telling us, so here are a few points to make note of:

▶ Any text that begins with an asterisk is a comment, and the rest of the line is not used by the processor;

▶ The instruction `org 0` is a *directive* that tells the processor to store the program in memory starting from location $0000. We will discuss directives in the next chapter;

▶ Within the main body of the program each instruction is shown as machine code, mnemonics and operands, and then finally comments. Note that the mnemonics and operands are not used by the processor at all - they are there to remind us what each machine code does. Each 16-bit machine code encodes the instruction completely.

Strictly speaking, when writing a program we only need to write the machine code - but it would make our programs very difficult to understand when we came back to them after even a short break.

The set of machine codes that make up this program need to be stored in memory in order for us to run it. When loaded into the memory of our system the first instruction, $9005, is stored at memory location $0000, the second instruction $9103 at location $0001 and so on - this is shown in figure 8.3.

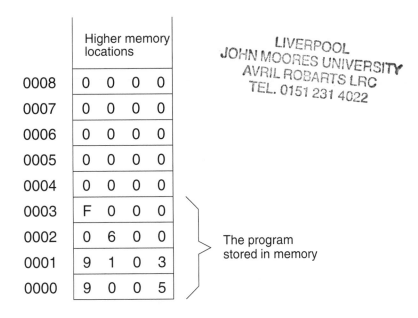

Figure 8.3 *The sum program stored in memory*

The task of the processor is to consecutively fetch each instruction and then decode and execute it. To do this it uses a process known as the *fetch-execute cycle*.

8.5 The Fetch-Execute Cycle

To understand how this processor system actually executes a program we will run the sum program that we've just looked at. This program adds two numbers together - effectively we will ask our processor to perform:

$5 + 3$

Hopefully, you will already have an idea of what the result will be! If you had to use pen and paper, rather than working the answer out in your head, how would you solve this problem? You would probably first write down both numbers on your paper, perform the addition in your head, and then write the result on your paper too. The program in figure 8.2 does pretty much the same thing:

▶ It stores the value 5 in the A register;

▶ It stores the value 3 in the B register;

▶ It adds the contents of A and B together (using the ALU), and stores the result in the A register;

▶ Finally it halts the processor.

Now we will examine how the processor executes this program using the fetch-execute cycle.

If we were to load this small program into JASPer, and execute it, let's try to figure out what we would expect to happen:

▶ The processor loads, or *fetches*, the first instruction from memory (stored in memory at location $0000) into the IR;

▶ Next it runs, or *executes*, this first instruction - it is the CU that does this, and as already seen, the A register takes the bit pattern $05;

▶ It then fetches the second instruction from memory and stores it in the IR;

▶ Next it executes this second instruction - the B register takes the bit pattern $03;

▶ It then fetches the third instruction from memory and stores it in the IR;

▶ It executes this third instruction, which adds the contents of A to B, storing the result in the A register;

▶ After that it fetches the final instruction and places it in the IR;

▶ It executes the final instruction which, as the mnemonic hints, stops the processor.

This process shows that the processor has to repeatedly *fetch* an instruction from memory, and *execute* it - hence this process is termed the *fetch-execute cycle*.

Like any assembly language instruction, the fetch-execute too is defined in terms of individual micro-instructions and we will look at the structure of the fetch-execute cycle next.

8.6 Inside The Fetch-Execute Cycle

The function of the fetch-execute cycle is exactly as it sounds. In order for a program to run, the processor must fetch each instruction in turn, and then execute it by running each individual micro-instruction that the instruction consists of. The only ways that the processor would cease to fetch the next instruction are:

▶ If the power to the processor is switched off;

▶ The halt microcode is executed;

▶ The processor reset button is pressed.

The fetch cycle is the same for every single instruction - no matter what the instruction is. This makes sense, because how otherwise could the processor fetch an instruction in a 'special' way if, as the instruction has not yet been fetched, it is impossible to tell what instruction it will be.

In our simple processor, the fetch cycle is defined as the following RTL sequence:

1 $MAR \leftarrow [PC]$
2 $INC \leftarrow [PC]$
3 $PC \leftarrow [INC]$
4 $MDR \leftarrow [M[MAR]]$
5 $IR \leftarrow [MDR]$
6 $CU \leftarrow [IR(opcode)]$

Here is what these RTL statements mean:

1 When fetching an instruction, we always assume that the PC contains the address of the next instruction to be fetched. For example, if a program is loaded into memory beginning at location $0000, then the PC needs to contain $0000 prior to running the program. Only then will the first instruction of the program actually be the first instruction fetched;

2 We tend to group micro-instructions 2 and 3 together, because together they perform the operation PC = PC + 1. As previously mentioned, moving a value into the INC results in the value plus 1 being stored, so in just two microcodes we are able to add 1 to the value of the PC. Why is this so necessary? We need to perform this for every single fetch cycle (so we do it *a lot*), so it is important that we can do it as quickly as possible. It means that the address of the next instruction to be fetched is already loaded into the PC, ready for the next fetch cycle. Also, using the INC to add 1 to the PC doesn't use the ALU, and therefore doesn't affect any of the PSR flags;

3 See point 2;

4 Next we access memory. We have seen this micro-instruction before, in chapter 7. It means access memory at the location stored in the MAR, and place the accessed bit pattern in the MDR. In other words, the MDR now contains the instruction to be executed;

5 But we still haven't finished there. Next we move the value from the MDR to the IR. This again is a special register, because it allows us to access either the opcode or the operand separately - we will see why this is useful next;

6 Finally, in the last part of the fetch cycle, we place the opcode of the instruction from the IR(opcode) - which is how we write 'the opcode part of the Instruction Register' (shown in figure 8.4) - and place it in the CU. It is the CU that is the heart of the processor, because it decodes this instruction

NOTES

It is worth noting that some micro-instructions can be performed in parallel, i.e. at the same time, for example $MAR \leftarrow [PC]$ and $INC \leftarrow [PC]$ in the fetch cycle. We don't need to consider this to understand our processor.

and sends the control signals to the rest of the processor in order to execute the instruction that has been fetched. Don't worry about *how* it does this - we will cover this in detail in chapter 17.

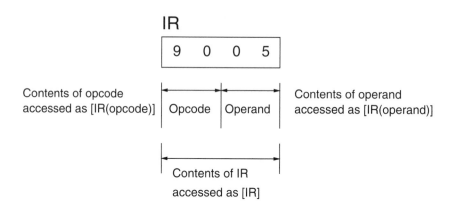

Figure 8.4 *Inside the IR*

Once the fetch cycle has completed, the CU will perform the execute cycle for the given opcode. For example, if we went back to the ADD B,A instruction the following micro-instructions would be executed for the execute cycle:

1 $ALUx \leftarrow [A]$
2 $ALUy \leftarrow [B]$
3 $ALUr = [ALUx] + [ALUy]$
4 $A \leftarrow [ALUr]$

Again, here is the explanation for this particular execution cycle:

1 We intend to add the contents of the A register to the contents of the B register, so the first micro-instruction copies the current bit pattern of the A register into the ALUx;

2 The second micro-instruction copies the contents of B into the ALUy;

3 We then add the two representations together. Incidentally it is worth noting that on the addition, the PSR will also be updated - as we saw when we described a simple addition circuit back in chapter 5;

4 Finally the result is stored in the A register.

Register	Size (bits)	Description
PC	16	Program counter - *is used to keep track of the memory address storing the next instruction to be executed*
INC	16	Incrementer - *is used to add one to the value held in the PC, something that needs to occur very often in most programs. Using the incrementer (effectively as a specialist register) is faster than using the ALU for this particular task, and importantly does not affect the PSR flags*
A	16	General Register A - *is the first of two general purpose registers, programmers can use the general purpose registers to store program bit patterns*
B	16	General Register B - *is the second of the two general purpose registers*
MAR	16	Memory Address Register - *is used as a specialist register to store the address of the memory location that we need to read from or write to*
MDR	16	Memory Data Register - *is used as a specialist register to store the data that we have just read from memory or need to write to memory*
IR	16	Instruction Register - *is the specialist register where we store the instruction once it has been fetched from memory*
ALUx	16	Arithmetic Logic Unit X Register *is the first of two specialist registers where we store bit patterns to be used in ALU operations*
ALUy	16	Arithmetic Logic Unit Y Register *is the second of two specialist registers where we store bit patterns to be used in ALU operations*
ALUr	16	Arithmetic Logic Unit Result Register *is the specialist register where the result from an ALU operation is stored*
SP	16	Stack Pointer - *is the specialist register used to store the address of the top of the stack held in memory - we will use the SP in chapter 10*
PSR	16	Processor Status Register - *is where we store information about the state of the processor, including the state of the last ALU operation*

Table 8.1 *Processor registers*

Once this execute cycle is completed, the CU would perform the next fetch cycle, and so on. It is worth noting that the execute cycle for any given opcode can consist of zero, one or many micro-instructions - and this can be different for any given opcode.

One further issue worth mentioning is the use of the IR(operand) field. This field, as we saw in figure 8.4 is eight bits wide, and therefore we need to understand the issue of performing data movements from the IR(operand) to a 16-bit wide register, as used in many instructions found in the instruction set used by our simple processor. When we perform a data movement from the

IR(operand) the data value is *sign extended* to 16 bits. This means that of the 8-bit IR(operand) value, the MSB is used to 'fill' eight left-most bits to produce a 16-bit value. This is demonstrated in figure 8.5. It is important to remember that, even though we have increased the number of bits representing the value, we are representing the *same value* - it has not changed. In figure 8.5 the 8-bit and the 16-bit values *both* represent the decimal number 43. The figure also shows the 8-bit and 16-bit values that *both* represent the decimal number -85.

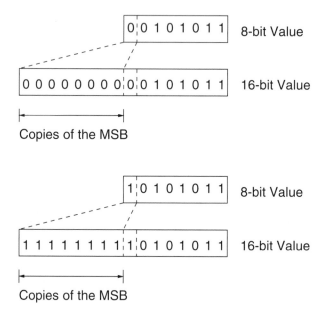

Figure 8.5 *Sign extension*

To recap the use of each of the registers, table 8.1 describes each of the registers in turn.

8.7 Running The Program In JASPer

Let's get back to running our example program from figure 8.2. We are going to load it into our processor system, and see what happens when we run it.

The file we want to run is stored on the CD that accompanies this book. On the CD, the sum program is stored in the location

```
\examples\chapter08\sum.jas
```

To load the program into JASPer use the 'file/open' menu option, or use the 'file open' button. Once you've done that, let's check the contents of memory using the 'view memory' button (or the 'memory/view' menu option) to ensure that the program has loaded successfully - if it has we can see the four lines of the program loaded in memory from address $0000.

The memory display is also useful because alongside the memory contents it also shows the instruction loaded in that location - it does this by looking at the most significant byte of each 16-bit machine code and checks what opcode this would represent (leaving a blank if the opcode is not a valid instruction in the instruction set). Notice that where we haven't loaded any program, like at address $0004, the mnemonic ADD #data,A is still listed - this is because the most significant byte, $00 indicates this instruction - the memory display cannot tell which 16-bit machine codes to treat as a program, so it blindly lists the instruction for all memory locations.

You can see how your memory view should look with the program loaded in figure 8.6. Note that unlike figure 8.3, JASPer lists memory addresses from top to bottom.

We are nearly ready to run our program, but let's have a brief think about what we are expecting to see.

- ▶ Firstly, we expect to have to run four instructions, so this means that we are going to see a fetch cycle followed by an execute cycle, four times;
- ▶ The first instruction, MOVE #$05,A (machine code $9005) will be fetched first from memory because when we start the program the value of the PC will be $0000 indicating the address of the first instruction of our program;
- ▶ For the execute phase, if we look up opcode $90 in appendix C we will find that the pattern moved into the IR(operand) during the fetch cycle (which will be $05) will be moved into the A register;
- ▶ Next we see another fetch cycle, identical to the first except that it is the second instruction of the program, from address $0001 that will be fetched;
- ▶ The execute phase for this instruction will store 3 into the B register;
- ▶ Next we see another fetch cycle fetching the instruction from address $0002;
- ▶ This third instruction will use the ALU to add the contents of A and B;
- ▶ Next we run the fourth and final fetch cycle - we should be getting used to seeing the fetch cycle now;
- ▶ The final execute cycle (for the HALT instruction) will unsurprisingly cause the processor to halt.

So let's run the program now.

1 The first time we run the program, we are going to *trace* through our program. This means that we are going to run each instruction separately - so that we can look at the values in the registers and make sure that we understand what is happening;

2 Use the 'trace' button, or the 'processor/trace' menu option to run the first instruction. You will see each micro-instruction being run in turn for firstly the fetch cycle and then the execute cycle. The fetch cycle matches exactly what we described before, while the execute cycle copies the number $05 to the A register as expected. By the way, if you've accidentally hit 'go' instead of 'trace' and you want to stop the processor, click on any part of the main processor display and the program will halt after the current cycle is completed;

3 Next, use the 'trace' button again to run the second instruction in the program (see how the PC is already pointing to the address of the next instruction?);

4 Next, use the 'trace' button again to run the third instruction in the program. Note that the ALU is used and that the PSR flags are set on the result;

5 Finally, run the last instruction in the same way. Once you've completed all of this your processor should look to be in the same *state* (the registers contain the same values) as shown in figure 8.7.

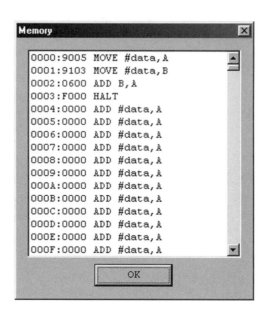

Figure 8.6 *Our program in memory*

After all of that what have we done? We successfully ran a program to add together $5 + 3$, and the result can be seen where we left it in the A register.

Even though this is a very small program it still demonstrates pretty much how any program on any von Neumann processor runs.

Before we finish this chapter we will briefly run our program one more time, not to see if the answer is any different (it won't be!), but to see how we can run a program without having to run each instruction individually.

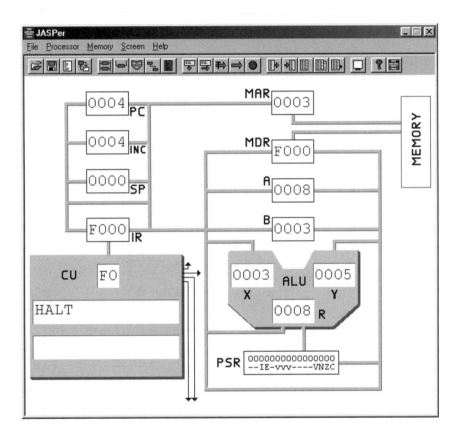

Figure 8.7   *The state of JASPer after running the program in trace mode*

1 Firstly, hit the processor reset button or use the menu option 'processor/reset'. This resets all the registers back to $0000, but leaves the contents of memory intact;

2 Instead of tracing through the program again, use the 'go' button or select 'processor/go' from the menu. This runs the whole program again and stops when the HALT instruction is encountered. If you've done this successfully, your processor will look like that in figure 8.8;

3 If you want to slow down the animation in JASPer, use the 'file/jumper set-tings' option and set a slower animation speed. Reset the processor and execute the program again.

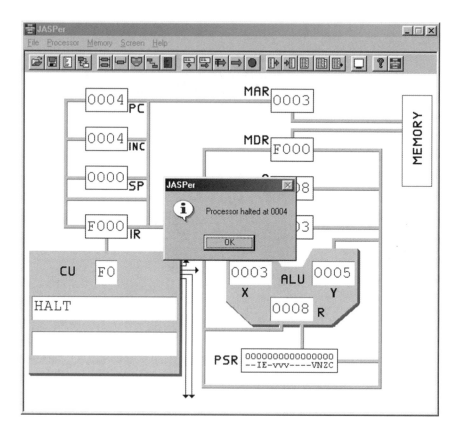

Figure 8.8 *The state of JASPer after running the program*

Now that we have a working processor system we will close this section on hardware issues. In the next section we will examine this system from the viewpoint of the programmer.

CHAPTER SUMMARY

Tasks for individual registers

▶ The PC is used to bookmark which instruction the processor is to execute next;

▶ The INC is used to add 1 to the PC;

▶ The MAR and MDR are used to access memory;

▶ A and B are general purpose registers;

▶ The IR is used to store the instruction;

▶ The ALUx and ALUy are the ALU inputs;

▶ The ALUr is the ALU output, and the PSR contains flags that are updated by the ALU.

Micro-instructions

▶ The four sets of micro-instructions understood by our simple processor are the data movement micro-instructions, the ALU micro-instructions, the test micro-instructions and the control micro-instructions;

▶ All micro-instructions can be represented by an RTL description;

▶ Assembly language instructions can be defined using micro-instructions.

Instruction sets

▶ The number of instructions within an instruction set is limited by the width of the opcode;

▶ Our simple processor has an opcode width of eight bits and therefore we can have a maximum of 256 instructions in an instruction set. In reality we do not need this many to write useful programs.

The format of a program

▶ The processor executes the machine codes of a program;

▶ Additionally we add mnemonics, operands and comments so that we can understand what the individual machine codes are to do.

The fetch-execute cycle

▶ The processor runs programs by using the fetch-execute cycle;

▶ Each instruction in memory is in turn, fetched, placed in the IR, and then executed by the CU.

Executing programs in JASPer

▶ JASPer can 'trace' a program, whereby each instruction is run individually;

▶ JASPer can execute a program whereby the program runs until either it completes, or the processor is reset.

SELF TEST QUESTIONS

1 Which instruction has the opcode $90? What micro-instructions make up the execute cycle for this opcode?

2 Which instruction has the opcode $C3? What micro-instructions make up the execute cycle for this opcode?

3 What function does the INC register have? Could we replace its use with the ALU? How would the fetch cycle have to be changed?

4 Which register decodes both the fetch and execute cycles?

EXERCISES

1 Which instruction has the opcode $06? What micro-instructions make up the execute cycle for this opcode?

2 Which instruction has the opcode $02? What micro-instructions make up the execute cycle for this opcode?

3 On the CD find \examples\chapter08\sum2.jas and load it into JASPer. Using the appendices, figure out what each line does - and then run the program a line at a time using the 'trace' button. If the program does something unexpected, reset the processor and run the program again.

Part II

Using the Processor

We look at the processor from the point of view of the programmer.

Writing Structured Programs

CHAPTER OVERVIEW

In this chapter we begin the task of focusing on the programmer's perspective of our processor system.

This chapter includes:

▶ The programming hierarchy;
▶ Structured programming concepts - sequences, selections and iterations;
▶ Writing assembly language programs;
▶ The assembly process;
▶ The debugging process;
▶ A comparison with using high-level languages;
▶ Tips on structured programming.

9.1 Introducing Programming

We've seen in part 1 that it is the program that actually makes the computer *do something*, whether that something is working out your bank balance, playing a ring-tone on your mobile phone, keeping your car engine efficient, or stopping a Boeing 737 from flying into a mountain.

Programs are *written* by human beings (to be pedantic it is also possible to have a program that writes programs - but someone had to *write* the program that writes the programs).

It is possible to write a program for a computer at one of a number of levels, known as a *programming hierarchy*. A simplified hierarchy is shown in figure 9.1. Different programming languages are written for each particular level, and each level has its own set of good and bad points. Also, each level sits on the level below it.

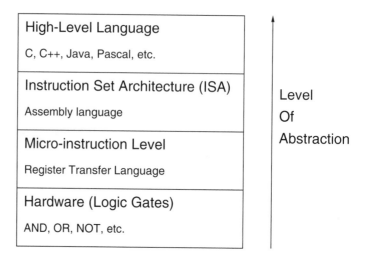

Figure 9.1   *A programming hierarchy*

Generally, the higher you are in the hierarchy, the more abstract a program can be. For example, high-level languages, such as *C* or *Java* include notions of *variables* (used as a named place where we can store a piece of data) and *data structures* (a way of storing related data items). At the second lowest level we have the micro-instruction level, which is totally aimed at effecting control of the lowest level, the hardware of the computer.

In this chapter we will concentrate on the *Instruction Set Architecture* (*ISA*) level, occasionally explaining concepts in a higher level language to show how the levels map onto each other.

9.2 Introducing Assembly Programming

At the instruction set architecture level we program our processor in assembly language instructions - we saw a brief glimpse of these in the previous chapter. Normally, we would apply the process as shown in figure 9.2, writing a program using assembly language mnemonics and running a program called an *assembler* to assemble our program into machine code. However, until chapter 14 we will act as our own assembler program.

Assembly language instructions correspond one to one (mostly) with the machine code instructions that we have seen so far, but are written in mnemonics to help we humans understand the machine code.

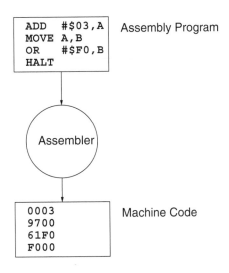

Figure 9.2 *The assembly process*

NOTES

For further information on programming constructs, and indeed many other computing issues, refer to [com02].

9.3 Programming Concepts

To understand how to program our processor we are going to look at something known as *procedural programming*. This is a form of programming that has been with us since the early days of computing. Lately, the trend has been to move to *object oriented programming*. Many modern languages, like Java for example, are object oriented languages. Object orientation is an abstraction used by programmers to more easily create programs.

Any procedural program is based on three fundamental constructs. These are:

► Sequences - executing one instruction sequentially after another;
► Selections - making a decision to do one thing or another;
► Iterations - doing something multiple times.

Let's look at each construct in turn, firstly using a high-level language, then moving to assembly language.

9.3.1 Sequences

A sequence is simply one instruction followed by another. For example, in a high-level language (this happens to be a pseudo-language (a made-up language) which is a cross between Java and C - designed to highlight the programming constructs rather than the idiosyncracies of any given real language) we could say something like:

```
number1 = 34;
number2 = 12;
number1 = number1 + number2;
```

In this sequence of three instructions (each instruction is terminated by a semi-colon) we have two variables (called `number1` and `number2`) having values assigned to them, and then the last instruction setting the first variable to be the sum of both variables.

In assembly code we could write something like

```
MOVE #^34,A    * store the decimal value 34 in A
MOVE #^12,B    * store the decimal value 12 in B
ADD B,A        * add A and B, storing the result in A
```

NOTES

What base is it? : A $ indicates hexadecimal, a ^ indicates decimal, a @ indicates octal, and a % indicates binary.

The first thing to notice about the assembly language program is that we can store variables on our processor in the A and B registers. We can also store variables in memory locations, but we will look at that later. Also, it is worth remembering that a ^ character indicates that the following number is decimal.

An assembly instruction does not end with a semi-colon, and indeed the comment at the end of the line is not necessary - however, *I recommend that you always write at least one comment for every line of assembly code you write. Your comments should describe, in as high a level as possible, what the assembly code actually does.* All comments in an assembly language program written for our processor begin with an asterisk and run to the end of the line.

9.3.2 Selections

Selections are more complicated than sequences, in fact there are a few ways to write a selection construct. The first of these is called an `if` construct, and we follow that with an `if-then-else` construct, which is just an embellishment of an `if` construct.

The If Construct

Here is the format for an if construct:

```
if (condition) {
    // payload to run if condition is true
    T_PAYLOAD
} // end if
```

We need to note the following points:

▶ '//' precedes any comment in our high-level language, the comment runs to the end of the line;

▶ The condition is used to decide whether to run our selection or not. More on this in a moment;

▶ If the condition is true, then the instructions between the curly braces (containing T_PAYLOAD, which means the *condition true payload*) are the instructions that are run;

▶ The payload of the selection can consist of other sequences, selections or iterations of program instructions.

Here is an example of an if construct in a high-level language.

```
A = 2;
B = 2;
if (A==B) {
    // payload to run if condition is true
    A = 0;
} // end if
```

In this example, we first assign the value of two variables, then we meet the if construct. In this construct A==B is known as the *condition*, which means if the two variables are equal, then the condition is *true*, else the condition is *false*. If the condition is true (it is), then the payload of the construct (setting A to be 0) is executed. If we were to change this example such that the first line reads

```
A = 1;
```

then the payload would not be executed as the condition of the if construct would be false. In assembly language we could write the example as follows:

```
        MOVE #^02,A  * initialize A
        MOVE #^02,B  * initialize B
        CMP A,B      * check the condition
        BEQ true     * if the condition is true, branch to
                     * the payload
        JMP end_if   * if it isn't, go to the end of the 'if'
true    MOVE #^00,A  * this line is the T_PAYLOAD
end_if  HALT
```

Here are the points to look out for in the assembly program example:

▶ true and end_if are both examples of *labels*. A label is used to refer to a memory address where a variable or an instruction can be stored. For example, the HALT instruction will be stored at a memory address that has been labelled as end_if - the instruction JMP end_if means jump to the address that contains the HALT instruction. It is important to note that in assembly language programs for JASPer, labels must always begin in the first column of the file, with no spaces before it on the line;

▶ Checking the condition takes *multiple* assembly language instructions - we'll cover these next.

To check the condition to see if both A and B registers contain the same value takes two assembly instructions. These are:

```
CMP A,B
BEQ true
```

The first of these, the CMP instruction, actually performs a subtract operation, setting the PSR flags, but does *not* store the result from the ALUr. We can see this by looking in appendix C to find that the execution cycle for this instruction is:

▶ $ALUx \leftarrow [B]$

▶ $ALUy \leftarrow [A]$

▶ $ALUr = [ALUx] - [ALUy]$

So, the act of executing the CMP instruction will set the PSR Z flag to one if the values were the same, or set it to zero if they weren't.

The next instruction (BEQ) checks to see if the Z flag is set to one, and if it is, the program *flow of control* (which instruction in the program should be run next) is moved to the line on which the label true can be found (the label is treated as an address). If the Z flag is not set to 1 then the next line of the program is executed. This occurs because the instruction uses a *test micro-instruction* as the first micro-instruction of the BEQ execute cycle. The complete execute cycle for the BEQ instruction is:

▶ $if(PSR(z) == 1)$

▶ $PC \leftarrow [IR(operand)]$

Essentially, if the test micro-instruction evaluates to be true, then any other micro-instructions following it in the execute cycle are executed (the one data movement micro-instruction in this example), otherwise all other micro-instructions for the execute cycle are ignored.

All conditions used to perform selections (and indeed, iterations) are controlled by the setting, and the checking, of the PSR flags, Z, N, V and C.

Lastly, it is worth noting that the JMP instruction near the end of the program is known as an *unconditional jump* as it immediately moves the flow of control to the line on which the end_if label can be found - ensuring that the condition payload (the final MOVE instruction) is only executed when the condition is true.

The If-Then-Else Construct

This is an extended form of the if construct. If a condition is true, some *true payload* will be executed, otherwise some *false payload* will be executed. This can be formatted as follows:

```
if (condition) {
    // payload to run if condition is true
    T_PAYLOAD
}
else {
    // payload to run if condition is false
    F_PAYLOAD
} // end if
```

As you can see, the condition controls which payload will be executed. This can be shown in an example as follows:

```
A = 2;
B = 2;
if (A==B) {
    // payload to run if condition is true
```

```
    A = 0;
}
else {
    // payload to run if condition is false
    A = 1;
} // end if
```

In this example, if the condition is true the true payload will be executed (setting A to 0), otherwise the false payload will be executed (setting A to 1). If we were to code this example into assembly language, we would have the following:

```
        MOVE #^02,A    * initialize A
        MOVE #^02,B    * initialize B
        CMP A,B        * check the condition
        BEQ true       * if the condition is true, branch to
                       * the T_PAYLOAD
                       * else execute the F_PAYLOAD
false   MOVE #^01,A    * this line is the F_PAYLOAD
        JMP end_if     * go to the end of the if-else
true    MOVE #^00,A    * this line is the T_PAYLOAD
end_if HALT           * halt the program
```

Again, in this example we see the condition being checked by use of first a CMP instruction followed by a BEQ instruction. Run through each line to ensure you understand what is happening.

9.3.3 Iterations

Iterations are a way of running particular instructions multiple times, for example if you wanted to count up to ten by adding one each time. In assembly language, iterations are relatively similar to sequence constructs.

I'll show you two forms of iteration constructs, known as the while construct and the for construct.

The While Construct

The format of the while construct is shown here.

```
while (condition) {
    // payload to run while condition is true
    PAYLOAD
} // end while
```

It is similar to what we have seen before except that, while the condition is true, the payload will keep executing (the flow of control will *loop* at the end of the *while* construct, back to check the condition again) - with the condition being checked *prior* to every payload execution. At the point that the condition becomes false, the flow of control leaves the while construct. It is worth noting that this form of construct is known as a *zero-based iteration*, in other words the payload can be executed zero, one or more times.

Another construct known as a `repeat-until` construct is similar to the `while` construct except that the payload always executes at least once, as the condition is checked *after* the payload has executed. It is a *non-zero based iteration*.

Both `while` constructs and `repeat-until` constructs are also sometimes referred to as a *condition-controlled loop*.

Let us have a look at a `while` construct example:

```
A = 10;
B =  0;
while (A > B) {
    // payload to run if condition is true
    B = B + 1;
} // end while
```

In this example, the payload executes while the condition $A > B$ is true, which is until the value of B also reaches 10. This is converted to assembly code as follows:

```
          MOVE #^10,A    * initialize A
          MOVE #^00,B    * initialize B
while     CMP A,B        * check the condition
          BMI true       * if the condition is true, branch to
                         * the payload
          JMP end_while  * if it isn't, go to the end of the 'while'
true      ADD #^01,B     * this line is the PAYLOAD
```

```
         JMP while      * run the loop again
end_while HALT          * halt program
```

You can see that this time the condition is checked with a BMI instruction, which uses the N flag to see if the value in the A register is greater than that in the B register (the CMP A,B instruction actually subtracts A from B, sets the PSR flags on the result, but does not store the result - it is used purely to ensure that the PSR flags are updated).

Generally, we tend to use a while construct when we don't know how many times we want to execute a particular instruction payload.

The For Construct

The for construct is similar again to the while construct, but it is used in a slightly different way in that we tend to use it whenever we know exactly how many times we wish the payload to be executed. The for construct is also sometimes referred to as a *count-controlled loop*.

The format of a for construct is as follows:

```
for (initialization; condition; increment) {
    // payload to run while the condition is true
    PAYLOAD
} // end for
```

As you can see the condition looks different to before, in that in this case it is built from three separate statements. The first statement deals with any variable initialization, the second is the condition itself, and the third is a statement to be executed after every payload execution. This can be demonstrated in an example.

```
B = 0;
for (A=0; A < 5; A++) {
    // payload to run while the condition is true
    B = B + 1;
} // end for
```

In this example, the condition is true for precisely five iterations, while A is set to 0, through to while A is set to 4. As soon as A is set to 5 the condition becomes false and the payload is no longer executed. This example can be converted to assembly instructions as follows:

```
            MOVE #^00,B     * initialize B
for         MOVE #^00,A     * initialize A
loop        CMP  #^05,A     * check the condition
            BEQ  end_for    * if the condition is false, branch to
                            *    the end of the for construct
                            *    otherwise run the PAYLOAD
            ADD  #^01,B     * this line is the PAYLOAD
            ADD  #^01,A     * increment A once the payload has executed
            JMP  loop       * run the loop again
end_for     HALT            * halt the program
```

This is very similar to the examples we have seen before.

It is worth mentioning that any for construct can just as easily be written as a while construct, as a while construct can also be used to execute a payload a given number of times. Here is the structure of a for construct expressed as a while construct:

```
initialization;
while (condition) {
    // payload to run while the condition is true
    PAYLOAD
    increment;
} // end while
```

9.4 Writing Our First Assembly Program

For our first program we will write a program to perform division. Let us first attempt to write our program in our higher level language, and then over a number of steps we will produce the machine code to run on the processor - this process is known as *stepwise refinement*.

```
count = 0;      // to store the quotient

dividend = 100;  // the number to be divided
```

```
divisor = 9;      // the number to divide by

while (dividend >= divisor) {
    count = count + 1;
    dividend = dividend - divisor;
}
```

This program will iteratively count how many times the `divisor` can be subtracted from the `dividend`, until the `dividend` value is less than the `divisor` value. Then the `count` variable will tell us the *quotient* and the final value will be the *remainder*.

9.4.1 Writing The Assembly Instructions

Writing the equivalent assembly instruction program is relatively simple once we make some decisions regarding where we are going to store the variables.

The problem is that our processor only has two registers to store variables in (register A and register B) and yet our program makes use of three variables (`divisor`, `dividend` and `count`). So where can we store the third variable? We will have to store it in a memory location (again, due to the von Neumann architecture, both program and data are stored in the same memory).

We will make the decision to store the `divisor` in the A register and the `dividend` in the B register. We could have done this the other way around, or indeed placed the `count` value in either register, but the point is that we have decided on our storage and we can now write our assembly program. The third variable, `count`, can go in a memory location.

So, using the previous `while` construct example as a template, let us have a first attempt at our assembly program. We will produce our solution in stages, so the first stage consists of coding the initializations and the `while` construct.

```
          MOVE #^0,count * initialize the count variable
          MOVE #^100,A   * initialize A with the dividend value
          MOVE #^9,B     * initialize B with the divisor value
while     CMP A,B        * check the condition
          BMI true       * if the condition is true, branch to
                         * the payload
          JMP end_while  * if it isn't, go to the end of the 'while'
true      PAYLOAD goes here
          JMP while
end_while HALT
```

So far we haven't added the payload to the `while` construct, but we can do that next.

```
            MOVE #^0,count   * initialize the count variable
            MOVE #^100,A     * initialize A with the dividend value
            MOVE #^9,B       * initialize B with the divisor value
while       CMP A,B          * check the condition
            BMI true         * if the condition is true, branch to
                             * the payload
            JMP end_while    * if it isn't, go to the end of the 'while'
true        SUB B,A          * } dividend = dividend - divisor
            ADD #^01,count   * } count = count + 1
            JMP while
end_while   HALT
```

Our second attempt is actually pretty close to our needs, and follows the structure of the high-level program in a format applied from the previous `while` example. However, it currently has one small flaw. It won't work.

The flaw is that we have treated `count` as if it were a register, and unfortunately we can't treat it like this, because when we look at the set of instructions available to us (listed in appendix B), there are no instructions that can add 1 directly to a memory location - instead we need to use registers A or B to add 1 to our `count` variable. Maybe you've spotted the problem by now - we are *already* storing variables in both of those registers. So what can we do? Simple, we transfer the current value from, say, the A register into a temporary storage area in a memory location, use A to add one to `count`, and then move the value from the temporary storage back into the A register.

Here is our finished assembly program:

```
            ORG 0            * load program in memory at location 0
            MOVE #^0,A       * } initialize the count variable
            MOVE A,count     * }
            MOVE #^100,A     * initialize A with the dividend value
            MOVE #^9,B       * initialize B with the divisor value
while       CMP A,B          * check the condition
            BMI true         * if the condition is true, branch to
                             * the payload
            JMP end_while    * if it isn't, go to the end of the 'while'
true        MOVE A,temp      * }
            MOVE count,A     * }
            ADD #^01,A       * } count = count + 1
            MOVE A,count     * }
```

```
            MOVE temp,A    * }
            SUB B,A        * dividend = dividend - divisor
            JMP while      * check the condition again
end_while   HALT           * stop the program on completion
count       DS.W 1         * store count variable here
temp        DS.W 1         * store temp variable here
```

Note the following in the finished program:

► Initializing count now takes two instructions, as we have to use the A register to pass the initial value to our memory location for count;

► In assembly code count = count + 1 has taken us five instructions, because we had to store count in memory;

► I have added an ORG 0 *directive* at the start of the program. Directives are normally instructions for the assembler program, but for the moment they are messages to ourselves as we will be the assembler program. ORG 0 means begin storing this program in memory starting at memory location 0;

► I have also added two DS.W directives at the end of the program. DS.W stands for *Define Storage - Word*, in other words, it tells the assembler to store our variables count and temp in memory. Each has one word put aside for it.

Now we have finished our assembly program, we need to convert it to machine code in order to execute it, so that we can see if it works.

9.4.2 The Assembly Process - Converting To Machine Code

NOTES

Assemblers that run on one instruction set architecture, and yet produce programs to run on a second architecture are known as cross-assemblers.

As I've said before, once we have a complete assembly program it is normal to run a program called an *assembler* to create the machine code that we can execute. However, until chapter 14 we will act as our own assembler program, so we can see how the assembly program is methodically converted into machine code.

We will use the following steps in order to produce our required machine code program:

► Convert any directives into the required machine code (discussed later);

► For each instruction, check the instruction set and find the opcode that represents the instruction;

► Figure out where each instruction will be stored in memory;

▶ Assign values to each instruction operand.

The first line of our program is an ORG directive, this is actually the only directive that JASPer can understand, and so we can include it directly in our machine code program to tell JASPer to load our program into memory starting at location 0. If we were to leave this directive out JASPer would load the program by default into memory starting at address 0 anyway, but the ORG directive is useful if we want to load a program into any other location in memory. It is also a reminder to us of where the program will load in memory.

The second line is our first instruction to convert into machine code. To do this we need to first think about the instruction MOVE #^0,A to ensure we understand what it is meant to do. It moves a number (which happens to be 0) into the A register. If we were to look for all the different MOVE instructions in the instruction set (as listed in appendix B) we would find many, but if we limited ourselves to moves where the result is transferred to the A register then we have the following MOVE instructions to choose from. These instructions use different addressing modes - we will discuss addressing modes in chapter 11.

We need to decide which of these is the correct match to our instruction:

```
90 MOVE #data,A   Move an immediate oper. into A
92 MOVE addr,A    Load reg. A from a direct addr.
94 MOVE (addr),A  Load reg. A from an indirect addr.
96 MOVE B,A       Move B reg. to A reg.
98 MOVE (B),A     Load A reg. with a reg. indirect oper.
9a MOVE B+addr,A  Load A reg from an indexed addr. (index in B)
```

Now, only the first of these transfers an immediate operand into the A register, so our opcode for this first instruction is $90.

The next instruction MOVE A,count is a little different, as we are treating count as the address of the memory location where this variable is stored, so the correct instruction is:

```
A2 MOVE A,addr    Store the A reg. in memory at a direct addr.
```

Therefore the correct opcode is $A2.

If we follow this process for all the instructions we end up with the following. I've numbered each line of the program to indicate where it will be stored in memory, the first instruction is stored in memory location $0000, while the temp variable is stored in memory location $0010.

Essentially, at this stage we attempt to match the *pattern* of the instruction to ensure we choose the correct opcode. In reality we are choosing between different addressing modes.

```
            Address              Instruction    Comment

ORG 0       0000                 ORG 0          * load program in memory at location 0
90??        0000                 MOVE #^0,A     * } initialize the count variable
A2??        0001                 MOVE A,count   * }
90??        0002                 MOVE #^100,A   * initialize A with the dividend value
91??        0003                 MOVE #^9,B     * initialize B with the divisor value
87??        0004    while        CMP A,B        * check the condition
BB??        0005                 BMI true       * if the condition is true, branch to
            0006                                * the payload
E0??        0006                 JMP end_while  * if it isn't, go to end of the 'while'
A2??        0007    true         MOVE A,temp    * }
92??        0008                 MOVE count,A   * }
00??        0009                 ADD #^01,A     * } count = count + 1
A2??        000A                 MOVE A,count   * }
92??        000B                 MOVE temp,A    * }
26??        000C                 SUB B,A        * dividend = dividend - divisor
E0??        000D                 JMP while      * check the condition again
F0??        000E    end_while    HALT           * stop the program on completion
0000        000F    count        DS.W 1         * store count variable here
0000        0010    temp         DS.W 1         * store temp variable here
```

Note that the DS.W directives simply convert into $0000 values stored in memory - to be used as the storage locations for the variables count and temp. Remember, these last two entries stored in memory are data locations, and not part of the machine code program.

Next, for each instruction we need to work out the missing operand for each instruction. Our first instruction, MOVE #^0,A is easy enough, because the immediate operand is 0, therefore as an 8-bit value (remember, all operands are 8 bits) we write down $00.

The second instruction count, as we said, is being used as an address where our variable is being stored. So, if we look towards the bottom of the program we can see that count is listed as being at address $000F, which in 8 bits (the lower 8 bits) becomes the operand value $0F.

There are also a number of other interesting operations. It is worth considering the operand for the instruction CMP A,B. This instruction requires no explicit operand when converted to machine code, and so we pad the operand field with $00 to form the complete 16-bit machine code. In theory, we could use any value - because the processor will never make use of the operand part of the machine code for this instruction, but it is convention that makes us pad out the unneeded operand with zeroes rather than use any other value.

Lastly, let us consider the instruction BMI true. Again, true is considered to be an address, and we use the address where the label true is shown at the start of the line, which is $0007 (shortened to $07 for our 8-bit operand).

If we continue this process we finally end up with the program as follows:

```
ORG 0   0000              ORG 0          * load program in memory at location 0
9000    0000              MOVE #^0,A     * } initialize the count variable      .
A20F    0001              MOVE A,count    * }
9064    0002              MOVE #^100,A   * initialize A with the dividend value
9109    0003              MOVE #^9,B     * initialize B with the divisor value
8700    0004   while      CMP A,B        * check the condition
BB07    0005              BMI true       * if the condition is true, branch to
        0006                             * the payload
E00E    0006              JMP end_while  * if it isn't, go to end of the 'while'
A210    0007   true       MOVE A,temp    * }
920F    0008              MOVE count,A    * }
0001    0009              ADD #^01,A     * } count = count + 1
A20F    000A              MOVE A,count    * }
9210    000B              MOVE temp,A     * }
2600    000C              SUB B,A        * dividend = dividend - divisor
E004    000D              JMP while       * check the condition again
F000    000E   end_while HALT           * stop the program on completion
0000    000F   count      DS.W 1         * store count variable here
0000    0010   temp       DS.W 1         * store temp variable here
```

After all that we have now completed the assembly process. Now to execute it, and see if it does what we expect!

9.4.3 Running The Program

Finally, we have reached the point where we can run our program. To do this we need to do the following in JASPer:

▶ Load the program (found in the file \examples\chapter09\divide.jas on the CD);

▶ Disable animation in the 'jumper settings' dialog box (otherwise the program will take a long time to complete, as we will see all the individual data movement animations);

▶ Run the program.

Once the program has completed, JASPer will look like figure 9.3.

Now, did our program work correctly? The result of the divide operation will be in memory location $000F (the storage for count). If we have a look at the memory contents, as shown in figure 9.4, we can see that the result is $000B, or converted to decimal, 11. So, we have proved that

$$100 \div 9 = 11$$

which is correct once we understand that we have performed an integer divide. In fact the remainder is left in the A register - it is set to $0001, so it's probably more correct to say that we have proved

$$100 \div 9 = 11, \; remainder \; 1$$

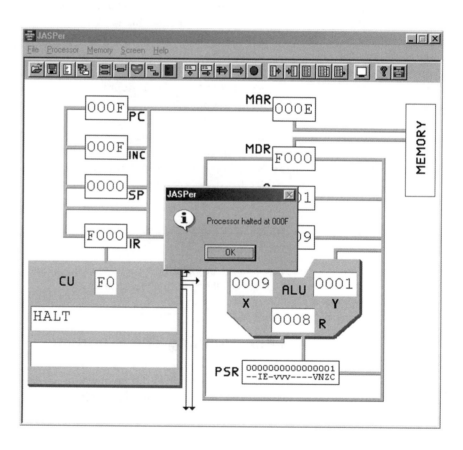

Figure 9.3 *JASPer after running* divide.jas

9.4.4 The Debugging Process

Is it this easy to write machine code programs? No, I'm afraid it isn't because even the slightest error (like using the wrong opcode, or the wrong address for an operand) can cause the program to malfunction - sometimes spectacularly. For example, it is possible to enter an *infinite loop*, which means that the program will *never* complete. When this happens the only solution is to click the mouse on the JASPer window to simulate the hitting of the processor reset button.

So how do we ensure our program *does* work correctly? We follow a process known as *debugging*.

Debugging allows us to remove *syntax errors* and *semantic errors* in our program. Syntax errors are those that cause the program to fail when entering them into memory (or more accurately fail during the assembly process), such as if we attempted to include a machine code value like $F00G, which is plainly incorrect hexadecimal. Semantic errors occur in programs that load correctly, but the program fails to do what we expect it to do, such as a condition that fails to ever set to true (possibly because we are checking the incorrect PSR flag).

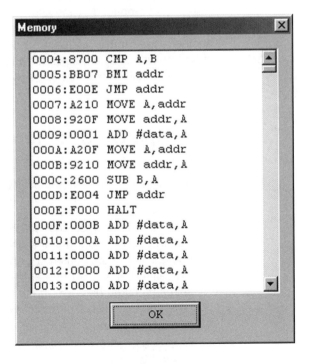

Figure 9.4 *Contents of memory after running* `divide.jas`

The aim of debugging is to remove all syntactic and semantic errors.

Syntactical errors, commonly known as syntax errors, are removed first (if your program won't load into JASPer then you have a syntax error), after which semantic errors are removed which is a *much* longer and more arduous process! Essentially, if your program doesn't work correctly, you need to logically and methodically work through your program a line at a time (known as *stepping through* your program), working from the first line until you reach the end of the program. It takes practice to become a good debugger!

9.5 Using High-Level Languages

Writing programs in high-level languages, like C, C++, Java or Pascal, is essentially a similar procedure to writing assembly programs.

If we were to write a high-level program for JASPer, we would use a *compiler* program to *compile* the program into machine code. A compiler is similar (but more complicated) to an assembler program and we'll talk more about compilers in chapter 14.

The machine code that the compiler produces would work in *exactly the same way* as that produced by the assembler program (or us mimicking an assembler). Just because one program can be written in a high-level language and another in assembly language, it doesn't mean that the resulting machine code acts differently on the underlying processor. The resulting machine code programs would work *in the same way*.

9.6 Tips On Structured Programming

When writing structured programs, try to remember the following:

▶ In all of the assembly instruction constructs displayed above, each has exactly *one entrance* (the first line of the construct), and exactly *one exit* (the last line of the construct). Any piece of code that contains constructs with either more than one entrance or more than one exit is known as *spaghetti code*, because of the convoluted route that the flow of control takes through such a program. *Writing spaghetti code is to be avoided at all costs!*

▶ Always use *stepwise refinement* for writing procedural programs. This method is also known as the *top down approach*, or *top down design*;

▶ It is worth emphasizing that, although all the above examples only show payloads consisting of short instruction sequences, a payload can itself consist of other sequences, selections or iterations of instructions. We will see this in future examples;

► Comment every line of assembly code! Otherwise, a few days later your own programs will be incomprehensible to you.

CHAPTER SUMMARY

Structured programming concepts

► The instruction set architecture level sits on top of the micro-instruction level, which in turn sits on the hardware level;

► The structured programming constructs are sequences, selections and iterations;

► `if` and `if-then-else` constructs are both examples of selections;

► `while` and `for` constructs are both examples of iterations;

► When writing any assembly language program, first write the program in a higher level language prior to your first attempt at writing it in assembly language.

The assembly and debugging processes

► To assemble a program, first code the opcodes, and then the operands to produce the 16-bit machine codes that constitute the program;

► Once the program has been successfully assembled, syntax errors have been removed. The task of the debugging process is to remove semantic errors;

► Once syntax and semantic errors have been removed from a program it will work correctly;

► High-level programs that are compiled execute on the processor in exactly the same way as assembled programs.

Tips on structured programming

► All structured programming constructs have one entrance and one exit;

► Use stepwise refinement to write and test program constructs iteratively;

► Comment all assembly language statements as fully as possible and as abstractly as possible.

SELF TEST QUESTIONS

1 Write a program to find the answer to the sum 6 + 5. Hint, you can store the values in A and B.

2 Modify your program to store the values to be added in memory. Hint, store 6 in location 0010 and 5 in location 0011.

3 Using the assembly language equivalent of a `for` construct, write a program to compute the sum of the first ten integers. Hint, use a `CMP #data,A` instruction to see if your program should halt.

4 Write a program to sort two values held at the addresses 0020 and 0021, such that the larger value is at the higher address. Describe your program in a high-level language first.

EXERCISES

1 Describe why a compiler can find syntax errors but not semantic errors.

2 Write a program to find the answer to the sum 23 + 56.

3 Write a program to find the answer to the sum 23 - 56.

4 Write a program to sort two values held at the addresses 0040 and 0041, such that the higher value is at the lower address. Describe your program in a high-level language first.

Stacks and Subroutines

In this chapter we introduce the concept of a stack, and describe how we can make use of stacks, most notably for implementing subroutines.

This chapter includes:

▶ The concept of the stack;
▶ Hardware support for the stack - the stack pointer;
▶ Using the stack;
▶ The concept of the subroutine, and how they can be implemented using the stack;
▶ Using subroutines in assembly language programs.

10.1 Introducing The Stack

Now we have begun writing simple assembly programs it is time to start introducing a very useful construct known as a *stack*. A stack is an example of an *abstract data type* (*ADT*), which is effectively a way to encapsulate data and operations on that data. The use of abstract data types in high-level languages is very common, and much less so at assembly level - the stack is the only ADT we will encounter in this text. A stack is a very common abstract data type, and we will see later how useful it can be to us in our role of assembly language programmer.

The most common analogy for a stack is a stack of plates. We can place another plate on top of the stack of plates, or we can take off a plate from the stack of plates. At all times we have a finite number of plates in the stack (either zero, one or more) and at any time we can only ever make use of the top plate on the stack.

The operation of placing an object on a stack is called a *push*, while removing an object from a stack is called a *pop*. This arrangement is shown in figure 10.1.

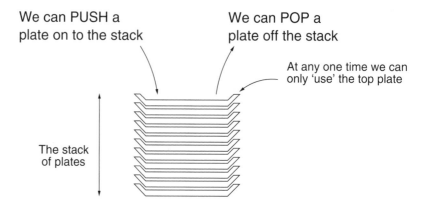

We can PUSH a plate on to the stack

We can POP a plate off the stack

At any one time we can only 'use' the top plate

The stack of plates

Figure 10.1 *A stack of plates*

So, now you can picture a stack of plates it is only a small jump to imagining a stack of anything - and for writing our programs we can imagine that instead of plates we want to stack numbers.

How can stacking numbers be useful? Well, we can go back to our divide example in chapter 9. Remember that we had to store a temporary value in a location we called temp? Even though we had to place this value in a particular memory location, in reality we didn't care where it was stored in memory - we just wanted a location that we could make use of briefly. You can imagine that, if we had a large number of temporary values used in different parts of the program, that life could get quite complicated keeping track of all the individual memory locations used for each temporary value. By using a stack instead, we actually make our life a little easier.

Here is the section of the divide program that made use of the temp variable.

```
MOVE A,temp    * }
MOVE count,A   * }
```

```
            ADD #^01,A      * } count = count + 1
            MOVE A,count    * }
            MOVE temp,A     * }
```

To use the `temp` variable we had to define exactly where it was in memory as shown here.

```
temp        DS.W 1          * store temp variable here
```

If we needed to have more temporary variables we would have to have multiple definitions like this in our program.

Using a stack we simply have to push the number we want to temporarily store onto the stack. Later on, when we can pop the value back from the stack.

```
            PUSH A          * save A on the stack
            MOVE count,A    * }
            ADD #^01,A      * } count = count + 1
            MOVE A,count    * }
            POP A           * restore A from the stack
```

When we push or pop values to or from a stack we don't *care* where individual values are stored - just that they *are* stored.

However, if we were to push multiple values on to the stack that we later wished to retrieve we need to remove them from the stack in *reverse* order.

10.2 Hardware Support For The Stack

Our stack is stored in memory, along with our program and any data, but so far we haven't considered how our processor knows where the stack is in memory, and how it knows where the top element is in memory. All we know is that our stack uses a number of *contiguous* (next to each other) memory locations to store values.

With the stack of plates analogy, we always know which plate is the top plate (no prizes for guessing it's the one on the top of the stack), but when our stack is just another part of memory with no clear 'top' or 'bottom' we need to keep track of what is happening with our stack in memory. Let us take a first look at our stack in memory in figure 10.2.

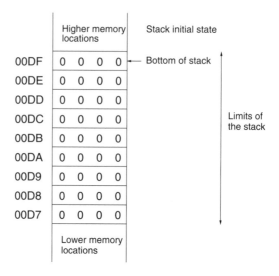

Figure 10.2 *Our stack in memory*

Points worth noting include:

► We have placed the stack inclusively between memory locations $00D7 and $00DF in contiguous locations;

► Stacks are placed in memory *upside down*, so memory location $00DF will be the first location used for the stack, then $00DE, etc;

► The bottom of the stack does not change, the stack grows *downwards in memory* as we push values on to the stack.

This can be quite confusing at first, but hopefully things become a little clearer if we push some numbers onto our stack. Firstly, we will push the value $FFFF onto our stack, and then have a look at the stack now in figure 10.3.

The operation *push* does 2 things:

► It places the value in memory at the location indicated by the top of the stack;

► It then moves the top of the stack to the next stack location (which is the address obtained by taking 1 from the current top of stack address).

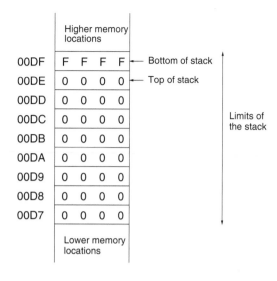

Figure 10.3 *Our stack in memory after a PUSH operation*

We can see the value we've pushed onto the stack at location $00DF. Also, we can see that the top of the stack has moved by one memory location. The bottom of the stack has remained in the same location (and will always do so - the bottom of the stack is fixed).

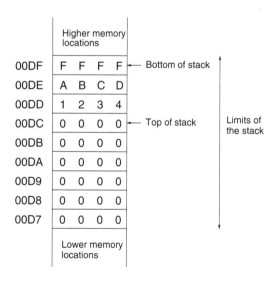

Figure 10.4 *Our stack in memory after two more PUSH operations*

To ensure we understand what is happening let us now push two more values onto the stack, these values are $ABCD and $1234. The stack after these push operations is shown in figure 10.4.

Now we have three values on our stack and the top of the stack has moved to location $00DC. The other operation we can perform on our stack is called *pop* - it is the act of taking a value from the stack.

The operation *pop* does 2 things:

▶ It moves the top of the stack to the previous stack location (which is effectively the address obtained by adding 1 to the current top of stack address);

▶ It copies the value from memory at the location indicated by the top of the stack into the location specified in the POP instruction.

Let us pop the most recent value and see what effect this has on the stack, as shown in figure 10.5.

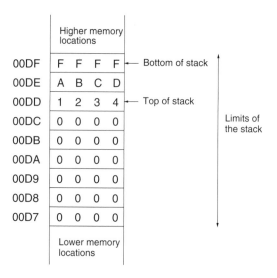

Figure 10.5 *Our stack in memory after 1 POP operation*

The top of the stack has now moved back to the location $00DD. It is worth noting that, even though we have popped a value from the stack, the value $1234 is still stored in memory location $00DD - it is not erased in any way. If we were to push another value on to the stack, only then would the value $1234 be overwritten with the newly pushed value.

10.2.1   Introducing The Stack Pointer

One thing we still haven't talked about is actually *how* we keep track of the current top of the stack.

We could simply use another memory location to contain the address of the top of the stack, but it so happens that using a stack is something we want to do so much (we'll see why when we cover subroutines later) that instead we use a special register in our processor called the *Stack Pointer*, or *SP*, to store the address of the top of the stack.

The stack pointer will, once it has been initialized, contain the address of the current top of the stack. We say that the stack pointer *points* to the top of the stack.

10.2.2   Stack Limitations

What would happen if we were to push so many values onto the stack that we used more locations than we had set aside for our stack? We could overwrite part of our program or data, and so cause the program to fail - this is known as *stack overflow*.

10.3   Using Stacks

Now that we understand the basic use of a stack, let us write a program to make use of a stack. We will write a program to reverse a list of numbers.

So, what do we want this program to do?

▶ We will store a list of values in memory, with the last value followed by a 0 value, to indicate the end of the list (when we use a 0 value in this way we often call it the *terminator*, although we could have chosen any bit pattern to be our terminator). Note that this also means that the list of values cannot include a 0;

▶ We will push each value in turn onto the stack, only stopping when we read the terminator value in our list, indicating that we have reached the end of the list and we have no more values to push onto the stack;

▶ Next, we will pop each value from the stack, writing it over the original list. We know we have reached the end of the list because the first value that we pushed onto the stack was a terminator value.

If we were to write this program in a higher level language we would have something like this:

```
initialize_the_stack_pointer;
push_terminator_onto_stack;

A = address_of_beginning_of_list;
while(value_held_at_A != 0) {
    push_value_held_at_A;
    A = A + 1;
}

// All values have now been placed on the stack
//

A = address_of_beginning_of_list;
B = first_popped_value;
while(B != 0) {
    write_B_to_address_in_A;
    A = A + 1;
    B = next_popped_value
}
```

A few points worth noting are:

▶ The first two lines initialize the stack by setting where we want to put the stack in memory, and by placing a terminator value onto the stack. Using this terminator we will later know when to stop popping values from the stack.

▶ The next section of the program deals with pushing values onto the stack. The condition `value_held_at_A != 0` means while the value held in memory at the address held in the A register is not equal to 0 - in other words, while we haven't yet reached the terminator value.

▶ The final section deals with popping the values back off the stack - which means that we pop values off the stack in the reverse order that they were first placed on the stack. A stack is often termed in computing a *LIFO* (*Last In, First Out*) data structure because of this feature.

We can, by using sequences, selections and iterations as described in the previous chapter, then turn the high-level program into an assembly program.

```
* This program uses the stack to reverse a set of
* values stored in memory, overwriting the original order
*
        ORG 0           * load program in memory at location 0
```

```
        MOVE #$D0,SP    * initialize the stack pointer

        MOVE #$00,A     * push 0 onto the stack, we can use
        PUSH A          * this later to show us we've finished
                        * popping values

        MOVE #list,A    * A contains the address of the 1st.
                        * list element

pushloop MOVE (A),B     * move the first element into B
        CMP  #$0,B      * } if the number is 0 we have gone
                        * } through the list
        BEQ  end_push   * }
        PUSH B          * otherwise push the value on to the
                        * stack
        ADD #$01,A      * get address of next list element
        JMP pushloop    * and run the loop again

end_push MOVE #list,A   * A contains the address of the 1st.
                        * list element
poploop POP  B          * get the element from the stack
        CMP  #$0,B      * if the number is 0 we have gone
                        * through the list
        BEQ  end_pop    * so we need to end the loop
        MOVE B,(A)      * otherwise, write the popped value
                        * to memory
        ADD #$01,A      * get to next list element
        JMP poploop     * and run the loop again
end_pop HALT            * stop the program on completion

* the list values
list        DC.W 1234
            DC.W 2345
            DC.W 3456
            DC.W 4567
            DC.W 5678
            DC.W 0000
```

A few things we haven't seen before are:

▶ The instruction MOVE (A),B treats the value held in the A register as an address in memory, it moves the value in memory at this location into the B register;

▶ The instruction MOVE #list,A transfers the address of the beginning of the list to the A register. We say that we are using the A register to *point* to the list;

▶ The instruction PUSH B places the contents of the B register on the stack, and the instruction POP B removes the top value from the stack and places it in the B register;

▶ The instruction DC.W $1234 is a directive to tell the assembler to store the value in memory. DC.W is short for *Define Constant - Word*.

Examine this program to ensure that you understand it.

If we were to convert this program into machine code, we would end up with the following:

```
ORG 0   0000            ORG 0          * load program in memory at location 0
A6D0    0000            MOVE #$D0,SP   * initialize the stack pointer
        0001
9000    0001            MOVE #$00,A    * push 0 onto the stack, we can use
8C00    0002            PUSH A         * this later to show us we've finished
        0003                           * popping values
        0003
9012    0003            MOVE #list,A   * A contains the address of the 1st.
        0004                           * list element
        0004
9900    0004  pushloop  MOVE (A),B     * move the first element into B
8100    0005            CMP  #$0,B      * } if the number is 0 we have gone
        0006                           * } through the list
C30A    0006            BEQ  end_push   * }
8D00    0007            PUSH B         * otherwise push the value on to the
        0008                           * stack
0001    0008            ADD #$01,A     * get next list element
E004    0009            JMP pushloop   * and run the loop again
        000A
9012    000A  end_push  MOVE #list,A   * A contains the address of the 1st.
        000B                           * list element
8F00    000B  poploop   POP  B         * get the element from the stack
8100    000C            CMP  #$0,B      * if the number is 0 we have gone
        000D                           * through the list
C311    000D            BEQ  end_pop    * so we need to end the loop
A900    000E            MOVE B,(A)     * otherwise, write the popped value
        000F                           * to memory
0001    000F            ADD #$01,A     * get to next list element
E00B    0010            JMP poploop    * and run the loop again
F000    0011  end_pop   HALT           * stop the program on completion
        0012
        0012  * the list values
```

```
1234    0012   list     DC.W 1234
2345    0013            DC.W 2345
3456    0014            DC.W 3456
4567    0015            DC.W 4567
5678    0016            DC.W 5678
0000    0017            DC.W 0000
```

You can now run the program, it's held on the CD in the examples directory in the file `reverse.jas`. Examine the contents of memory both before and after you run the program. After running the program the list held between memory locations $0012 and $0016 is now in reverse order.

It is worth remembering that we, the programmer, have to ensure that we don't overstep the limits of where we want the stack to be. If our stack (by pushing too many values) overwrites another part of our program or our program data then our program will cease to work correctly due to a stack overflow.

10.4 Introducing Subroutines

So far we have only seen relatively small programs, but what if our programs had to perform an operation on many different values? How could we deal with that?

Let's look first at a high-level language example. Let's imagine that we needed to work out the total wages for three different workers. As things stand right now, we would have to duplicate the part of our program that works out each workers wages - so parts of our program will appear three times over.

Here is our program:

```
// employee 1
hourly_rate  = employee1_hourly_rate;
hours_worked = employee1_hours_worked;
employee1_wages = hourly_rate * hours_worked;

// employee 2
hourly_rate  = employee2_hourly_rate;
hours_worked = employee2_hours_worked;
employee2_wages = hourly_rate * hours_worked;

// employee 3
hourly_rate  = employee3_hourly_rate;
```

```
hours_worked = employee3_hours_worked;
employee3_wages = hourly_rate * hours_worked;
```

However there is a better method that we can use, rather than just have duplicate sections within our program. This is by using *subroutines*.

A subroutine can be thought of as a mini-program within our program, that we can make use of as many times as we like. If we were to use subroutines in the program above, it would look something like this:

```
subroutine wages (hourly_rate, hours_worked) {
    emp_wages = hourly_rate * hours_worked;
    return(emp_wages);
}

employee1_wages = wages(employee1_hourly_rate, employee1_hours_worked);

employee2_wages = wages(employee2_hourly_rate, employee2_hours_worked);

employee3_wages = wages(employee3_hourly_rate, employee3_hours_worked);
```

A number of points are worth noting.

▶ The subroutine is defined in its own section of the program, and it is executed only when it is *called*. The subroutine `wages` takes two parameters (known as *formal parameters*) called `hourly_rate` and `hours_worked`. It *returns* a value called `emp_wages`. We'll cover how this works in a moment;

▶ The main part of the program is where we work out the wages for each employee. If we looked at the first employee's details, you can see that the `wages` subroutine is used and takes two parameters (the values passed to the subroutine, known as *actual parameters*). When the subroutine has completed, the variable `employee1_wages` will be set to whatever value the subroutine has returned.

When we make use of a subroutine (or *make a subroutine call* as it is sometimes known), the actual parameters map onto the formal parameters for the subroutine to make use of. For example, in the above example we pass two parameters to the subroutine, called `employee1_hourly_rate` and `employee1_hours_worked`. These map onto the formal parameters of `hourly_rate` and `hours_worked`, and we can treat them effectively within the subroutine as the same as the parameters passed to the subroutine.

So, imagine that

`employee1_hourly_rate = 10`

and

`employee1_hours_worked = 5`

These values are passed to the subroutine, so

`hourly_rate = 10`

and `hours_worked = 5`

Within the subroutine the calculation

`10 * 5`

is executed, with the variable `emp_wages` being set to the result, which is 50. Once the subroutine completes this value is returned to the variable `employee1_wages` in the main program.

Both of the above programs look roughly the same size, but if we were to work on larger programming problems you would see that the use of subroutines greatly simplifies the programmer's task. Also, the use of subroutines maps very well with the process of stepwise refinement as we discussed briefly in the previous chapter, and as we will see in a larger programming example in chapter 15.

10.5 Implementing Subroutine Calls Using Stacks

Subroutines in assembly language are implemented using the JSR and RTS instructions and we'll see what each of these does in a moment.

When we make use of a subroutine it must follow the following structure:

```
ORG 0             * load program in memory at location 0
MOVE #$DF,SP      * initialize the stack pointer

     .            * the main program
     .
JSR subroutine1   * demonstrate a subroutine call
     .
     .
HALT              * end our main program
```

```
subroutine1
            .               * here is our subroutine code
            .
      RTS                   * ending with a return from subroutine
```

As we can see, subroutines are called with a JSR (which means *jump to subroutine*) instruction, and the end of the subroutine must have an RTS (which means *ReTurn from Subroutine*) instruction.

So what has the use of subroutines to do with stacks? Simply this: without stacks we couldn't write programs, whether high-level or assembly programs, that make use of subroutines. This is because when we jump to a subroutine we need to remember *where* we need to return to in our program once the subroutine has completed. It is the stack that is used to store the value of the PC when the JSR instruction is executed, and to restore the PC from the stack when the RTS instruction is executed.

We can see this by looking firstly at the micro-instructions that make up a JSR instruction. This particular instruction is a JSR address:

▶ $ALUx \leftarrow [PC]$
▶ $MDR \leftarrow [ALUx]$
▶ $MAR \leftarrow [SP]$
▶ $M[MAR] \leftarrow [MDR]$
▶ $ALUx \leftarrow [SP]$
▶ $ALUr = [ALUx] - 1$
▶ $SP \leftarrow [ALUr]$
▶ $PC \leftarrow [IR(operand)]$

In the JSR instruction the PC is saved on the stack in the first four micro-instructions, the next three micro-instructions update the SP to point to the next free stack location, and finally the last micro-instruction updates the PC.

Next we can see how the value of the PC is popped from the stack in the RTS instruction. Execution of the program will now continue from the next instruction after the original JSR.

▶ $ALUx \leftarrow [SP]$
▶ $ALUr = [ALUx] + 1$
▶ $SP \leftarrow [ALUr]$
▶ $MAR \leftarrow [SP]$
▶ $MDR \leftarrow [M[MAR]]$

▶ $PC \leftarrow [MDR]$

In the RTS instruction we can see that the first three micro-instructions decrement the SP, and the final three micro-instructions update the PC with the saved value from the stack.

We can pass parameters to subroutines via the use of the A and B registers, the stack, or named memory locations.

Subroutines can also be called by other subroutines, this is called *nesting*. A common programming error is for programmers to forget to place RTS instructions at the end of subroutines - leading to buggy code.

Many subroutines tend to be useful in many different programs, and so it is normal practice to include the most useful subroutines in a *library*. A library is a file that can be included in our programs with a special directive called USE. We'll see this in chapter 14.

10.6 Using Subroutines In Assembly Language

Finally in this chapter, we will write a program to make use of subroutines. This program is a modification of the *Hello World* program from chapter 1, it has been updated to include a subroutine called putchar to write a character on the screen.

The main program places each data word from the sequence of characters to be printed into the A register prior to calling putchar. The sequence of characters is in a format known as unpacked ASCII - this means that each character (remember that an ASCII character is 7 bits wide) is stored in a 16-bit word. This is a very easy format to work with. Another format, known as packed ASCII, places two ASCII characters into a 16-bit word - packed ASCII requires more processing to print.

The subroutine putchar is designed to print the character that has been transferred into the A register by the main program. It does this in such a way that only the character defined in the lo-byte of the A register is sent to the I/O device. We will cover I/O in greater depth in chapter 12.

Here is the program:

```
* Memory mapped I/O
ODR        EQU $E2        * } definitions
OSR        EQU $E3        * }
```

```
            ORG  0           * load program in memory at location 0
            MOVE #$D0,SP     * initialize the stack pointer

            MOVE #data,B     * point at data
next        MOVE (B),A       * get a character
            CMP  #$0,A       * is this the terminator?
            BEQ  done        * yes - stop
            JSR  putchar     * call the print sub-routine
            ADD  #$1,B       * increment data address
            JMP  next        * repeat loop
done        HALT             * halt the program

*
* putchar routine (char in lo-byte of A)
*
putchar     PUSH B          * save B on the stack
_putch1     MOVE OSR,B      * move OSR to B
            CMP  #$00,B     * can we print ?
            BEQ  _putch1    * if not, grab OSR again
            MOVE A,ODR      * otherwise print lo-byte of A
            POP  B          * retrieve B from the stack
            RTS             * return from subroutine

* data string
* (stored as unpacked ASCII)
data        DC.W 0048       * H
            DC.W 0065       * e
            DC.W 006C       * l
            DC.W 006C       * l
            DC.W 006F       * o
            DC.W 0020       *
            DC.W 0057       * W
            DC.W 006F       * o
            DC.W 0072       * r
            DC.W 006C       * l
            DC.W 0064       * d
            DC.W 0021       * !
            DC.W 000D       * <cr>
            DC.W 000A       * <lf>
            DC.W 0000       * Terminator
```

We can take note of a number of points in this program:

► The main program is quite short, it begins with a couple of definitions (EQU, which stands for *equates* which is an assembler directive for *constants* (values in our program that don't change) used in the `putchar` subroutine. The main program includes one call to our subroutine;

► After the main program the subroutine is defined, and we can see some interesting features within it. Firstly, it is important to note that the subroutine ends with an `RTS` statement. Next, we can see that a parameter is passed to the subroutine in the A register - the ASCII character to be printed;

► We can also see a label (`_putch1`) that we only want to be used within the subroutine. By convention we prefix an underscore to any label that we want to limit in usage to the subroutine. Please note that this doesn't stop a programmer from using the label from anywhere in a program - it is just bad practice to do so;

► It is worth noticing that we make use of the B register inside the subroutine as temporary storage and, as the B register could be used by the main program, it is good practice to push the current value of the B register to the stack before we use it in the subroutine, and to pop the value from the stack prior to returning to the main program;

► Finally the data is listed in the unpacked ASCII format, for us to print out as our message.

This program can be found on the CD - it is called `subroutines.jas`. Run this program in black-box mode to see what it does. Once it has completed running, look at the stack area to see what has been written there.

We can also see a useful program structure emerging in this example. This structure is:

► Definitions;
► The main program;
► Subroutine definitions;
► Data storage.

We will refine this structure in coming chapters.

CHAPTER SUMMARY

The concept of the stack

► A stack is an example of an abstract data type;
► We *push* an object onto a stack;

▶ We *pop* an object from a stack.

Hardware support for the stack

▶ To keep track of the top of stack we make use of a specialist register, the stack pointer;

The concept of the subroutine

▶ A subroutine is a section of program code that we can call from other locations in the program;

▶ When we call a subroutine, the contents of the PC are stored on the stack prior to the PC being set with the address of the subroutine;

▶ When we exit a subroutine, the PC is updated from the stack.

Using subroutines in assembly language programs

▶ We call subroutines using the JSR family of instructions;

▶ We return from a subroutine with an RTS instruction.

SELF TEST QUESTIONS

1 Modify your sorting program from the previous chapter's self test questions to use a subroutine to sort the two numbers.

2 Look at the file reverse.jas. What would we need to change so that the program could sort 10 values instead of the current 5 values?

3 Add a subroutine to subroutines.jas (within putchar) to count the number of letters that putchar prints. Store the result in the A register when the program terminates.

EXERCISES

1 Modify reverse.jas such that the stack pointer is set to memory location $0018. Trace through the program and see what happens - does the program complete successfully? If not, why not?

2 Modify your answer to self test question 3 to allow putchar to only be used a maximum of 10 times within the program.

3 Modify subroutines.jas so that the message is printed five times.

Addressing Modes

We introduce the concept of addressing modes and their particular uses within our assembly language programs.

This chapter includes:

▶ An introduction to addressing modes, including immediate, register direct, register indirect, memory direct, memory indirect, register indexed and relative addressing;
▶ How we can build up more complex instruction addressing modes;
▶ An addressing example.

11.1 Introducing Addressing Modes

An *addressing mode* is how we tell the processor where to find the data that it needs to use with each instruction. There are many different forms of addressing, the most common being *immediate addressing*, *direct addressing*, *indirect addressing*, *indexed addressing* and *relative addressing*. We will look at these each in turn.

Every operand to an instruction has an addressing mode, so to understand each mode we will look at a set of instructions where only one parameter is different in each instruction.

To look at each we will examine the MOVE instructions available to us in the JASP instruction set that place their result in the A register. If we were to examine this set in appendix B, we would see that we could perform a MOVE operation with the result being placed in the A register using the following instructions:

- ▶ MOVE #data,A
- ▶ MOVE addr,A
- ▶ MOVE (addr),A
- ▶ MOVE B,A
- ▶ MOVE (B),A
- ▶ MOVE B+addr,A

We have already seen some of these addressing modes, we will look at each in turn.

11.2 Immediate Addressing

Immediate addressing is the most simple form of addressing, and we have already seen this a number of times in example programs so far.

Immediate addressing takes the following form:

- ▶ MOVE #data,A - where data is the data value to use.

Immediate addressing is where we specify the value we wish to put into the register as an operand to the instruction. Figure 11.1 shows the instruction MOVE #$0F,A where we want to set the A register to contain the hexadecimal value $0F. We can always tell when immediate addressing is used as the parameter will always be preceded by a hash character (#).

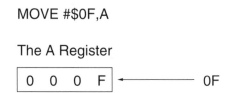

MOVE #$0F,A

The A Register

| 0 | 0 | 0 | F | ◄——————— 0F

Figure 11.1   *An immediate addressing example*

With immediate addressing, the value from the IR(operand) is copied into the A register - which actually limits the size of the number that we can place in the A register using this instruction. Why is this? It is because the IR(operand) is 8-bits wide (as we have seen previously) whereas the A register is 16-bits wide. The hi-byte of the A register is set to zero. As the IR(operand) is only 8 bits wide, it means that we can only move values in the range 0 (00000000_2) through to 255 (11111111_2) into the A register using this form of addressing. If we want to move larger values in, then we must use a different form of addressing. This is a limitation of the implementation of the standard JASP instruction set.

11.3 Direct Addressing

Direct addressing is where we can transfer a value from one location, either in a register or in memory, to our destination register. Let us look at each of these in turn.

Direct addressing takes the following forms:

▶ MOVE B,A - Register direct addressing.
▶ MOVE addr,A - Memory direct addressing, where addr is the address to use.

11.3.1 Register Direct Addressing

In figure 11.2 we can see an example of register direct addressing.

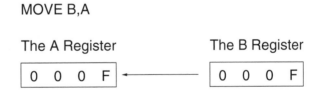

MOVE B,A

The A Register   The B Register

| 0 | 0 | 0 | F | ◀————— | 0 | 0 | 0 | F |

Figure 11.2 *A register direct addressing example*

We can simply copy the value from one register to another.

11.3.2 Memory Direct Addressing

Memory direct addressing is very similar to register direct addressing, as we can see in figure 11.3.

Figure 11.3 *A memory direct addressing example*

The address (we can tell it is an address because it does *not* have a hash prefix) is used to look up a value in memory, which is then transferred to the target location.

Note that in JASPer this form of addressing also suffers from the size limitation of the IR(operand), and so we can only address memory from $0000 to $00FF.

11.4 Indirect Addressing

Indirect addressing is a little more complex than direct addressing. Using indirect addressing we use the value stored in a register or in a memory location to store the address of the value that is then moved into the target location.

We will look at register indirect addressing and memory indirect addressing in turn. We can always see that indirect addressing is used when we see round brackets around an operand.

Indirect addressing takes the following forms:

▶ MOVE (B),A - Register indirect addressing.
▶ MOVE (addr),A - Memory indirect addressing.

11.4.1 Register Indirect Addressing

We can see an example of register indirect addressing in figure 11.4.

MOVE (B),A

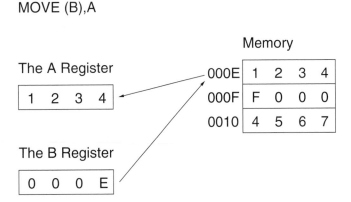

Figure 11.4 *A register indirect addressing example*

In this example we can see that the instruction MOVE (B),A means:

▶ Look up memory at the location stored in the B register. This gives us the value $1234;

▶ Transfer that value into the A register.

11.4.2 Memory Indirect Addressing

Memory indirect addressing is again similar to register indirect addressing, and our example for this mode is shown in figure 11.5.

MOVE ($0F),A

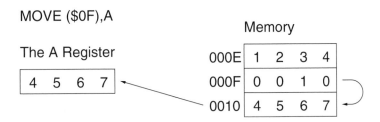

Figure 11.5 *A memory indirect addressing example*

In this example we can see that the instruction MOVE ($0F),A means:

▶ Look up memory at the location stored in the memory location $0F. This gives us the value $0010;

▶ Use the value $0010 as a memory address, obtaining the value $4567;

▶ Transfer that value into the A register.

Note that this mode in JASPer also suffers from the size limitation of the IR(operand), and so the initial memory address can only address memory from $0000 to $00FF.

11.5 Indexed Addressing

With indexed addressing we will only consider register indexed addressing.

Indexed addressing takes the following form.

▶ MOVE B+addr,A - Indexed addressing, the address of the memory location is formed by adding the contents of the B register to addr.

11.5.1 Register Indexed Addressing

An example using register indexed addressing is shown in figure 11.6.

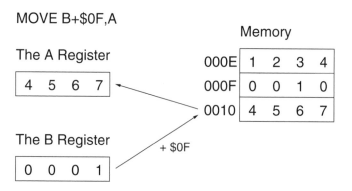

Figure 11.6 *A register indexed addressing example*

In this example we can see that the instruction MOVE B+$0F,A means:

▶ Add the value stored in the B register to $0F to obtain the address $0010;

▶ Look up memory at the location stored in the memory location $0010. This value is $4567;

▶ Transfer that value into the A register.

This mode of addressing is very useful to process a set of values held in contiguous memory locations (also known as an *array*), as the value in B can be quickly and easily increased by 1 on each iteration (B is known as the index, while the given address - $0F in our example - is known as the base address).

This form of addressing is sometimes given the forms:

▶ `MOVE addr(B),A`
▶ `MOVE (B)addr,A`

But it means the same thing.

11.6 Relative Addressing

Relative addressing is often used in branching. For example, so far we have only used branch instructions of the form:

▶ `JMP addr`

Where `addr` is the address to branch to. With relative addressing we can say the equivalent of 'branch 3 instructions forward', or 'branch 10 instructions back'. Such an instruction is defined as:

▶ `JMP #dis`

Where `dis` is the *displacement* value, that is, the number of instructions we wish to jump forward or back within the program. The displacement is added onto the PC during the instruction execution - you must remember that the PC has already been incremented by 1 during the fetch cycle, and adjust your displacement accordingly.

11.7 More Complex Instructions

Other forms of addressing are used in larger processors, but they tend to be extensions of what we have already seen, or a way in which multiple instructions can be combined into single instructions.

For example, some processors allow instructions of the form:

▶ `MOVE (B)+,A`

which means, copy the value pointed to by register B to register A (as in register indirect addressing), but the plus sign indicates that this instruction will then add one to the value stored in the B register. This is known as *post-incrementing* (adding one to the register after the main function of the instruction has executed). If the plus sign is shown before the symbol for the B register, as in

▶ `MOVE +(B),A`

This is known as *pre-incrementing*, as 1 is added to the B register before the address stored in the B register is used to access the value to be transferred to the A register. *Post-decrementing* (taking 1 from the contents of the register after the main function of the instruction), or *pre-decrementing* (taking 1 off before the main function of the instruction) is also possible. As shown here:

▶ `MOVE (B)-,A` This is post-decrementing
▶ `MOVE -(B),A` This is pre-decrementing

With our processor we can perform the function of

▶ `MOVE (B)+,A`

with two instructions as follows:

▶ `MOVE (B),A`
▶ `ADD #$01,B`

It is worth mentioning that instructions can be made that are far more complex.

For example, we could define an instruction of the form:

▶ `MOVE (B)+,(addr)`

This means the following:

▶ Look up memory at the address held in the B register (register indirect addressing);
▶ Move that value to the memory location obtained by looking up the address held in the second operand (memory indirect addressing);
▶ Write the value into memory at the memory address held in the second operand;
▶ Add one to the B register (post-incrementing B).

However, this instruction too can be built up from the modes that we have already discussed. We will return to this subject again in chapter 16 where we will see how to write our own instructions rather than having to rely on the standard instruction set.

11.8 An Addressing Example

Here is an example program that tests all the common modes of addressing for the JASPer processor.

```
* This program demonstrates the addressing
* modes used by our processor
*

        ORG 0           * load program in memory at location 0

        MOVE #$0E,B      * for use in the examples

        MOVE #$0F,A      * immediate addressing
        MOVE B,A         * register direct addressing
        MOVE $0F,A       * memory direct addressing
        MOVE (B),A       * register indirect addressing
        MOVE ($0F),A     * memory indirect addressing

        MOVE B+$01,A     * register indexed addressing

        HALT             * should not be needed as you should
                         * trace through this program!

* the data for the instructions to use
        ORG 0E
        DC.W 1234       *
        DC.W 0010       *
        DC.W 4567       *
```

This program is called addressing.jas and is available on the CD. Set the JASPer animation to off, and execute the program an instruction at a time using the 'trace' button. Prior to executing each instruction, try to figure out what you think the A register will be set to.

CHAPTER SUMMARY

Addressing modes

▶ Immediate addressing, e.g. MOVE #$03,A - a # indicates this mode;

▶ Register direct addressing, e.g. MOVE B,A - only registers listed as operands indicate this mode;

▶ Memory direct addressing, e.g. MOVE $03,A - no # indicates this mode;

▶ Register indirect addressing, e.g. MOVE (B),A - only registers listed as parameters, and round brackets used, indicates this mode;

▶ Memory indirect addressing, e.g. MOVE ($03),A - no # and round brackets used indicates this mode;

▶ Register indexed addressing, e.g. MOVE B+$03,A - no # and a + sign indicates this mode;

▶ Relative addressing, e.g. JMP #$03 - a # used in branch instructions indicates this mode.

Building instruction addressing modes

▶ Other addressing modes include pre and post incrementing and pre and post decrementing;

▶ Some processors have many dozens of addressing modes - for our simple processor we can simply use multiple assembly instructions.

SELF TEST QUESTIONS

1 Modify a copy of reverse.jas from the last chapter such that the JMP addr instructions are replaced with JMP #dis instructions that use relative addressing.

2 Write a program to add $12D5 to $073A. Which addressing modes can you use to do this?

3 Write a program to add a sequence of data values, storing the result in the A register. Use register indexed addressing to access the sequence of data values.

EXERCISES

1 Write a program that stores $1234 in memory address $0100. Which addressing modes can you use to do this?

2 Write a program to add a sequence of data values, storing the result in the A register. Use register indirect addressing to access the sequence of data values.

3 Modify your answer to exercise three to store the list of values in memory starting at memory address $0100. What addressing modes can you use to access these values?

Input/Output

It's time to allow our processor to talk to the rest of the world, at least in some rudimentary sense. To do this we introduce the concept of I/O.

This chapter includes:

▶ The concept of memory-mapped peripheral devices;

▶ The concepts of polled I/O, interrupt driven I/O and Direct Memory Access (DMA) - we look at each I/O method in turn, concentrating on the use of polled I/O;

▶ A discussion of the memory-mapped peripherals available to JASPer.

12.1 Introducing Input/Output

To pass data to programs we've had to place it directly in memory, and to see the results of our programs once they are executed we've had to look at the contents of memory. This allows us to see what our program has done, but it's not exactly very practical. Wouldn't it be easier if we could connect some devices to our processor to allow us to more easily input data and output data? We tend to call devices that we want to connect to our processor *peripherals* (because they are peripheral to our processor system).

A computer system can use many different types of peripherals, if we were to list the most common, we would end up with a list like this:

▶ Keyboard;

- ► Mouse;
- ► Modem (to connect to the telephone line);
- ► Network card (to connect to a network, like the Internet);
- ► Graphics card (to connect to a monitor screen);
- ► Sound card;
- ► Games joystick interface card;
- ► Hard disk (for storage - but still effectively a peripheral);
- ► DVD/CD-ROM drives.

Of course, this list isn't complete, but we can see the sort of peripherals that we mean. We can pretty much group these sort of peripherals into those that send input to our computer system, those that use output from our computer system, and those that do both.

We will concentrate mostly on one of the most simple peripherals, an I/O device which gives us the ability to use a keyboard connected to our processor system (to send characters to our system) and a monitor attached so we can see output from our system (like we have already seen with the *Hello World* program back in chapter 1).

12.1.1 Connecting Peripherals

We need to think about how to physically connect our peripheral to our processor system, and then how to use them within our programs.

We need to connect our peripheral to:

- ► The address bus - to pass addresses to the peripheral;
- ► The data bus - to pass data to and from the peripheral;
- ► The control bus - to send control signals to the peripheral.

A very common way of doing this is to build the peripheral device into the memory map. We had a glimpse of how this could be done in chapter 7. We saw in that chapter that we could build a complete memory by connecting up many different memory chips to build a larger memory. We can also wire in other forms of devices, other than memory chips, that we can use as if they were like memory but can actually perform other tasks - such a device is known as a *memory-mapped* device. We can actually see this in the memory map, shown in figure 12.1.

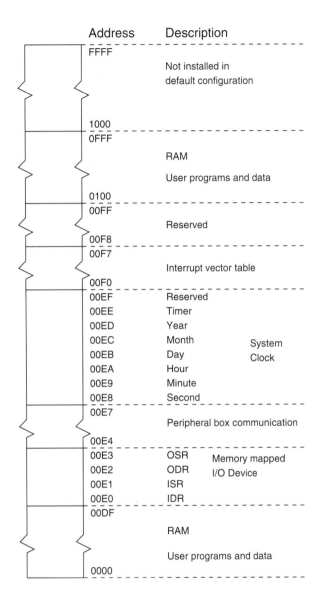

Figure 12.1 *The JASPer memory map*

The part of the memory map that we are interested in is the area between $00E0 and $00E3, as this is where our memory-mapped device (an I/O device) is situated. These four memory locations are not actually memory at all, but can be used in the same manner as memory - so making I/O easy to use without introducing any new complexities to our processor.

When we want to use our peripheral, there are three steps that we need to follow to ensure that our processor communicates with the device correctly.

We need to:

1   Select the device we want to communicate with;
2   Transfer any data to or from the peripheral device;
3   Arrange synchronization for the I/O operation (we'll see what this means shortly).

We'll look at each of these points in detail later.

There are three key forms of I/O. The first form of I/O we will look at is called *polled* I/O, then we will look at *interrupt driven* I/O, and then finally we will look at *Direct Memory Access* (*DMA*). In this chapter we will spend the most time looking at polled I/O.

12.2 Polled I/O

The device situated in the memory map between locations $00E0 and $00E3 is actually a polled I/O device. Polled I/O is the simplest form of I/O that we can use.

We can imagine that we have wired our I/O device into the memory map for us to use the peripheral - and to communicate with our device we can do the following.

▶   Firstly, the CPU puts the device address on the address bus (just like addressing memory). This meets point one above;

▶   Next, the data is transmitted on the data bus to or from the device. To do this the device uses a device *data register*. This meets point two;

▶   Finally we perform synchronization, often known as *hand-shaking* (more on this in a moment) using a device *status register*. This meets point three.

We generally put all the circuitry to control these tasks on a single I/O interface chip, which is an integrated circuit built just for this type of task. The memory map of our polled I/O device is shown in figure 12.2.

00E3		Output Status Register (OSR)
00E2		Output Data Register (ODR)
00E1		Input Status Register (ISR)
00E0		Input Data Register (IDR)

Figure 12.2 *The polled I/O device*

As you can see, this device has four registers, that we can use in the same way as accessing memory.

▶ Two of these registers deal with input - the *Input Status Register* (*ISR*) and the *Input Data Register* (*IDR*);
▶ Two of these registers deal with output - the *Output Status Register* (*OSR*) and the *Output Data Register* (*ODR*).

Each of these is 16 bits wide, exactly the same as the rest of the memory locations in the memory map, so that the device can be accessed exactly like memory. It is worth remembering that these I/O data registers only use the lowest seven bits to transfer characters, while the status registers only use the LSB to indicate status.

To use this device we can use a very simple protocol which demonstrates why this is called polled I/O. Let us imagine that we want to print a character on the monitor screen, how could we go about this? Our processor needs to do the following:

▶ When the peripheral is ready (not still dealing with a character sent previously), we say that the peripheral is idle. When it is in an idle state, the LSB in the OSR will be set to 1;
▶ If the OSR is set to one, the processor sends a character to the device's ODR. While the processor is dealing with this character the peripheral sets the LSB of the OSR to 0;
▶ While the LSB of the OSR is still set to 0 we cannot send another character to this device. We can check the OSR many times (called polling) until it is set back to 1 by the peripheral to indicate that the device is in an idle state;
▶ Once the peripheral indicates that it is ready, with the LSB of the OSR set to 1, we can then send another character.

Input using polled I/O works in a similar way as the output protocol shown above.

Why do we need such a protocol? Many devices work at different speeds, and if we were not to follow this polled approach then the communication might not work successfully - we will see examples of this shortly. If you imagine that our output device was printing the sent character on a very slow printer, it could be that the processor has to check the OSR of the peripheral many thousands of times before it can send the next character, as our processor is so much faster.

12.2.1 A Polled I/O Example Program

First of all we will look at some programs that use polled I/O incorrectly to understand the most common mistakes, and then we will examine a program that uses polled I/O correctly.

The programs listed here are designed to show both the flawed and the correct way to use polled I/O. When executed, they attempt to take ten key presses from the user, storing each character sent to the processor in a storage area, and then finally they attempt to print out all ten characters to the screen.

Incorrect Input

Below we have an example of a program that uses polled I/O incorrectly for input. Reading through this program you will see that the ISR is never checked to see if the input device is ready with a character in the IDR. Instead, the IDR value is moved directly to the character storage area of the program.

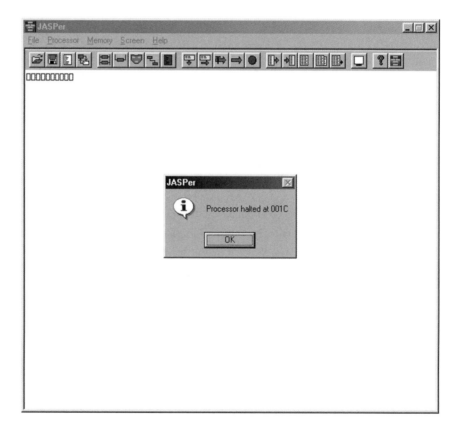

Figure 12.3 *JASPer - after running the program with incorrect input*

```
* A demonstration of polled I/O
*
* This program is supposed to read 10 characters from the keyboard
* and then print them all out once they've been entered
*
* The ISR is not used. Therefore the input will not
* work correctly.
*
OSR       EQU    $E3        * Output Status Register (OSR)
ODR       EQU    $E2        * Output Data Register   (ODR)
ISR       EQU    $E1        * Input Status Register  (ISR)
IDR       EQU    $E0        * Input Data Register    (IDR)

          ORG    0
          MOVE   #$00,B     * count is storage for our
          MOVE   B,count    *   counter value

loop      MOVE   IDR,A      * read the char

          MOVE   count,B    * the address to write the
          ADD    #data,B    * value to is count+data
          MOVE   A,(B)      * write the char in there

          MOVE   count,B    * add 1 to count
          ADD    #$01,B     *
          CMP    #$0A,B     * and see if we have reached 10
          BEQ    gotchars   * and move to next section if we have
          MOVE   B,count    * otherwise write count back
          JMP    loop       * and get another char
gotchars  MOVE   #$00,B     * count is storage for our
          MOVE   B,count    *   counter value

write     MOVE   OSR,A      * get OSR
          CMP    #$00,A     * OSR 1 can print, OSR 0 can't print
          BEQ    write      * not yet, wait some more

          MOVE   count,B    * the address to read the
          ADD    #data,B    * value from is count+data
          MOVE   (B),A      * get the char in there
          MOVE   A,ODR      * print the char

          MOVE   count,B    * add 1 to count
          ADD    #$01,B     *
          CMP    #$0A,B     * and see if we have reached 10
          BEQ    done       * and move to end if we have
```

```
        MOVE  B,count   * otherwise write count back
        JMP   write     * and write another char
done    HALT            * done

count   DS.W $01        * the counter
data    DS.W $0A        * storage for our 10 characters
```

*If you fail to use correct
polled I/O for input, the
same character can be
read many times.*

If we were to run this program (it can be found on the CD in the directory for this chapter, called `polled-io-bad-input.jas`), then the program would output something similar to that in figure 12.3.

As you can see, we don't have the output that we would like. Instead we see a sequence of 'square boxes', this is the character that JASPer displays when it attempts to print a non-printable character. It prints this because the initial IDR value of $00 is being used, before any key has been pressed.

Incorrect Output

So now let's take a look at what happens when we fail to use polled I/O with the output. Here we have a program that does not poll the OSR in order to check if the output device is ready to receive another character.

```
* A demonstration of polled I/O
*
* This program is supposed to read 10 characters from the keyboard
* and then print them all out once they've been entered
*
* The OSR is not used. Therefore the output will not
* work correctly.
*
OSR     EQU  $E3         * Output Status Register (OSR)
ODR     EQU  $E2         * Output Data Register   (ODR)
ISR     EQU  $E1         * Input Status Register  (ISR)
IDR     EQU  $E0         * Input Data Register    (IDR)

        ORG  0
        MOVE #$00,B      * count is storage for our
        MOVE B,count     *   counter value

loop    MOVE ISR,A       * Get ISR
```

```
           CMP    #$00,A    * is a char available?
           BEQ    loop      * no - wait some more
           MOVE   IDR,A     * read the char

           MOVE   count,B   * the address to write the
           ADD    #data,B   * value to is count+data
           MOVE   A,(B)     * write the char in there

           MOVE   count,B   * add 1 to count
           ADD    #$01,B    *
           CMP    #$0A,B    * and see if we have reached 10
           BEQ    gotchars  * and move to next section if we have
           MOVE   B,count   * otherwise write count back
           JMP    loop      * and get another char
gotchars   MOVE   #$00,B    * count is storage for our
           MOVE   B,count   *   counter value

write      MOVE   count,B   * the address to read the
           ADD    #data,B   * value from is count+data
           MOVE   (B),A     * get the char in there
           MOVE   A,ODR     * print the char

           MOVE   count,B   * add 1 to count
           ADD    #$01,B    *
           CMP    #$0A,B    * and see if we have reached 10
           BEQ    done      * and move to end if we have
           MOVE   B,count   * otherwise write count back
           JMP    write     * and write another char
done       HALT             * done

count      DS.W $01         * the counter
data       DS.W $0A         * storage for our 10 characters
```

NOTES

If you fail to use correct polled I/O for output, characters will not all be printed, data will be lost.

If we were to run this program (also available on the CD, called `polled-io-bad-output.jas`), using the input values 1, 2, 3, 4, 5, 6, 7, 8, 9 and 0 we would expect the output appearing on the screen to be 1234567890. This doesn't happen as some data is lost, resulting in the output shown in figure 12.4.

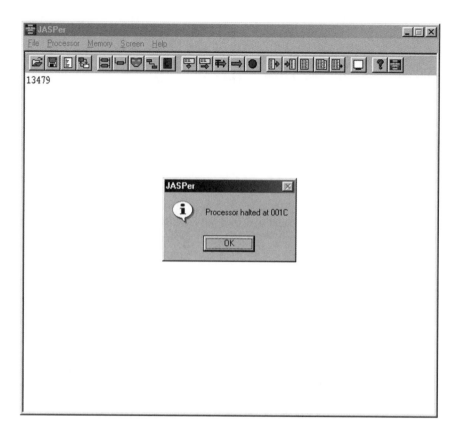

Figure 12.4   *JASPer - after running the program with incorrect output*

Using Polled I/O Correctly

Finally, here is a program that uses polled I/O correctly.

```
* A demonstration of polled I/O
*
* This program reads 10 characters from the keyboard
* and then prints them all out once they've been entered
*
OSR       EQU    $E3        * Output Status Register (OSR)
ODR       EQU    $E2        * Output Data Register   (ODR)
ISR       EQU    $E1        * Input Status Register  (ISR)
IDR       EQU    $E0        * Input Data Register    (IDR)
```

```
        ORG    0
        MOVE   #$00,B      * count is storage for our
        MOVE   B,count     *   counter value

loop    MOVE   ISR,A       * Get ISR
        CMP    #$00,A      * is a char available?
        BEQ    loop        * no - wait some more
        MOVE   IDR,A       * read the char

        MOVE   count,B     * the address to write the
        ADD    #data,B     * value to is count+data
        MOVE   A,(B)       * write the char in there

        MOVE   count,B     * add 1 to count
        ADD    #$01,B      *
        CMP    #$0A,B      * and see if we have reached 10
        BEQ    gotchars    * and move to next section if we have
        MOVE   B,count     * otherwise write count back
        JMP    loop        * and get another char
gotchars MOVE  #$00,B      * count is storage for our
        MOVE   B,count     *   counter value

write   MOVE   OSR,A       * get OSR
        CMP    #$00,A      * OSR 1 can print, OSR 0 can't print
        BEQ    write       * not yet, wait some more

        MOVE   count,B     * the address to read the
        ADD    #data,B     * value from is count+data
        MOVE   (B),A       * get the char in there
        MOVE   A,ODR       * print the char

        MOVE   count,B     * add 1 to count
        ADD    #$01,B      *
        CMP    #$0A,B      * and see if we have reached 10
        BEQ    done        * and move to end if we have
        MOVE   B,count     * otherwise write count back
        JMP    write       * and write another char
done    HALT               * done

count   DS.W   $01         * the counter
data    DS.W   $0A         * storage for our 10 characters
```

When we run this program (again available on the CD, as polled-io.jas), with the input values 1, 2, 3, 4, 5, 6, 7, 8, 9 and 0 we would expect the output

1234567890, and as we can see in figure 12.5, this is what we get - finally we are using polled I/O for both input and output correctly.

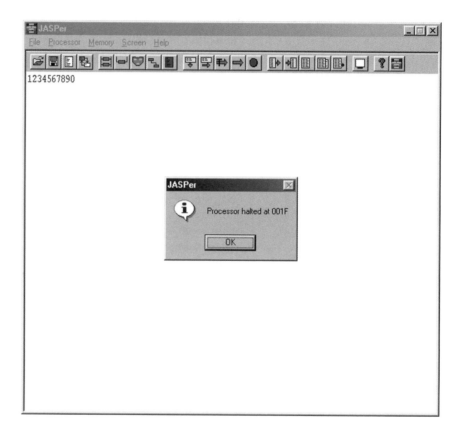

Figure 12.5   *JASPer - after running the program using correct polled I/O*

Polled I/O is very wasteful of processor clock cycles, but if the processor does not need to be doing anything else, it really doesn't matter. A method exists that can be more complicated than using polled I/O, but is much more efficient. This is interrupt driven I/O which we briefly discuss next.

12.3 Interrupt Driven I/O

The idea behind interrupt driven I/O is substantially different from the concept of polled I/O. Instead of constantly checking a device to see if it is ready to communicate, with interrupt driven I/O the processor can be sent a signal by a device when it is ready to communicate with the processor.

Interrupt driven I/O is much more efficient than polled I/O, as it depends on the peripheral to signal to the processor when it is ready to communicate. This means that the processor only has to deal with the peripheral at the moment that it is ready to send or receive data, so no polling is required.

Interrupt driven I/O depends on the implementation of an interrupt mechanism, and we'll examine such a mechanism in chapter 13.

We won't spend any more time now looking at interrupt driven I/O, as we will look at the interrupt mechanism itself in detail in the next chapter.

12.4 I/O Using Direct Memory Access

The third of the three I/O methods is called *Direct Memory Access* (or *DMA*). It is quite different from the two previous methods, in that although the process is controlled by the processor, the data does not actually pass through the processor as it did using other I/O methods.

We would use DMA to, for example, transfer large amounts of data between a CD and a sound card. Within DMA the processor allows the two devices to talk directly to each other using the data bus. The processor controls the data transfer, but the data does not pass through the processor. This is a good idea for a large amount of data as it is much faster than if the data actually had to route from one device to another via the processor itself.

JASPer does not make use of DMA, as it does not show any fundamental aspects that differ from before, apart from a speed increase. We will not mention DMA again in this book.

12.5 Other Memory-Mapped Devices

JASPer has two other peripherals within its memory map, a system clock and an I/O device that can communicate with an external peripherals box.

12.5.1 The System Clock

The system clock resides in the memory map between memory locations $00E8 and $00EF. Using the clock we can access the current hour, minute, second, day, month or year - by accessing the correct memory location. The clock also has a facility to trigger interrupts at specified intervals.

We will use the clock, and its interrupt facility, in the next chapter.

12.5.2 The Peripheral Box

The peripheral box is an external device with a number of input and output devices built into it. These include LEDs, digital read outs, a potentiometer and a buzzer.

Figure 12.6   *A clock display running on the JASPer peripheral box - a PDA is included to give scale*

CHAPTER SUMMARY

The concept of memory-mapped peripheral devices

▶ Peripherals need to connect to the data bus, the address bus and the control bus;

▶ Peripheral devices can be built into the memory map in a similar way to building in memory chips;

The concepts of I/O

▶ Polled I/O is the simplest form of I/O. We need to use a polling loop to successfully use such a device;

▶ If we fail to use correct polled I/O for input, then the same character can be read multiple times;

▶ If we fail to use correct polled I/O for output, characters will not all be printed, data will be lost;

▶ Polled I/O is very inefficient;

▶ Interrupt driven I/O relies on the implementation of an interrupt mechanism. It is much more efficient than polled I/O;

▶ Direct Memory Access does not pass data through the processor, although the processor controls the operation.

The memory-mapped peripherals in JASPer

▶ JASPer has a memory-mapped I/O device, system clock and an I/O device for a peripheral box all built into its memory map.

SELF TEST QUESTIONS

1 Modify a copy of the `polledio.jas` program so that a space character is printed between each character of the output.

2 Write a program to read in lowercase characters from the keyboard, terminated by a space character. As each character is input it should be printed as the uppercase equivalent of the letter. For example, typing the letter 'a' should result in a 'A' being printed. Use the ASCII table in chapter 2 to determine the connection in the ASCII character set between upper and lowercase letters.

3 Write a program the use inputs a character in the range '0' to '9'. The program must then print out a corresponding number of asterisks. For example, if the user enters '2' then ** is printed.

EXERCISES

1 Write a program to read in a number of characters, and then prints out the characters in the reverse order to what they were typed. Hint, limit the number of characters that can be entered to 10.

2 Write a program to read in uppercase characters from the keyboard, terminated by a space character. As each character is input it should be

printed as the lowercase equivalent of the letter. For example, typing the letter 'A' should result in a 'a' being printed.

3 Write a program where the use inputs a character in the range '0' to '9'. This character must be converted into it's associated numeric value and then stored in the A register. For example, if the user types a '9' character, then the A register should be set to $0009.

The Interrupt Mechanism

In this chapter we introduce the concept of the interrupt mechanism. We describe an implementation of an interrupt mechanism, and how interrupts can be used within our processor.

This chapter includes:

▶ The concept of the interrupt;
▶ The concept of the interrupt mechanism;
▶ Comparing the use of subroutines with interrupts;
▶ How interrupts are used within our processor;
▶ The features of more complex interrupt mechanisms.

13.1 Introducing Interrupts

Interrupts are signals that can be sent to the processor by either hardware or software. Interrupts can be used to implement interrupt driven I/O as mentioned briefly in the previous chapter, but they can also be used in many more contexts, for example in the use of timers.

The implementation of interrupts on a processor is known as an interrupt mechanism and before we can write programs that can make use of interrupts we need to explore how interrupts are implemented.

First of all, how can we see the effects of the interrupt mechanism in our processor? We can see them by looking inside the PSR. Certain flags in the

PSR are used to control the activity of interrupts. These flags, shown in figure 13.1, are:

▶ The *Interrupt Enable* flag, or *E* flag;
▶ The *Interrupt Request* flag, or *I* flag;
▶ The *Interrupt vector*, a 3-bit value indicated in JASPer by the label 'vvv'.

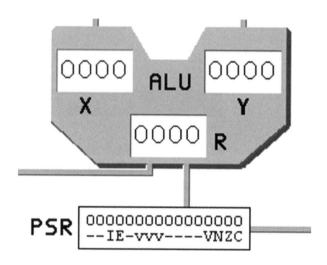

Figure 13.1 *The PSR flags*

I will describe the use of each of these flags in turn.

▶ The interrupt enable flag indicates, not surprisingly, whether or not interrupts are enabled. If the flag is set to 1 then interrupts are enabled, if the flag is set to 0 then interrupts are disabled and the interrupt mechanism cannot be used;

▶ The interrupt request flag indicates when an interrupt has been requested. An interrupt request is sometimes referred to as an *IRQ*. If the flag is set to 1 then an interrupt has been requested, if the flag is set to 0 then an interrupt has not been requested;

▶ Finally, the interrupt vector indicates how the interrupt should be dealt with, or *serviced*, by the processor. In JASPer, the vector can have a value between 0 and 7 as it is limited to three bits in size. This means that eight different types of interrupt can be dealt with by the processor - as when a device raises an interrupt it will indicate which type of interrupt to use by placing the vector value on the data bus. The interrupt vector is then copied to the PSR.

As well as the flags in the PSR, there is also a set of eight memory locations known as the *vector table*. These eight locations can be used to store the addresses of the individual *interrupt servicing routines*, or *interrupt handlers*. For example, if an interrupt sets the interrupt vector to seven, then it is the eighth memory location of the vector table where the address of that particular interrupt handler is stored. If an interrupt is raised, for example with a vector of three, we can say that we have a level three interrupt.

This is shown in figure 13.2.

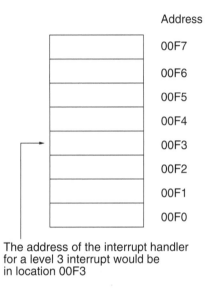

Address

00F7

00F6

00F5

00F4

00F3

00F2

00F1

00F0

The address of the interrupt handler
for a level 3 interrupt would be
in location 00F3

Figure 13.2   *The interrupt vector table*

The default location for the vector table is between the memory locations $00F0 and $00F7.

13.2 Introducing A Simple Interrupt Mechanism

So, this is all very interesting, but we need to understand how the processor deals with interrupts.

Interrupts, sometimes known as *exceptions*, depend on updating our description of the fetch-execute cycle. When we described the fetch-execute cycle in chapter 8 we effectively said that it could be described as:

```
while(true) {
    fetch_cycle;
    execute_cycle;
}
```

This means that we run a fetch cycle, followed by an execute cycle, and then repeat the process forever. To use interrupts we need to modify our fetch-execute cycle to this:

```
while(true) {
    fetch_cycle;
    execute_cycle;
    if ((interrupts_enabled) && (interrupt_requested)) {
        save_PSR_on_stack;
        save_PC_on_stack;
        PC = address_of_interrupt_handling_routine;
    }
}
```

This means run the fetch and execute cycles as before apart from when interrupts have been enabled, and an interrupt has also been requested. When both of these events are true, the processor is to save the current value of the PSR on the stack, save the current value of the PC on the stack, and then compute the address of the interrupt handling routine and then place it in the PC.

Our simple processor can only deal with one interrupt at a time, so a second interrupt cannot be raised while the processor is dealing with the first interrupt.

The interrupt mechanism to save the PSR and the PC on the stack, and to set the PC to the address of the correct interrupt routine can be found in the micro-instruction file that defines our basic instruction set, instruct.mco, for our processor - the interrupt cycle is listed prior to the individual microprograms for individual opcodes. Here it is:

1 $PSR(I) = 0$
2 $MAR \leftarrow [SP]$
3 $MDR \leftarrow [PSR]$
4 $M[MAR] \leftarrow [MDR]$
5 $ALUx \leftarrow [SP]$
6 $ALUr = [ALUx] - 1$

7 $SP \leftarrow [ALUr]$

8 $ALUx \leftarrow [PC]$

9 $MDR \leftarrow [ALUx]$

10 $MAR \leftarrow [SP]$

11 $M[MAR] \leftarrow [MDR]$

12 $ALUx \leftarrow [SP]$

13 $ALUr = [ALUx] - 1$

14 $SP \leftarrow [ALUr]$

15 $PSR(E) = 0$

16 $ALUy \leftarrow [JUMPERS(IntBase)]$

17 $ALUx \leftarrow [PSR(IntVec)]$

18 $ALUr = [ALUx] + [ALUy]$

19 $MAR \leftarrow [ALUr]$

20 $MDR \leftarrow [M[MAR]]$

21 $PC \leftarrow [MDR]$

Here is an explanation of the key parts to this interrupt mechanism:

▶ Micro-instruction 1 clears the interrupt request flag, as we are now dealing with the interrupt request;

▶ Micro-instructions 2 – 4 save the PSR on the stack;

▶ Micro-instructions 5 – 7 decrement the SP;

▶ Micro-instructions 8 – 11 save the PC on the stack;

▶ Micro-instructions 12 – 14 decrement the SP again;

▶ Micro-instruction 15 disables the interrupt enable flag, disallowing any further interrupts until this interrupt has been dealt with;

▶ Micro-instructions 16 – 18 work out the address of the interrupt handler in the interrupt vector table by adding the interrupt base address to the interrupt vector value;

▶ Micro-instructions 19 – 21 gets the address of the interrupt handler from the interrupt vector table and loads it into the PC.

So, how can we write a program to make use of this? Interrupts can be raised by both hardware, known as *hard* interrupts, and software, known as *soft interrupts*.

A soft interrupt can be triggered by an assembly instruction called a TRAP instruction. Here is the definition of the TRAP instruction:

1 $PSR(IntVec) \leftarrow [IR(operand)]$

2 $PSR(I) = 1$

You can see that the TRAP assembly instruction sets the interrupt vector value in the PSR, and then sets the interrupt request flag.

Hard interrupts can be triggered by hardware devices within our processor system. We will shortly see an example where interrupts are generated by a *hardware timer*.

The last assembly instruction to mention is the RTI instruction - in the same way as a subroutine must end with an RTS instruction, an interrupt handling routine must end with an RTI instruction. RTI stands for *ReTurn from Interrupt*.

The RTI instruction restores the previously saved versions of the PSR and the PC (saved when the interrupt was first requested). It is listed here:

1 $ALUx \leftarrow [SP]$
2 $ALUr = [ALUx] + 1$
3 $SP \leftarrow [ALUr]$
4 $MAR \leftarrow [SP]$
5 $MDR \leftarrow [M[MAR]]$
6 $PC \leftarrow [MDR]$
7 $ALUx \leftarrow [SP]$
8 $ALUr = [ALUx] + 1$
9 $SP \leftarrow [ALUr]$
10 $MAR \leftarrow [SP]$
11 $MDR \leftarrow [M[MAR]]$
12 $PSR \leftarrow [MDR]$

Here is a breakdown of what this instruction does:

▶ Micro-instructions 1 – 3 increment the SP;
▶ Micro-instructions 4 – 6 recover the previously stored value to the PC;
▶ Micro-instructions 7 – 9 increment the SP again;
▶ Micro-instructions 10 – 12 recover the previously stored value of the PSR.

Compare the breakdown of the RTI instruction with that of the interrupt routine that we saw before. Within the RTI instruction we don't have to explicitly re-enable interrupts, as the previously stored value of the PSR will have the E flag set to 1.

13.3 An Example Interrupt Program

It's now time to look at a program that makes use of interrupts.

It's a program that prints '.' characters, until the user either hits any key, or until the processor is halted. However, what makes this programming interesting for us is that a timer, which for the moment we can think of as a sort of alarm clock, requests an interrupt every second. When this happens, an interrupt handler is executed which prints the current time on the screen.

Typical output from this program is shown in figure 13.3.

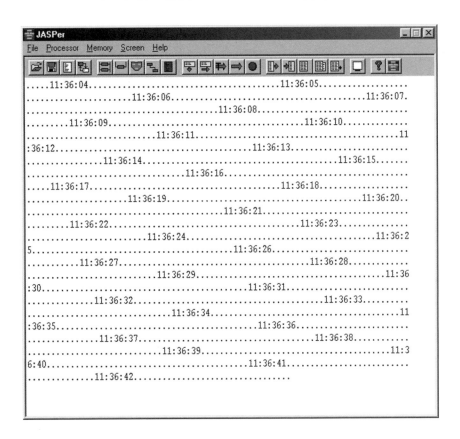

Figure 13.3 *Running the* `clock2.jas` *program*

It isn't the prettiest of clocks, but it does show graphically that the processor is executing the main program continuously, as shown by the sequence of '.' characters. At one second intervals the interrupt is requested by the timer, so causing the interrupt handler to display the current time. After the interrupt routine has finished, the main program continues from where it was interrupted.

The program is listed here and it is also available as `clock2.jas` on the CD.

```
* This program uses a timer to raise an interrupt every
* one second to display the time.

* Memory mapped I/O
IDR             EQU $E0         * Input Data Register
ISR             EQU $E1         * Input Status Register
ODR             EQU $E2         * Output Data Register
OSR             EQU $E3         * Output Status Register

* Time subsystem
_SECS           EQU $E8         * Current seconds
_MINS           EQU $E9         * Current minutes
_HOURS          EQU $EA         * Current hours
_DAY            EQU $EB         * Current day
_MONTH          EQU $EC         * Current month
_YEAR           EQU $ED         * Current year
_TIMER          EQU $EE         * Current timer interval

                * load handler address in interrupt vector table
                * timer is triggered on interrupt 6
                ORG $f6
                DC.W #timerhandler

                ORG $0
                INTE            * Enable interrupts
                MOVE #$D0,SP     * initialize stack pointer ($D0)
                MOVE #$01,A      *
                MOVE A,_TIMER    * intialize timer with 1 second
main
                MOVE #$2e,B      * move a '.' into B
                JSR putchar      * jump to sub-routine putchar
                MOVE ISR,A       * get the ISR
                CMP  #$00,A       * check if a key has been pressed
                BEQ  main        * if it hasn't then goto main
                HALT             * finished

* trap 6
timerhandler
                PUSH A
                PUSH B
                MOVE _HOURS,A    * move hours value into A
                JSR putdbyte     * jump to sub-routine put-dec-byte
                MOVE #$3a,B      * move a ':' into B
                JSR putchar      * jump to sub-routine putchar
                MOVE _MINS,A     * move mins value into A
```

```
                 JSR putdbyte     * jump to sub-routine put-dec-byte
                 MOVE #$3a,B       * move a ':' into B
                 JSR putchar       * jump to sub-routine putchar
                 MOVE _SECS,A      * move seconds value into A
                 JSR putdbyte      * jump to sub-routine put-dec-byte
                 POP B
                 POP A
                 RTI
*
* putchar routine (char in lo-byte of B)
*
putchar          PUSH A            * save A on the stack
_putch1          MOVE OSR,A        * move OSR to A
                 CMP  #$00,A       * Can we print ?
                 BEQ  _putch1      * If not, grab OSR again
                 MOVE B,ODR        * otherwise print lo-byte of B
                 POP  A            * retrieve a from the stack
                 RTS               * return from subroutine
*
* put-dec-byte (value in A)
*
putdbyte         PUSH A
                 PUSH B
                 MOVE #$00,B       * set B to 0
                 MOVE B,_tens      * clear the tens variable
                 MOVE A,_units     * set the units variable to A
_decloop         CMP  #$0a,A       * compare A with 10
                 BMI  _print       * goto print if less than 10
                 SUB  #$0a,A       * otherwise A = A-10
                 MOVE _tens,B      * B = tens   }
                 ADD  #$01,B       * B++        } i.e tens++
                 MOVE B,_tens      * tens = B   }
                 MOVE A,_units     * A = units
                 JMP  _decloop     * goto decloop
_print           MOVE _tens,A      * move tens into A
                 ADD  #$30,A       * add 30hex (i.e. its a char value now)
                 PUSH B            *
                 MOVE A,B          *
                 JSR  putchar      * print it
                 POP  B            *
                 MOVE _units,A     * move units to A
                 ADD  #$30,A       * add 30hex (i.e. its a char value now)
                 PUSH B            *
                 MOVE A,B          *
                 JSR  putchar      * print it
                 POP  B            *
                 POP  B            *
```

```
            POP   A            *
            RTS                *
* data storage
_tens       DS.W 1             * storage for tens variable
_units      DS.W 1             * storage for units variable
```

If we break down this program we can see the following:

► The first section consists of a set of EQU statements which are used to set up some constant values used by the rest of the program. The first four are constants we have seen previously in chapter 12, and the others are there to enable us to easily use the system clock. The system clock is a memory-mapped device that enables us to use the current time within our programs as well as a timer that we can use to trigger interrupts;

► Next, the interrupt vector table is initialized with the address of the interrupt handler. When the timer requests an interrupt (more on how it actually does this in a moment) it requests an interrupt at level six (when the vector value equals six). This is a hardware interrupt, the timer has been wired to only use this interrupt level, as is common in processor systems. The address of the interrupt handling routine is placed in location $00F6, which is the value of the vector table base address, plus 6;

► The next section of the program contains program initialization, followed by the main function;

► As part of the initialization, the INTE instruction enables the interrupt mechanism by setting the E flag in the PSR to 1, and the stack pointer is initialized. In the last part of the initialization, the timer is set to trigger an interrupt every 1 second, by placing the value $01 into the TIMER memory location. This timer can trigger interrupts between 1 second and 255 seconds apart. A 0 value would cause the timer to never trigger an interrupt;

► The main program is the next section. It prints a '.' character, checks to see if a key has been pressed, and if it hasn't loops back to print another '.' character. If a key has been pressed, the program terminates. To print the '.' character it calls a subroutine called putchar, which is defined later;

► After the main program, the interrupt handler, called timerhandler is defined. This saves the current values from the A and B registers on to the stack, and then displays the current time (using the subroutines putdbyte and putchar). Afterwards the interrupt handler restores the previously saved values of the A and B registers so that the program can resume successfully once the interrupt routine is completed. After the RTI instruction is executed the program will continue where it was before the interrupt occurred;

▶ Finally, we have the definitions of the `putchar` and the `putdbyte` sub-routines. We have already seen `putchar` in a previous example - it uses polled I/O as described in the previous chapter. The subroutine `putdbyte` converts a hexadecimal value, that must be less than $64 (decimal 100), stored in the A register into two decimal digits that are then displayed on the monitor. For example, if register A contains $001C when `putdbyte` is called, then '28' is displayed on the monitor.

So, to recap:

▶ The program prints '.' characters;
▶ Every second an interrupt is requested which interrupts the program wherever it is;
▶ The interrupt handling routine displays the time;
▶ Once the interrupt has been serviced, the program continues from where it was interrupted.

13.4 Comparing Subroutines With Interrupt Handling

In our example, we demonstrated the interrupt mechanism by using hard interrupts, in other words the interrupts were triggered by an external device (the timer in the clock system).

However, as mentioned before, not all interrupts are hard interrupts. Soft interrupts can also be triggered, and unlike hardware interrupts which are triggered at any point in the program execution, software interrupts are triggered at the same location in the program every time.

For example TRAP #$02 will trigger an interrupt with a vector of two. Software TRAP instructions are often used in real processor systems to make *system calls*. A system call is a subroutine that is provided, most probably in ROM, by the makers of the processor system.

It is very important to note that the use of interrupt handlers is very different to the use of subroutines. Let us compare the two different methods:

▶ The interrupt mechanism saves both the PC and the PSR on the stack;
▶ The subroutine mechanism saves only the PC;
▶ A call to a subroutine occurs at the same address during program execution each time;
▶ When a hard interrupt is triggered, program execution could be at any address within the program.

13.5 The Features Of A More Complex Interrupt Mechanism

It's worth mentioning some of the features offered by a more complex interrupt mechanism.

13.5.1 Layered Interrupts

Firstly, many processors offer layered interrupts. This means that some interrupts can be classed as being more important than other interrupts that are requested at the same time.

For example, if an aircraft's flight control system has two interrupts requested at the same time, the first at level one indicates that someone is smoking in the toilet, while the second interrupt at level four indicates that you are about to fly into a mountain, then the interrupt with the higher level will be dealt with first. Once the more important interrupt has been dealt with, the second less important interrupt can then be dealt with.

13.5.2 Non-Maskable Interrupts

Next, many processors offer non-maskable interrupts. This means that some interrupts cannot be 'switched off' in software, and must always be dealt with.

Neither of these features are offered within JASPer, and won't be mentioned again in this book as they are not required for a fundamental understanding of interrupts.

CHAPTER SUMMARY

The concept of the interrupt

▶ An interrupt is a signal sent to the processor by either hardware or software;

▶ The processor uses its interrupt mechanism to either call an interrupt handling routine or to ignore the interrupt;

▶ In our simple processor we use the I and E PSR flags and the interrupt vector in the PSR to indicate the status of the interrupt mechanism;

▶ The interrupt vector can be from 0 through to 7;

▶ A segment of memory is used to store the addresses of the different interrupt serving routines;

▶ The interrupt mechanism is based on an extended fetch-execute cycle.

Comparing the use of subroutines with interrupts

▶ An interrupt saves the PC and the PSR on the stack, while a subroutine call saves only the PC;

▶ A subroutine call happens at the same point in a program, while a hard interrupt can occur at any point within the program flow of execution.

The features of more complex interrupt mechanisms

▶ More complex interrupt mechanisms implement layered interrupts, where different interrupts can have a different importance;

▶ More complex interrupt mechanisms can implement non-maskable interrupts, which are interrupts that cannot be disabled.

SELF TEST QUESTIONS

1 Modify a copy of the `clock2.jas` program to include a `INTD` instruction instead of the `INTE`. An `INTD` instruction will disable interrupts. Run the program and see what is different to the previous execution of the program.

2 Modify your program to display the time every five seconds instead of every one second. Hint, you need to change the value in the `TIMER` memory location.

3 Modify the `subroutines.jas` program to use a `TRAP` instruction to trigger an interrupt that calls the subroutine instead of the `JSR` call. Hint, you need to set up a handler for the interrupt.

EXERCISES

1 Write a program that uses an interrupt mechanism to count the number of complete seconds between two key presses by the user.

2 Write a program that allows a user to enter a 10 character word. If they enter the word before 5 seconds has elapsed, the program prints out the word. If they do not enter the word in time, then the program prints 'Too late!' instead.

3 Write a program that generates a random time value between 5 and 20 seconds. The user can hit the space bar at any point in time, but if the user hits the space bar within 3 seconds before the timer is triggered, then the message 'You win!' is displayed. If the interrupt is triggered before a key has been pressed then the message 'You lose!' is displayed.

14

Systems Software

In this chapter we discuss the tools available to the programmer to aid program development.

This chapter includes:

▶ An overview of systems software, including operating systems and systems development software;
▶ The concepts of translators, including the assembler and the compiler;
▶ Comparing the assembler with the compiler;
▶ Using the assembler and compiler with our processor;
▶ Other systems tools, including the use of software libraries.

14.1 Introducing Systems Software

As we have found in the course of using our processor, the task of writing, running and debugging our programs is not straightforward. Very early on in the history of electronic computers it was discovered that there was a need for software to make the whole process much easier. This software is known as *systems software*. Systems software is the software that you can use so that you don't have to deal with the 'raw' machine.

Systems software tends to fall into two broad categories, these are the *operating system software* and *systems development software*. We will look at both of these in turn, but our main emphasis will be on systems development software.

14.2 The Operating System

The most common form of system software today is the operating system. The operating system can be as simple as a single *monitor* program, or as complex as a suite of programs, such as *Microsoft Windows XP* or the *Linux* operating system.

Many novice computer users never realize that the operating system is a set of programs that are written by programmers just like any other program.

The aim of an operating system is to provide a useful working environment to a user, who does not have to understand how the underlying machine works, but just wants to complete a particular task. This task might be writing a document, or emailing friends on the Internet, or calculating the monthly budget. Whatever the task, the operating system will provide a common working environment for the user.

At its core the operating system provides a number of services to the user. The most common of these include:

▶ Process management - running multiple programs at the same time;

▶ Memory management - managing the limited memory resource for all running programs;

▶ File system management - providing a standard interface to all the files available to the operating system;

▶ Interfacing with hardware devices - so that all programs can use the attached devices through a standard interface.

Although the operating system is the most often used piece of software that most users actually see, it is beyond the scope of this text to discuss operating systems in any greater detail than this.

14.3 Systems Development Software

Now we move on to the second key category of systems software, that of systems development software.

The point of systems development software is to ease the program development process.

The most important programs that aid this task are a form of program called a *translator*. We will look at two types of translator programs - the *assembler* and the *compiler*.

A translator program takes an input file written in one programming language and converts, or *translates*, it into another. This could be from an assembly language into machine code, as in an *assembler*, or it could be from a high-level language into machine code or assembly language, as with a *compiler*.

Firstly, we will take a look at the operation of the assembler, which takes assembly language and converts it into machine code.

14.3.1 The Assembler

If you have been attempting all of the chapter exercises, creating programs for our processor, then you will have found out a key truth in creating machine code programs. It is difficult! Firstly you have to work out the function of the program itself, and then you have to convert the program into assembly code, and then convert that into machine code - this includes working out opcodes and operands as well as addresses of labels that loops will make use of.

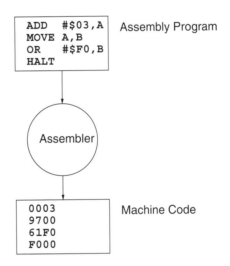

Figure 14.1 *The assembly process*

For this reason, early programmers soon created a program that would take over most of this laborious task for them. They still had to write the assembly language programs, but the task of turning assembly programs into machine code was automated. An *assembler program* is possible because our program and data are held in the same memory. The data output of one program (the assembler program) can in turn be a program in its own right.

Assembler programs translate assembly language into machine code. Both the assembly language source program and the machine code are *machine dependent*. This means that the source program and the machine code are related directly to a particular type of machine architecture. For example, assembly programs written for the Intel X86 architecture will not work on the Motorola 68000 architecture, and vice versa.

Our processor too has an assembler program, and now you have completed all your programming exercises so far I wish to make a confession. All but one (the 'Hello World' example from chapter 1) of the machine code example programs that you have seen in this book were created by the assembler program rather than by hand. I don't feel too guilty about this, because I had to write the assembler program!

So what does an assembler program do for us? Essentially it automates the process that you have had to do by hand so far:

- ▶ It converts instructions into machine code;
- ▶ It works out the memory locations of address labels;
- ▶ It decodes directives;
- ▶ It ignores comments;
- ▶ It reports any syntax errors found.

It means that when we use the assembler, if our program has been successfully assembled then we only have to concentrate on looking for semantic errors in our program, rather than syntax errors.

Apart from when processing some directives, an assembler program writes one machine code instruction for every assembly code instruction.

The use of an assembler program also gives us greater flexibility with our programs because it makes it much easier to use libraries of useful subroutines.

14.3.2 Using An Assembler

The assembler program for JASP is imaginatively named the *JASP Cross Assembler*. It is written in a language called *Perl*, and therefore to use the assembler on your own computer system you need an installation of Perl running on your machine. It is outside the scope of this book to tell you how to do this, instead take a look at [SOC97].

Assuming that you have an installation of Perl, and that you have copied the directory `jasp` from the CD, it is possible to assemble assembly language files.

Place the file `polled-io.txt` (from the examples directory tree on the CD, and shown below) in the same directory as the assembler program and run the following from a command prompt:

```
        jasm -a polled-io.txt
```

```
* A demonstration of polled I/O
*
* This program reads 10 characters from the keyboard
* and then prints them all out once they've been entered
*
OSR       EQU   $E3        * Output Status Register (OSR)
ODR       EQU   $E2        * Output Data Register   (ODR)
ISR       EQU   $E1        * Input Status Register  (ISR)
IDR       EQU   $E0        * Input Data Register    (IDR)

          ORG   0
          MOVE  #$00,B     * count is storage for our
          MOVE  B,count    *   counter value

loop      MOVE  ISR,A      * Get ISR
          CMP   #$00,A     * is a char available?
          BEQ   loop       * no - wait some more
          MOVE  IDR,A      * read the char

          MOVE  count,B    * the address to write the
          ADD   #data,B    * value to is count+data
          MOVE  A,(B)      * write the char in there

          MOVE  count,B    * add 1 to count
          ADD   #$01,B     *
          CMP   #$0A,B     * and see if we have reached 10 and
          BEQ   gotchars   * move to next section if we have
          MOVE  B,count    * otherwise write count back
          JMP   loop       * and get another char
gotchars  MOVE  #$00,B     * count is storage for our
          MOVE  B,count    *   counter value

write     MOVE  OSR,A      * get OSR
          CMP   #$00,A     * OSR 1 can print, OSR 0 can't print
          BEQ   write      * not yet, wait some more

          MOVE  count,B    * the address to read the
          ADD   #data,B    * value from is count+data
          MOVE  (B),A      * get the char in there
          MOVE  A,ODR      * print the char

          MOVE  count,B    * add 1 to count
          ADD   #$01,B     *
          CMP   #$0A,B     * and see if we have reached 10
```

```
          BEQ    done      * and move to end if we have
          MOVE   B,count   * otherwise write count back
          JMP    write     * and write another char
done      HALT             * done

count     DS.W $01         * the counter
data      DS.W $0A         * storage for our 10 characters
```

You should now see the machine code file, with the original assembly program included as comments, scroll up your command window. If you want to capture the output of the assembler program into a file so it can be executed in JASPer, you can type the following:

```
jasm -a polled-io.txt -o polled-io.jas
```

It is the resulting file polled-io.jas, shown below, that can then be loaded into JASPer and executed.

The JASPer assembler understands a typical set of directives. Directives can be thought of as shorthand for processing the assembly language program in particular ways, this could be saying where the program is to be loaded into memory (the ORG directive) or including complete library files (the USE directive).

For more information on the JASP Assembler, see appendix A.

```
            # 0000 # * A demonstration of polled I/O
            # 0000 # *
            # 0000 # * This program reads 10 characters from the keyboard
            # 0000 # * and then prints them all out once they've been entered
            # 0000 # *
            # 0000 # OSR    EQU    $E3       * Output Status Register (OSR)
            # 0000 # ODR    EQU    $E2       * Output Data Register   (ODR)
            # 0000 # ISR    EQU    $E1       * Input Status Register  (ISR)
            # 0000 # IDR    EQU    $E0       * Input Data Register    (IDR)
            # 0000 #
ORG $0000   # 0000 #        ORG    0
9100        # 0000 #        MOVE   #$00,B    * count is storage for our
A31F        # 0001 #        MOVE   B,count   *    counter value
            # 0002 #
92E1        # 0002 # loop   MOVE   ISR,A     * Get ISR
```

```
8000        # 0003 #          CMP    #$00,A     * is a char available?
C302        # 0004 #          BEQ    loop       * no - wait some more
92E0        # 0005 #          MOVE   IDR,A      * read the char
            # 0006 #
931F        # 0006 #          MOVE   count,B    * the address to write the
0120        # 0007 #          ADD    #data,B    * value to is count+data
A800        # 0008 #          MOVE   A,(B)      * write the char in there
            # 0009 #
931F        # 0009 #          MOVE   count,B    * add 1 to count
0101        # 000A #          ADD    #$01,B     *
810A        # 000B #          CMP    #$0A,B     * and see if we have reached 10 and
C30F        # 000C #          BEQ    gotchars   * move to next section if we have
A31F        # 000D #          MOVE   B,count    * otherwise write count back
E002        # 000E #          JMP    loop       * and get another char
9100        # 000F # gotchars MOVE   #$00,B     * count is storage for our
A31F        # 0010 #          MOVE   B,count    *   counter value
            # 0011 #
92E3        # 0011 # write    MOVE   OSR,A      * get OSR
8000        # 0012 #          CMP    #$00,A     * OSR 1 can print, OSR 0 can't print
C311        # 0013 #          BEQ    write      * not yet, wait some more
            # 0014 #
931F        # 0014 #          MOVE   count,B    * the address to read the
0120        # 0015 #          ADD    #data,B    * value from is count+data
9800        # 0016 #          MOVE   (B),A      * get the char in there
A2E2        # 0017 #          MOVE   A,ODR      * print the char
            # 0018 #
931F        # 0018 #          MOVE   count,B    * add 1 to count
0101        # 0019 #          ADD    #$01,B     *
810A        # 001A #          CMP    #$0A,B     * and see if we have reached 10
C31E        # 001B #          BEQ    done       * and move to end if we have
A31F        # 001C #          MOVE   B,count    * otherwise write count back
E011        # 001D #          JMP    write      * and write another char
F000        # 001E # done     HALT              * done
            # 001F #
0000        # 001F # count    DS.W   $01        * the counter
0000        # 0020 # data     DS.W   $0A        * storage for our 10 characters
0000        #      #
0000        #      #
0000        #      #
0000        #      #
0000        #      #
0000        #      #
0000        #      #
0000        #      #
0000        #      #
```

14.3.3 The Compiler

A compiler program is similar in many ways to an assembler. It takes input in one language and translates it into another. However, a compiler translates a high-level language into either assembly language or machine code.

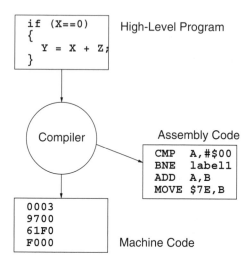

Figure 14.2   *The compilation process*

The key aspect of a high-level language is that it is generally *machine indepen-dent*, which means that different compilers can convert the same source code into either machine code or assembly language for different architectures.

NOTES

C-- is pronounced 'See minus minus'.

14.3.4 Using A Compiler

There is also a compiler written for JASP. It is called the *JASP C-- Cross Compiler*. This is a compiler for a language called C-- that produces output in JASP assembly language.

NOTES

C++ is pronounced 'See plus plus'.

A cross compiler is a compiler that creates programs to be run on a different machine architecture.

C-- is a purely educational language and is a very small sub-set of a popular high-level language called C++. C--, written by David Harrison, can be used to demonstrate the workings of a typical compiler.

A small program to demonstrate the use of the compiler can be seen here.

```
// add four numbers together

int a = 40;          // first value
int b = 45;          // second value
int c = 10;          // third value
int d =  5;          // fourth value

{
  a = a + b + c + d; // add them
  cout << a;         // and print the result result
}

// End of program
```

This is very similar to the pseudo-language we've used since chapter 9.

This program adds four numbers together, and outputs the result to the screen. To run this program on our processor, we first have to compile the C−− program into assembly language (by using the cross compiler) and then convert the resulting assembly language program into machine code (by using the cross assembler program we briefly described earlier). Once we've done all that we can load the machine code into JASPer and run the program.

So, to begin the process we need to run the cross compiler:

```
jcc < add.c-- > add.asm
```

This produces the assembly file add.asm, shown shortly.

We can then assemble this program using the cross assembler as follows:

```
jasm -a add.asm -o add.jas
```

It is the file add.jas which can then be executed on our processor. Even running the machine code isn't as simple as we've seen before, because the program has to be executed using the advanced instruction set, advanced.mco, which can be loaded from the JASPer 'file/open' dialog (the advanced instruction set can address all of memory with no addressing limitations - it is not intended for novice users). When the program is executed you will see the value 100 printed on the screen and then the program will halt.

If you take a look at the assembly program add.asm produced by the compiler (shown below), you will see that the assembly code that it produces looks exactly the same as that you would write yourself, except that there are no comments in the program. Don't worry if at first glance the assembly language looks complicated - it is! The compiler actually writes assembly programs that use the stack often, more so than a human would write.

```
      MCO  "advanced.mco"
      ORG  $0100
      LPC  $0100
      MOVE #$DF,SP
      JMP  main
_Eintegeroverflow DC.B 'Integer overflow!\n',0

_Edividebyzero    DC.B 'Divide by zero!\n',0

sym_d    DS.W 1
sym_c    DS.W 1
sym_b    DS.W 1
sym_a    DS.W 1

main
      MOVE #^5,B
      MOVE B,sym_d
      MOVE #^10,B
      MOVE B,sym_c
      MOVE #^45,B
      MOVE B,sym_b
      MOVE #^40,B
      MOVE B,sym_a
      MOVE sym_a,A
      PUSH A
      MOVE sym_b,A
      PUSH A
      MOVE sym_c,A
      PUSH A
      MOVE sym_d,A
      PUSH A
      POP  B
      POP  A
      ADD  B,A
      BVS  L0
      PUSH A
      POP  B
      POP  A
      ADD  B,A
```

```
        BVS   LO
        PUSH  A
        POP   B
        POP   A
        ADD   B,A
        BVS   LO
        PUSH  A
        POP   A
        MOVE  A,sym_a
        MOVE  sym_a,A
        JSR   putdword
        HALT
LO
        MOVE  #_Eintegeroverflow,A
        JSR   putstring
        HALT

Ldividebyzero
        MOVE  #_Edividebyzero,A
        JSR   putstring
        HALT

        USE   "advancedio.lib"
```

NOTES

*The issues of optimization
are described in [BO03].*

Also, you may see that the assembly language that it produces is not *optimized* - this means that the code isn't as efficient as it could be. *Optimizing compilers* attempt to create the most efficient assembly programs, but we don't need to concern ourselves with advanced features of this sort.

We won't make use of the compiler again in this text.

For more information on the JASP C−− Cross Compiler, see appendix A.

14.3.5 Comparing The Assembler With The Compiler

Now we have looked at both assemblers and compilers it is important to stress their similarities and their differences:

▶ Both the compiler and the assembler are examples of translators;

▶ Generally one assembly language statement will produce one line of machine code, whereas one line from a high-level language will compile into multiple assembly language statements;

▶ Assembly language focuses on the use of a particular hardware architecture. For example, an assembly program for JASPer will not be correctly assembled for any other processor. A high-level language program can (providing a compiler for the task exists) be compiled for any given hardware architecture. For example, the same C−− program can be compiled to any hardware architecture to which the compiler has been *ported* (written to work on a given architecture).

▶ A high-level language program is said to be *portable*, if it can be compiled for many different architectures. However, the effect of this is that high-level languages do not offer the full facilities of a given architecture, such as particular hardware features (for example, direct access to the PSR flags), to a programmer. Some functions of a program, for example to access a disk drive, are still written in assembly language to allow a high-level program to access specific hardware. The use of assembly language in a high-level program is called *in-line assembler*, and is not offered by all compilers.

▶ Most programs these days are written in high-level languages rather than assembly language due to this need for portability.

14.3.6 Other Systems Software Tools

Compilers and assemblers are not the only tools available to the program developer. Other tools exist to aid the program development process.

One such tool is the software library, wherein useful programming subroutines are written once, and used each time that they are required. This means that the developer doesn't have to be constantly re-inventing the wheel.

For example, a library might contain subroutines that print a character on the screen, get a character from the keyboard, etc. Such libraries exist for our processor, and can be used by the assembler we discussed earlier by using the USE directive within your program. An example of this is shown below, which is a version of the interrupt program we looked at in the previous chapter updated to use libraries. The subroutines `putchar` and `putdbyte` no longer need to be written as part of the program, as there are versions available in the library used.

Please note that when you include a library in your program, the entire contents are included and not just the functions you wish to make use of.

```
* This program uses a timer to raise an interrupt every
```

```
* one second to display the time.

          MCO "advanced.mco"

          * load handler address in interrupt vector table
          * timer is triggered on interrupt 6
          ORG $f6
          DC.W #timerhandler

          ORG $100
          LPC $100

          INTE                * Enable interrupts
          MOVE #$D0,SP        * initialize stack pointer ($D0)
          MOVE #$01,A         *
          MOVE A,_TIMER       * intialize timer with 1 second
main
          MOVE #$2e,B         * move a '.' into B
          JSR putchar         * jump to sub-routine putchar
          MOVE ISR,A          * get the ISR
          CMP  #$00,A         * check if a key has been pressed
          BEQ  main           * if it hasn't then goto main
          HALT                * finished

* trap 6
timerhandler
          PUSH A
          PUSH B
          MOVE _HOURS,A       * move hours value into A
          JSR putdbyte        * jump to sub-routine put-dec-byte
          MOVE #$3a,B         * move a ':' into B
          JSR putchar         * jump to sub-routine putchar
          MOVE _MINS,A        * move mins value into A
          JSR putdbyte        * jump to sub-routine put-dec-byte
          MOVE #$3a,B         * move a ':' into B
          JSR putchar         * jump to sub-routine putchar
          MOVE _SECS,A        * move seconds value into A
          JSR putdbyte        * jump to sub-routine put-dec-byte
          POP B
          POP A
          RTI

          USE "advancedio.lib"
```

CHAPTER SUMMARY

Systems software

▶ System software is used so that users do not have to work with the 'bare' processor;

▶ The two broad categories of system software are operating systems and systems development software.

Translators

▶ The most common form of systems development software is the translator;

▶ A translator takes a program in one form of the programming hierarchy and outputs another. A compiler inputs a high-level language program and outputs either an assembly language program or a machine code program. An assembler inputs an assembly language program and outputs a machine code program;

▶ A high-level program is said to be portable, because it is not written for any one specific architecture. An assembly language program is not portable because it *is* written for one specific architecture;

▶ An assembly language statement generally produces one machine code, while a high-level statement will generally produce many machine codes.

Other systems tools

▶ The software library is a useful tool, as it means that subroutines for particular tasks can be re-used.

SELF TEST QUESTIONS

1 Run the `polled-io.jas` program, then modify the `polled-io.txt` source by altering the `ORG` statement to begin the program load at memory location $0010. Re-assemble the program, examine the new `polled-io.jas` program, and then execute it from its new start location.

2 Use the compiler and the assembler to produce the machine code for the program `add.c--`.

3 In the program `add.c--` modify the variable b to the value 55, then re-compile, re-assemble, and re-run the program.

4 Write a program to display 'The time is now xx:xx', where xx:xx is the current hours and minutes in hexadecimal. Hint, there is a subroutine in the `basicio.lib` library called `putbyte` that you can make use of.

5 Write a program to read in the user's name, and then prints out 'Hello name!', where `name` is the name entered. Hint, limit the number of characters that can be entered to 10 characters, not including the carriage return.

EXERCISES

1 Re-write the `polled-io.txt` program making use of the `putchar` and `getchar` subroutines from within the `basicio.lib` library. Use the assembler to produce the new `polled-io.jas` - debug any syntax and semantic errors. Run the debugged program in JASPer.

2 Write a program to input your name in lowercase and display it in uppercase.

3 Write a program to read in a number of characters, terminated by a carriage return (the ASCII code 0D) and then print out the number of characters typed.

4 Use the compiler and the assembler to produce the machine code for the program `fact.c--`, and then run the program.

15

Bringing It All Together - The Programmer's Perspective

CHAPTER OVERVIEW

In the final chapter of this section we take a problem specification and design and write an assembly language program that requires many of the features described in previous chapters.

This chapter includes:

▶ The introduction of a problem specification;
▶ The development of a solution, using stepwise refinement;
▶ Testing the solution;
▶ Documenting the solution.

15.1 Problem Specification

The problem we will attempt to solve is the creation of a stopwatch program to run on our processor system. This stopwatch will count seconds, up to a limit of 59 minutes and 59 seconds, at which point the stopwatch will count from 0 seconds once more.

The stopwatch will have two functions that can be controlled by the user to control the stopwatch, as well as a third function to quit the program. These functions can be attached to key presses, and so the program will understand the following keys:

▶ A '1' key press will cause the stopwatch to start counting seconds. If the stopwatch is already running, then hitting the '1' key will cause the stopwatch to pause;

▶ A '2' key press will cause the stopwatch to reset itself, so whatever the current stopwatch time it is reset to 0. If the stopwatch is running at the point the '2' key is pressed then the stopwatch will also be paused;

▶ A '3' key press will halt the program.

The time is updated by the use of an interrupt handler being triggered by the hardware timer, but more on that in a later refinement.

The first task we need to perform is to sketch out in a high-level language the functionality of our program.

Here is the high-level description of our program:

```
print_opening_message;
while (keypress != 3) {
    keypress = getchar();
    if (keypress == '1') {
        // run the stopwatch
        runStopwatch();
    }
    else if (keypress == '2') {
        // reset the stopwatch
        resetStopwatch();
    }
    else if (keypress == '3') {
        // quit the program
    }
    else {
        // ignore keypress
    }
}
print_closing_message;
```

Basically, we can see from the high-level description that the program consists of a processing loop based on a `while` construct. Each time around the loop the program checks to see which function, based on a key press of '1', '2' or '3', has been selected and runs an appropriate piece of code for that function.

▶ If a '1' key has been pressed, then the subroutine `runStopwatch` is called;

▶ If a '2' key has been pressed, then the subroutine `resetStopwatch` is called;

▶ And if a '3' key has been pressed, the flow of control leaves the `while` construct so that the program can complete.

Initially, it appears that the time displayed by the stopwatch can never be updated, but we must remember that independently of the main program, there is also an interrupt handler being executed every time the clock timer requests an interrupt. The interrupt routine, in a high-level language, appears like this:

```
seconds++;
if (seconds == 60) {
    seconds = 0;
    minutes++;
}
if (minutes == 60) {
    minutes = 0;
}
```

So, you can see that the interrupt handler actually increments the time to be displayed by the stopwatch.

We will start by writing an equivalent assembly language program to match the high-level definition of the main program.

15.2 Program Refinement One

Our first draft program will create the 'bones' of our program without us having to yet worry about the detail of the functionality, and so this is the first stage of our step-wise refinement.

An assembly language program should typically take a structure similar to that shown in figure 15.1. If you follow such a structure it actually makes the program easier to read and understand, as well as helps us focus on the issues we need to solve.

Constant Definitions
Main Program
Subroutines
Library Definitions
Global Variables
String Constants

Figure 15.1 *The structure of a typical assembly language program*

Using this structure, we can already map out our first draft program and test its simple functionality. We have to make a number of decisions before we can begin:

▶ Constants: we will make use of polled I/O, and therefore we must include the definitions of the I/O registers;

▶ Main program: the main program will be required to initialize the stack as we expect to use a number of subroutine calls;

▶ Subroutines: we can use empty subroutines for the running and resetting of the stopwatch for the moment. We have encountered subroutines to print character strings in chapter 14;

▶ Library definitions: to simplify this program, and ensure that our program will fit into the memory space between $0000 and $00DF, we will not make use of any libraries. Examine the memory map in figure 12.1 to understand this limitation;

▶ Global variables: we will need storage for the stopwatch time, and it makes sense to store minutes and seconds in separate locations;

▶ String constants: we can define our character strings to be printed as the program starts, and as it completes.

15.2.1 Constants

Here is a first draft of our constants section:

```
* Memory mapped I/O
IDR    EQU $E0      * Input Data Register
ISR    EQU $E1      * Input Status Register
ODR    EQU $E2      * Output Data Register
OSR    EQU $E3      * Output Status Register
```

15.2.2 Main Program

Here is a first draft of our main program:

```
        ORG $0
        MOVE #$D0,SP            * initialise stack pointer

        MOVE #$00,A            *
        MOVE A,minutes         * minutes = 0
        MOVE A,seconds         * seconds = 0

        MOVE #message,A        * print opening message
        JSR  putstring         *
_main_loop                     *
        JSR  displayTime       * print the stopwatch time
        JSR  getchar           * get a keypress from the user
        CMP  #$31,A            * if it is a '1' we
        BEQ  _main_runStopwatch   *   want to run the stopwatch
        CMP  #$32,A            * if it is a '2' we
        BEQ  _main_resetStopwatch *   want to reset the stopwatch
        CMP  #$33,A            * if it is a '3' we
        BEQ  _main_done        *   want to stop the program
        JMP  _main_loop        * any other keypress is ignored
_main_runStopwatch             *
        JSR  runStopwatch      * run the stopwatch
        JMP  _main_loop        *   then go through the loop again
_main_resetStopwatch           *
        JSR  resetStopwatch    * reset the stopwatch
        JMP  _main_loop        *   then go through the loop again
_main_done                     *
        MOVE #message2,A       * print closing message
        JSR  putstring         *
        HALT                   * finished
```

Our program performs some initialization by setting the SP and setting the stopwatch minutes and seconds to zero. Then it prints the opening message to the screen prior to entering the while construct. Inside the while construct the program accepts key presses from the user, using '1', '2' or '3' key presses to perform program functionality (checking for ASCII codes $31, $32 and $33 respectively). The while construct is exited when the key press '3' has been entered. Finally, the program prints a final message to the screen prior to halting.

15.2.3 Subroutines

Here is a first draft of our subroutines section:

```
displayTime             *
        RTS             * return from subroutine

runStopwatch            *
        RTS             * return from subroutine

resetStopwatch          *
        RTS             * return from subroutine

putchar PUSH A          * save A on the stack
_pc_check
        MOVE OSR,A       * move OSR to A
        CMP  #$00,A      * Can we print ?
        BEQ  _pc_check   * If not, grab OSR again
        MOVE B,ODR       * otherwise print lo-byte of B
        POP  A           * retrieve A from the stack
        RTS              * return from subroutine

getchar
        MOVE ISR,A       * move ISA to A
        CMP  #$00,A      * if it is 0 we have no char
        BEQ  #getchar    * so branch to check again
        MOVE IDR,A       * when we have a char put it in A
        RTS              * return from subroutine

putstring               *
        MOVE (A),B       * move the word pointed to by A into B
        SWAP B           * swap bytes in B
        PUSH A           *
        MOVE #$ff,A      * place a mask of $00ff into A
        AND  A,B         *    and use the mask on B (to look at
        POP  A           *    the lo-byte only)
        CMP  #$00,B      * if the lo-byte is a 0, we are
        BEQ  #_ps_done   *    finished
        JSR  putchar     * otherwise print the character
        MOVE (A),B       *    and get the next byte into
        PUSH A           *    the lo-byte of B
        MOVE #$ff,A      *
        AND  A,B         * apply the same mask as before
        POP  A           *
        CMP  #$00,B      * if the lo-byte of B is a 0, we are
        BEQ  #_ps_done   *    finished
        JSR  putchar     * otherwise print the character
```

```
        ADD   #$01,A        * point to the next word
        JMP   #putstring    *   and run the subroutine again
_ps_done
        RTS                 * return from subroutine
```

The subroutine `displayTime`, `runStopwatch` and `resetStopwatch` are empty subroutines, in that they can be called, but merely return without doing anything. Putting in these subroutines means that we can attempt to assemble the complete program and test it prior to adding to the complexity of the program.

The subroutines `putchar`, `getchar` and `putstring` have been seen before. Don't be afraid to use subroutines that you have written previously, provided that they are well documented and 'self-contained'. By 'self-contained' I mean that they must not change the contents of the A or B register (unless this is required for parameter passing to the subroutine), and any data storage required by the subroutine is kept within the subroutine. Of course, if we had decided to use the `basicio.lib` library, then we would not have need to include these subroutines directly in the program. If we included the contents of the library however, our program would be too large to fit in memory between $0000 and $00DF.

15.2.4 Global Variables

Here is a first draft of our global variables section:

```
minutes  DS.W 1     * stopwatch minutes
seconds  DS.W 1     * stopwatch seconds
```

As you can see, we are setting aside a word of memory for each of our variables.

15.2.5 String Constants

Here is a first draft of our string constants section:

```
message  DC.B 'Stopwatch Facility [1]Start/stop [2]Reset [3]Quit\n\n',0
message2 DC.B '\nProgram completed.\n',0
```

The DC.B directive allows us to specify strings that we can use within our program. These strings are called *null-terminated strings*, as each character in turn is printed until a $00 (that we have placed as the last character of each string) is encountered. Also, \n means print a line feed - the assembler converts this into a $0A code. These strings are displayed at the start and at the end of the program respectively.

15.2.6 Assembling The First Refinement

These sections have been placed in a file called sw1.txt, it is available on the CD. Assuming that you have the assembler set up on your system (see appendix A for a description of how to do this), and you have the sw1.txt copied to your current directory, at a command-line prompt you can type:

```
jasm -a sw1.txt -o sw1.jas
```

The program assembles with no errors and can be run by loading into JASPer and executed. It doesn't currently do much, it displays the character strings and accepts the key presses from the user, but only pressing key '3' will actually do anything - it will complete the program.

Figure 15.2 shows the output of the program after being executed in JASPer.

15.3 Program Refinement Two

In the second refinement of our program we will build the stopwatch functionality into our existing program.

We need to define the functionality of the runStopwatch, resetStopwatch, and displayTime subroutines.

15.3.1 Subroutine displayTime

Starting with the easiest first, we will write the subroutine displayTime. This subroutine has to display the current stopwatch time, as stored in the minutes and seconds global variables, and print it in the format MM:SS. To ensure that we continually overwrite the 'old' printed value we will also first print a carriage return character.

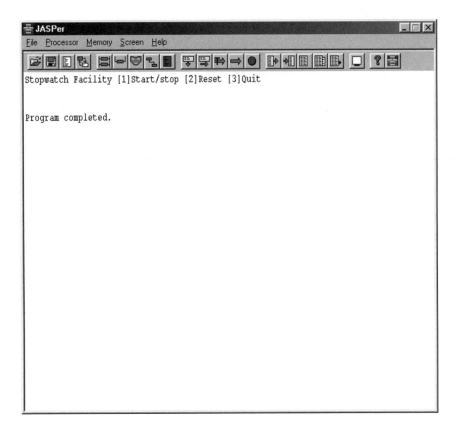

Figure 15.2 *The output after running the first refinement in JASPer*

Here is a first draft of our displayTime subroutine:

```
displayTime             *
        PUSH A          * store A on the stack
        PUSH B          * store B on the stack
        MOVE #$0D,B      *
        JSR  putchar    * print a CR
        MOVE minutes,A   *
        JSR  putdbyte   * print minutes
        MOVE #$3A,B      *
        JSR  putchar    * print a :
        MOVE seconds,A   *
        JSR  putdbyte   * print seconds
        POP  B          * restore B from the stack
        POP  A          * restore A from the stack
        RTS             * return from subroutine
```

This subroutine firstly prints a carriage return character, then it uses a subroutine called `putdbyte` to print the number of minutes in a decimal format, it prints a ':' character, and then finally prints the number of seconds in a decimal format.

We encountered the `putdbyte` subroutine in an earlier clock example program. Here it is:

```
putdbyte
        PUSH A              * store A on the stack
        PUSH B              * store B on the stack
        MOVE #$00,B         * set B to 0
        MOVE B,_pdb_tens    * clear the tens variable
        MOVE A,_pdb_units   * set the units variable to A
_pdb_decloop
        CMP  #$0a,A         * compare A with 10
        BMI  _pdb_print     * goto print if less than 10
        SUB  #$0a,A         * otherwise A = A-10
        MOVE _pdb_tens,B    * B = tens  }
        ADD  #$01,B         * B++       } i.e tens++
        MOVE B,_pdb_tens    * tens = B  }
        MOVE A,_pdb_units   * A = units
        JMP  _pdb_decloop   * goto decloop
_pdb_print
        MOVE _pdb_tens,A    * move tens into A
        ADD  #$30,A         * add 30hex (i.e. its a char number now)
        PUSH B              * store B on the stack
        MOVE A,B            *
        JSR  putchar        * print it
        POP  B              *
        MOVE _pdb_units,A   * move units to A
        ADD  #$30,A         * add 30hex (i.e. its a char number now)
        PUSH B              *
        MOVE A,B            *
        JSR  putchar        * print it
        POP  B              * restore B from the stack
        POP  B              * restore B from the stack
        POP  A              * restore A from the stack
        RTS                 * return from subroutine
* data storage
_pdb_tens       DS.W 1     * storage for tens variable
_pdb_units      DS.W 1     * storage for units variable
```

The `putdbyte` subroutine prints the lower byte of the contents of the A register as two decimal digits, so we can use it to print both the minutes and the seconds of the stopwatch time. Note that the subroutine uses two words of storage internally to compute the correct output.

15.3.2 Subroutine runStopwatch

Next we will write the subroutine `runStopwatch`. This subroutine keeps check whether the stopwatch is running or paused, and for every time it is called, it switches the state between running and paused. To do this it needs to store which state it is currently in, so we make use of an extra global variable called `state`. This variable is set to 0, representing a paused state, in the main program as an addition to the program initialization code. These changes a shown below:

```
* main program
            .
            .

        * further initialization
        MOVE #$00,A      *
        MOVE A,state     * state = 0, stopwatch not running
            .
            .

* global variables
            .
            .

state   DS.W 1           * stopwatch state, 0=stopped, 1=running
            .
            .
```

Our `runStopwatch` subroutine can be defined as:

```
    if (state == 0) {
        state = 1;
        // enable timer
    }
    else {
        state = 0;
        // disable timer
    }
```

This can be drafted as:

```
runStopwatch               *
        PUSH  A            * store A on the stack
        MOVE  state,A      *
        CMP   #$00,A       * if (state == 0)
        BEQ   _rsw_stopped *   then ...
        JMP   _rsw_started *
_rsw_stopped               *
        MOVE  #$01,A       *
        MOVE  A,state      * state = 1
        JMP   _rsw_done    *
_rsw_started               * else ...
        MOVE  #$00,A       *
        MOVE  A,state      * state = 0
_rsw_done                  *
        POP   A            * restore A from the stack
        RTS                * return from subroutine
```

Currently, this subroutine doesn't control how the interrupt is requested, but that will come in the next refinement.

15.3.3 Subroutine resetStopwatch

This subroutine is to reset the stopwatch time. It will also pause the stopwatch if it is currently running.

Here is the first draft of this subroutine:

```
resetStopwatch             *
        PUSH  A            * store A on the stack
        MOVE  #$00,A       *
        MOVE  A,state      * state = 0 (paused)
        MOVE  A,minutes    * minutes = 0
        MOVE  A,seconds    * seconds = 0
        POP   A            * restore A from the stack
        RTS                * return from subroutine
```

15.3.4 Assembling The Second Refinement

We can assemble and execute this latest refinement to our program. It is stored on the CD in a file called sw2.txt. When we run it we see the output as shown in figure 15.3. The stopwatch still does very little, apart from take the key presses as before, and display the stopwatch time as 00:00.

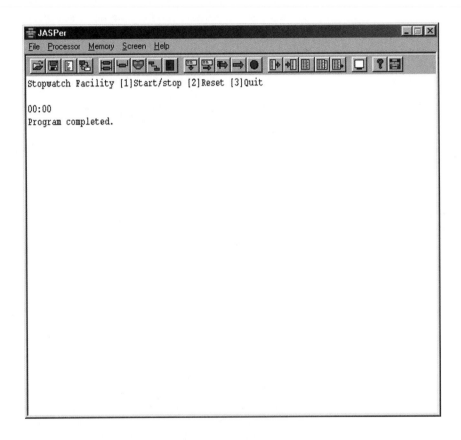

Figure 15.3 *The output after running the second refinement in JASPer*

15.4 Program Refinement Three

Our program, for all our hard work so far, still can't actually provide a stopwatch facility, as the stored time is not yet updated. In this third and final refinement of our program we will build the interrupt handler to count the seconds and look at what we have to do to ensure the timer requests the interrupts.

The interrupt mechanism, as described in chapter 13, can request a timed interrupt by the use of the timer register, which is at memory location $00EE. The timer can be used to request interrupts anything from 1 to 255 seconds apart, so we can cause an interrupt to be requested every one second by placing the value $01 into the register.

Provided that interrupts are enabled and the address of the interrupt handler is in the interrupt vector table at location $00F6, to handle the level 6 interrupts generated by the timer, we can make our processor call our interrupt handler every second, thus becoming the heart of our stopwatch.

15.4.1 The Interrupt Handler

So, assuming that our interrupt handler is going to be called every second by the interrupt mechanism, what do we actually want it to do?

As we said at the start of the chapter, here is the high-level definition of its functionality:

```
seconds++;
if (seconds == 60) {
    seconds = 0;
    minutes++;
}
if (minutes == 60) {
    minutes = 0;
}
```

The handler needs to add one to the current value of seconds, and if this means that the number of seconds is now 60, to set seconds to 0 and add 1 to the current value of minutes. If the number of minutes is now 60 it also needs to set the number of minutes back to 0. In this way the stopwatch display can count up to 59:59 before going back to 00:00.

Here is the first draft of our interrupt handler:

```
intHandler
          PUSH A                  * store A on the stack
          MOVE seconds,A          * }
          ADD  #$01,A             * } seconds++
          MOVE A,seconds          * }
          CMP  #^60,A             * if (seconds == 60)
          BEQ  _ih_update_secs    *   then ...
```

```
            JMP   _ih_mins          *
_ih_update_secs                     *
            MOVE #$00,A             *
            MOVE A,seconds          * seconds = 0
            MOVE minutes,A          * }
            ADD  #$01,A             * } minutes++
            MOVE A,minutes          * }
_ih_mins                            *
            CMP  #^60,A             * if (minutes == 60)
            BEQ  _ih_update_mins    *   then ...
            JMP  _ih_done           *
_ih_update_mins                     *
            MOVE #$00,A             *
            MOVE A,minutes          * minutes = 0
_ih_done                            *
            JSR  displayTime        * display the stopwatch time
            POP  A                  * restore A from the stack
            RTI                     * return from interrupt
```

As you can see, the interrupt handler also displays the current stopwatch time once the time has been updated. Also, note that the interrupt handler is terminated with an RTI (Return from Interrupt) instruction and not an RTS instruction. Remember, these two instructions do slightly different things, and if we were to mistakenly have used an RTS instruction, our program would fail to work correctly.

15.4.2 Setting Up The Interrupt Mechanism

We are not quite finished yet, as we still need to make the appropriate updates to the rest of our program to allow interrupts to be triggered, to load the address of the interrupt handler into the interrupt vector table, and to update a number of subroutines to make use of the TIMER memory location.

To allow interrupts, we update the beginning of our main program as follows:

```
    ORG $0
    INTE      * Enable interrupts
    .
    .
    .
```

We add the TIMER constant:

```
TIMER  EQU $EE      * TIMER register used to set the timer
                    * interval to trigger the interrupts
```

We also add a section prior to our main program to install the address of our interrupt handler into the interrupt vector table for an interrupt level 6:

```
        ORG $F6             * Load the handler address in
        DC.W #intHandler *    interrupt vector table.
```

Finally we need to update the main program, the runStopwatch subroutine and the resetStopwatch subroutine to include setting the TIMER register. The updates to the main program are:

```
* main program
        .
        .
        * more initialization
        MOVE #$00,A    *
        MOVE A,TIMER   * TIMER = 0, interrupts not triggered
        MOVE A,state   * state = 0, stopwatch not running
        .
        .
_main_done             *
        MOVE #$00,A    *
        MOVE A,TIMER   * TIMER = 0
        .
        .
```

The runStopwatch subroutine becomes:

```
runStopwatch               *
        PUSH A             * store A on the stack
        MOVE state,A       *
        CMP  #$00,A        * if (state == 0)
        BEQ _rsw_stopped *    then ...
        JMP _rsw_started *
_rsw_stopped               *
        MOVE #$01,A        *
```

```
        MOVE  A,state        * state = 1
        MOVE  A,TIMER        * TIMER = 1
        JMP   _rsw_done      *
_rsw_started                 * else ...
        MOVE  #$00,A         *
        MOVE  A,state        * state = 0
        MOVE  A,TIMER        * TIMER = 0
_rsw_done                    *
        POP   A              * restore A from the stack
        RTS                  * return from subroutine
```

While the `resetStopwatch` subroutine becomes:

```
resetStopwatch               *
        PUSH  A              * store A on the stack
        MOVE  #$00,A         *
        MOVE  A,state        * state = 0
        MOVE  A,TIMER        * TIMER = 0
        MOVE  A,minutes      * minutes = 0
        MOVE  A,seconds      * seconds = 0
        POP   A              * restore A from the stack
        RTS                  * return from subroutine
```

15.4.3 Assembling The Final Refinement

We can assemble and execute this final refinement to our program. It is stored on the CD in a file called `sw3.txt`. When we run it we see the output as shown in figure 15.4 - you can see that the stopwatch has been run for 38 seconds.

15.5 Final Testing Of The Program

NOTES

It is worth noting that black box testing has nothing to do with the black-box mode in JASPer - don't confuse the two.

As we have seen, testing new functionality as we put it in is vital to ensure that our program runs as expected. However, once the program is in its final stage we need to formalize the tests that ensure our complete program meets the original specification.

To do this we can use a method known as *black box testing*. It is outside the scope of this text to cover the issues of testing in detail, but the broad concepts of black box testing are described below.

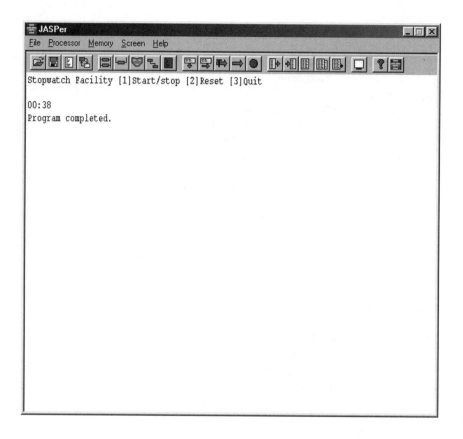

Figure 15.4 *The output after running the final refinement in JASPer*

15.5.1 Black Box Testing

Black box testing means that we test our program against our initial specification without reference to the program code in the solution. We treat our program as a black box, where it can do particular functions and yet we are not interested in how it actually performs these functions.

Using black box testing, we can check the functionality of our program against the initial specification. We can do this in a tabular form as seen in table 15.1. We document eight test cases that describe what we expect our program to do under particular actions.

It is worth mentioning that this set of test cases could be expanded to also test that the stopwatch correctly works between the times of $00{:}00$ to $59{:}59$, but as I said before, a more thorough discussion of testing is outside the scope of this text.

Test Case	Action	State	Expected Result	Actual Result
1	Key '1' pressed	Stopwatch paused	Stopwatch to start	
2	Key '1' pressed	Stopwatch running	Stopwatch to pause	
3	Key '2' pressed	Stopwatch paused	Stopwatch to reset time to 00:00	
4	Key '2' pressed	Stopwatch running	Stopwatch to reset time to 00:00 and stop running	
5	Key '3' pressed	Stopwatch paused	Program quits	
6	Key '3' pressed	Stopwatch running	Program quits	
7	Any other key pressed	Stopwatch paused	Key press ignored	
8	Any other key pressed	Stopwatch running	Key press ignored	

Table 15.1 *Using black box testing - example test cases*

15.6 Documenting The Program

We have a working program that meets our specification, so are we finished? No we are not! Throughout the writing of the program we commented on the low level workings of individual subroutines, but it is time to complete the documentation. With assembly language programs it is wise to add comments to:

▶ Document what the program is expected to do, and any restrictions on the program;

▶ Document at a higher level the functionality of individual subroutines, including descriptions of *pre-conditions* and *post-conditions*. Pre-conditions are those conditions that have to be true prior to the subroutine being used, while post-conditions are those conditions that have to be true once the subroutine has completed;

▶ Document any other information that you think another programmer (or yourself at some later date) will need to understand the program to a level by which they could update or maintain it.

The completed program is on the CD in a file called `stopwtch.txt`. It has had documentation added to describe the usage of the program as a whole and individual subroutines.

Here is an example of the level of documentation added to explain an individual subroutine:

```
* Name: runStopwatch
*
* Description    : Starts or pauses the stopwatch
*                  subroutine.  The state of the
*                  stopwatch is stored in the 'state'
*                  variable. If the state is
*                  currently 0 (paused), then the
*                  state is set to 1 (running) and
*                  the TIMER is set to 1 to trigger
*                  an interrupt every one second.
*                  If the state is already 1 then
*                  the state is set to 0 (paused),
*                  and the TIMER is set to 0 to stop
*                  interrupts being raised.
*
* Preconditions : state is expected to be 1 or 0.
* Postconditions: The state is updated and the TIMER
*                  updated.
* Stack use      : 1 word
* Calls          : None
* Called by      : main program
*
* Algorithm to check state:
*
*    if (state == 0) {
*        state = 1;
*        TIMER = 1;
*    }
*    else {
*        state = 0;
*        TIMER = 0;
*    }
```

All this, as well as the individual comments for particular assembly language statements, are to explain only 14 assembly language statements! This level of documentation is vital for assembly language programs; it is worth getting into the habit of writing this level of documentation early on in your programming career as it will pay dividends to you when you have to update programs long after you originally wrote them, or when you have to pass your programs on to someone else to support.

15.6.1 Stack Usage

This level of detail also helps us better understand our program in ways not immediately obvious. For example, now we have fully documented individual subroutines we can see categorically how much stack usage is required by our program.

No subroutines are *recursive* (where a subroutine can make a call to itself) - if they were we would have documented that fact, and so we can work out exactly what our stack usage requirements are.

Before we documented our program we might not have considered checking the issues of stack usage, but remember, the stack is an ADT that is completely under our control and if we provide too small a stack our program could fail. To check usage we can draw a tree of subroutine calls, as shown in figure 15.5 to work out maximum stack usage.

From figure 15.5 we can see that the maximum stack usage is only nine words, which consists of the interrupt handler calling `displayTime`, which calls `putdbyte`, which calls `putchar`. However, we must also remember that the interrupt handler can be called at any point in the program. The greatest use of the stack therefore would be 11 words if the timer triggered while the `runStopwatch` subroutine was executing.

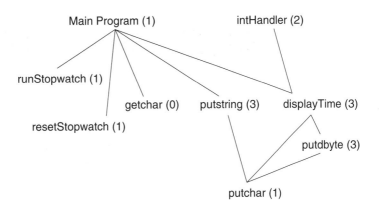

Figure 15.5 *A tree to work out maximum stack usage*

As the last part of our program is the string constants we can check where the end of our program is in memory. It occurs at memory location $00B7. We know that our stack begins at memory location $00DF, so we can see that we have more than enough stack space to ensure that the program will never suffer from a stack overflow - where parts of the program are overwritten by the usage of the stack.

CHAPTER SUMMARY

Using stepwise refinement

▶ Use stepwise refinement to test partial programs as the program is being written;

▶ Comment your program wisely, don't just duplicate the assembly language literally;

▶ Stick to the program structure of constants, main program, subroutines, library definitions, global variables and string constants. Doing so will aid the readability of your program.

Testing and documenting the solution

▶ To ensure the removal of semantic errors, perform both white box and black box testing on your solution;

▶ Fully document each subroutine of your program, listing a full description of what it does, pre-conditions, post-conditions, stack usage, etc. This level of documentation will make the program easier to update when you come back to it months or even years later.

EXERCISES

1 Modify the stopwatch program so that it could be used to count up to 24 hours, rather than the current one hour limit.

2 Modify the stopwatch program so that it could be used to count up to a full 7 days. How can you test such a program? Hint, without having to sit at your computer for 7 days!

3 Write a program to count down from a value that can be set by the user. The user should be able to set the timer to a particular start time, pause the timer, and reset the timer in a similar fashion to the stopwatch program described in this chapter.

Part III

Under The Bonnet

We return to the viewpoint of the hardware engineer, in order to examine the control of our processor.

Building An Instruction Set

In this first chapter that looks 'under the bonnet' we discuss how to build instructions from micro-instructions.

This chapter includes:

▶ Micro-instructions revisited - data movement operations, ALU operations, test operations and processor control operations;
▶ How to construct instructions from micro-instructions;
▶ Building new instruction sets.

16.1 The Instruction Set

We have now used our instruction set in anger, and it is time to revisit how instructions actually work, looking at the types of micro-instructions, and then seeing how to create new instructions.

16.2 Micro-Instructions Revisited

We have seen before, in chapter 8 and earlier, how micro-instructions are used to build assembly language instructions.

To remind ourselves, each micro-instruction belongs to one of the following groups:

▶ Data transfer micro-instructions;

▶ ALU micro-instructions;

▶ Test micro-instructions;

▶ Processor control micro-instructions.

Each micro-instruction is actually defined at the hardware level of our processor, and when a micro-instruction is executed it performs certain actions at that level, and we will look into this in chapter 17. To describe the action of a micro-instruction, we have described it in RTL, such as with the data movement

$$A \leftarrow [MDR]$$

We will look at each group in turn, to make sure we are acquainted with what they do in our processor.

16.2.1 Data Transfer Micro-Instructions

Data transfer microcodes copy a bit pattern from one location to another.

For example, $A \leftarrow [MDR]$ describes the micro-instruction that copies a bit pattern from the MDR into the A register.

16.2.2 ALU Micro-Instructions

ALU micro-instructions control the functionality of the ALU, they are used to make the ALU perform a logical or arithmetic operation.

For example, the operation to add the contents of the ALUx and the ALUy registers is described as $ALUr = [ALUx] + [ALUy]$.

16.2.3 Test Micro-Instructions

Test micro-instructions are used to allow assembly language programs to have conditional branches. For example, the assembly language instruction BEQ address would not be possible without the test micro-instruction to check the condition of the Z flag. Let's take a deeper look at that, here is the definition of the BEQ address instruction:

▶ $if(PSR(z) == 1)$

▶ $PC \leftarrow [IR(operand)]$

To perform the branch this is what happens:

▶ If the Z flag is set to 1, then the condition of the test micro-instruction is true and the following micro-instructions in the assembly instruction are executed, in this case the data movement micro-instruction to place a new value in the PC, performing the branch operation;

▶ If the Z flag is set to 0, then the condition of the test micro-instruction is false, and the following micro-instructions that make up the assembly instruction are ignored, so for this example the PC is never updated, and so no branch is executed.

So, without test micro-instructions it would be impossible for our assembly language programs to ever use any conditional branching, and so severely limit the usefulness of our processor.

16.2.4 Processor Control Micro-Instructions

Processor control micro-instructions do exactly that, they control the processor. There are not many processor control instructions. One example is the $PSR(E) = 1$ micro-instruction, which enables the interrupt mechanism by setting the E flag in the PSR. This micro-instruction is used in the INTE assembly instruction that we used in the example program in chapter 13.

16.3 Creating An Instruction

Now we have re-examined the different types of micro-instructions available to us, we can attempt to create our own instructions. Once we have created a new instruction we can write an assembly language program to make use of it.

16.3.1 Our First New Instruction

Our first example is relatively simple. We will write an instruction to transfer the value from the A register to the B register, and then increment the A register. The instruction can be written as:

▶ MOVE (A)+,B

To do this we first need to be able to describe our new instruction in terms of pre-conditions and post-conditions. Here are our pre-conditions and post-conditions:

▶ Pre-condition: The address of the value to be transferred has been placed in the A register;

► Post-condition: B will contain the transferred value, and the A register will be incremented.

We will give our new instruction the unused opcode of $F5 - we know that this opcode is unused because it is not listed in the basic instruction set quick reference in appendix B. Let us make an attempt at writing this instruction:

```
Opcode f5
Mnemonic "MOVE (A)+,B"
Description "MOVE (A) to B, post-increment A"
MAR<-[A]        * }
MDR<-[M[MAR]]   * } B = (A)
B<-[MDR]        * }
ALUx<-[A]       *   }
ALUr=[ALUx]+1   *   } A = A+1
A<-[ALUr]       *   }
```

This instruction is stored in \examples\chapter16\move_ab.mco.

This solution successfully loads into our processor when we use the 'file/open' dialog (don't forget to select the microcode filetype), and if we were to list all available micro-instructions now using the menu option 'processor/view opcodes', we can see our new instruction listed at opcode $F5. The next stage is to write a program to test our new instruction. This test program can be seen below, it is called move_ab.txt.

Here is the command to assemble the test program:

```
jasm -a move_ab.txt -m instruct.mco:move_ab.mco -o move_ab.jas
```

The option -m to the assembler tells it to use the instruction set provided by the following one or more micro-instruction files. If more than one micro-instruction file is to be used, then they are separated from each other by a colon, as seen with -m instruct.mco:move_ab.mco above.

```
* A program to use our new instruction MOVE (A)+,B

        ORG   0
        MOVE  #value,A    * initialize A with addr of value
```

```
          MOVE   #$00,B        * initialize B with 0
          MOVE   (A)+,B        * test our new instruction
          HALT                 * program complete
value     DC.W   $1234
```

When we assemble this program using our assembler program we have the finished machine code program as shown here. To test this program we can use the JASPer 'trace' option to step through each line of our program individually.

```
          # 0000 # * A program to use our new instruction MOVE (A)+,B
          # 0000 #
ORG $0000 # 0000 #          ORG   0
9004      # 0000 #          MOVE  #value,A    * initialize A with addr of value
9100      # 0001 #          MOVE  #$00,B      * initialize B with 0
F500      # 0002 #          MOVE  (A)+,B      * test our new instruction
F000      # 0003 #          HALT              * program complete
1234      # 0004 # value    DC.W  $1234
```

When we trace through the program we can see that initially the A register is set to $0004 (the address of the value to transfer) and the B register set to $0000, and after running our new instruction then we have A set to $0005 and B set to $1234, as we would have expected. Our new instruction has worked successfully.

16.3.2 Our Second New Instruction

For our second, more complex example, let us assume that we want to build the instruction to move a data value into a memory location, so that initializing variables in our programs doesn't take two instructions as we have seen so far. For example, we currently have to use instructions such as:

▶ MOVE #$00,A
▶ MOVE A,counter

Wouldn't it be better if we could create an instruction that could be used like:

▶ `MOVE #$00,counter`

To do this we again first need to be able to describe our new instruction in terms of pre-conditions and post-conditions.

▶ Pre-condition: The value to move into the variable `counter` located in memory consists of one byte (#$00), and is contained in the first operand to the instruction;

▶ Pre-condition: The address of the `counter` variable has a length of one word, and is contained in the second operand;

▶ Post-condition: The 8-bit value is transferred, sign extended, to the 16-bit counter variable, located in memory.

We can formally describe this instruction as:

▶ `MOVE #databyte,addrword`

This means that we wish to transfer the data byte from the initial operand into the word contained in the address which is the second operand. This particular form is used because it is clear to us the sizes and usage of the individual operands, and the assembler program can also understand this format. Note that this instruction will use two 16-bit machine codes, the first to contain the opcode and the first operand, the second to contain the second operand. Note that this allows us to use 16-bit addressing.

First of all, we need to write the micro-instruction to define our instruction. This instruction needs to:

▶ Read the next word in memory to obtain the address to store the data byte to;

▶ Perform the data movement;

▶ Ensure that the address of the next instruction to be executed is stored in the PC.

One possible solution, found on the CD at

`\examples\chapter16\move.mco`

is shown in here:

```
* An example instruction
*
Opcode f5
```

```
Mnemonic "MOVE #databyte,addrword"
Description "MOVE a data value into a memory location"
MAR<-[PC]           * move the address of the storage location into the MAR
INC<-[PC]           * } update PC to point to next address
PC<-[INC]           * } ready to fetch the next instruction
MDR<-[M[MAR]]       *   } read the address of the location
MAR<-[MDR]          *   } to move the data value into
ALUx<-[IR(operand)] * } move the IR(operand) into the MDR via the
MDR<-[ALUx]         * } ALUx (causes the value to be sign extended)
M[MAR]<-[MDR]       * Write the data value to the address
```

Note that for testing I've used the same opcode that we used in the previous example.

Again, we need to use a test program, stored in

\examples\chapter16\move.txt

to check that our new instruction performs as expected. The test program is shown in below.

```
* A program to use our new instruction
* MOVE #databyte,addrword

        ORG    $0

        MOVE   #$05,store   * move #$05 to store
        HALT                * done
store   DS.W   1
```

Once assembled, with the command

jasm -a move.txt -m instruct.mco:move.mco -o move.jas

we have the program listed below to run within our processor.

```
            # 0000 # * A program to use our new instruction
            # 0000 # * MOVE #databyte,addrword
            # 0000 #
ORG $0000   # 0000 #          ORG   $0
            # 0000 #
F505        # 0000 #          MOVE  #$05,store   * move #$05 to store
0003        #      #
F000        # 0002 #          HALT              * done
0000        # 0003 # store    DS.W  1
```

To check that our new instruction works, load both the test program and the new instruction into JASPer and trace through the program. You will find that after completing the new MOVE instruction the PC is pointing at the next instruction (the HALT) and on examining the contents of memory you will find that the memory location $0003 (containing the store variable) now contains $0005 as expected.

16.4 Building New Instruction Sets

The JASPer basic instruction set gives a typical set of instructions available to programmers within the Instruction Set Architecture, or ISA, of a typical 16-bit processor.

As it uses 16-bit instructions the basic instruction set is limited to an operand of only eight bits, this means that some instructions, like MOVE A,$12 are limited to only addressing the first 256 locations in memory or to moving 8-bit values to a register like in MOVE #$7F,A.

So far we have looked at how to build individual ISA level instructions using micro-instructions, but it is worth remembering that the complete instruction set contains not only instructions but also the definitions of the fetch and interrupt cycles too.

It is possible to avoid the limitation in the basic instruction set by implementing a full 32-bit instruction set, where operands can be 16 bits in size. It is actually quite simple to do this, by making slight modifications to individual instructions, but mainly by re-implementing the fetch cycle.

The major change is by removing the use of the IR(operand), as this is only 8 bits wide and the limiting factor in operand size. Instead, we can redefine the fetch cycle such that the first word is always the opcode (with a further 8 bits - the old IR(operand) as padding) and the second word is a mandatory 16-bit operand. To replace the IR(operand), we can decide to always store the operand in the MDR once it is fetched, in other words we can use the MDR as a 16-bit operand field.

We can then redefine the fetch cycle to be:

1 $MAR \leftarrow [PC]$
2 $INC \leftarrow [PC]$
3 $PC \leftarrow [INC]$
4 $MDR \leftarrow [M[MAR]]$
5 $IR \leftarrow [MDR]$
6 $MAR \leftarrow [PC]$
7 $INC \leftarrow [PC]$
8 $PC \leftarrow [INC]$
9 $MDR \leftarrow [M[MAR]]$
10 $CU \leftarrow [IR(opcode)]$

In this new fetch cycle, micro-instructions 1 to 5 fetch the instruction and place it in the IR, micro-instructions 6 to 9 fetch the operand and place it in the MDR and micro-instruction 10 transfers the opcode to the CU.

What are the effects of using such a fetch cycle in an advanced instruction set?

▶ All operations are at least 32 bits long;
▶ The whole address space can be addressed in a single operand;
▶ 16-bit data transfers can be easily undertaken;
▶ The fetch cycle takes longer to complete;
▶ Instructions that require no operand still have to have the operand word fetched, so wasting clock cycles;
▶ Programs written using this advanced instruction set use double the amount of memory used by programs written using the basic instruction set.

To see how instructions themselves have to be updated, here is the execution cycle for the `MOVE #$dataword,A` instruction, which moves a 16-bit immediate value into the A register:

▶ $A \leftarrow [MDR]$

We can see that the immediate value is transferred from the MDR, where it has been placed by the extended fetch cycle. In the basic instruction set the operand was placed in the 8-bit IR(operand) field.

To assemble our previous example program to use the advanced instruction set we can use the following command:

```
jasm -a move.txt -m advanced.mco:move.mco -o move2.jas
```

The output from this command can be seen below. Note the differences between this program and that produced for our second new instruction that used the basic JASPer instruction set. Basically, we can see that all instructions are now 32-bit, as the HALT instruction also has a 16-bit operand that contains $0000.

```
            # 0000 # * A program to use our new instruction
            # 0000 # * MOVE #databyte,addrword
            # 0000 #
ORG $0000   # 0000 #         ORG    $0
            # 0000 #
F505        # 0000 #         MOVE   #$05,store   * move #$05 to store
0004        #      #
F000        # 0002 #         HALT                * done
0000        #      #
0000        # 0004 # store   DS.W   1
```

Finally, it is worth noting that the cross compiler discussed in chapter 14 writes assembly instructions using this advanced instruction set.

CHAPTER SUMMARY

Building assembly instructions

▶ Be clear as to what you want your new instruction to do, and understand the micro-instructions available to you;

▶ Always test your new instruction within a short assembly language program, and step through it to ensure that your new instruction works successfully, and has no side-effects;

▶ Understand the limitations placed on you by the architecture, and ensure that your new instructions either bypasses these limitations or document the fact that they don't.

SELF TEST QUESTIONS

1 Write an instruction to perform the operation MOVE -A,B, which pre-decrements the A register prior to transferring the contents of the A register to the B register.

2 Write a test program to test your MOVE -A,B instruction.

3 Write an instruction that can move any 16-bit value into the A register, as in MOVW #$FFFF,A. Hint, your instruction will consist of two 16-bit words.

4 Write a test program to test your MOVW #dataword,A instruction.

EXERCISES

1 Write an instruction to perform the operation MOVE A+,B, which post-increments the A register after transferring the contents of the A register to the B register.

2 Write a test program to test your MOVE A+,B instruction.

3 Write an instruction to perform an operation like ADDW #$1234,A, which adds a 16-bit value to the A register.

4 Write a test program to test your instruction from exercise three.

The Control Unit

CHAPTER OVERVIEW

In this chapter we get to grips with the engine of the processor - the control unit. The use of the control unit is explained, together with how it uses sets of micro-instructions to implement each opcode and run the fetch-execute cycle.

This chapter includes:

▶ The concepts of a microcoded processor;
▶ A look inside the CU;
▶ How the CU decodes and executes instructions.

17.1 Introducing The Control Unit

We have looked at the construction of instruction sets using groups of micro-instructions to describe individual instructions. Now it is time to look inside the control unit of our processor to understand how machine instructions are actually run by the hardware.

It is now worth mentioning that our processor is an example of a well-known architecture known as a CISC architecture, where CISC stands for *Complex Instruction Set Computer*. It has a microcoded processor at its heart that runs individual micro-instructions to perform the execution of instructions and hence our programs.

Later on in chapter 19 we will compare this with another form of processor design known as the RISC architecture, where RISC stands for *Reduced Instruction Set Computer*.

Meanwhile, let us take another look at our simple processor, but this time concentrating on the hardware level again, showing the control signals between the control unit and the other various components that make up our processor system. This view of our processor is shown in figure 17.1.

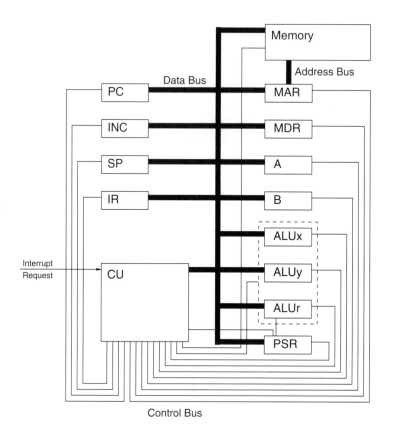

Figure 17.1 *The hardware level of our processor*

This view of our processor has been simplified by the removal of many control signals. As we saw in chapter 4 individual registers are controlled by the use of Output Enable and Clock control lines, whereas in figure 17.1 for simplicity only single control lines between the control unit and each component has been shown. However, even with this simple diagram, we can see that the other components within our system are controlled completely by the control unit, as all control lines emanate from the CU.

In fact, as we will see shortly, it is the CU that performs the extended fetch-execute cycle that we saw in chapter 13. To remind ourselves, here is the complete fetch-execute cycle for the basic instruction set, shown in the form of a high-level language algorithm:

```
while(true) {
    fetch_cycle;
    execute_cycle;
    if ((interrupts_enabled) && (interrupt_requested)) {
        save_PSR_on_stack;
        save_PC_on_stack;
        PC = address_of_interrupt_handling_routine;
    }
}
```

Let us imagine that we want to perform an operation such as MOVE A,B which copies the value held in the A register into the B register.

Firstly, the control unit has to perform a fetch cycle, which as we saw in chapter 8, within our processor is defined as follows:

1 $MAR \leftarrow [PC]$
2 $INC \leftarrow [PC]$
3 $PC \leftarrow [INC]$
4 $MDR \leftarrow [M[MAR]]$
5 $IR \leftarrow [MDR]$
6 $CU \leftarrow [IR(opcode)]$

If we were to look at the definition of the MOVE A,B instruction we would find that it is:

1 $MDR \leftarrow [A]$
2 $B \leftarrow [MDR]$

So, to complete this instruction, the CU needs to execute the six steps of the fetch cycle and the two steps of the execute cycle. How does it do this? Let us take the first of these micro-instructions and look at it in more detail.

The micro-instruction $MAR \leftarrow [PC]$ is a data movement, and we learned back in chapter 4 that it can be performed by setting the PC Output Enable to 1, setting the clock input of the MAR to 1 (known as *clocking* the MAR), and then back to 0, and then finally setting the PC Output Enable back to 0. This sequence of micro-operations can be written as:

$$PC_{en} = 1; MAR_c; PC_{en} = 0$$

where $PC_{en} = 1$ means set the output enable of the PC to 1, and MAR_c means clock the MAR. We can list these actions for all steps as shown in figure

17.2. This grid defines all of the operations required to perform the instruction MOVE A,B. Each line of signals is sent out on the control lines at each step to perform the actions required for that step, whether it is clocking particular registers or performing a memory access. Once a step is completed, the next step is executed.

Step	Register Output Enable											Register Clock											Memory		ALU Control Lines	ALU Data Bus Lines	Micro-instruction	Comments
	PC	INC	SP	IR	MAR	MDR	A	B	ALUx	ALUy	ALUr	PC	INC	SP	IR	MAR	MDR	A	B	ALUx	ALUy	ALUr	R/W	CS				
1	1	0	0	0	0	0	0	0	0	0	0	0	0	0	0	1	0	0	0	0	0	0	0	0	0	0	MAR ← [PC]	
2	1	0	0	0	0	0	0	0	0	0	0	0	1	0	0	0	0	0	0	0	0	0	0	0	0	0	INC ← [PC]	
3	0	1	0	0	0	0	0	0	0	0	0	1	0	0	0	0	0	0	0	0	0	0	0	0	0	0	PC ← [INC]	The fetch cycle
4	0	0	0	0	1	0	0	0	0	0	0	0	0	0	0	0	1	0	0	0	0	0	1	1	0	0	MDR ← [M[MAR]]	
5	0	0	0	0	0	1	0	0	0	0	0	0	0	0	1	0	0	0	0	0	0	0	0	0	0	0	IR ← [MDR]	
6	0	0	0	1	0	0	0	0	0	0	0	0	0	0	0	0	0	0	0	0	0	0	0	0	0	0	CU ← [IR(opcode)]	
7	0	0	0	0	0	0	1	0	0	0	0	0	0	0	0	0	1	0	0	0	0	0	0	0	0	0	MDR ← [A]	The execute cycle
8	0	0	0	0	0	1	0	0	0	0	0	0	0	0	0	0	0	0	1	0	0	0	0	0	0	0	B ← [MDR]	

Figure 17.2 *The instruction defined at the hardware level*

It is worth noting that steps one and two could be executed concurrently, as they both consist of a register taking the value from the data bus placed there by the PC.

17.2 Inside The Control Unit

Now we have a direct link between the execution of our program and the enabling and clocking of individual registers at the hardware level.

However, we still need to define how the CU itself works, and we will move on to that now by introducing the internal structure of the CU, as shown in figure 17.3.

As you can see, inside the CU we have a device that looks very much like our processor, but in miniature. In fact this device works in a similar fashion to the overall processor, the difference being that this level is aimed entirely at running individual instructions. Each instruction has been allocated a *microprogram*, which is the sequence of micro-instructions that execute that instruction.

The control unit has a *micromemory* for storing all the micro-instructions that make up individual instructions (as we saw for just one instruction in figure 17.2), it has a *microMAR* and a *microMDR* to access this memory, and it has a *microPC* to step through the micro-instructions that make up a particular instruction. The *microCU* is the engine of the CU. This is a complex circuit that is built from gate logic as we saw back in chapter 3. There is not another tiny control unit inside the microCU - we are now at the lowest level of our processor. We won't take a look inside the microCU (it will be implemented as gate logic), instead we will focus on what it does.

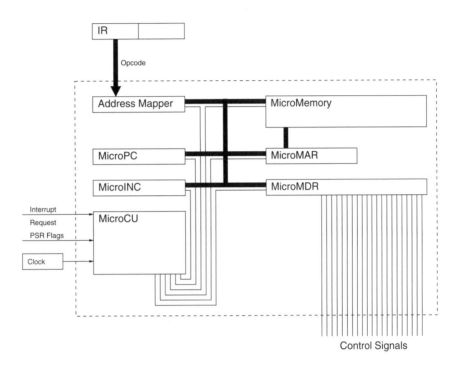

Figure 17.3   *Inside the control unit*

We will now work through what the CU does to process an instruction.

▶ Firstly, the opcode is passed into the CU from the IR;

▶ The address mapper is used to find the start address of the microprogram for this opcode in the micromemory, and the address is accessed from the micromemory by the use of the microMAR;

▶ The first micro-instruction is now in the microMDR and it is now important to note the difference between what we've seen of the MDR and the functionality of this microMDR. The microMDR is a very wide register - this consists of a number of bits that the microCU uses to control the processor, whereas the rest, which could be up to 200 bits on real processors, are the control signals that we saw emanating from the control unit back in figure 17.1.

► The microcontrol unit uses values from the microMDR and the PSR flag values to choose where to get the next micro-instruction to run, which could be from the next micromemory location, or to run a different cycle, or to run a new microprogram for a different opcode;

► Once the microprogram for a given instruction has been executed then the CU runs the next fetch cycle, which itself consists of just another microprogram stored in the micromemory.

This is a very powerful structure. It means that we can load different instruction sets into our processor to model different instruction set architectures. This idea was first proposed in the 1950s by Maurice Wilkes (a description can be found in [RH00]), and has been in use since the 1960s. It can be found still in processors today. Instruction sets that can be loaded into a processor have been labelled *firmware*, to emphasize their position between hardware and software.

We started many chapters ago by introducing simple electronic circuitry, and seeing how complex useful circuits could be built. From there we saw how we could write programs based on our newly built processor. Finally, we have now moved back down to the hardware level to see how our processor, at the electronic level, actually executes our programs.

CHAPTER SUMMARY

The concept of a microcoded processor

► A microcoded processor has its instruction set in firmware;

► The firmware can be updated, even to the extent that the complete instruction set is changed.

The work of the CU

► The CU fetches and executes all instructions - it is the engine of the processor;

► The individual micro-instructions that perform a single instruction are fetched in turn from a micromemory and control signals to perform that micro-instruction are placed on the control bus;

► The fetch and interrupt sequences of micro-instructions are stored in the micromemory just like that of every other instruction;

SELF TEST QUESTIONS

1 For the instruction POP A, write down the complete list of micro-instructions that are executed, and then specify the instruction at the hardware level in a table like figure 17.2.

2 For the instruction AND addr,A, write down the complete list of micro-instructions that are executed, and then specify the instruction at the hardware level in a table like figure 17.2.

EXERCISES

1 For the instruction PUSH A, write down the complete list of micro-instructions that are executed, and then specify the instruction at the hardware level.

2 For the instruction NOT (B), write down the complete list of micro-instructions that are executed, and then specify the instruction at the hardware level.

3 For the interrupt mechanism, write down the complete list of micro-instructions that are executed, and then specify the cycle at the hardware level.

Extending The Hardware

In the final chapter within this section we discuss the possible extensions to our basic design that we could make.

This chapter includes:

▶ Adding more general purpose registers.
▶ Implementing further ALU functions;
▶ The implementation of a supervisor mode, and its implications for creating an operating system;
▶ Implications on the instruction set.

18.1 Introduction

I will discuss more wide-ranging architectural issues in chapter 19. In the meanwhile it is interesting to look at some of the simple 'tweaks' we could make to our processor design and see what effects they could have on our processor.

18.2 Adding More General Purpose Registers

One thing that you will have already found while writing programs for our simple processor, is that the limitation of only two general purpose registers causes you to have to think more ingeniously! If a subroutine makes use of three or more variables, then it is currently impossible to store them in the general purpose registers available to you, instead you have to either store the variables in named memory locations all the time, or make heavy use of the stack (which is still in memory). This means our program executes more slowly, as memory accesses could be an order of magnitude (or more) slower than the use of register transfers.

18.2.1 The Origins Of Limiting General Purpose Registers

Early processors were limited in the number of general purpose registers they had available to them purely because they had to be built from vacuum tubes that failed very often. More general purpose registers meant more vacuum tubes, which meant the computer system needed more maintenance work and hence was less available for processing.

This limitation is no longer with us as we now build our general purpose registers from much more reliable components. The trend today is to have many general purpose registers in a processor and we will look at this in chapter 19.

18.2.2 The Implications Of Adding Extra General Purpose Registers To JASPer

Getting back to our simple processor, yes, we could quite simply add more registers to our processor design, however this would have a number of implications.

Firstly, let us imagine that we have added two more general purpose registers. We will call them register C and register D. To build these in to our design we would have to:

► Add two copies of our register circuit to our processor design;
► Update the CU such that the two new registers are controlled - effectively we would have had to expand the contents of the micromemory, as described in chapter 17;
► This would have the effect of adding in many more data movement operations to our processor to cope with data movements to and from the new registers.

If the memory usage in our micromemory was already high, then by adding these extra general purpose registers we may also need to increase the size of our micromemory.

The largest impact on adding extra general purpose registers is actually on the design of the instruction set. For example, if we wanted to have the same functionality for our new general purpose registers as our existing general purpose registers then we would have to add at least 87 instructions per general purpose register to our instruction set, to have instructions available to us like:

▶ `ADD #data,C`

▶ `MOVE C,addr`

▶ `JSR C`

However, the number of instructions we can have in a JASP instruction set is limited by the width of the opcode field, and so we can only have a maximum of 256 instructions in an instruction set. The standard instruction set already has over 170 instructions, and so there is just enough room to add instructions for one extra general purpose register, but certainly not enough for two.

A possible compromise might be to reduce the number of addressing modes used in the standard instruction set to reduce the number of instructions required to use each additional general purpose register.

NOTES

An instruction format that uses bits in the opcode field to specify registers is described for the hypothetical microprocessor NeMiSyS in [SACR91].

A further compromise might be to use the newer general purpose registers with only a limited number of instructions, but that limitation means that a programmer would have to remember to use individual general purpose registers with different instructions - and so negating any usefulness of this sort of limited general purpose register.

In reality, rather than limit instructions in this way, modern processors actually have larger opcode fields with a number of bits within the field to represent which general purpose registers to use with the instruction, therefore a single instruction can be used with any general purpose registers available on the processor.

18.3 Increasing ALU Functionality

Like adding general purpose registers, increasing ALU functionality seems like something we can do quite easily, and yet there are a number of fundamental issues to consider.

Actually, over the years that JASPer has been in use, the ALU *has* increased in functionality. Originally it didn't perform any multiplication, division or remainder operations, but these functions were added relatively recently to the ALU. These operations increase dramatically the amount of logic circuitry required, but this increase in complexity is easily counterbalanced by the greater flexibility in functionality.

The ALU however is now very close to a key limit of the ALU, in that the ALU control code is only four bits wide, limiting the number of ALU functions to 16. Currently there are 15 ALU functions, leaving only one free control code. If we wanted to extensively increase ALU functionality we would have to increase the size of the ALU control code, which is not a major issue in itself, but to do this we would need to update the micromemory of the control unit and increase the complexity of the ALU control signal decoder.

What further functionality could we actually add? The only key type of arithmetic and logical operations that are not included in the ALU of our simple processor is a set of floating point functions. However, adding floating point functionality to our simple processor would be a huge undertaking as it would involve very complex circuitry. Early microprocessors didn't include floating point functionality because as it required such a large number of transistors it couldn't be fitted onboard the processor. Instead in those days computer systems used floating point co-processors - whole chips dedicated to floating point only. These days modern processors do include floating point functionality. A large percentage of the transistors on board modern processors are dedicated to providing floating point functions.

18.4 The Use Of A Supervisor Mode

Firstly, I'll explain what is meant by a supervisor mode, and then we can see if it would be appropriate to add this feature into our simple processor.

Our simple processor currently runs in a single *state*, in that all programs can use all features of the processor. In larger computer systems, where you would make use of an operating system, this would be a severe limitation. The first program to cause problems, for example by locking up all system resources, would stop the whole computer system from working.

NOTES

For a detailed discussion of the supervisor mode, see [Cle00].

The solution to this is that modern processors can be run in any one of a set of different states, typically the two states *user mode* and *supervisor mode* (sometimes known as the *privileged mode*). Generally, operating systems, or their junior siblings, monitors, would make use of privileged mode. Individual programs run by the operating system would then make use of user mode (allowing the user program to run a safer subset of all possible instructions, or by limiting resource access), and if a program in user mode failed in some way, then the operating system could recover rather than causing the whole computer system to fail. Generally, a user program communicates with the operating system via the interrupt mechanism by using TRAP calls.

Within processors that have multiple modes, a bit within the PSR, known as the supervisor bit is used to indicate whether the processor is in user mode or supervisor mode.

Now we have examined the principles behind supervisor mode, let us see what we would have to do to our simple processor to build in a supervisor mode.

Firstly, the easiest part of adding a supervisor mode would be to add an S flag into the PSR to store the supervisor bit. After that, updating our processor gets a little trickier. We would probably have to update the whole interrupt mechanism to ensure that user mode programs couldn't control certain parts of the hardware, such as the I/O devices.

All things being equal, adding a supervisor mode into our processor is probably overkill given the severe limitations of what our processor can actually do. Supervisor modes are most useful in multi-user or multi-tasking situations, neither of which our processor is designed to do. Adding a supervisor mode into our design would give us few practical benefits, and would make the design more complex than it needs to be.

18.5 Adding Instructions To The Instruction Set

As we have already seen when we discussed the addition of extra general purpose registers, the standard instruction set contains around 170 of a maximum of 256 instructions. This leaves quite a large number of possible instructions that we could implement, as we discussed back in chapter 16. Apart from the limitation on the maximum number of instructions that we could use at any one time, writing new instructions has no further implications on the use of our simple processor.

It is interesting to see how some of the features we have discussed would be rather simple to implement, while others actually have far reaching consequences. In chapter 19 we will look at some of the decisions made by processor designers when building their processors.

CHAPTER SUMMARY

More general purpose registers

▶ It would be easy to add further registers to our processor;

▶ We would have to update the CU to accommodate extra control signals being required;

▶ Limitations with the instruction set however would mean that we would have to completely change the format of our instruction set.

Further ALU functions

▶ We could add further ALU functions quite easily, but we would have to increase the width of the ALU control code;

▶ However, adding floating point support would make our processor much more complex.

A supervisor mode

▶ A supervisor bit could be added to the PSR, and updates added to the CU to use a supervisor mode;

▶ However, our simple processor would gain little benefit from such a mode.

Implications on the instruction set

▶ The instruction set currently has over 80 free opcodes, and therefore new instructions could be added quite easily.

Part IV

The Real World

In this final section we take a look at the features of real microprocessors and point out the similarities they share with our simple processor.

CISC and RISC Architectures: An Overview

This chapter discusses the rise of the CISC architecture and the RISC architecture; it then discusses modern hybrid processor architectures.

This chapter includes:

▶ A discussion of RISC and CISC processors;
▶ A brief comparison of RISC and CISC;
▶ Modern hybrid processors.

19.1 CISC Processors

As I mentioned in chapter 17, our simple processor is an example of a *CISC*, *Complex Instruction Set Computer*, processor. CISC processors have been with us since the dawn of the electronic computer, even if the term CISC hasn't.

Generally, as they were initially built using vacuum tube components that often failed, CISC processors began life with a very limited number of registers, and a simple hardwired control unit. Over time, newer more reliable technologies were used, leading to more complex processor designs. To give these newer complex processors greater flexibility the control unit was switched from a hardware design to a microcoded control unit similar to what we saw in chapter 17, making it possible to update instruction sets using firmware. Instruction sets grew more complex to better utilize these new processors.

However, as technologies changed, philosophies didn't. The trend was to build more and more complex processors, with very complicated instruction sets, and so it was time for a paradigm shift.

19.2 RISC Processors

A group of individuals around the globe began to see this level of complexity in processors as self-defeating. It was leading to instruction sets that were difficult to understand and use, which in turn lead to difficulties in writing compilers for such an architecture, which lead to less efficient programs.

By the 1980s, a back-to-basics approach was mooted, whereby a simpler processor design could actually lead to less power hungry and higher performance processors.

This new architecture included as its key features:

▶ More general purpose registers, typically 32;

▶ A limited, uniform, and faster instruction set;

▶ Very limited addressing modes;

▶ Hardware compiler support;

▶ A hardwired control unit.

NOTES

Patterson, in league with another major RISC pioneer, John Hennessy, has written two major texts on the subject of computer architecture focusing inevitably on the RISC architecture, [PH98] and [HP02].

This approach was termed the RISC, Reduced Instruction Set Computer, architecture by one of the leading RISC pioneers, David Patterson. He also coined the term CISC, as a thinly veiled jibe against the complex architectures of the time.

The RISC philosophy is best explained by referring to the four design principles described by Hennessy and Patterson in [PH98]:

▶ *Simplicity favours regularity.* If we were to look at the instruction set of our simple processor, we would find instructions that took zero, one, two or three operands. It is even possible to design instructions that make use of even more operands, and this is relatively easy to do given that our processor has a microcoded control unit. If we were to use the RISC philosophy it makes sense to use the simplest hardwired control unit possible, and this leads us into needing a very regular instruction set. Most RISC instruction sets have this level of regularity. For example, rather than having ADD instructions that can have different numbers of operands (depending on the addressing modes), all ADD instructions on a RISC processor will always take the same number of operands;

▶ *Smaller is faster*. Provide the hardware to fulfil the requirements of the processor. Don't fall into the trap of adding hardware features that are rarely used, they add significant complexity with very little gain;

▶ *Good design demands good compromises*. On the other hand, don't try to fit all instructions into exactly the same format if this doesn't make sense. Many RISC instruction sets have types of instructions (arithmetic, data transfer) that have their own instruction format, possibly not the simplest format but the most pragmatic when viewed with the other design principles;

▶ *Make the common case fast*. Even the most complex program written for our simple processor will use very few instructions, the RISC approach would optimize for these broad types of instructions, at the expense of much less used instructions.

19.3 Comparing RISC To CISC

A comparison of the CISC and RISC design philosophies leads to a list of classical differences in architectural features.

CISC	RISC
Typically, a small number of general purpose registers	Typically many (e.g. 32) general purpose registers
Microcoded control unit	Hardwired control unit
Large number of instructions	Smaller number of instructions
Many addressing modes	Smaller number of addressing modes
Slow bulky instructions	Faster sleeker instructions
Needs less instructions per high-level function	Needs more instructions per high-level function

Table 19.1 *The classical differences between CISC and RISC*

These classical differences between the CISC and RISC approaches are shown in table 19.1. In reality, the lines between CISC and RISC architectures are much more blurred and we'll examine some of these factors in a moment.

19.3.1 Number Of Registers

Although we tend to think of RISC processors having more general purpose registers, in reality typical RISC and CISC designs these days tend to have roughly similar numbers. The typical number of registers in modern processors is 32.

19.3.2 Format Of The Control Unit

Due to its simpler design, the control unit of a RISC processor is hardwired.

CISC designs tend to use many different types of instruction, many addressing modes, etc. This leads to the requirement of a much more complex control unit for which a microcoded control unit is most appropriate. With complex instruction sets it is more likely that the instruction set designer will make mistakes. By using a microcoded control unit these mistakes can be repaired simply by replacing the instruction set in firmware.

19.3.3 Addressing Modes

RISC processors typically use far less addressing modes than their CISC counterparts. For example, within typical RISC processors the only instructions that are allowed to reference memory locations are LOAD and STORE instructions, which often leads this form of design to be known as a *load/store architecture*. This limitation immediately removes addressing modes such as memory indirect addressing. The most common forms of addressing used by RISC architectures are register addressing, displacement addressing, immediate addressing, and relative addressing.

19.3.4 Instruction Types And Functionality

The simpler nature of the RISC approach vastly simplifies the instruction set. As only LOAD and STORE instructions are used to reference memory, all other instructions only need to make use of the general purpose registers on the processor. This approach tends to be faster per instruction, but typically RISC programs are a little longer than the equivalent CISC program.

In comparison, CISC instruction sets are typically far more complex than their RISC counterparts, using many more addressing modes.

NOTES

See [TT00] and [NG99] for descriptions of the Intel processors and their competitors. [HVZ02] describes a number of processor families including the Intel family. The PowerPC, a competitor to the Intel family with a RISC core is briefly described in [Cri01]. [CCW02] includes a section that describes how to build your own Intel-based PC system.

DEFINITION

Backwardly compatible : A processor that will run programs written for processors with earlier versions of the instruction set architecture family.

19.4 Modern Hybrid Processors

The debate over the merits of CISC versus RISC architectures raged for a number of years, leading to CISC designs being seen as monolithic and anti-quated. However, the majority of today's processors are now a hybrid of both forms of architecture - they implement the best features of both classes of processor architectures.

The Intel Pentium Pro and its derivatives are a case in point. It's roots lie firmly in the CISC camp, and yet it has a RISC core to provide further speed benefits. This processor actually converts the CISC instructions from the instruction set architecture level into RISC instructions and then runs them internally in the RISC core. This does add overheads, but the overall gains make this process worthwhile.

This hybrid approach brings the benefits of the RISC architecture to the largest family of processors available on the planet, the Intel X86 range, while ensuring that it remains *backwardly compatible* and so able to run the many millions of programs that have been written to use this architectural family.

Modern processors are a hybrid of both RISC and CISC architectures, using the best of each architecture where it is most appropriate. In the next, and final, chapter we will investigate further features used by modern processors to speed up program execution.

CHAPTER SUMMARY

RISC and CISC processors

▶ CISC processors emerged in the 1940s;

▶ RISC processors emerged in the 1980s;

▶ RISC processors follow four key rules - simplicity favours regularity, smaller is faster, good design demands good compromises and make the common case fast;

▶ Traditionally, RISC processors are seen to have more registers than their CISC counterpart;

▶ Traditionally, RISC processors are seen to have less addressing modes, less instructions and faster instructions than their CISC counterpart;

▶ CISC processors traditionally have a microcoded CU, while RISC processors have a hardwired CU.

Modern hybrid processors

▶ The reality is that most modern processors have features of both classical RISC and CISC designs;

▶ A hybrid approach brings the benefits of a faster RISC architecture, while maintaining the backward compatibility with older CISC processors, as required by the user community.

Advanced Architecture Features

This final chapter looks at some of the features available in modern processors. All processors have something like our simple processor as their ancestor but are changed out of all recognition by the use of these advanced features to produce more powerful processors.

This chapter includes:

▶ Issues of increasing clock speeds;
▶ The use of specialized instructions;
▶ The use of caches;
▶ An introduction to pipelining;
▶ An introduction to superscalar architectures;
▶ An introduction to multiprocessor systems.

20.1 Introduction

There is a very good reason why computer architectures have moved on from something like our simple processor. It's not very powerful in its current design, and would soon be beaten by competitors, because what we mostly want from a processor in our modern world is to be able to run our programs as fast as possible, as cheaply as possible.

Most microprocessors in use today are much removed from our simple processor; they are much more complex in many different ways. However, it is important to realize that all von Neumann processors that you use in your mobile phone, your microwave, and indeed in your desktop computer, are based on exactly the same principles as have been demonstrated by our simple processor throughout this text.

All of the real processors that you make use of use a number of *advanced architectural features* in order to run your programs faster. This chapter will look at some of these features.

20.2 Increasing Clock Speed

At first sight it would seem that the easiest way to speed up a processor is to increase the clock speed. To some extent this can be the case, but there are limits to how fast we can clock any processor, due to the latency of the circuitry within our processor. The other issue with increasing the clock speed of our processor is that it will tend to require more power, and it will generate more heat which your system will have to dissipate by using heat sinks, fans or a combination of both.

NOTES

Embedded systems issues are described in [HVZ02].

The use of more power is a major issue for processor designers, as the trend today is towards embedded processors. An embedded processor, such as in a laptop or a mobile phone, needs to use as little power as possible otherwise the device would need batteries the size of small bricks! RISC processors, due to their simpler design (they can contain as little as a quarter of the number of transistors of equivalent CISC designs) are used heavily in the embedded processor market due to their lower power consumption.

It is worth noting that each new generation of processor tends to run at higher clock speeds, as each design pushes the boundaries of manufacture that little bit extra to make each design more power efficient than before. Clock speeds move so quickly (no pun intended) that if I were to include here the clock speeds of typical standard desktop PC processors, this sentence would be out of date before you had this text in your hands.

20.3 Adding Specialized Instructions

Another feature used by modern processors is the use of specialized instructions within the instruction set to deal with particular types of data. Multimedia data is a case in point, where many megabytes of data can make up a single graphic image or sound file.

Multimedia data tends to be a little different to, say, that entered from your keyboard and we can process it differently. So far we have only seen a form of instruction in our simple processor known as *SISD* (*Single Instruction Single Data*) instructions. With multimedia data, for example a graphic image, we can often process that data using a form of instruction known as a *SIMD* (*Single Instruction Multiple Data*) instruction, which can process the data much faster than using SISD instructions. Basically it means that one single instruction can process a larger amount of data.

NOTES

Intel claimed that the initials MMX didn't stand for anything, but they are widely known as the MultiMedia eXtensions.

Intel added a set of 57 specialized instructions known as the *MMX* (*MultiMedia eXtensions*) to its Pentium design in 1997, and added another set of specialized instructions, the *SSE* (Streaming SIMD extensions) set, to the Pentium III a few years later. The SSE set was a further 70 instructions to deal with multimedia data.

Although RISC instruction sets have grown over the years, adding sets of complex instructions for very specialized uses runs counter to the RISC philosophy and so you are unlikely to find such highly specialized instructions on RISC processors.

20.4 Moving Memory Into Our Processor

One particular limit to the use of our simple processor at the moment is that many instructions require a memory access. Compared to something like a data movement operation, a memory access is relatively slow. One way in which to speed up our processor would be to place some very fast memory actually inside our processor. This technique is called *cache memory*. Cache memory is faster than, but also more expensive than, conventional memory.

The use of cache memory can give us the impression that all of our memory is as fast as cache memory. We would also have to implement a method by which we place data from memory into the cache memory, but we are helped by the fact that our programs when stored in memory exhibit the properties of both *spatial locality* and *temporal locality*. Spatial locality means that our program in memory contains instructions and data that are close to each other - our program is unlikely to be spread in small pockets all over memory. With temporal locality, we mean that we are very likely to use instructions and data nearby to what we have just made use of - again, we are unlikely to use instructions placed in separate parts of memory, unless our program is the worst piece of spaghetti code ever written!

In fact, there are two accepted levels of cache memory, known as *level one*, and *level two* cache memory. Level one cache memory is situated actually on the processor chip, which is the best location for cache memory, as well as being the most expensive form of memory, and so most modern processors limit level one cache memory to something like 16 kilobytes, where a kilobyte (Kb) is 1024 bytes. Level two caches mostly reside in special chips associated with the processor chip, although it is not uncommon for level two caches to also sit on the same chip as the processor these days. Level two caches are generally larger than level one caches with sizes typically between 256Kb to 512Kb.

Cache memory does tend to be more expensive than main memory, and so there is a tradeoff between speed and cost. This is why we don't build systems that only make use of faster cache memory.

The use of cache memory can give a major speed increase in program execution, as we can greatly reduce the delays caused by having to access memory. All modern processor systems make use of both level one and level two caches.

20.5 Running More Instructions Per Clock Cycle

Another key way to build more powerful processors is to structure them such that they can run more instructions per clock cycle.

Typical instructions for our simple processor show that the average time to fetch and execute a typical instruction from the default instruction set is something like 12 clock cycles if we assume that each micro-instruction takes one clock cycle to complete. In other words we can run something like 0.08 instructions per clock cycle. This is fine for our simple processor that is designed to show us the inner workings of processors, but it could hardly be termed efficient.

By revising our design we could manage to run something like one instruction per clock cycle, or even better. At first it seems inconceivable that we could run multiple instructions per clock cycle, but it can be done. To investigate this we need to examine *pipelining* and *superscalar architectures*.

20.5.1 Pipelining

NOTES

For a complete pipelined example, see [PH98].

The implementation of pipelining involves dividing up the functional aspects of the processor into distinct stages, where each stage is designed to perform its function in one clock cycle and pass data on to the next stage.

Modern processors have in the order of five or more stages. For example, the typical RISC stages are:

▶ Instruction fetch;
▶ Instruction decode;
▶ Instruction execution;
▶ Memory access;

▶ Write back.

Each instruction still has to go through each of these stages sequentially, and assuming each stage takes one clock cycle then each instruction will still take five clock cycles to complete. However, the use of a pipeline allows parallelism, in that it means that once the first instruction has moved on to the second stage of the pipeline, a second instruction can be in the first stage of the pipeline. At it's most efficient, this means that this pipelined approach can complete an instruction every clock cycle - which is a major increase on throughput to the non-pipelined approach.

Some processors have many pipeline stages, eight or over, but as the number of stages are increased, it becomes more complex to use them efficiently.

There are particular issues with pipelining when it is impossible to make use of them efficiently, but that is beyond the scope of this text.

NOTES

For further information on pipelining and superscalar architectures, see [PH98], [HP02] or the more advanced text [SFK97].

20.5.2 Superscalar Architecture

The next step from the use of pipelining is the use of superscalar architectures. This purely means that a processor with a superscalar architecture has duplicate components within it. By duplicating the pipelines such that a processor has two or more pipelines the processor can achieve greater throughput of instructions. Again, it is important to note that this further complexity brings its own problems, and it is very difficult to keep a superscalar architecture running as efficiently as possible.

It is important to note that a superscalar processor still conforms to a von Neumann architecture.

NOTES

A useful introduction to parallel architectures is [Cha96], while [Tan99] dedicates a complete chapter to the issues of parallel computer architectures.

20.6 Adding More Processors

Finally, another way to increase the power of our computer system is to add more processors. This is, in a sense, similar to superscalar architectures, albeit instead of trying to build very complex processors, a computer system can make use of multiple simpler designed processors.

NOTES

See [HP02] for a detailed discussion on multiprocessor systems.

This approach still gives concurrency, but in a different level of granularity to the superscalar approach. The use of more processors in systems is a very popular solution, as it means that off the shelf processors can be used to give very powerful computing power to a system. Most large servers these days have multiple processors. In this configuration, the problems of concurrency have to be solved by the operating systems designers as opposed to the processor architects.

20.7 Full Circle

Modern processors, at their heart, perform the same functions as our simple processor. They still conform to the structure of the von Neumann architecture, as described nearly fifty years ago [vN00].

For all their advanced features, the core of our modern processors would be instantly recognizable to the likes of Alan Turing and John von Neumann.

CHAPTER SUMMARY

Clock speeds

▶ Increased speed means increased power requirements and increased heat;

▶ Embedded systems require low power requirements.

Specialized instructions

▶ SIMD instructions are proving popular for multimedia data.

Caches

▶ The use of cache memory has been popular for many years now - all modern processors make use of cache memory;

▶ Cache memory is possible due to the fact that programs have the properties of spatial and temporal locality.

Pipelining

▶ Pipelining means dividing the fetch-execute process into distinct stages that can be run concurrently;

▶ All modern processors use pipelining to increase instruction throughput;

▶ Five to eight pipelined stages are now common.

Superscalar architectures

▶ A superscalar architecture duplicates components within the processor to increase the number of pipelines;

▶ Increasing the number of pipelines again increase throughput.

Multiprocessor systems

▶ A much lower level of granularity of concurrency is given by multiprocessor systems;

▶ These type of systems are very popular because they can use off the shelf processors - most large servers today have multiple processors within them.

Part V

Appendices

The JASP Toolkit

A.1 Introducing JASP

The JASP toolkit is based around the design of a simple processor named JASP - *Just Another Simulated Processor*. A diagram of this processor is shown in figure A.1.

The original JASP design was by William Henderson of the School of Informatics, Northumbria University.

JASP consists of a small set of registers, a microcoded control unit and an ALU. This processor is connected to a memory to form a rudimentary computer system.

JASP is deliberately meant to be simple technology - containing the simplest elements from a microcoded processor. JASP is designed as an educational tool to demonstrate fundamental concepts in a generic way, so allowing students to gain an understanding of them prior to transferring to 'real world' processors.

Within the toolkit we have two simulations of the JASP processor, the main one being JASPer (*Just Another Simulated Processor emulator*), the second being Aspen (*Another Simulated Processor emulation*). The toolkit also contains an assortment of useful tools to aid the use of the processor simulators.

The set of tools includes:

- ▶ *JASPer* - the main simulated processor, JASPer will run on Windows 95 and above;
- ▶ *Aspen* - a command-line version of JASPer that can be used with DOS or Linux;
- ▶ *The JASP cross-assembler* - a cross-assembler, written in Perl, that assembles programs for the JASP architecture. The assembler should work on any platform with a Perl installation, but it has been tested under DOS and Linux only;

▶ *The JASP C−− cross-compiler* - a cross-compiler for the JASP architecture. It can be used with DOS or Linux;

▶ The basic and advanced JASP instruction sets;

▶ Two software libraries, for use with each instruction set.

A reference to the functionality of the JASP processor is given below, followed by descriptions of each tool in the toolkit.

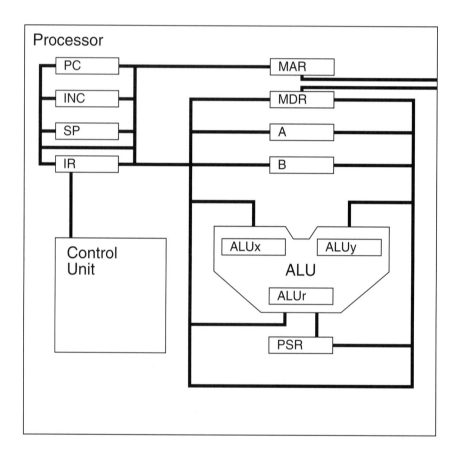

Figure A.1 *The JASP processor*

A.1.1 Obtaining The JASP Toolkit

All the tools within the JASP toolkit are copyright Mark Burrell, except for the C−− cross-compiler which is copyright David Harrison.

The authors of this toolkit, and the distributors, cannot accept responsibility for any disruption, damage and/or loss to your data or computer system that may occur while using this package. This is free software and comes with no warranty.

To obtain a copy of the JASP toolkit go to this website:

▶ http://www.palgrave.com/science/computing/burrell/

Additionally, a copy of the JASP toolkit is available on the accompanying CD.

While the authors hold copyright on all JASP executables and documentation, it may be freely distributed at no cost (excluding minimal expenses), providing that it is distributed intact, and not subsumed into any other work.

A.1.2 Installing The JASP Toolkit

The JASP toolkit has various tools, some of which work in Microsoft Windows, while others work on Linux systems. The installation instructions for each environment are given below.

Refer to the `readme.txt` file within the toolkit for a detailed description of each file, and how it can be used.

Installing On Windows

The JASP toolkit is distributed as a zipped archive, and you need to unzip this archive into a directory on your computer. None of the JASP tools make use of the Windows registry, and so no further installation is necessary, apart from you may set up any desktop icons or menu options as you prefer.

You can additionally set up an environment variable called `JASP`, and update your path as listed below - but this is only really required if you intend to make use of the JASP assembler or Aspen.

If you do wish to update your path and use the `JASP` environment variable then place the following lines in your `autoexec.bat` file (this assumes you have installed the JASP toolkit at the location `c:\jasp\`):

```
set path=%path%;c:\jasp\
```

```
set JASP=c:\jasp\
```

Installing on Linux

Once again, unzip the archive into a directory on your computer - something like ~/jasp.

As all the tools for Linux are command-line driven, it makes sense to set up the path and the JASP environment. You may need to do this differently, depending on your flavour of Linux, but on my system, using the bash shell, all I need to do is update .bash_profile with:

```
PATH="$PATH:~/jasp/"

export JASP=~/jasp/
```

Additionally, to make the assembler work successfully, you will need to ensure that the first line of the jasm.pl program uses the correct location for Perl on your system. You may also want to set up a logical file to point to the jasm.pl like this:

```
cd $JASP
ln -s jasm.pl jasm
```

A.2 The JASP Processor - A Reference

This section covers:

▶ A description of the function of each register;

▶ The micro-instructions understood by the JASP control unit;

▶ A description of the memory map, including a description of the memory-mapped peripherals;

▶ The interrupt mechanism;

▶ The file formats used by JASP for both instruction sets and machine code.

A.2.1 Registers

The processor registers are listed in table A.1.

Register	Width (bits)	Description
PC	16	Program counter - *is used to keep track of the memory address storing the next instruction to be executed*
INC	16	Incrementer - *is used to add one to the value held in the PC, something that needs to occur very often in most programs. Using the incrementer (effectively as a specialist register) is faster than using the ALU for this particular task, and importantly does not affect the PSR flags*
A	16	General Register A - *is the first of two general purpose registers, programmers can use the general purpose registers to store program bit patterns*
B	16	General Register B - *is the second of the two general purpose registers*
MAR	16	Memory Address Register - *is used as a specialist register to store the address of the memory location that we need to read from or write to*
MDR	16	Memory Data Register - *is used as a specialist register to store the data that we have just read from memory or need to write to memory*
IR	16	Instruction Register - *is the specialist register where we store the instruction once it has been fetched from memory*
ALUx	16	Arithmetic Logic Unit X Register *is the first of two specialist registers where we store bit patterns to be used in ALU operations*
ALUy	16	Arithmetic Logic Unit Y Register *is the second of two specialist registers where we store bit patterns to be used in ALU operations*
ALUr	16	Arithmetic Logic Unit Result Register *is the specialist register where the result from an ALU operation is stored*
SP	16	Stack Pointer - *is the specialist register used to store the address of the top of the stack held in memory*
PSR	16	Processor Status Register - *is where we store information about the state of the processor, including the state of the last ALU operation*

Table A.1 *Processor registers*

A.2.2 Micro-Instructions

The JASP processor has a micro-programmed control unit, where each machine code instruction is defined as a sequence of micro-instructions known as a micro-program. These micro-programs are used by the control unit to execute individual instructions.

These micro-programs can be grouped together in an instruction set file, sometimes referred to as a microcode file. Two instruction set are distributed with the JASP toolkit, and it is a simple process to define and use new instructions.

All the micro-instructions that are recognized by the processor can be separated into one of four distinct micro-instruction groups. These are:

► Data movement micro-instructions;
► ALU micro-instructions;
► Test micro-instructions;
► Processor control micro-instructions.

All the micro-instructions within each group are described below.

Data Movement Micro-Instructions

There are over forty data movements, as listed in tables A.2 and A.3.

RTL	Notes
A←[MDR]	
A←[ALUr]	
A←[IR(operand)]	8-bit transfer, hi-byte of result = 0x00
B←[MDR]	
B←[ALUr]	
B←[IR(operand)]	8-bit transfer, hi-byte of result = 0x00
B←[PC]	
PC←[IR(operand)]	8-bit transfer, hi-byte of result = 0x00
PC←[ALUr]	
PC←[B]	
PC←[MDR]	
PC←[INC]	
INC←[PC]	
ALUx←[MDR]	
ALUx←[A]	
ALUx←[B]	
ALUx←[IR(operand)]	8-bit transfer, value is sign-extended

Table A.2 *Data movement micro-instructions*

RTL	Notes
ALUx←[PC]	
ALUx←[ALUr]	
ALUx←[SP]	
ALUy←[A]	
ALUy←[B]	
ALUy←[MDR]	
ALUy←[IR(operand)]	8-bit transfer, value is sign-extended
MAR←[PC]	
MAR←[IR(operand)]	8-bit transfer, hi-byte of result = 0x00
MAR←[ALUr]	
MAR←[A]	
MAR←[B]	
MAR←[SP]	
MAR←[MDR]	
MDR←[A]	
MDR←[B]	
MDR←[ALUr]	
MDR←[ALUx]	
MDR←[PSR]	Moves flag contents
MDR←[M[MAR]]	Performs a memory read operation
M[MAR]←[MDR]	Performs a memory write operation
CU←[IR(opcode)]	8-bit transfer
IR←[MDR]	
SP←[ALUx]	
SP←[ALUr]	
SP←[MDR]	
SP←[IR(operand)]	8-bit transfer, hi-byte of result = 0x00
PSR←[MDR]	Restore 16-bit PSR contents
ALUy←[JUMPERS(IntBase)]	Transfer the interrupt base address to ALUy
ALUx←[PSR(IntVec)]	Transfer the interrupt vector to ALUx
PSR(IntVec)←[IR(operand)]	Set the interrupt vector
PSR(IntVec)←[MDR]	Set the interrupt vector with low 3-bits of MDR

Table A.3 *Data movement micro-instructions - continued*

ALU Micro-Instructions

The ALU micro-instructions are listed in table A.4.

Code	Operation	RTL	Notes
0000	ADD	ALUr=[ALUx]+[ALUy]	Perform a 2's complement ADD operation, adding the ALUx and ALUy bit patterns together and storing the result in the ALUr register
0001	ADC	ALUr=[ALUx]+[ALUy]+[PSR(c)]	Perform a 2's complement ADC operation, adding the ALUx and ALUy and C flag together and storing the result in the ALUr register
0010	SUB	ALUr=[ALUx]-[ALUy]	Perform a 2's complement SUB operation, subtracting the ALUy from the ALUx bit pattern and storing the result in the ALUr register
0011	SL	ALUr=[ALUx]<<1	Perform a logical shift left on the ALUx, storing the result in the ALUr
0100	SR	ALUr=[ALUx]>>1	Perform a logical shift right on the ALUx, storing the result in the ALUr
0101	AND	ALUr=[ALUx]&[ALUy]	Perform a logical AND operation on the ALUx and ALUy bit patterns and storing the result in the ALUr register
0110	OR	ALUr=[ALUx]|[ALUy]	Perform a logical OR operation on the ALUx and ALUy bit patterns and storing the result in the ALUr register
0111	NOT	ALUr=~[ALUx]	Perform a logical NOT operation on the ALUx and storing the result in the ALUr register
1000	NEG	ALUr=~[ALUx]+1	Perform a 2's complement negative operation on the ALUx and storing the result in the ALUr register
1001	INC	ALUr=[ALUx]+1	Add 1 to the ALUx bit pattern, storing the result in the ALUr
1010	DEC	ALUr=[ALUx]-1	Subtract 1 from the ALUx bit pattern, storing the result in the ALUr
1011	SWAP	ALUr(7:0)=[ALUx(15:8)]; ALUr(15:8)=[ALUx(7:0)]	Swap the most significant byte and the least significant byte of the ALUx, storing the result in the ALUr
1100	MUL	ALUr=[ALUx]*[ALUy]	Multiply the ALUx value by the ALUy value, storing the result in the ALUr
1101	DIV	ALUr=[ALUx]/[ALUy]	Divide the ALUx value by the ALUy value, storing the result in the ALUr
1110	MOD	ALUr=[ALUx]%[ALUy]	Divide the ALUx value by the ALUy value, storing the remainder in the ALUr

Table A.4   *ALU micro-instructions*

Whenever an ALU operation is executed, the PSR flags V, N, C and Z are updated. Table A.5 shows how the flags are updated by each ALU operation - a key to this table is given in table A.6.

Operation	V	N	Z	C
ADD	*	*	*	*
ADC	*	*	*	*
SUB	*	*	*	*
SL	0	*	*	*
SR	0	*	*	*
AND	0	*	*	0
OR	0	*	*	0
NOT	0	*	*	0
NEG	*	*	*	*
INC	*	*	*	*
DEC	*	*	*	*
SWAP	0	*	*	0
MUL	*	*	*	0
DIV	*	*	*	0
MOD	*	*	*	0

Table A.5 *How ALU operations affect the PSR flags*

Flag	Meaning
V	* means that if 2's complement overflow occurs then V=1 else V-0 (division overflow in cases of DIV and MOD) 0 means that V=0
N	* means N=MSB(ALUr)
Z	* means if (ALUr==0) then Z=1 else Z=0
C	* means if (carry from MSB of ALUr) then C=1 else C=0 * except with SR this means if (carry from LSB of ALUr) then C=1 else C=0 0 means that C=0

Table A.6 *The key to figure A.5*

Test Micro-Instructions

The four PSR flags may be tested. If a test evaluates to TRUE, any remaining micro-instructions in that microprogram are executed. Otherwise the micro-instructions following the test are ignored.

The valid test micro-instructions are listed in table A.7.

RTL	Notes
if(PSR(c)==1)	Carry flag set
if(PSR(c)==0)	Carry flag clear
if(PSR(n)==1)	Negative flag set
if(PSR(n)==0)	Negative flag clear
if(PSR(z)==1)	Zero flag set
if(PSR(z)==0)	Zero flag clear
if(PSR(v)==1)	Overflow flag set
if(PSR(v)==0)	Overflow flag clear

Table A.7 *Test micro-instructions*

Processor Control Micro-Instructions

The valid processor control micro-instructions are listed in table A.9.

ALU Connectivity To The Data Bus

The individual registers of the ALU are connected to the data bus via the ALU data bus connection circuitry. A 2-bit code is given to this circuitry to connect or disconnect ALU registers from the bus. The codes are listed in table A.8.

Code	Notes
00	All ALU registers disconnected from the bus
01	ALUx is connected to the bus
10	ALUy is connected to the bus
11	ALUr is connected to the bus

Table A.8 *ALU connectivity to the data bus*

A.2.3 Memory

JASP has 8Kb of memory, accessed as 4096 16-bit words (addresses $0000 to $0FFF). Some implementations of JASP can have extra memory installed. For example, JASPer can have a maximum of 65536 words of memory (addresses $0000 to $FFFF).

An address points to a 16-bit word and all memory accesses are words. Note that this may not be the case with some popular microprocessors which have byte-addressable memories.

RTL	Notes
PSR(I)=0	Set the interrupt flag to 0
PSR(I)=1	Set the interrupt flag to 1
PSR(E)=0	Set the interrupt enable flag to 0
PSR(E)=1	Set the interrupt enable flag to 1
HALT	Processor halt
NOP	No operation

Table A.9 *Processor control micro-instructions*

Two registers are associated with memory accesses. The Memory Data Register (MDR) contains the data value which is about to be written to memory or a value which has been read from memory. The Memory Address Register (MAR) contains the memory address of a read or write operation.

Think of MAR as a pointer to a word of memory. The pointer may be moved by altering the value held in MAR. Values may be transferred from the MDR to memory (Write) or from Memory to the MDR (Read).

To write a value into memory you do the following:

```
RTL               Description

MDR<-00FF         Place data in MDR
MAR<-0010         Place address in MAR
M[MAR]<-[MDR]     Update memory
```

Note the sequence of operations performed when writing data into memory. The address and data values are loaded into the MAR and MDR respectively and a write cycle is performed.

A memory read is as follows:

```
RTL                    Description

MAR<-0010              Place address in MAR
MDR<-[M[MAR]]          Read memory
                       MDR now contains [M[0010]]
```

The memory map is shown in figure A.2.

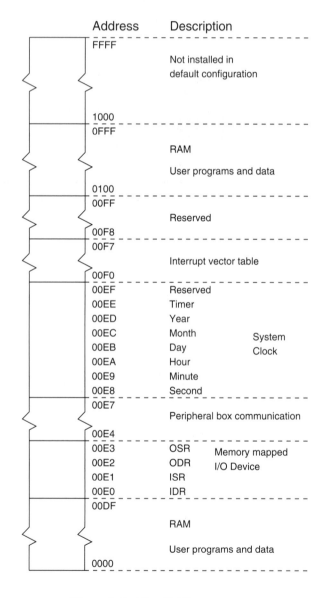

Figure A.2 *The JASP memory map*

When accessing or writing to memory, all addresses are wrapped. So for example, if memory is installed up to $0FFF, then writing to the address $1FFF *will still cause memory to be updated.*

It can be seen that the small memory of the JASPER processor is used for a variety of purposes. The bulk of the memory is available for storing user data and instructions.

All peripherals have default locations within the memory map, but their locations are configurable.

Memory Mapped I/O

Handshaking needs to be used in order to perform I/O.

To write a character to the screen, first check that the OSR port is set to 1, if it's not go into a loop until it is. Only then write the character to the ODR.

To read a character from the keyboard, keep checking until the ISR is set to 1, only then should you read the character from the IDR.

Here is a piece of code that shows handshaking for both input and output:

```
* A demonstration of polled I/O
*
* This program reads 10 characters from the keyboard
* and then prints them all out once they've been entered
*
OSR      EQU   $E3      * Output Status Register (OSR)
ODR      EQU   $E2      * Output Data Register   (ODR)
ISR      EQU   $E1      * Input Status Register  (ISR)
IDR      EQU   $E0      * Input Data Register    (IDR)


         ORG   0
         MOVE  #$00,B   * count is storage for our
         MOVE  B,count  *   counter value

loop     MOVE  ISR,A    * Get ISR
         CMP   #$00,A   * is a char available?
         BEQ   loop     * no - wait some more
         MOVE  IDR,A    * read the char

         MOVE  count,B  * the address to write the
         ADD   #data,B  * value to is count+data
         MOVE  A,(B)    * write the char in there
```

```
          MOVE   count,B    * add 1 to count
          ADD    #$01,B     *
          CMP    #$0A,B     * and see if we have reached 10 and
          BEQ    gotchars   * move to next section if we have
          MOVE   B,count    * otherwise write count back
          JMP    loop       * and get another char
gotchars  MOVE   #$00,B     * count is storage for our
          MOVE   B,count    *   counter value

write     MOVE   OSR,A      * get OSR
          CMP    #$00,A     * OSR 1 can print, OSR 0 can't print
          BEQ    write      * not yet, wait some more

          MOVE   count,B    * the address to read the
          ADD    #data,B    * value from is count+data
          MOVE   (B),A      * get the char in there
          MOVE   A,ODR      * print the char

          MOVE   count,B    * add 1 to count
          ADD    #$01,B     *
          CMP    #$0A,B     * and see if we have reached 10
          BEQ    done       * and move to end if we have
          MOVE   B,count    * otherwise write count back
          JMP    write      * and write another char
done      HALT             * done

count     DS.W $01          * the counter
data      DS.W $0A          * storage for our 10 characters
```

Current System Time

Additionally, JASP has a system clock device. The current date and time is accessible from $00E8 to $00ED. No handshaking is required, simply access the particular memory location for the required date/time value. You cannot write to these memory locations, although no errors are raised if you try.

Peripheral Box Communication

A prototype peripherals board has been configured to work with the JASP processor - it was defined and built by Ian Chilton, under the supervision of Mark Burrell.

The peripherals board uses four memory locations, by default installed between $00E4 and $00E7, and the JASP processor can communicate with various input and output devices on the board. These include DIP switches, a buzzer, various LEDs and digit displays.

The peripherals board is purely a prototype for demonstration purposes only.

Reserved Addresses

It is recommended that you do not use the reserved memory addresses for storage - it could make your programs incompatible with future versions of JASP.

A.2.4 The Interrupt Mechanism

The interrupt mechanism makes use of an interrupt vector table stored in memory, and the I and E flags of the PSR.

The JASP processor can only deal with a single interrupt at any given time - any further interrupts generated while the first interrupt is being handled will be ignored. The actual details of the interrupt mechanism are definable within the instruction set. Within the default instruction set the interrupt mechanism is defined as:

```
PSR(I)=0                      interrupt flag = 0
MAR<-[SP]                       }      save PSR
MDR<-[PSR]                      }      on the stack
M[MAR]<-[MDR]                   }
ALUx<-[SP]                    }  decrement
ALUr=[ALUx]-1                 }  SP
SP<-[ALUr]                    }
ALUx<-[PC]                      }
MDR<-[ALUx]                     }      write PC
MAR<-[SP]                       }      to the stack
M[MAR]<-[MDR]                   }
ALUx<-[SP]                    }  decrement
ALUr=[ALUx]-1                 }  SP
SP<-[ALUr]                    }
PSR(E)=0                      interrupt enable flag = 0
ALUy<-[JUMPERS(IntBase)]        }
ALUx<-[PSR(IntVec)]             } build the vector address
ALUr=[ALUx]+[ALUy]              }
MAR<-[ALUr]                   } obtain the handler address
MDR<-[M[MAR]]                 }
```

```
PC<-[MDR]                        load address of handler into PC
```

The position of the vector table is configurable, but it defaults to the locations $00F0 to $00F7.

A.2.5 JASP Files Reference

The JASP engine understands two file formats, these are the micro-instruction and machine code formats. In previous versions these formats proved to be somewhat stringent, and so have been made much more flexible.

Micro-Instruction File Format

Each micro-instruction file consists of a set of zero or more instruction definitions. These definitions begin with an opcode directive and an opcode, and then a set of micro-instructions to enter into the control unit micro-memory. Blank lines can exist anywhere within the file, and comments can be written after an asterisk. Each line in the micro-instruction file can be a maximum of 250 characters.

An instruction definition can also include two further directives, these are the mnemonic and description directives. The mnemonic directive describes the form of the mnemonic while the description directive gives a brief description of the opcodes function. Both the mnemonic and description directives expect their values to be within double quotes. Neither of these tags are mandatory, both being set to null strings if they are not included. If the line is not a directive and not a comment it is expected to hold a valid micro-instruction, followed by an optional comment.

A typical micro-instruction file might consist of a number of micro-programs each like the following instruction definition:

```
Opcode d0
* addr 00 to FF
Mnemonic "JSR addr"
Description "Jump to subroutine at a direct address"
ALUx<-[PC]              }
MDR<-[ALUx]             }      write PC
MAR<-[SP]               }      to the stack
M[MAR]<-[MDR]           }
ALUx<-[SP]                  } decrement
ALUr=[ALUx]-1               } SP
```

```
SP<-[ALUr]                    }
PC<-[IR(operand)]
```

Instruction Sets

JASP is provided with a default instruction set (instruct.mco). This instruction set contains all single word instructions where the hi-byte is the opcode. This set is limited to addressing memory in the range $0000 to $00FF.

To use the full memory available, use the advanced instruction set in `advanced.mco`, however it is advisable to only use this instruction set in conjunction with the assembler rather than with hand coding.

Machine Code File Format

Each machine code file consists of a set of zero or more machine code segments. These segments begin with an `org` directive and address, and then a set of 16-bit values to enter into memory. Blank lines can exist anywhere within the machine code file, and comments can be written after an asterisk character. A simple program is shown below. Each line in the machine code file can be a maximum of 250 characters. If a line does not begin as a comment and does not have an `org` directive, then it is assumed to be a 16-bit value.

```
org 0400
45FF
3200
0001
F000   * this is the only comment in this program
```

A.3 JASPer

JASPer originally came into being as a clone of part of a software package for VAX/VMS known as *ASP*, or *Animated Simple Processor*, designed and written by William Henderson. The first Windows clone was known as *WinASP*, but when the VAX/VMS version was no longer supported then this package (which had grown into a package in its own right) became known as ASP. It has now changed its name (again!) to JASPer, to avoid any confusion with Microsoft ASP which is something totally different altogether.

So what is JASPer? It is a package that simulates the JASP processor. It can be used in one of two modes - either white-box mode where the internal registers of the processor are visible, or black-box mode where the user can see the output produced by their programs. What this figure does not demonstrate is that, when instructions are run (either individual micro-instructions or whole machine code programs) all data movements are animated within the package - graphically showing the inner workings of the processor.

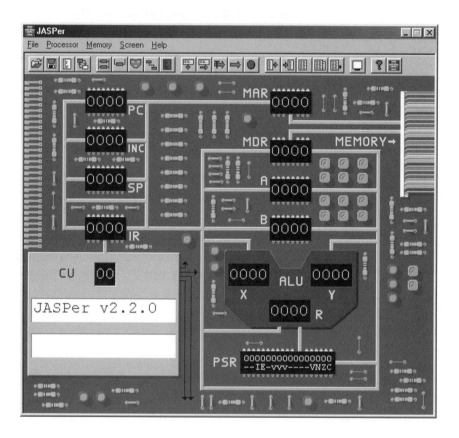

Figure A.3   *JASPer - the main graphic display*

There are actually two different white-box views of the processor that can be selected. The first, as illustrated in figure A.3 is the main animated display. A second, simpler display, can be used instead - it is used for a number of screen-shots in the main text of the book - the simpler display is shown in figure A.4.

A.3.1   How To Use JASPer

The functionality of JASPer is accessed via the menu bar and the buttons below the menu bar:

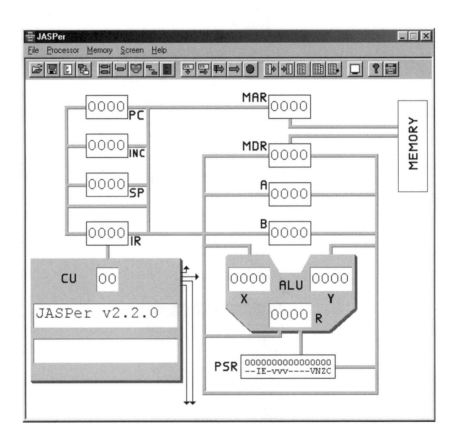

Figure A.4   *JASPer - the simple display*

The Menu Bar

The menu bar has five entries. These are for controlling the processor, memory functions, etc. The menu bar looks like this:

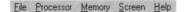

As you can see, each entry has one letter underlined, pressing this letter together with the ALT key is the keyboard equivalent of clicking on the entry. For example, typing ALT-M will bring up the memory menu.

The Buttons

The buttons provide the same functionality as the menu bar, only in a graphical manner.

Usage

Both the menu bar and the buttons can be broken down into the same five key function areas, and these are now described in turn.

The File Menu

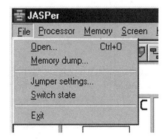

The file menu accessed from the keyboard provides the same functionality as the following set of buttons.

Button	Menu Option	Description
	Open	This option brings up a file open dialogue, allowing the user to open either a microcode file (MCO), or a macrocode file (JAS).
	Memory Dump	Save JAS file containing all the contents of memory.

Button	Menu Option	Description
	Jumper Settings	This allows the user to control the animation features, including animation speed.
	Switch State	This option switches between black-box mode and white-box mode. JASPer always starts in white-box mode, where the registers and data paths of the processor can be seen. In black-box mode the JASPer window switches to a view of JASPer's output - any I/O output will be seen here.

The Processor Menu

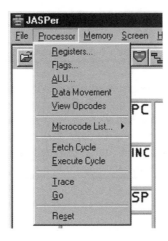

The processor menu is equivalent to the following set of buttons:

Button	Menu Option	Description
	Registers	Brings up a dialogue where the user can change register values.
	Flags	Brings up a dialogue where the user can change flag values.
	ALU	Brings up a dialogue where the user can perform ALU operations.
	Data Movement	Allows the user to perform all data movement operations. Click on the destination register first, followed by the source register in order to perform the data movement.

Button	Menu Option	Description
■	View Opcodes	This option displays a summary of all the currently loaded opcodes loaded into the processor. There are three parts to the display, the opcode, the mnemonic and the brief description.
	Microcode List	This option doesn't have an equivalent button - it combines both the ALU and data movement operations. On using this option a further menu is displayed, allowing the user to select a particular micro-instruction to run - divided into ALU and data movement micro-instructions. The data movement micro-instructions are displayed by destination - one can select the destination and then an appropriate source register.
⊞	Fetch Cycle	This option runs a single fetch cycle.
⊞	Execute Cycle	This option runs a single execute cycle.
⇥	Trace	This option runs one fetch-execute cycle
⇒	Go	This runs the processor. The processor stops when either the Escape key (acting as a reset button) is pressed, the mouse is clicked on the JASPer window, or a halt instruction is executed. Note that, if animation is turned on, even if the Escape key or the mouse is clicked on the JASPer Window, the animation displays until either the current fetch or the current execute cycle completes.
●	Reset	This option resets the processor, as if the processor power switch has been cycled.

The Memory Menu

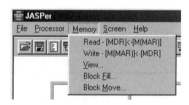

The memory menu accessed from the keyboard provides the same functionality as the following set of buttons.

Button	Menu Option	Description
	Read	Perform a memory read operation
	Write	Perform a memory write operation
	View	This option brings up a dialogue which allows the user to view the contents of memory. For each location it displays the address, value and mnemonic (of the opcode that is stored in the most significant byte of the memory address)
	Block Fill	This option brings up a dialogue that allows the user to fill user defined memory locations with a definable word value.
	Block Move	This option brings up a dialogue that allows the user to copy the contents of a given set of contiguous memory locations to another memory location. The original contiguous memory is unaffected.

The Screen Menu

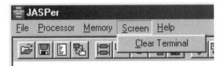

The memory menu accessed from the keyboard provides the same functionality as the following button.

Button	Menu Option	Description
	Clear Terminal	Terminal Clears the screen when JASPer is in black-box mode.

The Help Menu

The help menu accessed from the keyboard provides the same functionality as the following set of buttons.

Button	Menu Option	Description
?	Help Index	This option displays the Windows help file for JASPer.
	About JASPer	This option brings up a dialogue that displays the current version of JASPer and build date, together with a copyright statement.

A.3.2 JASPer Parameters

Parameters for JASPER are:

```
JASPER [/h*elp]

  or

JASPER [/l*oad={macrocodefile}][/m*co={microcodefile}] [/pc={addr}]
       [/n*odefault] [/bw] [/anim_off]
```

The meaning of each parameter is as follows:

```
/help       - displays the parameters for the program.
/load       - loads the given macrocode file
/mco        - loads the given microcode file
/pc         - sets the PC to the given value prior to running
/nodefault  - instructs the processor not to load the default
              instruction set
/bw         - use the simple display rather than the full
              graphic
/anim_off   - animation switched off by default
```

A.4 Aspen

Aspen is a command-line version of JASPer, obviously without any graphical display apart from a simple text output. Aspen actually uses the same processor engine as JASPer, and so the two programs share the (nearly) exact same functionality. Figure A.5 shows Aspen running in a Windows 95 DOS window. Versions of Aspen will run on any version of DOS (from V5.0 upwards), any version of Microsoft Windows and Linux (ELF binary).

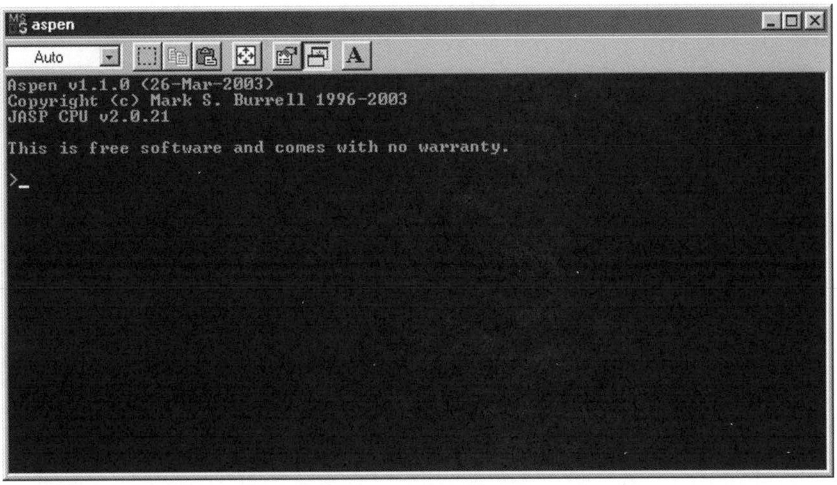

Figure A.5 *Aspen*

When you use Aspen, you need to either make sure the default instruction set and the Aspen help file (aspen.hco) is in the same directory, or make use of the JASP environment variable as detailed previously. Using Aspen, and any text editor of your choice, it is possible to use even the lowliest 386 PC to develop programs for JASPer.

If you have the JASP environment set, then when you attempt to open either a microcode or a program file from within Aspen it will first attempt to find that file within the current directory, and if it can't find the file it will then look for it in the directory named in the JASP environment. Please note that the 16-bit version of Aspen only understands the 8.3 DOS naming convention.

Use the help facility within Aspen by typing help at the chevron prompt.

A.4.1 Aspen Parameters

Parameters for Aspen are:

```
ASPEN [/h*elp]

  or

ASPEN [/l*oad={macrocodefile}][/m*co={microcodefile}] [/g*o] [/q*uit]
      [/pc={addr}] [/n*odefault]
```

The meaning of each parameter is as follows:

```
/help        - displays the parameters for the program.
/load        - loads the given macrocode file
/mco         - loads the given microcode file
/go          - instructs the processor to begin executing
/quit        - instructs the program to close once the given
               execution process has finished
/pc          - sets the PC to the given value prior to running
/nodefault   - instructs the processor not to load the default
               instruction set
```

A.4.2 Example Programs Running on the JASP

Here is the same program, *clock.jas* as distributed with the JASPer package, seen running in both JASPer and in Aspen.

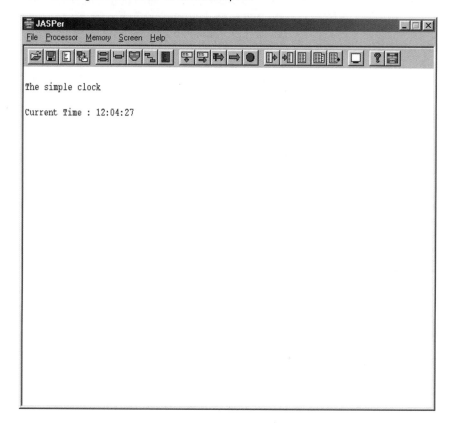

```
MS
S aspen                                                          _ □ ✕
┌─────────┬─────────────────────────────────┐
│ Auto  ▾ │ ▢ ▤ ▦ ⊡ ⊞ ▢ A │
Aspen v1.1.0 (26-Mar-2003)
Copyright (c) Mark S. Burrell 1996-2003
JASP CPU v2.0.21

This is free software and comes with no warranty.

>load clock.jas
Loading [clock.jas] - success

>go

The simple clock

Current Time : 12:05:53
```

A.5 The JASP Assembler

The JASP Cross-Assembler, to give it its full title, is a program written in Perl that can be used to ease the process of creating assembly language programs for the JASP processor.

The assembler should work on any system with a Perl installation, although it has only been test on DOS and Linux systems.

A.5.1 The Instruction Set Used

By default the assembler uses instruct.mco as the default instruction set. It then attempts to assemble your assembly language program using the information it finds within the instruction set file.

A.5.2 Directives

It understands a limited set of directives, listed here:

Directive	Example	Description
ORG	`org $0000`	Sets the program origin
DC.B	`DC.B 'hello',0`	Stores a byte in memory, can also be used to specify text strings
DC.W	`DC.W $1234`	Stores a word in memory
DS.W	`DS.W 1`	Defines storage in words
EQU	`IDR EQU $E0`	Defines a constant
MCO	`MCO "advanced.mco"`	Specifies the instruction set to use
LPC	`LPC $0100`	Sets the PC to a particular value
USE	`USE "advancedio.lib"`	Include a library file in the program

When a USE directive is encountered, the assembler attempts to load the file from the current directory, and if that fails then it attempts to load the file from the directory listed in the the JASP environment variable.

A.5.3 Usage

The options of the assembler are as follows:

```
jasm [-h]

   or

jasm [-m mco] [-a asm] [-l type] [-o filename]
```

The meaning of each parameter is as follows:

```
-m mco      : loads a microcode file (can be multiple files
              separated by a ':')
-a asm      : loads a JASP assembler file
-l type     : output type can be default|debug|code|printout
-o filename : send assembler listing to filename listed
-h          : list this help information.
```

Additionally, the assembler understands a `force_32bit` directive that can be placed in instruction set files. This has the effect of forcing all machine code instructions to be written in 32 bits rather than the standard 16 bits.

A.5.4 Operand Sizes

The assembler, not understanding anything about assembly language, has to make assumptions about the bit length of operands. To do this it makes use of information within the instruction mnemonics.

For example, if the assembler sees something like `data`, `addr` or `dis` in a mnemonic then it assumes that this operand should be 8 bits wide. However, if the assembler sees something like `dataword`, `addrword` or `disword` in a mnemonic then it assumes that this operand should be 16 bits wide.

The assembler also makes sure that words begin and end on word boundaries, and will pad out any odd bytes, to form 16-bit words, with zeroes to ensure that all words are word aligned.

A.5.5 Error Messages

As the assembler has no real understanding of assembly language, but rather can only read an instruction set and output machine code following very strict rules, this means that often its error message leave a little to be desired. Please treat this as part of the learning process - after all, without the assembler you would have to encode every assembly language program by hand!

A.6 The JASP C−− Compiler

The JASP C−− cross compiler is written by David Harrison. The program, `jcc`, compiles programs written in a small educational language called C−− into assembly language files that can then be assembled by the JASP assembler. The name of the language is a pun on the language C++; David admits it isn't a great pun.

The syntax rules for high-level languages tend to be written in a form known as Extended Backus-Naur Form, or EBNF. Within EBNF, symbols are defined in terms of other symbols. For example, an `if` construct in C−− is described as:

```
if ::= 'if' '(' express ')' statement 'else' statement
     | 'if' '(' express ')' statement
```

This means that an `if` construct begins with the word `if` followed by a condition expression that is within brackets. If the condition is true then `statement` is executed (the definition of `statement` is elsewhere), and the statement after the `else` is executed if the condition is false. Alternatively, the `if` statement can omit the `else` section.

Lastly, any entries within square brackets, as shown below are optional.

```
variable dec ::= type ident [ '=' literal ]
```

The production rules for C−− are given here:

```
program ::= declarations compstat

declarations ::= { declaration ';' }

compstat ::= '{'  statement statements '}'

statements ::= { statement }

declaration ::= constant_dec | variable_dec

statement ::= compstat | assign | input | output | if | while

constant dec ::= 'const' type ident '=' literal

variable dec ::= type ident [ '=' literal ]

assign ::= variable '=' express ';'

input ::= 'cin' '>>' ident ';'

output ::= 'cout' '<<' express ';'

if ::= 'if' '(' express ')' statement 'else' statement
       | 'if' '(' express ')' statement

while ::= 'while' '(' express ')' statement

type ::= 'bool' | 'string' | 'int'

ident ::= letter ident_chars

literal ::= boolit | stringlit | intlit

letter ::= 'A' | .. | 'Z' | 'a' | .. | 'z'
```

```
ident_chars ::= { ident_char }

boolit ::= 'false' | 'true'

stringlit ::= '"' { printable } '"'

intlit ::= sign uint | uint

ident_char ::= letter | digit | '_'

printable ::= ' ' | .. | '~'        {ASCII codes 0x20 to 0x7F)

sign ::= '+' | '-'

uint ::= digit { digit }

digit ::= '0' | '1' | '2' | '3' | '4' | '5' | '6' | '7' | '8' | '9'

express ::= basic relop express | basic

basic ::= term addop basic | term

term ::= factor mulop term | factor

factor ::= literal | ident | '(' express ')' | '!' factor

mulop ::= '*' | '/' | '%' | '&&'

addop ::= '+' | '-' | '||'

relop> ::= '<' | '<=' | '==' | '>=' | '>' | '!='
```

Using these rules we can compile programs such as the example below, provided by David:

```
// Computes the maximum, minimum, total and average of a list
// of integers read from input. The input is terminated by a
// 0 on the input.

int n      = 0     ;        // Number read in
int max    = 0     ;        // Maximum
int min    = 32767 ;        // Minimum
int total  = 0     ;        // Total
```

```
int count   = 0     ;          // Number of inputs
int average = 0     ;          // Average
bool done   = false ;          // Input done flag.
bool done2  = true  ;          // Input done flag.
const string prompt            // Prompt for input
            = "Number  : " ;
const string mess1             // Output messages
            = "Maximum : " ;
const string mess2
            = "Minimum : " ;
const string mess3
            = "Total   : " ;
const string mess4
            = "Average : " ;
const string endl              // End of line for output
            = "\n" ;
const string countzero
            = "count was zero" ;

{
  // Prompt for and read integer. If number is 0 we're done, otherwise
  // increment count, add number into running total, check if it's
  // the maximum or minimum so far and prompt for the next number.
  while (!done)
  { cout << prompt ;
    cin >>  n ;
    if (n == 0)
    { done = true ; }
    else
    { count = count + 1 ;
      total = total + n ;

      if (n > max)
      { max = n ; } ;
      if (n < min)
      { min = n ; } ;
    } ;
  } ;

  // Compute the average.
  if (count != 0)
  {
    average = total / count ;
  }
  else
  {
    cout << countzero;
```

```
        cout << endl;
    };

    // Output results
    cout << mess1 ;
    cout << max ;
    cout << endl ;
    cout << mess2 ;
    cout << min ;
    cout << endl ;
    cout << mess3 ;
    cout << total ;
    cout << endl ;
    cout << mess4 ;
    cout << average ;
    cout << endl ;
}
// End of program
```

The compiler doesn't take any parameters, instead re-direction is used to pass a C-- program to it, and the assembly language output can be re-directed into an assembly language program file.

For example, imagine that we have a C-- program called `myprog.c--` that we want to run in Aspen. Provided that the program compiles with no errors we would do the following:

```
jcc < myprog.c-- > myprog.asm
jasm -a myprog.asm -o myprog.jas
aspen /l=myprog.jas /m=advanced.mco
```

The first line uses the compiler to produce the assembly language program. In the second line we assemble this to the machine code program. The third line loads the program into Aspen, along with the advanced instruction set as used by all programs created with the compiler. Once loaded into Aspen (or JASPer) we can run the program.

Lastly, it is worth noting that the program `jcc` doesn't make use of the JASP environment variable, but then again it doesn't need to.

A.7 The JASP Software Libraries

Two libraries of subroutines are part of the JASP toolkit. The first library, `basicio.lib` offers a few subroutines that are useful for text input and output, and is only really intended to demonstrate the usefulness of libraries. It can only be used in relatively small programs if they are intended to fit into memory between $0000 and $00DF.

The second library, `advancedio.lib`, is more useful and offers a number of extra subroutines not offered by `basicio.lib`.

To use a library in your assembly language program you need to use a USE directive as shown here:

```
* include a library
USE "basicio.lib"
```

A.7.1 The Basic I/O Library

The subroutines provided by `basicio.lib` are:

```
* putstring - prints packed strings, address has to be in register A.
* putchar   - prints a single character from lo-byte of register B.
* putword   - prints a word held as 4 hex chars (from A)
* putbyte   - prints a word held as 2 hex chars (from lo-byte of A)
* getchar   - get a character from the keyboard, char in A register.
* newline   - print a CR/LF pair
```

A.7.2 The Advanced I/O Library

The subroutines provided by `advancedio.lib` are superset of those offered by `basicio.lib`. This library is so large that it can only usefully be used in programs written for above $0100 in memory using the advanced instruction set.

Here are the subroutines offered by this library:

```
* putdbyte   - prints lo-byte of register A as decimal value.
```

```
* putdword   - prints a word held as a decimal number
* putstring  - prints packed strings, address has to be in register A.
* putchar    - prints a single character from lo-byte of register B.
* putbyte    - prints a word held as 2 hex chars (lo-byte of A)
* putword    - prints a word held as 4 hex chars (from A)
* getchar    - get a character from the keyboard, char in A register.
* newline    - print a CR/LF pair
* getustring - read in an unpacked character string, address in A
*              and required size in B
* putustring - print an unpacked character string, address in A
* inkey      - read a character from the keyboard if available.
* getdword   - read up to 6 chars and interpret as a signed decimal value
* getbyte    - read 2 chars and interpret as a hexadecimal value
* getword    - read 4 chars and interpret as a hexadecimal value
* getdbyte   - read up to 4 chars and interpret as a signed decimal value
```

The Basic Instruction Set Quick Reference

This is a quick reference listing of the instructions available in the basic JASP instruction set.

The mnemonic and description is listed for each opcode in the instruction set.

```
00 ADD  #data,A    Add to reg. A an immediate oper.
01 ADD  #data,B    Add to reg. B an immediate oper.
02 ADD  addr,A     Add to reg. A from a direct addr.
03 ADD  addr,B     Add to reg. B from a direct addr.
04 ADD  (addr),A   Add to reg. A from an indirect addr.
05 ADD  (addr),B   Add to reg. B from an indirect addr.
06 ADD  B,A        Add B reg. to contents of A reg.
07 ADD  A,B        Add A reg. to contents of B reg.
08 ADD  (B),A      Add B reg. indirect oper. to A reg.
09 ADD  (A),B      Add A reg. indirect oper. to B reg.
0A ADD  B+addr,A   Add to reg. A from an indexed addr. (index in B)
0B ADD  A+addr,B   Add to reg. B from an indexed addr. (index in A)
10 ADC  #data,A    Add with carry to reg. A an immediate oper.
11 ADC  #data,B    Add with carry to reg. B an immediate oper.
12 ADC  addr,A     Add with carry to reg. A from a direct addr.
13 ADC  addr,B     Add with carry to reg. B from a direct addr.
14 ADC  (addr),A   Add with carry to reg. A from an indirect addr.
15 ADC  (addr),B   Add with carry to reg. B from an indirect addr.
16 ADC  B,A        Add with carry to A reg. from B reg.
17 ADC  A,B        Add with carry to B reg. from A reg.
18 ADC  (B),A      Add with carry to B reg. a reg. indirect oper.
19 ADC  (A),B      Add with carry to B reg. a reg. indirect oper.
1A ADC  B+addr,A   Add with carry to reg. A an indexed oper. (index in B)
1B ADC  A+addr,B   Add with carry to reg. B an indexed oper. (index in A)
20 SUB  #data,A    Subtract an immediate oper. from A reg
21 SUB  #data,B    Subtract an immediate oper. from B reg
22 SUB  addr,A     Subtract from reg. A a direct oper.
```

```
23 SUB  addr,B     Subtract from reg. B a direct oper.
24 SUB  (addr),A   Subtract from reg. A an indirect oper.
25 SUB  (addr),B   Subtract from reg. B an indirect oper.
26 SUB  B,A        Subtract from reg. A the contents of reg. B
27 SUB  A,B        Subtract from reg. B the contents of reg. A
28 SUB  (B),A      Subtract from reg. A a reg. indirect oper.
29 SUB  (A),B      Subtract from reg. B a reg. indirect oper.
2A SUB  B+addr,A   Subtract an indexed oper. from the reg. A (index in B)
2B SUB  A+addr,B   Subtract an indexed oper. from the reg. B (index in A)
32 SHL  addr       Shift left a memory direct oper.
34 SHL  (addr)     Shift left a memory indirect oper.
36 SHL  A          Shift left reg. A
37 SHL  B          Shift left reg. B
38 SHL  (A)        Shift left a reg. indirect oper., addr. in A
39 SHL  (B)        Shift left a reg. indirect oper., addr. in B
3A SHL  A+addr     Shift left an indexed oper. (index in A)
3B SHL  B+addr     Shift left an indexed oper. (index in B)
42 SHR  addr       Shift right a direct oper.
44 SHR  (addr)     Shift right a memory indirect oper.
46 SHR  A          Shift right the contents of reg. A
47 SHR  B          Shift right the contents of reg. B
48 SHR  (A)        Shift right a reg. indirect oper.
49 SHR  (B)        Shift right a reg. indirect oper.
4A SHR  A+addr     Shift right a memory indexed oper. (index in A)
4B SHR  B+addr     Shift right a memory indexed oper. (Index in B)
50 AND  #data,A    AND operation on A reg and an immediate oper.
51 AND  #data,B    AND operation on B reg and an immediate oper.
52 AND  addr,A     AND operation on A and a direct oper.
53 AND  addr,B     AND operation on B and a direct oper.
54 AND  (addr),A   AND operation on A and an indirect oper.
55 AND  (addr),B   AND operation on B and an indirect oper.
56 AND  B,A        AND on A and B, result in A
57 AND  A,B        AND on B and A, result in B
58 AND  (B),A      AND on A and a reg. indirect oper.
59 AND  (A),B      AND on B and a reg. indirect oper.
5A AND  B+addr,A   AND operation on A and an indexed oper.
5B AND  A+addr,B   AND operation on B and an indexed oper.
60 OR   #data,A    OR operation on A reg and an immediate oper.
61 OR   #data,B    OR operation on B reg and an immediate oper.
62 OR   addr,A     OR operation on A and a direct oper.
63 OR   addr,B     OR operation on B and a direct oper.
64 OR   (addr),A   OR operation on A and an indirect oper.
65 OR   (addr),B   OR operation on B and an indirect oper.
66 OR   B,A        OR on A and B, result in A
67 OR   A,B        OR on B and A, result in B
68 OR   (B),A      OR on A and a reg. indirect oper.
69 OR   (A),B      OR on B and a reg. indirect oper.
6A OR   B+addr,A   OR operation on A and an indexed oper.
6B OR   A+addr,B   OR operation on B and an indexed oper.
```

```
72 NOT   addr      NOT operation on a direct oper.
74 NOT   (addr)    NOT operation on an indirect oper.
76 NOT   A         NOT operation on A reg.
77 NOT   B         NOT operation on B reg.
78 NOT   (A)       NOT on a reg. indirect oper. (address in A)
79 NOT   (B)       NOT on a reg. indirect oper. (address in B)
7A NOT   A+addr    NOT on an indexed oper. (index in A)
7B NOT   B+addr    NOT on an indexed oper. (index in B)
7C SWAP  A         Swap A register lo and hi bytes
7D SWAP  B         Swap B register lo and hi bytes
80 CMP   #data,A   Compare an immediate oper. with A reg
81 CMP   #data,B   Compare an immediate oper. with B reg
82 CMP   addr,A    Compare a direct oper. with A reg.
83 CMP   addr,B    Compare a direct oper. with B reg.
84 CMP   (addr),A  Compare an indirect oper. with A reg.
85 CMP   (addr),B  Compare an indirect oper. with B reg.
86 CMP   B,A       Compare A and B reg.
87 CMP   A,B       Compare B and A reg.
88 CMP   (B),A     Compare A with a reg. indirect oper.
89 CMP   (A),B     Compare B with a reg. indirect oper.
8A CMP   B+addr,A  Compare with A an indexed oper.
8B CMP   A+addr,B  Compare with B an indexed oper.
8C PUSH  A         Push A onto the stack
8D PUSH  B         Push B onto the stack
8E POP   A         Pop A from the stack
8F POP   B         Pop B from the stack
90 MOVE  #data,A   Move an immediate oper. into A
91 MOVE  #data,B   Move an immediate oper. into B
92 MOVE  addr,A    Load reg. A from a direct addr.
93 MOVE  addr,B    Load reg. B from a direct addr.
94 MOVE  (addr),A  Load reg. A from an indirect addr.
95 MOVE  (addr),B  Load reg. B from an indirect addr.
96 MOVE  B,A       Move B reg. to A reg.
97 MOVE  A,B       Move A reg. to B reg.
98 MOVE  (B),A     Load A reg. with a reg. indirect oper.
99 MOVE  (A),B     Load B reg. with a reg. indirect oper.
9A MOVE  B+addr,A  Load A reg from an indexed addr. (index in B)
9B MOVE  A+addr,B  Load B reg from an indexed addr. (index in A)
A2 MOVE  A,addr    Store the A reg. in memory at a direct addr.
A3 MOVE  B,addr    Store the B reg. in memory at a direct addr.
A4 MOVE  A,(addr)  Store reg. A at a mem. indirect addr.
A5 MOVE  B,(addr)  Store reg. B at a mem. indirect addr.
A6 MOVE  #data,SP  Move an immediate oper. into SP
A7 MOVE  addr,SP   Load reg. SP from a direct addr.
A8 MOVE  A,(B)     Store A reg. at an addr. held in B
A9 MOVE  B,(A)     Store B reg. at an addr. held in A
AA MOVE  A,B+addr  Store A reg. at an indexed addr. (index in B)
AB MOVE  B,A+addr  Store B reg. at an indexed addr. (index in A)
AC MOVE  (addr),SP Load reg. SP from an indirect addr.
```

```
AD MOVE A,SP       Move A reg. to SP reg.
AE MOVE B,SP       Move B reg. to SP reg.
B0 BCC  #dis       Branch on carry clear to a PC relative addr.
B1 BCS  #dis       Branch on carry set to a PC relative addr.
B2 BCC  addr       Branch to a direct addr. if carry flag clear (C=0)
B3 BCS  addr       Branch to a direct addr. if carry flag set (C=1)
B4 BCC  (addr)     Branch to an indirect addr. if carry flag is clear
B5 BCS  (addr)     Branch to an indirect addr. if carry flag is set
B8 BPL  #dis       Branch on negative clear to a PC relative addr.
B9 BMI  #dis       Branch on negative set to a PC relative addr.
BA BPL  addr       Branch to a direct addr. if negative flag clear (N=0)
BB BMI  addr       Branch to a direct addr. if negative flag set (N=1)
BC BPL  (addr)     Branch to an indirect addr. if negative flag is clear
BD BMI  (addr)     Branch to an indirect addr. if negative flag is set
C0 BNE  #dis       Branch on zero clear to a PC relative addr.
C1 BEQ  #dis       Branch on zero set to a PC relative addr.
C2 BNE  addr       Branch to a direct addr. if zero flag clear (Z=0)
C3 BEQ  addr       Branch to a direct addr. if zero flag set (Z=1)
C4 BNE  (addr)     Branch to an indirect addr. if zero flag is clear
C5 BEQ  (addr)     Branch to an indirect addr. if zero flag is set
C8 BVC  #dis       Branch on no overflow to a PC relative addr.
C9 BVS  #dis       Branch on overflow to a PC relative addr.
CA BVC  addr       Branch to a direct addr. if overflow flag clear (V=0)
CB BVS  addr       Branch to a direct addr. if overflow flag set (V=1)
CC BVC  (addr)     Branch to an indirect addr. if overflow flag is clear
CD BVS  (addr)     Branch to an indirect addr. if overflow flag is set
D0 JSR  addr       Jump to subroutine at a direct address
D1 JSR  (addr)     Jump to subroutine at an indirect address
D2 JSR  A          Jump to subroutine at an addr. held in the A reg.
D3 JSR  B          Jump to subroutine at an addr. held in the B reg.
D4 JSR  (A)        Jump to subroutine at an indirect addr. held in the A reg.
D5 JSR  (B)        Jump to subroutine at an indirect addr. held in the B reg.
D6 JSR  A+addr     Jump to subroutine at an indexed addr. (index in A)
D7 JSR  B+addr     Jump to subroutine at an indexed addr. (index in B)
D8 JSR  #dis       Jump to subroutine at a PC relative address
E0 JMP  addr       Jump to a direct addr.
E1 JMP  (addr)     Jump to an indirect addr.
E2 JMP  A          Jump to an addr. held in the A reg.
E3 JMP  B          Jump to an addr. held in the B reg.
E4 JMP  (A)        Jump to a reg. indirect addr.
E5 JMP  (B)        Jump to a reg. indirect addr.
E6 JMP  A+addr     Jump to an indexed addr. (index in A)
E7 JMP  B+addr     Jump to an indexed addr. (index in B)
E8 JMP  #dis       Jump to a PC relative address
F0 HALT            Halt processor
F1 RTS             Return from subroutine
F2 NOP             No operation
F3 INTE            Enable interrupts
F4 INTD            Disable interrupts
```

FA TRAP #data   Software interrupt mechanism

The Basic Instruction Set

This is a complete reference to the basic instruction set that ships with the JASP toolkit. It details the microcode lists for each opcode.

```
* A basic instruction set for the JASP architecture.
*
* Originally based on an instruction set
* by William Henderson.
*
* This instruction set is purely for use in
* memory locations $00 to $FF.  Many instructions
* make use of movements from the ir(operand),
* and so cannot address memory locations above $FF.
*
* All instructions are one word, the hi-byte
* of each is the opcode.
*
* Revision : 2.0.7
* Author   : Mark Burrell
* Date     : 16-FEB-2003
*
*
Fetch
* fetch cycle definition
MAR<-[PC]
INC<-[PC]
PC<-[INC]
MDR<-[M[MAR]]
IR<-[MDR]
CU<-[IR(opcode)]

Interrupt
* interrupt routine
```

```
PSR(I)=0                        interrupt flag = 0
MAR<-[SP]                          }       save PSR
MDR<-[PSR]                         }       on the stack
M[MAR]<-[MDR]                      }
ALUx<-[SP]                      }  decrement
ALUr=[ALUx]-1                   }  SP
SP<-[ALUr]                      }
ALUx<-[PC]                         }
MDR<-[ALUx]                        }       write PC
MAR<-[SP]                          }       to the stack
M[MAR]<-[MDR]                      }
ALUx<-[SP]                      }  decrement
ALUr=[ALUx]-1                   }  SP
SP<-[ALUr]                      }
PSR(E)=0                        interrupt enable flag = 0
ALUy<-[JUMPERS(IntBase)]           }
ALUx<-[PSR(IntVec)]                } build the vector address
ALUr=[ALUx]+[ALUy]                 }
MAR<-[ALUr]                     } obtain the handler address
MDR<-[M[MAR]]                   }
PC<-[MDR]                       load address of handler into PC


Opcode fa
Mnemonic "TRAP #data"
Description "Software interrupt mechanism"
* programmably trigger the interrupt routine
*
* The #data value is masked with %00000111
* to produce the interrupt number
*
PSR(IntVec)<-[IR(operand)]     } Load the PSR with the Interrupt Vector
PSR(I)=1                       } Fire the interrupt


Opcode 00
* data 00 to FF, sign extended
Mnemonic "ADD #data,A"
Description "Add to reg. A an immediate oper."
ALUx<-[A]
ALUy<-[IR(operand)]
ALUr=[ALUx]+[ALUy]
A<-[ALUr]


Opcode 01
* data 00 to FF, sign extended
Mnemonic "ADD #data,B"
Description "Add to reg. B an immediate oper."
ALUx<-[B]
ALUy<-[IR(operand)]
ALUr=[ALUx]+[ALUy]
```

```
B<-[ALUr]


Opcode 02
* addr 00 to FF
Mnemonic "ADD addr,A"
Description "Add to reg. A from a direct addr."
MAR<-[IR(operand)]
MDR<-[M[MAR]]
ALUy<-[MDR]
ALUx<-[A]
ALUr=[ALUx]+[ALUy]
A<-[ALUr]


Opcode 03
* addr 00 to FF
Mnemonic "ADD addr,B"
Description "Add to reg. B from a direct addr."
MAR<-[IR(operand)]
MDR<-[M[MAR]]
ALUy<-[MDR]
ALUx<-[B]
ALUr=[ALUx]+[ALUy]
B<-[ALUr]


Opcode 04
* addr and (addr) 00 to FF
Mnemonic "ADD (addr),A"
Description "Add to reg. A from an indirect addr."
MAR<-[IR(operand)]
MDR<-[M[MAR]]
IR<-[MDR]
MAR<-[IR(operand)]
MDR<-[M[MAR]]
ALUy<-[MDR]
ALUx<-[A]
ALUr=[ALUx]+[ALUy]
A<-[ALUr]


Opcode 05
* addr and (addr) 00 to FF
Mnemonic "ADD (addr),B"
Description "Add to reg. B from an indirect addr."
MAR<-[IR(operand)]
MDR<-[M[MAR]]
IR<-[MDR]
MAR<-[IR(operand)]
MDR<-[M[MAR]]
ALUy<-[MDR]
ALUx<-[B]
```

```
ALUr=[ALUx]+[ALUy]
B<-[ALUr]


Opcode 06
Mnemonic "ADD B,A"
Description "Add B reg. to contents of A reg."
ALUy<-[A]
ALUx<-[B]
ALUr=[ALUx]+[ALUy]
A<-[ALUr]


Opcode 07
Mnemonic "ADD A,B"
Description "Add A reg. to contents of B reg."
ALUy<-[A]
ALUx<-[B]
ALUr=[ALUx]+[ALUy]
B<-[ALUr]


Opcode 08
Mnemonic "ADD (B),A"
Description "Add B reg. indirect oper. to A reg."
MAR<-[B]
MDR<-[M[MAR]]
ALUy<-[MDR]
ALUx<-[A]
ALUr=[ALUx]+[ALUy]
A<-[ALUr]


Opcode 09
Mnemonic "ADD (A),B"
Description "Add A reg. indirect oper. to B reg."
MAR<-[A]
MDR<-[M[MAR]]
ALUy<-[MDR]
ALUx<-[B]
ALUr=[ALUx]+[ALUy]
B<-[ALUr]


Opcode 0a
* addr 00 to FF
Mnemonic "ADD B+addr,A"
Description "Add to reg. A from an indexed addr. (index in B)"
ALUy<-[IR(operand)]
ALUx<-[B]
ALUr=[ALUx]+[ALUy]
MAR<-[ALUr]
MDR<-[M[MAR]]
ALUy<-[MDR]
```

```
ALUx<-[A]
ALUr=[ALUx]+[ALUy]
A<-[ALUr]


Opcode 0b
* addr 00 to FF
Mnemonic "ADD A+addr,B"
Description "Add to reg. B from an indexed addr. (index in A)"
ALUy<-[IR(operand)]
ALUx<-[A]
ALUr=[ALUx]+[ALUy]
MAR<-[ALUr]
MDR<-[M[MAR]]
ALUy<-[MDR]
ALUx<-[B]
ALUr=[ALUx]+[ALUy]
B<-[ALUr]


Opcode 10
* data 00 to FF, sign extended
Mnemonic "ADC #data,A"
Description "Add with carry to reg. A an immediate oper."
ALUx<-[A]
ALUy<-[IR(operand)]
ALUr=[ALUx]+[ALUy]+[PSR(c)]
A<-[ALUr]


Opcode 11
* data 00 to FF, sign extended
Mnemonic "ADC #data,B"
Description "Add with carry to reg. B an immediate oper."
ALUx<-[B]
ALUy<-[IR(operand)]
ALUr=[ALUx]+[ALUy]+[PSR(c)]
B<-[ALUr]


Opcode 12
* addr 00 to FF
Mnemonic "ADC addr,A"
Description "Add with carry to reg. A from a direct addr."
MAR<-[IR(operand)]
MDR<-[M[MAR]]
ALUy<-[MDR]
ALUx<-[A]
ALUr=[ALUx]+[ALUy]+[PSR(c)]
A<-[ALUr]


Opcode 13
* addr 00 to FF
```

```
Mnemonic "ADC addr,B"
Description "Add with carry to reg. B from a direct addr."
MAR<-[IR(operand)]
MDR<-[M[MAR]]
ALUy<-[MDR]
ALUx<-[B]
ALUr=[ALUx]+[ALUy]+[PSR(c)]
B<-[ALUr]


Opcode 14
* addr and (addr) 00 to FF
Mnemonic "ADC (addr),A"
Description "Add with carry to reg. A from an indirect addr."
MAR<-[IR(operand)]
MDR<-[M[MAR]]
IR<-[MDR]
MAR<-[IR(operand)]
MDR<-[M[MAR]]
ALUy<-[MDR]
ALUx<-[A]
ALUr=[ALUx]+[ALUy]+[PSR(c)]
A<-[ALUr]


Opcode 15
* addr and (addr) 00 to FF
Mnemonic "ADC (addr),B"
Description "Add with carry to reg. B from an indirect addr."
MAR<-[IR(operand)]
MDR<-[M[MAR]]
IR<-[MDR]
MAR<-[IR(operand)]
MDR<-[M[MAR]]
ALUy<-[MDR]
ALUx<-[B]
ALUr=[ALUx]+[ALUy]+[PSR(c)]
B<-[ALUr]


Opcode 16
Mnemonic "ADC B,A"
Description "Add with carry to A reg. from B reg."
ALUy<-[B]
ALUx<-[A]
ALUr=[ALUx]+[ALUy]+[PSR(c)]
A<-[ALUr]


Opcode 17
Mnemonic "ADC A,B"
Description "Add with carry to B reg. from A reg."
ALUy<-[A]
```

```
ALUx<-[B]
ALUr=[ALUx]+[ALUy]+[PSR(c)]
B<-[ALUr]


Opcode 18
Mnemonic "ADC (B),A"
Description "Add with carry to B reg. a reg. indirect oper."
MAR<-[B]
MDR<-[M[MAR]]
ALUy<-[MDR]
ALUx<-[A]
ALUr=[ALUx]+[ALUy]+[PSR(c)]
A<-[ALUr]


Opcode 19
Mnemonic "ADC (A),B"
Description "Add with carry to B reg. a reg. indirect oper."
MAR<-[A]
MDR<-[M[MAR]]
ALUy<-[MDR]
ALUx<-[B]
ALUr=[ALUx]+[ALUy]+[PSR(c)]
B<-[ALUr]


Opcode 1a
* addr 00 to FF
Mnemonic "ADC B+addr,A"
Description "Add with carry to reg. A an indexed oper. (index in B)"
ALUy<-[IR(operand)]
ALUx<-[B]
ALUr=[ALUx]+[ALUy]
MAR<-[ALUr]
MDR<-[M[MAR]]
ALUy<-[MDR]
ALUx<-[A]
ALUr=[ALUx]+[ALUy]+[PSR(c)]
A<-[ALUr]


Opcode 1b
* addr 00 to FF
Mnemonic "ADC A+addr,B"
Description "Add with carry to reg. B an indexed oper. (index in A)"
ALUy<-[IR(operand)]
ALUx<-[A]
ALUr=[ALUx]+[ALUy]
MAR<-[ALUr]
MDR<-[M[MAR]]
ALUy<-[MDR]
ALUx<-[B]
```

```
ALUr=[ALUx]+[ALUy]+[PSR(c)]
B<-[ALUr]


Opcode 20
* data 00 to FF, sign extended
Mnemonic "SUB #data,A"
Description "Subtract an immediate oper. from A reg"
ALUx<-[A]
ALUy<-[IR(operand)]
ALUr=[ALUx]-[ALUy]
A<-[ALUr]


Opcode 21
* data 00 to FF, sign extended
Mnemonic "SUB #data,B"
Description "Subtract an immediate oper. from B reg"
ALUx<-[B]
ALUy<-[IR(operand)]
ALUr=[ALUx]-[ALUy]
B<-[ALUr]


Opcode 22
* addr 00 to FF
Mnemonic "SUB addr,A"
Description "Subtract from reg. A a direct oper."
MAR<-[IR(operand)]
MDR<-[M[MAR]]
ALUx<-[A]
ALUy<-[MDR]
ALUr=[ALUx]-[ALUy]
A<-[ALUr]


Opcode 23
* addr 00 to FF
Mnemonic "SUB addr,B"
Description "Subtract from reg. B a direct oper."
MAR<-[IR(operand)]
MDR<-[M[MAR]]
ALUx<-[B]
ALUy<-[MDR]
ALUr=[ALUx]-[ALUy]
B<-[ALUr]


Opcode 24
* addr and (addr) 00 to FF
Mnemonic "SUB (addr),A"
Description "Subtract from reg. A an indirect oper."
MAR<-[IR(operand)]
MDR<-[M[MAR]]
```

```
IR<-[MDR]
MAR<-[IR(operand)]
MDR<-[M[MAR]]
ALUx<-[A]
ALUy<-[MDR]
ALUr=[ALUx]-[ALUy]
A<-[ALUr]


Opcode 25
* addr and (addr) 00 to FF
Mnemonic "SUB (addr),B"
Description "Subtract from reg. B an indirect oper."
MAR<-[IR(operand)]
MDR<-[M[MAR]]
IR<-[MDR]
MAR<-[IR(operand)]
MDR<-[M[MAR]]
ALUx<-[B]
ALUy<-[MDR]
ALUr=[ALUx]-[ALUy]
B<-[ALUr]


Opcode 26
Mnemonic "SUB B,A"
Description "Subtract from reg. A the contents of reg. B"
ALUx<-[A]
ALUy<-[B]
ALUr=[ALUx]-[ALUy]
A<-[ALUr]


Opcode 27
Mnemonic "SUB A,B"
Description "Subtract from reg. B the contents of reg. A"
ALUx<-[B]
ALUy<-[A]
ALUr=[ALUx]-[ALUy]
B<-[ALUr]


Opcode 28
Mnemonic "SUB (B),A"
Description "Subtract from reg. A a reg. indirect oper."
MAR<-[B]
MDR<-[M[MAR]]
ALUx<-[A]
ALUy<-[MDR]
ALUr=[ALUx]-[ALUy]
A<-[ALUr]


Opcode 29
```

```
Mnemonic "SUB (A),B"
Description "Subtract from reg. B a reg. indirect oper."
MAR<-[A]
MDR<-[M[MAR]]
ALUx<-[B]
ALUy<-[MDR]
ALUr=[ALUx]-[ALUy]
B<-[ALUr]


Opcode 2a
* addr 00 to FF
Mnemonic "SUB B+addr,A"
Description "Subtract an indexed oper. from the reg. A (index in B)"
ALUy<-[IR(operand)]
ALUx<-[B]
ALUr=[ALUx]+[ALUy]
MAR<-[ALUr]
MDR<-[M[MAR]]
ALUy<-[MDR]
ALUx<-[A]
ALUr=[ALUx]-[ALUy]
A<-[ALUr]


Opcode 2b
* addr 00 to FF
Mnemonic "SUB A+addr,B"
Description "Subtract an indexed oper. from the reg. B (index in A)"
ALUy<-[IR(operand)]
ALUx<-[A]
ALUr=[ALUx]+[ALUy]
MAR<-[ALUr]
MDR<-[M[MAR]]
ALUy<-[MDR]
ALUx<-[B]
ALUr=[ALUx]-[ALUy]
B<-[ALUr]


Opcode 32
* addr 00 to FF
Mnemonic "SHL addr"
Description "Shift left a memory direct oper."
MAR<-[IR(operand)]
MDR<-[M[MAR]]
ALUx<-[MDR]
ALUr=[ALUx]<<1
MDR<-[ALUr]
M[MAR]<-[MDR]


Opcode 34
```

```
* addr and (addr) 00 to FF
Mnemonic "SHL (addr)"
Description "Shift left a memory indirect oper."
MAR<-[IR(operand)]
MDR<-[M[MAR]]
IR<-[MDR]
MAR<-[IR(operand)]
MDR<-[M[MAR]]
ALUx<-[MDR]
ALUr=[ALUx]<<1
MDR<-[ALUr]
M[MAR]<-[MDR]


Opcode 36
Mnemonic "SHL A"
Description "Shift left reg. A"
ALUx<-[A]
ALUr=[ALUx]<<1
A<-[ALUr]


Opcode 37
Mnemonic "SHL B"
Description "Shift left reg. B"
ALUx<-[B]
ALUr=[ALUx]<<1
B<-[ALUr]


Opcode 38
Mnemonic "SHL (A)"
Description "Shift left a reg. indirect oper., addr. in A"
MAR<-[A]
MDR<-[M[MAR]]
ALUx<-[MDR]
ALUr=[ALUx]<<1
MDR<-[ALUr]
M[MAR]<-[MDR]


Opcode 39
Mnemonic "SHL (B)"
Description "Shift left a reg. indirect oper., addr. in B"
MAR<-[B]
MDR<-[M[MAR]]
ALUx<-[MDR]
ALUr=[ALUx]<<1
MDR<-[ALUr]
M[MAR]<-[MDR]


Opcode 3a
* addr 00 to FF
```

```
Mnemonic "SHL A+addr"
Description "Shift left an indexed oper. (index in A)"
ALUy<-[IR(operand)]
ALUx<-[A]
ALUr=[ALUx]+[ALUy]
MAR<-[ALUr]
MDR<-[M[MAR]]
ALUx<-[MDR]
ALUr=[ALUx]<<1
MDR<-[ALUr]
M[MAR]<-[MDR]

Opcode 3b
* addr 00 to FF
Mnemonic "SHL B+addr"
Description "Shift left an indexed oper. (index in B)"
ALUy<-[IR(operand)]
ALUx<-[B]
ALUr=[ALUx]+[ALUy]
MAR<-[ALUr]
MDR<-[M[MAR]]
ALUx<-[MDR]
ALUr=[ALUx]<<1
MDR<-[ALUr]
M[MAR]<-[MDR]

Opcode 42
* addr 00 to FF
Mnemonic "SHR addr"
Description "Shift right a direct oper."
MAR<-[IR(operand)]
MDR<-[M[MAR]]
ALUx<-[MDR]
ALUr=[ALUx]>>1
MDR<-[ALUr]
M[MAR]<-[MDR]

Opcode 44
* addr and (addr) 00 to FF
Mnemonic "SHR (addr)"
Description "Shift right a memory indirect oper."
MAR<-[IR(operand)]
MDR<-[M[MAR]]
IR<-[MDR]
MAR<-[IR(operand)]
MDR<-[M[MAR]]
ALUx<-[MDR]
ALUr=[ALUx]>>1
MDR<-[ALUr]
```

```
M[MAR]<-[MDR]


Opcode 46
Mnemonic "SHR A"
Description "Shift right the contents of reg. A"
ALUx<-[A]
ALUr=[ALUx]>>1
A<-[ALUr]


Opcode 47
Mnemonic "SHR B"
Description "Shift right the contents of reg. B"
ALUx<-[B]
ALUr=[ALUx]>>1
B<-[ALUr]


Opcode 48
Mnemonic "SHR (A)"
Description "Shift right a reg. indirect oper."
MAR<-[A]
MDR<-[M[MAR]]
ALUx<-[MDR]
ALUr=[ALUx]>>1
MDR<-[ALUr]
M[MAR]<-[MDR]


Opcode 49
Mnemonic "SHR (B)"
Description "Shift right a reg. indirect oper."
MAR<-[B]
MDR<-[M[MAR]]
ALUx<-[MDR]
ALUr=[ALUx]>>1
MDR<-[ALUr]
M[MAR]<-[MDR]


Opcode 4a
* addr 00 to FF
Mnemonic "SHR A+addr"
Description "Shift right a memory indexed oper. (index in A)"
ALUy<-[IR(operand)]
ALUx<-[A]
ALUr=[ALUx]+[ALUy]
MAR<-[ALUr]
MDR<-[M[MAR]]
ALUx<-[MDR]
ALUr=[ALUx]>>1
MDR<-[ALUr]
M[MAR]<-[MDR]
```

```
Opcode 4b
* addr 00 to FF
Mnemonic "SHR B+addr"
Description "Shift right a memory indexed oper. (Index in B)"
ALUy<-[IR(operand)]
ALUx<-[B]
ALUr=[ALUx]+[ALUy]
MAR<-[ALUr]
MDR<-[M[MAR]]
ALUx<-[MDR]
ALUr=[ALUx]>>1
MDR<-[ALUr]
M[MAR]<-[MDR]


Opcode 50
* data 00 to FF, sign extended
Mnemonic "AND #data,A"
Description "AND operation on A reg and an immediate oper."
ALUy<-[IR(operand)]
ALUx<-[A]
ALUr=[ALUx]&[ALUy]
A<-[ALUr]


Opcode 51
* data 00 to FF, sign extended
Mnemonic "AND #data,B"
Description "AND operation on B reg and an immediate oper."
ALUy<-[IR(operand)]
ALUx<-[B]
ALUr=[ALUx]&[ALUy]
B<-[ALUr]


Opcode 52
* addr 00 to FF
Mnemonic "AND addr,A"
Description "AND operation on A and a direct oper."
MAR<-[IR(operand)]
MDR<-[M[MAR]]
ALUy<-[MDR]
ALUx<-[A]
ALUr=[ALUx]&[ALUy]
A<-[ALUr]


Opcode 53
* addr 00 to FF
Mnemonic "AND addr,B"
Description "AND operation on B and a direct oper."
MAR<-[IR(operand)]
```

```
MDR<-[M[MAR]]
ALUy<-[MDR]
ALUx<-[B]
ALUr=[ALUx]&[ALUy]
B<-[ALUr]


Opcode 54
* addr and (addr) 00 to FF
Mnemonic "AND (addr),A"
Description "AND operation on A and an indirect oper."
MAR<-[IR(operand)]
MDR<-[M[MAR]]
IR<-[MDR]
MAR<-[IR(operand)]
MDR<-[M[MAR]]
ALUy<-[MDR]
ALUx<-[A]
ALUr=[ALUx]&[ALUy]
A<-[ALUr]


Opcode 55
* addr and (addr) 00 to FF
Mnemonic "AND (addr),B"
Description "AND operation on B and an indirect oper."
MAR<-[IR(operand)]
MDR<-[M[MAR]]
IR<-[MDR]
MAR<-[IR(operand)]
MDR<-[M[MAR]]
ALUy<-[MDR]
ALUx<-[B]
ALUr=[ALUx]&[ALUy]
B<-[ALUr]


Opcode 56
Mnemonic "AND B,A"
Description "AND on A and B, result in A"
ALUy<-[B]
ALUx<-[A]
ALUr=[ALUx]&[ALUy]
A<-[ALUr]


Opcode 57
Mnemonic "AND A,B"
Description "AND on B and A, result in B"
ALUy<-[A]
ALUx<-[B]
ALUr=[ALUx]&[ALUy]
B<-[ALUr]
```

```
Opcode 58
Mnemonic "AND (B),A"
Description "AND on A and a reg. indirect oper."
MAR<-[B]
MDR<-[M[MAR]]
ALUx<-[MDR]
ALUy<-[A]
ALUr=[ALUx]&[ALUy]
A<-[ALUr]

Opcode 59
Mnemonic "AND (A),B"
Description "AND on B and a reg. indirect oper."
MAR<-[A]
MDR<-[M[MAR]]
ALUx<-[MDR]
ALUy<-[B]
ALUr=[ALUx]&[ALUy]
B<-[ALUr]

Opcode 5a
* addr 00 to FF
Mnemonic "AND B+addr,A"
Description "AND operation on A and an indexed oper."
ALUy<-[IR(operand)]
ALUx<-[B]
ALUr=[ALUx]+[ALUy]
MAR<-[ALUr]
MDR<-[M[MAR]]
ALUy<-[MDR]
ALUx<-[A]
ALUr=[ALUx]&[ALUy]
A<-[ALUr]

Opcode 5b
* addr 00 to FF
Mnemonic "AND A+addr,B"
Description "AND operation on B and an indexed oper."
ALUy<-[IR(operand)]
ALUx<-[A]
ALUr=[ALUx]+[ALUy]
MAR<-[ALUr]
MDR<-[M[MAR]]
ALUy<-[MDR]
ALUx<-[B]
ALUr=[ALUx]&[ALUy]
B<-[ALUr]
```

```
Opcode 60
* data 00 to FF, sign extended
Mnemonic "OR #data,A"
Description "OR operation on A reg and an immediate oper."
ALUy<-[IR(operand)]
ALUx<-[A]
ALUr=[ALUx]|[ALUy]
A<-[ALUr]

Opcode 61
* data 00 to FF, sign extended
Mnemonic "OR #data,B"
Description "OR operation on B reg and an immediate oper."
ALUy<-[IR(operand)]
ALUx<-[B]
ALUr=[ALUx]|[ALUy]
B<-[ALUr]

Opcode 62
* addr 00 to FF
Mnemonic "OR addr,A"
Description "OR operation on A and a direct oper."
MAR<-[IR(operand)]
MDR<-[M[MAR]]
ALUy<-[MDR]
ALUx<-[A]
ALUr=[ALUx]|[ALUy]
A<-[ALUr]

Opcode 63
* addr 00 to FF
Mnemonic "OR addr,B"
Description "OR operation on B and a direct oper."
MAR<-[IR(operand)]
MDR<-[M[MAR]]
ALUy<-[MDR]
ALUx<-[B]
ALUr=[ALUx]|[ALUy]
B<-[ALUr]

Opcode 64
* addr and (addr) 00 to FF
Mnemonic "OR (addr),A"
Description "OR operation on A and an indirect oper."
MAR<-[IR(operand)]
MDR<-[M[MAR]]
IR<-[MDR]
MAR<-[IR(operand)]
MDR<-[M[MAR]]
```

```
ALUy<-[MDR]
ALUx<-[A]
ALUr=[ALUx]|[ALUy]
A<-[ALUr]


Opcode 65
* addr and (addr) 00 to FF
Mnemonic "OR (addr),B"
Description "OR operation on B and an indirect oper."
MAR<-[IR(operand)]
MDR<-[M[MAR]]
IR<-[MDR]
MAR<-[IR(operand)]
MDR<-[M[MAR]]
ALUy<-[MDR]
ALUx<-[B]
ALUr=[ALUx]|[ALUy]
B<-[ALUr]


Opcode 66
Mnemonic "OR B,A"
Description "OR on A and B, result in A"
ALUy<-[B]
ALUx<-[A]
ALUr=[ALUx]|[ALUy]
A<-[ALUr]


Opcode 67
Mnemonic "OR A,B"
Description "OR on B and A, result in B"
ALUy<-[A]
ALUx<-[B]
ALUr=[ALUx]|[ALUy]
B<-[ALUr]


Opcode 68
Mnemonic "OR (B),A"
Description "OR on A and a reg. indirect oper."
MAR<-[B]
MDR<-[M[MAR]]
ALUx<-[MDR]
ALUy<-[A]
ALUr=[ALUx]|[ALUy]
A<-[ALUr]


Opcode 69
Mnemonic "OR (A),B"
Description "OR on B and a reg. indirect oper."
MAR<-[A]
```

```
MDR<-[M[MAR]]
ALUx<-[MDR]
ALUy<-[B]
ALUr=[ALUx]|[ALUy]
B<-[ALUr]


Opcode 6a
* addr 00 to FF
Mnemonic "OR B+addr,A"
Description "OR operation on A and an indexed oper."
ALUy<-[IR(operand)]
ALUx<-[B]
ALUr=[ALUx]+[ALUy]
MAR<-[ALUr]
MDR<-[M[MAR]]
ALUy<-[MDR]
ALUx<-[A]
ALUr=[ALUx]|[ALUy]
A<-[ALUr]


Opcode 6b
* addr 00 to FF
Mnemonic "OR A+addr,B"
Description "OR operation on B and an indexed oper."
ALUy<-[IR(operand)]
ALUx<-[A]
ALUr=[ALUx]+[ALUy]
MAR<-[ALUr]
MDR<-[M[MAR]]
ALUy<-[MDR]
ALUx<-[B]
ALUr=[ALUx]|[ALUy]
B<-[ALUr]


Opcode 72
* addr 00 to FF
Mnemonic "NOT addr"
Description "NOT operation on a direct oper."
MAR<-[IR(operand)]
MDR<-[M[MAR]]
ALUx<-[MDR]
ALUr=~[ALUx]
MDR<-[ALUr]
M[MAR]<-[MDR]


Opcode 74
* addr and (addr) 00 to FF
Mnemonic "NOT (addr)"
Description "NOT operation on an indirect oper."
```

```
MAR<-[IR(operand)]
MDR<-[M[MAR]]
IR<-[MDR]
MAR<-[IR(operand)]
MDR<-[M[MAR]]
ALUx<-[MDR]
ALUr=~[ALUx]
MDR<-[ALUr]
M[MAR]<-[MDR]
```

```
Opcode 76
Mnemonic "NOT A"
Description "NOT operation on A reg."
ALUx<-[A]
ALUr=~[ALUx]
A<-[ALUr]
```

```
Opcode 77
Mnemonic "NOT B"
Description "NOT operation on B reg."
ALUx<-[B]
ALUr=~[ALUx]
B<-[ALUr]
```

```
Opcode 78
Mnemonic "NOT (A)"
Description "NOT on a reg. indirect oper. (address in A)"
MAR<-[A]
MDR<-[M[MAR]]
ALUx<-[MDR]
ALUr=~[ALUx]
MDR<-[ALUr]
M[MAR]<-[MDR]
```

```
Opcode 79
Mnemonic "NOT (B)"
Description "NOT on a reg. indirect oper. (address in B)"
MAR<-[B]
MDR<-[M[MAR]]
ALUx<-[MDR]
ALUr=~[ALUx]
MDR<-[ALUr]
M[MAR]<-[MDR]
```

```
Opcode 7a
* addr 00 to FF
Mnemonic "NOT A+addr"
Description "NOT on an indexed oper. (index in A)"
ALUx<-[A]
```

```
ALUy<-[IR(operand)]
ALUr=[ALUx]+[ALUy]
MAR<-[ALUr]
MDR<-[M[MAR]]
ALUx<-[MDR]
ALUr=~[ALUx]
MDR<-[ALUr]
M[MAR]<-[MDR]
```

```
Opcode 7b
* addr 00 to FF
Mnemonic "NOT B+addr"
Description "NOT on an indexed oper. (index in B)"
ALUx<-[B]
ALUy<-[IR(operand)]
ALUr=[ALUx]+[ALUy]
MAR<-[ALUr]
MDR<-[M[MAR]]
ALUx<-[MDR]
ALUr=~[ALUx]
MDR<-[ALUr]
M[MAR]<-[MDR]
```

```
Opcode 7c
Mnemonic "SWAP A"
Description "Swap A register lo and hi bytes"
ALUx<-[A]
ALUr(7:0)=[ALUx(15:8)];ALUr(15:8)=[ALUx(7:0)]
A<-[ALUr]
```

```
Opcode 7d
Mnemonic "SWAP B"
Description "Swap B register lo and hi bytes"
ALUx<-[B]
ALUr(7:0)=[ALUx(15:8)];ALUr(15:8)=[ALUx(7:0)]
B<-[ALUr]
```

```
Opcode 80
* data 00 to FF, sign extended
Mnemonic "CMP #data,A"
Description "Compare an immediate oper. with A reg"
ALUx<-[A]
ALUy<-[IR(operand)]
ALUr=[ALUx]-[ALUy]
```

```
Opcode 81
* data 00 to FF, sign extended
Mnemonic "CMP #data,B"
Description "Compare an immediate oper. with B reg"
```

```
ALUx<-[B]
ALUy<-[IR(operand)]
ALUr=[ALUx]-[ALUy]


Opcode 82
* addr 00 to FF
Mnemonic "CMP addr,A"
Description "Compare a direct oper. with A reg."
MAR<-[IR(operand)]
MDR<-[M[MAR]]
ALUy<-[MDR]
ALUx<-[A]
ALUr=[ALUx]-[ALUy]


Opcode 83
* addr 00 to FF
Mnemonic "CMP addr,B"
Description "Compare a direct oper. with B reg."
MAR<-[IR(operand)]
MDR<-[M[MAR]]
ALUy<-[MDR]
ALUx<-[B]
ALUr=[ALUx]-[ALUy]


Opcode 84
* addr and (addr) 00 to FF
Mnemonic "CMP (addr),A"
Description "Compare an indirect oper. with A reg."
MAR<-[IR(operand)]
MDR<-[M[MAR]]
IR<-[MDR]
MAR<-[IR(operand)]
MDR<-[M[MAR]]
ALUy<-[MDR]
ALUx<-[A]
ALUr=[ALUx]-[ALUy]


Opcode 85
* addr and (addr) 00 to FF
Mnemonic "CMP (addr),B"
Description "Compare an indirect oper. with B reg."
MAR<-[IR(operand)]
MDR<-[M[MAR]]
IR<-[MDR]
MAR<-[IR(operand)]
MDR<-[M[MAR]]
ALUy<-[MDR]
ALUx<-[B]
ALUr=[ALUx]-[ALUy]
```

```
Opcode 86
Mnemonic "CMP B,A"
Description "Compare A and B reg."
ALUx<-[A]
ALUy<-[B]
ALUr=[ALUx]-[ALUy]


Opcode 87
Mnemonic "CMP A,B"
Description "Compare B and A reg."
ALUx<-[B]
ALUy<-[A]
ALUr=[ALUx]-[ALUy]


Opcode 88
Mnemonic "CMP (B),A"
Description "Compare A with a reg. indirect oper."
MAR<-[B]
MDR<-[M[MAR]]
ALUx<-[A]
ALUy<-[MDR]
ALUr=[ALUx]-[ALUy]


Opcode 89
Mnemonic "CMP (A),B"
Description "Compare B with a reg. indirect oper."
MAR<-[A]
MDR<-[M[MAR]]
ALUx<-[B]
ALUy<-[MDR]
ALUr=[ALUx]-[ALUy]


Opcode 8a
* addr 00 to FF
Mnemonic "CMP B+addr,A"
Description "Compare with A an indexed oper."
ALUx<-[B]
ALUy<-[IR(operand)]
ALUr=[ALUx]+[ALUy]
MAR<-[ALUr]
MDR<-[M[MAR]]
ALUx<-[A]
ALUy<-[MDR]
ALUr=[ALUx]-[ALUy]


Opcode 8b
* addr 00 to FF
Mnemonic "CMP A+addr,B"
```

```
Description "Compare with B an indexed oper."
ALUx<-[A]
ALUy<-[IR(operand)]
ALUr=[ALUx]+[ALUy]
MAR<-[ALUr]
MDR<-[M[MAR]]
ALUx<-[B]
ALUy<-[MDR]
ALUr=[ALUx]-[ALUy]

Opcode 8c
Mnemonic "PUSH A"
Description "Push A onto the stack"
MAR<-[SP]
MDR<-[A]
M[MAR]<-[MDR]
ALUx<-[SP]
ALUr=[ALUx]-1
SP<-[ALUr]

Opcode 8d
Mnemonic "PUSH B"
Description "Push B onto the stack"
MAR<-[SP]
MDR<-[B]
M[MAR]<-[MDR]
ALUx<-[SP]
ALUr=[ALUx]-1
SP<-[ALUr]

Opcode 8e
Mnemonic "POP A"
Description "Pop A from the stack"
ALUx<-[SP]
ALUr=[ALUx]+1
SP<-[ALUr]
MAR<-[SP]
MDR<-[M[MAR]]
A<-[MDR]

Opcode 8f
Mnemonic "POP B"
Description "Pop B from the stack"
ALUx<-[SP]
ALUr=[ALUx]+1
SP<-[ALUr]
MAR<-[SP]
MDR<-[M[MAR]]
B<-[MDR]
```

```
Opcode 90
* data 00 to FF
Mnemonic "MOVE #data,A"
Description "Move an immediate oper. into A"
A<-[IR(operand)]

Opcode 91
* data 00 to FF
Mnemonic "MOVE #data,B"
Description "Move an immediate oper. into B"
B<-[IR(operand)]

Opcode 92
* addr 00 to FF
Mnemonic "MOVE addr,A"
Description "Load reg. A from a direct addr."
MAR<-[IR(operand)]
MDR<-[M[MAR]]
A<-[MDR]

Opcode 93
* addr 00 to FF
Mnemonic "MOVE addr,B"
Description "Load reg. B from a direct addr."
MAR<-[IR(operand)]
MDR<-[M[MAR]]
B<-[MDR]

Opcode 94
* addr and (addr) 00 to FF
Mnemonic "MOVE (addr),A"
Description "Load reg. A from an indirect addr."
MAR<-[IR(operand)]
MDR<-[M[MAR]]
IR<-[MDR]
MAR<-[IR(operand)]
MDR<-[M[MAR]]
A<-[MDR]

Opcode 95
* addr and (addr) 00 to FF
Mnemonic "MOVE (addr),B"
Description "Load reg. B from an indirect addr."
MAR<-[IR(operand)]
MDR<-[M[MAR]]
IR<-[MDR]
MAR<-[IR(operand)]
MDR<-[M[MAR]]
```

```
B<-[MDR]


Opcode 96
Mnemonic "MOVE B,A"
Description "Move B reg. to A reg."
MDR<-[B]
A<-[MDR]


Opcode 97
Mnemonic "MOVE A,B"
Description "Move A reg. to B reg."
MDR<-[A]
B<-[MDR]


Opcode 98
Mnemonic "MOVE (B),A"
Description "Load A reg. with a reg. indirect oper."
MAR<-[B]
MDR<-[M[MAR]]
A<-[MDR]


Opcode 99
Mnemonic "MOVE (A),B"
Description "Load B reg. with a reg. indirect oper."
MAR<-[A]
MDR<-[M[MAR]]
B<-[MDR]


Opcode 9a
* addr 00 to FF
Mnemonic "MOVE B+addr,A"
Description "Load A reg from an indexed addr. (index in B)"
ALUy<-[IR(operand)]
ALUx<-[B]
ALUr=[ALUx]+[ALUy]
MAR<-[ALUr]
MDR<-[M[MAR]]
A<-[MDR]


Opcode 9b
* addr 00 to FF
Mnemonic "MOVE A+addr,B"
Description "Load B reg from an indexed addr. (index in A)"
ALUy<-[IR(operand)]
ALUx<-[A]
ALUr=[ALUx]+[ALUy]
MAR<-[ALUr]
MDR<-[M[MAR]]
B<-[MDR]
```

```
Opcode a2
* addr 00 to FF
Mnemonic "MOVE A,addr"
Description "Store the A reg. in memory at a direct addr."
MAR<-[IR(operand)]
MDR<-[A]
M[MAR]<-[MDR]

Opcode a3
* addr 00 to FF
Mnemonic "MOVE B,addr"
Description "Store the B reg. in memory at a direct addr."
MAR<-[IR(operand)]
MDR<-[B]
M[MAR]<-[MDR]

Opcode a4
* addr and (addr) 00 to FF
Mnemonic "MOVE A,(addr)"
Description "Store reg. A at a mem. indirect addr."
MAR<-[IR(operand)]
MDR<-[M[MAR]]
IR<-[MDR]
MAR<-[IR(operand)]
MDR<-[A]
M[MAR]<-[MDR]

Opcode a5
* addr and (addr) 00 to FF
Mnemonic "MOVE B,(addr)"
Description "Store reg. B at a mem. indirect addr."
MAR<-[IR(operand)]
MDR<-[M[MAR]]
IR<-[MDR]
MAR<-[IR(operand)]
MDR<-[B]
M[MAR]<-[MDR]

Opcode a6
* data 00 to FF
Mnemonic "MOVE #data,SP"
Description "Move an immediate oper. into SP"
SP<-[IR(operand)]

Opcode a7
* addr 00 to FF
Mnemonic "MOVE addr,SP"
Description "Load reg. SP from a direct addr."
```

```
MAR<-[IR(operand)]
MDR<-[M[MAR]]
SP<-[MDR]


Opcode a8
Mnemonic "MOVE A,(B)"
Description "Store A reg. at an addr. held in B"
MAR<-[B]
MDR<-[A]
M[MAR]<-[MDR]


Opcode a9
Mnemonic "MOVE B,(A)"
Description "Store B reg. at an addr. held in A"
MAR<-[A]
MDR<-[B]
M[MAR]<-[MDR]


Opcode aa
* addr 00 to FF
Mnemonic "MOVE A,B+addr"
Description "Store A reg. at an indexed addr. (index in B)"
ALUy<-[IR(operand)]
ALUx<-[B]
ALUr=[ALUx]+[ALUy]
MAR<-[ALUr]
MDR<-[A]
M[MAR]<-[MDR]


Opcode ab
* addr 00 to FF
Mnemonic "MOVE B,A+addr"
Description "Store B reg. at an indexed addr. (index in A)"
ALUy<-[IR(operand)]
ALUx<-[A]
ALUr=[ALUx]+[ALUy]
MAR<-[ALUr]
MDR<-[B]
M[MAR]<-[MDR]


Opcode ac
* addr and (addr) 00 to FF
Mnemonic "MOVE (addr),SP"
Description "Load reg. SP from an indirect addr."
MAR<-[IR(operand)]
MDR<-[M[MAR]]
IR<-[MDR]
MAR<-[IR(operand)]
MDR<-[M[MAR]]
```

```
SP<-[MDR]

Opcode ad
Mnemonic "MOVE A,SP"
Description "Move A reg. to SP reg."
MDR<-[A]
SP<-[MDR]

Opcode ae
Mnemonic "MOVE B,SP"
Description "Move B reg. to SP reg."
MDR<-[B]
SP<-[MDR]

Opcode b0
* dis 00 to FF, sign extended
Mnemonic "BCC #dis"
Description "Branch on carry clear to a PC relative addr."
if(PSR(c)==0)
ALUx<-[PC]
ALUy<-[IR(operand)]
ALUr=[ALUx]+[ALUy]
PC<-[ALUr]

Opcode b1
* dis 00 to FF, sign extended
Mnemonic "BCS #dis"
Description "Branch on carry set to a PC relative addr."
if(PSR(c)==1)
ALUx<-[PC]
ALUy<-[IR(operand)]
ALUr=[ALUx]+[ALUy]
PC<-[ALUr]

Opcode b2
* addr 00 to FF
Mnemonic "BCC addr"
Description "Branch to a direct addr. if carry flag clear (C=0)"
if(PSR(c)==0)
PC<-[IR(operand)]

Opcode b3
* addr 00 to FF
Mnemonic "BCS addr"
Description "Branch to a direct addr. if carry flag set (C=1)"
if(PSR(c)==1)
PC<-[IR(operand)]

Opcode b4
```

```
* addr and (addr) 00 to FF
Mnemonic "BCC (addr)"
Description "Branch to an indirect addr. if carry flag is clear"
if(PSR(c)==0)
MAR<-[IR(operand)]
MDR<-[M[MAR]]
IR<-[MDR]
MAR<-[IR(operand)]
MDR<-[M[MAR]]
IR<-[MDR]
PC<-[IR(operand)]


Opcode b5
* addr and (addr) 00 to FF
Mnemonic "BCS (addr)"
Description "Branch to an indirect addr. if carry flag is set"
if(PSR(c)==1)
MAR<-[IR(operand)]
MDR<-[M[MAR]]
IR<-[MDR]
MAR<-[IR(operand)]
MDR<-[M[MAR]]
IR<-[MDR]
PC<-[IR(operand)]


Opcode b8
* dis 00 to FF, sign extended
Mnemonic "BPL #dis"
Description "Branch on negative clear to a PC relative addr."
if(PSR(n)==0)
ALUx<-[PC]
ALUy<-[IR(operand)]
ALUr=[ALUx]+[ALUy]
PC<-[ALUr]


Opcode b9
* dis 00 to FF, sign extended
Mnemonic "BMI #dis"
Description "Branch on negative set to a PC relative addr."
if(PSR(n)==1)
ALUx<-[PC]
ALUy<-[IR(operand)]
ALUr=[ALUx]+[ALUy]
PC<-[ALUr]


Opcode ba
* addr 00 to FF
Mnemonic "BPL addr"
Description "Branch to a direct addr. if negative flag clear (N=0)"
```

```
if(PSR(n)==0)
PC<-[IR(operand)]


Opcode bb
* addr 00 to FF
Mnemonic "BMI addr"
Description "Branch to a direct addr. if negative flag set (N=1)"
if(PSR(n)==1)
PC<-[IR(operand)]


Opcode bc
* addr and (addr) 00 to FF
Mnemonic "BPL (addr)"
Description "Branch to an indirect addr. if negative flag is clear"
if(PSR(n)==0)
MAR<-[IR(operand)]
MDR<-[M[MAR]]
IR<-[MDR]
MAR<-[IR(operand)]
MDR<-[M[MAR]]
IR<-[MDR]
PC<-[IR(operand)]


Opcode bd
* addr and (addr) 00 to FF
Mnemonic "BMI (addr)"
Description "Branch to an indirect addr. if negative flag is set"
if(PSR(n)==1)
MAR<-[IR(operand)]
IR<-[MDR]
MAR<-[IR(operand)]
MDR<-[M[MAR]]
IR<-[MDR]
PC<-[IR(operand)]


Opcode c0
* dis 00 to FF, sign extended
Mnemonic "BNE #dis"
Description "Branch on zero clear to a PC relative addr."
if(PSR(z)==0)
ALUx<-[PC]
ALUy<-[IR(operand)]
ALUr=[ALUx]+[ALUy]
PC<-[ALUr]


Opcode c1
* dis 00 to FF, sign extended
Mnemonic "BEQ #dis"
Description "Branch on zero set to a PC relative addr."
```

```
if(PSR(z)==1)
ALUx<-[PC]
ALUy<-[IR(operand)]
ALUr=[ALUx]+[ALUy]
PC<-[ALUr]


Opcode c2
* addr 00 to FF
Mnemonic "BNE addr"
Description "Branch to a direct addr. if zero flag clear (Z=0)"
if(PSR(z)==0)
PC<-[IR(operand)]


Opcode c3
* addr 00 to FF
Mnemonic "BEQ addr"
Description "Branch to a direct addr. if zero flag set (Z=1)"
if(PSR(z)==1)
PC<-[IR(operand)]


Opcode c4
* addr and (addr) 00 to FF
Mnemonic "BNE (addr)"
Description "Branch to an indirect addr. if zero flag is clear"
if(PSR(z)==0)
MAR<-[IR(operand)]
MDR<-[M[MAR]]
IR<-[MDR]
MAR<-[IR(operand)]
MDR<-[M[MAR]]
IR<-[MDR]
PC<-[IR(operand)]


Opcode c5
* addr and (addr) 00 to FF
Mnemonic "BEQ (addr)"
Description "Branch to an indirect addr. if zero flag is set"
if(PSR(z)==1)
MAR<-[IR(operand)]
MDR<-[M[MAR]]
IR<-[MDR]
MAR<-[IR(operand)]
MDR<-[M[MAR]]
IR<-[MDR]
PC<-[IR(operand)]


Opcode c8
* dis 00 to FF, sign extended
Mnemonic "BVC #dis"
```

```
Description "Branch on no overflow to a PC relative addr."
if(PSR(v)==0)
ALUx<-[PC]
ALUy<-[IR(operand)]
ALUr=[ALUx]+[ALUy]
PC<-[ALUr]


Opcode c9
Mnemonic "BVS #dis"
Description "Branch on overflow to a PC relative addr."
if(PSR(v)==1)
ALUx<-[PC]
ALUy<-[IR(operand)]
ALUr=[ALUx]+[ALUy]
PC<-[ALUr]


Opcode ca
Mnemonic "BVC addr"
Description "Branch to a direct addr. if overflow flag clear (V=0)"
if(PSR(v)==0)
PC<-[IR(operand)]


Opcode cb
Mnemonic "BVS addr"
Description "Branch to a direct addr. if overflow flag set (V=1)"
if(PSR(v)==1)
PC<-[IR(operand)]


Opcode cc
* addr and (addr) 00 to FF
Mnemonic "BVC (addr)"
Description "Branch to an indirect addr. if overflow flag is clear"
if(PSR(v)==0)
MAR<-[IR(operand)]
MDR<-[M[MAR]]
IR<-[MDR]
MAR<-[IR(operand)]
MDR<-[M[MAR]]
IR<-[MDR]
PC<-[IR(operand)]


Opcode cd
* addr and (addr) 00 to FF
Mnemonic "BVS (addr)"
Description "Branch to an indirect addr. if overflow flag is set"
if(PSR(v)==1)
MAR<-[IR(operand)]
MDR<-[M[MAR]]
IR<-[MDR]
```

```
MAR<-[IR(operand)]
MDR<-[M[MAR]]
IR<-[MDR]
PC<-[IR(operand)]


Opcode d0
* addr 00 to FF
Mnemonic "JSR addr"
Description "Jump to subroutine at a direct address"
ALUx<-[PC]              }
MDR<-[ALUx]             }       write PC
MAR<-[SP]              }       to the stack
M[MAR]<-[MDR]           }
ALUx<-[SP]                  } decrement
ALUr=[ALUx]-1               } SP
SP<-[ALUr]                  }
PC<-[IR(operand)]


Opcode d1
* addr and (addr) 00 to FF
Mnemonic "JSR (addr)"
Description "Jump to subroutine at an indirect address"
ALUx<-[PC]              }
MDR<-[ALUx]             }       write PC
MAR<-[SP]              }       to the stack
M[MAR]<-[MDR]           }
ALUx<-[SP]                  } decrement
ALUr=[ALUx]-1               } SP
SP<-[ALUr]                  }
MAR<-[IR(operand)]
MDR<-[M[MAR]]
PC<-[MDR]


Opcode d2
Mnemonic "JSR A"
Description "Jump to subroutine at an addr. held in the A reg."
ALUx<-[PC]              }
MDR<-[ALUx]             }       write PC
MAR<-[SP]              }       to the stack
M[MAR]<-[MDR]           }
ALUx<-[SP]                  } decrement
ALUr=[ALUx]-1               } SP
SP<-[ALUr]                  }
MDR<-[A]
PC<-[MDR]


Opcode d3
Mnemonic "JSR B"
Description "Jump to subroutine at an addr. held in the B reg."
```

```
ALUx<-[PC]              }
MDR<-[ALUx]             }      write PC
MAR<-[SP]               }      to the stack
M[MAR]<-[MDR]           }
ALUx<-[SP]                 } decrement
ALUr=[ALUx]-1              } SP
SP<-[ALUr]                 }
PC<-[B]
```

Opcode d4
Mnemonic "JSR (A)"
Description "Jump to subroutine at an indirect addr. held in the A reg."
```
ALUx<-[PC]              }
MDR<-[ALUx]             }      write PC
MAR<-[SP]               }      to the stack
M[MAR]<-[MDR]           }
ALUx<-[SP]                 } decrement
ALUr=[ALUx]-1              } SP
SP<-[ALUr]                 }
MAR<-[A]
MDR<-[M[MAR]]
PC<-[MDR]
```

Opcode d5
Mnemonic "JSR (B)"
Description "Jump to subroutine at an indirect addr. held in the B reg."
```
ALUx<-[PC]              }
MDR<-[ALUx]             }      write PC
MAR<-[SP]               }      to the stack
M[MAR]<-[MDR]           }
ALUx<-[SP]                 } decrement
ALUr=[ALUx]-1              } SP
SP<-[ALUr]                 }
MAR<-[B]
MDR<-[M[MAR]]
PC<-[MDR]
```

Opcode d6
* addr 00 to FF
Mnemonic "JSR A+addr"
Description "Jump to subroutine at an indexed addr. (index in A)"
```
ALUx<-[PC]              }
MDR<-[ALUx]             }      write PC
MAR<-[SP]               }      to the stack
M[MAR]<-[MDR]           }
ALUx<-[SP]                 } decrement
ALUr=[ALUx]-1              } SP
SP<-[ALUr]                 }
ALUy<-[IR(operand)]
```

```
ALUx<-[A]
ALUr=[ALUx]+[ALUy]
MAR<-[ALUr]
MDR<-[M[MAR]]
PC<-[MDR]
```

```
Opcode d7
* addr 00 to FF
Mnemonic "JSR B+addr"
Description "Jump to subroutine at an indexed addr. (index in B)"
ALUx<-[PC]              }
MDR<-[ALUx]             }      write PC
MAR<-[SP]               }      to the stack
M[MAR]<-[MDR]           }
ALUx<-[SP]                  } decrement
ALUr=[ALUx]-1               } SP
SP<-[ALUr]                  }
ALUy<-[IR(operand)]
ALUx<-[B]
ALUr=[ALUx]+[ALUy]
MAR<-[ALUr]
MDR<-[M[MAR]]
PC<-[MDR]
```

```
Opcode d8
Mnemonic "JSR #dis"
Description "Jump to subroutine at a PC relative address"
ALUx<-[PC]              }
MDR<-[ALUx]             }      write PC
MAR<-[SP]               }      to the stack
M[MAR]<-[MDR]           }
ALUx<-[SP]                  } decrement
ALUr=[ALUx]-1               } SP
SP<-[ALUr]                  }
ALUx<-[PC]
ALUy<-[IR(operand)]
ALUr=[ALUx]+[ALUy]
PC<-[ALUr]
```

```
Opcode e0
* addr 00 to FF
Mnemonic "JMP addr"
Description "Jump to a direct addr."
PC<-[IR(operand)]
```

```
Opcode e1
* addr and (addr) 00 to FF
Mnemonic "JMP (addr)"
Description "Jump to an indirect addr."
```

```
MAR<-[IR(operand)]
MDR<-[M[MAR]]
IR<-[MDR]
MAR<-[IR(operand)]
MDR<-[M[MAR]]
IR<-[MDR]
PC<-[IR(operand)]

Opcode e2
Mnemonic "JMP A"
Description "Jump to an addr. held in the A reg."
MDR<-[A]
PC<-[MDR]

Opcode e3
Mnemonic "JMP B"
Description "Jump to an addr. held in the B reg."
PC<-[B]

Opcode e4
Mnemonic "JMP (A)"
Description "Jump to a reg. indirect addr."
MAR<-[A]
MDR<-[M[MAR]]
PC<-[MDR]

Opcode e5
Mnemonic "JMP (B)"
Description "Jump to a reg. indirect addr."
MAR<-[B]
MDR<-[M[MAR]]
PC<-[MDR]

Opcode e6
* addr 00 to FF
Mnemonic "JMP A+addr"
Description "Jump to an indexed addr. (index in A)"
ALUy<-[IR(operand)]
ALUx<-[A]
ALUr=[ALUx]+[ALUy]
MAR<-[ALUr]
MDR<-[M[MAR]]
PC<-[MDR]

Opcode e7
* addr 00 to FF
Mnemonic "JMP B+addr"
Description "Jump to an indexed addr. (index in B)"
ALUy<-[IR(operand)]
```

```
ALUx<-[B]
ALUr=[ALUx]+[ALUy]
MAR<-[ALUr]
MDR<-[M[MAR]]
PC<-[MDR]
```

```
Opcode e8
Mnemonic "JMP #dis"
Description "Jump to a PC relative address"
ALUx<-[PC]
ALUy<-[IR(operand)]
ALUr=[ALUx]+[ALUy]
PC<-[ALUr]
```

```
Opcode f0
Mnemonic "HALT"
Description "Halt processor"
HALT
```

```
Opcode f1
Mnemonic "RTS"
Description "Return from subroutine"
ALUx<-[SP]              }      increment
ALUr=[ALUx]+1           }      SP
SP<-[ALUr]              }
MAR<-[SP]                 }  recover PC
MDR<-[M[MAR]]             }  from the stack
PC<-[MDR]                 }
```

```
Opcode f2
Mnemonic "NOP"
Description "No operation"
NOP
```

```
Opcode ff
Mnemonic "RTI"
Description "Return from interrupt"
*
* Recover PC and PSR from the stack
*
ALUx<-[SP]              }      increment
ALUr=[ALUx]+1           }      SP
SP<-[ALUr]              }
MAR<-[SP]                 }  recover PC
MDR<-[M[MAR]]             }  from the stack
PC<-[MDR]                 }
ALUx<-[SP]              }      increment
ALUr=[ALUx]+1           }      SP
?<-[ALUr]              }
```

```
MAR<-[SP]              }  recover PSR
MDR<-[M[MAR]]          }  from the stack
PSR<-[MDR]             }

Opcode f3
Mnemonic "INTE"
Description "Enable interrupts"
PSR(E)=1

Opcode f4
Mnemonic "INTD"
Description "Disable interrupts"
PSR(E)=0
```

The Advanced Instruction Set Quick Reference

This is a quick reference listing of the instructions available in the advanced JASP instruction set.

The mnemonic and description is listed for each opcode in the instruction set.

```
00 ADD  #dataword,A   Add to reg. A an immediate oper.
01 ADD  #dataword,B   Add to reg. B an immediate oper.
02 ADD  addrword,A    Add to reg. A from a direct addr
03 ADD  addrword,B    Add to reg. B from a direct addr
04 ADD  (addrword),A  Add to reg. A from an indirect addr
05 ADD  (addrword),B  Add to reg. B from an indirect addr.
06 ADD  B,A           Add B reg. to contents of A reg.
07 ADD  A,B           Add A reg. to contents of B reg.
08 ADD  (B),A         Add B reg. indirect oper. to A reg.
09 ADD  (A),B         Add A reg. indirect oper. to B reg.
0A ADD  B+addrword,A  Add to reg. A from an indexed addr (index in B)
0B ADD  A+addrword,B  Add to reg. B from an indexed addr (index in A)
10 ADC  #dataword,A   Add with carry to reg. A an immediate oper.
11 ADC  #dataword,B   Add with carry to reg. B an immediate oper.
12 ADC  addrword,A    Add with carry to reg. A from a direct addr
13 ADC  addrword,B    Add with carry to reg. B from a direct addr
14 ADC  (addrword),A  Add with carry to reg. A from an indirect addr
15 ADC  (addrword),B  Add with carry to reg. B from an indirect addr
16 ADC  B,A           Add with carry to A reg. from B reg.
17 ADC  A,B           Add with carry to B reg. from A reg.
18 ADC  (B),A         Add with carry to B reg. a reg. indirect oper.
19 ADC  (A),B         Add with carry to B reg. a reg. indirect oper.
1A ADC  B+addrword,A  Add with carry to reg. A an indexed oper. (index in B)
1B ADC  A+addrword,B  Add with carry to reg. B an indexed oper. (index in A)
```

```
20 SUB   #dataword,A      Subtract an immediate oper. from A reg
21 SUB   #dataword,B      Subtract an immediate oper. from B reg
22 SUB   addrword,A       Subtract from reg. A a direct oper.
23 SUB   addrword,B       Subtract from reg. B a direct oper.
24 SUB   (addrword),A     Subtract from reg. A an indirect oper.
25 SUB   (addrword),B     Subtract from reg. B an indirect oper.
26 SUB   B,A              Subtract from reg. A the contents of reg. B
27 SUB   A,B              Subtract from reg. B the contents of reg. A
28 SUB   (B),A            Subtract from reg. A a reg. indirect oper.
29 SUB   (A),B            Subtract from reg. B a reg. indirect oper.
2A SUB   B+addrword,A     Subtract an indexed oper. from the reg. A (index in B)
2B SUB   A+addrword,B     Subtract an indexed oper. from the reg. B (index in A)
32 SHL   addrword         Shift left a memory direct oper.
34 SHL   (addrword)       Shift left a memory indirect oper.
36 SHL   A                Shift left reg. A
37 SHL   B                Shift left reg. B
38 SHL   (A)              Shift left a reg. indirect oper., addr in A
39 SHL   (B)              Shift left a reg. indirect oper., addr in B
3A SHL   A+addrword       Shift left an indexed oper. (index in A)
3B SHL   B+addrword       Shift left an indexed oper. (index in B)
42 SHR   addrword         Shift right a direct oper.
44 SHR   (addrword)       Shift right a memory indirect oper.
46 SHR   A                Shift right the contents of reg. A
47 SHR   B                Shift right the contents of reg. B
48 SHR   (A)              Shift right a reg. indirect oper.
49 SHR   (B)              Shift right a reg. indirect oper.
4A SHR   A+addrword       Shift right a memory indexed oper. (index in A)
4B SHR   B+addrword       Shift right a memory indexed oper. (Index in B)
50 AND   #dataword,A      AND operation on A reg and an immediate oper.
51 AND   #dataword,B      AND operation on B reg and an immediate oper.
52 AND   addrword,A       AND operation on A and a direct oper.
53 AND   addrword,B       AND operation on B and a direct oper.
54 AND   (addrword),A     AND operation on A and an indirect oper.
55 AND   (addrword),B     AND operation on B and an indirect oper.
56 AND   B,A              AND on A and B, result in A
57 AND   A,B              AND on B and A, result in B
58 AND   (B),A            AND on A and a reg. indirect oper.
59 AND   (A),B            AND on B and a reg. indirect oper.
5A AND   B+addrword,A     AND operation on A and an indexed oper.
5B AND   A+addrword,B     AND operation on B and an indexed oper.
60 OR    #dataword,A      OR operation on A reg and an immediate oper.
61 OR    #dataword,B      OR operation on B reg and an immediate oper.
62 OR    addrword,A       OR operation on A and a direct oper.
63 OR    addrword,B       OR operation on B and a direct oper.
64 OR    (addrword),A     OR operation on A and an indirect oper.
65 OR    (addrword),B     OR operation on B and an indirect oper.
66 OR    B,A              OR on A and B, result in A
67 OR    A,B              OR on B and A, result in B
68 OR    (B),A            OR on A and a reg. indirect oper.
```

```
69 OR    (A),B           OR on B and a reg. indirect oper.
6A OR    B+addrword,A    OR operation on A and an indexed oper.
6B OR    A+addrword,B    OR operation on B and an indexed oper.
72 NOT   addrword        NOT operation on a direct oper.
74 NOT   (addrword)      NOT operation on an indirect oper.
76 NOT   A               NOT operation on A reg.
77 NOT   B               NOT operation on B reg.
78 NOT   (A)             NOT on a reg. indirect oper. (addr in A)
79 NOT   (B)             NOT on a reg. indirect oper. (addr in B)
7A NOT   A+addrword      NOT on an indexed oper. (index in A)
7B NOT   B+addrword      NOT on an indexed oper. (index in B)
7C SWAP  A               Swap A register lo and hi bytes
7D SWAP  B               Swap B register lo and hi bytes
80 CMP   #dataword,A     Compare an immediate oper. with A reg
81 CMP   #dataword,B     Compare an immediate oper. with B reg
82 CMP   addrword,A      Compare a direct oper. with A reg.
83 CMP   addrword,B      Compare a direct oper. with B reg.
84 CMP   (addrword),A    Compare an indirect oper. with A reg.
85 CMP   (addrword),B    Compare an indirect oper. with B reg.
86 CMP   B,A             Compare A and B reg.
87 CMP   A,B             Compare B and A reg.
88 CMP   (B),A           Compare A with a reg. indirect oper.
89 CMP   (A),B           Compare B with a reg. indirect oper.
8A CMP   B+addrword,A    Compare with A an indexed oper.
8B CMP   A+addrword,B    Compare with B an indexed oper.
8C PUSH  A               Push A onto the stack
8D PUSH  B               Push B onto the stack
8E POP   A               Pop A from the stack
8F POP   B               Pop B from the stack
90 MOVE  #dataword,A     Move an immediate oper. into A
91 MOVE  #dataword,B     Move an immediate oper. into B
92 MOVE  addrword,A      Load reg. A from a direct addr
93 MOVE  addrword,B      Load reg. B from a direct addr
94 MOVE  (addrword),A    Load reg. A from an indirect addr
95 MOVE  (addrword),B    Load reg. B from an indirect addr
96 MOVE  B,A             Move B reg. to A reg.
97 MOVE  A,B             Move A reg. to B reg.
98 MOVE  (B),A           Load A reg. with a reg. indirect oper.
99 MOVE  (A),B           Load B reg. with a reg. indirect oper.
9A MOVE  B+addrword,A    Load A reg from an indexed addr (index in B)
9B MOVE  A+addrword,B    Load B reg from an indexed addr (index in A)
A2 MOVE  A,addrword      Store the A reg. in memory at a direct addr
A3 MOVE  B,addrword      Store the B reg. in memory at a direct addr
A4 MOVE  A,(addrword)    Store reg. A at a mem. indirect addr
A5 MOVE  B,(addrword)    Store reg. B at a mem. indirect addr
A6 MOVE  #dataword,SP    Move an immediate oper. into SP
A7 MOVE  addrword,SP     Load reg. SP from a direct addr
A8 MOVE  A,(B)           Store A reg. at an addr held in B
A9 MOVE  B,(A)           Store B reg. at an addr held in A
```

```
AA MOVE A,B+addrword  Store A reg. at an indexed addr (index in B)
AB MOVE B,A+addrword  Store B reg. at an indexed addr (index in A)
AC MOVE (addrword),SP Load reg. SP from an indirect addr
AD MOVE A,SP          Move A reg. to SP reg.
AE MOVE B,SP          Move B reg. to SP reg.
B0 BCC  #disword      Branch on carry clear to a PC relative addr
B1 BCS  #disword      Branch on carry set to a PC relative addr
B2 BCC  addrword      Branch to a direct addr if carry flag clear (C=0)
B3 BCS  addrword      Branch to a direct addr if carry flag set (C=1)
B4 BCC  (addrword)    Branch to an indirect addr if carry flag is clear
B5 BCS  (addrword)    Branch to an indirect addr if carry flag is set
B8 BPL  #disword      Branch on negative clear to a PC relative addr
B9 BMI  #disword      Branch on negative set to a PC relative addr
BA BPL  addrword      Branch to a direct addr if negative flag clear (N=0)
BB BMI  addrword      Branch to a direct addr if negative flag set (N=1)
BC BPL  (addrword)    Branch to an indirect addr if negative flag is clear
BD BMI  (addrword)    Branch to an indirect addr if negative flag is set
C0 BNE  #disword      Branch on zero clear to a PC relative addr
C1 BEQ  #disword      Branch on zero set to a PC relative addr
C2 BNE  addrword      Branch to a direct addr if zero flag clear (Z=0)
C3 BEQ  addrword      Branch to a direct addr if zero flag set (Z=1)
C4 BNE  (addrword)    Branch to an indirect addr if zero flag is clear
C5 BEQ  (addrword)    Branch to an indirect addr if zero flag is set
C8 BVC  #disword      Branch on no overflow to a PC relative addr
C9 BVS  #disword      Branch on overflow to a PC relative addr
CA BVC  addrword      Branch to a direct addr if overflow flag clear (V=0)
CB BVS  addrword      Branch to a direct addr if overflow flag set (V=1)
CC BVC  (addrword)    Branch to an indirect addr if overflow flag is clear
CD BVS  (addrword)    Branch to an indirect addr if overflow flag is set
D0 JSR  addrword      Jump to subroutine at a direct addr
D1 JSR  (addrword)    Jump to subroutine at an indirect addr
D2 JSR  A             Jump to subroutine at an addr held in the A reg.
D3 JSR  B             Jump to subroutine at an addr held in the B reg.
D4 JSR  (A)           Jump to subroutine at an indirect addr held in the A reg.
D5 JSR  (B)           Jump to subroutine at an indirect addr held in the B reg.
D6 JSR  A+addrword    Jump to subroutine at an indexed addr (index in A)
D7 JSR  B+addrword    Jump to subroutine at an indexed addr (index in B)
D8 JSR  #disword      Jump to subroutine at a PC relative addr
E0 JMP  addrword      Jump to a direct addr
E1 JMP  (addrword)    Jump to an indirect addr
E2 JMP  A             Jump to an addr held in the A reg.
E3 JMP  B             Jump to an addr held in the B reg.
E4 JMP  (A)           Jump to a reg. indirect addr.
E5 JMP  (B)           Jump to a reg. indirect addr
E6 JMP  A+addrword    Jump to an indexed addr (index in A)
E7 JMP  B+addrword    Jump to an indexed addr (index in B)
E8 JMP  #disword      Jump to a PC relative addr
E9 MUL  B,A           Multiply A by B, result in A
EA DIV  B,A           Divide A by B, result in A
```

```
EB MOD  B,A            Mod of divide A by B, result in A
EC MOD  B,#dataword    Mod of divide B by dataword, result in B
ED DIV  B,#dataword    Divide B by dataword, result in B
EE DIV  A,#dataword    Divide A by dataword, result in A
FO HALT                Halt processor
F1 RTS                 Return from subroutine
F2 NOP                 No operation
F3 INTE                Enable interrupts
F4 INTD                disable interrupts
FA TRAP #dataword      Software interrupt mechanism
```

The Advanced Instruction Set

A listing of the complete advanced JASP instruction set including microcode information, as shipped with the simulation package.

```
* A 32-bit instruction set for the JASP architecture.
*
* Originally based on an instruction set
* by William Henderson.
*
* Revision : 0.9.3
* Author   : Mark Burrell
* Date     : 29-MAR-2003
*
*
* Force the JASM assembler to use 32-bit operations
Force_32bit
*
Fetch
* fetch cycle definition
MAR<-[PC]
INC<-[PC]
PC<-[INC]
MDR<-[M[MAR]]
IR<-[MDR]
MAR<-[PC]              } operand in MDR
INC<-[PC]             }
PC<-[INC]             }
MDR<-[M[MAR]]         }
CU<-[IR(opcode)]

Interrupt
* interrupt routine
PSR(I)=0                        interrupt flag = 0
```

```
MAR<-[SP]                        }       save PSR
MDR<-[PSR]                       }       on the stack
M[MAR]<-[MDR]                    }
ALUx<-[SP]                    } decrement
ALUr=[ALUx]-1                 } SP
SP<-[ALUr]                    }
ALUx<-[PC]                       }
MDR<-[ALUx]                      }       write PC
MAR<-[SP]                        }       to the stack
M[MAR]<-[MDR]                    }
ALUx<-[SP]                    } decrement
ALUr=[ALUx]-1                 } SP
SP<-[ALUr]                    }
PSR(E)=0                      interrupt enable flag = 0
ALUy<-[JUMPERS(IntBase)]         }
ALUx<-[PSR(IntVec)]              } build the vector address
ALUr=[ALUx]+[ALUy]               }
MAR<-[ALUr]                   } obtain the handler address
MDR<-[M[MAR]]                 }
PC<-[MDR]                     load address of handler into PC


Opcode fa
Mnemonic "TRAP #dataword"
Description "Software interrupt mechanism"
* programmably trigger the interrupt routine
*
* The #dataword value is masked with %00000111
* to produce the interrupt vector
*
PSR(IntVec)<-[MDR]               } Load the PSR with the Interrupt Vector
PSR(I)=1                         } Fire the interrupt


Opcode 00
Mnemonic "ADD #dataword,A"
Description "Add to reg. A an immediate oper."
ALUx<-[A]
ALUy<-[MDR]
ALUr=[ALUx]+[ALUy]
A<-[ALUr]


Opcode 01
Mnemonic "ADD #dataword,B"
Description "Add to reg. B an immediate oper."
ALUx<-[B]
ALUy<-[MDR]
ALUr=[ALUx]+[ALUy]
B<-[ALUr]


Opcode 02
```

```
Mnemonic "ADD addrword,A"
Description "Add to reg. A from a direct addr"
MAR<-[MDR]
MDR<-[M[MAR]]
ALUy<-[MDR]
ALUx<-[A]
ALUr=[ALUx]+[ALUy]
A<-[ALUr]


Opcode 03
Mnemonic "ADD addrword,B"
Description "Add to reg. B from a direct addr"
MAR<-[MDR]
MDR<-[M[MAR]]
ALUy<-[MDR]
ALUx<-[B]
ALUr=[ALUx]+[ALUy]
B<-[ALUr]


Opcode 04
Mnemonic "ADD (addrword),A"
Description "Add to reg. A from an indirect addr"
MAR<-[MDR]
MDR<-[M[MAR]]
MAR<-[MDR]
MDR<-[M[MAR]]
ALUy<-[MDR]
ALUx<-[A]
ALUr=[ALUx]+[ALUy]
A<-[ALUr]


Opcode 05
Mnemonic "ADD (addrword),B"
Description "Add to reg. B from an indirect addr."
MAR<-[MDR]
MDR<-[M[MAR]]
MAR<-[MDR]
MDR<-[M[MAR]]
ALUy<-[MDR]
ALUx<-[B]
ALUr=[ALUx]+[ALUy]
B<-[ALUr]

Opcode 06
Mnemonic "ADD B,A"
Description "Add B reg. to contents of A reg."
ALUy<-[A]
ALUx<-[B]
ALUr=[ALUx]+[ALUy]
```

```
A<-[ALUr]


Opcode 07
Mnemonic "ADD A,B"
Description "Add A reg. to contents of B reg."
ALUy<-[A]
ALUx<-[B]
ALUr=[ALUx]+[ALUy]
B<-[ALUr]


Opcode 08
Mnemonic "ADD (B),A"
Description "Add B reg. indirect oper. to A reg."
MAR<-[B]
MDR<-[M[MAR]]
ALUy<-[MDR]
ALUx<-[A]
ALUr=[ALUx]+[ALUy]
A<-[ALUr]


Opcode 09
Mnemonic "ADD (A),B"
Description "Add A reg. indirect oper. to B reg."
MAR<-[A]
MDR<-[M[MAR]]
ALUy<-[MDR]
ALUx<-[B]
ALUr=[ALUx]+[ALUy]
B<-[ALUr]


Opcode 0a
Mnemonic "ADD B+addrword,A"
Description "Add to reg. A from an indexed addr (index in B)"
ALUy<-[MDR]
ALUx<-[B]
ALUr=[ALUx]+[ALUy]
MAR<-[ALUr]
MDR<-[M[MAR]]
ALUy<-[MDR]
ALUx<-[A]
ALUr=[ALUx]+[ALUy]
A<-[ALUr]


Opcode 0b
Mnemonic "ADD A+addrword,B"
Description "Add to reg. B from an indexed addr (index in A)"
ALUy<-[MDR]
ALUx<-[A]
ALUr=[ALUx]+[ALUy]
```

```
MAR<-[ALUr]
MDR<-[M[MAR]]
ALUy<-[MDR]
ALUx<-[B]
ALUr=[ALUx]+[ALUy]
B<-[ALUr]
```

Opcode 10
Mnemonic "ADC #dataword,A"
Description "Add with carry to reg. A an immediate oper."
```
ALUx<-[A]
ALUy<-[MDR]
ALUr=[ALUx]+[ALUy]+[PSR(c)]
A<-[ALUr]
```

Opcode 11
Mnemonic "ADC #dataword,B"
Description "Add with carry to reg. B an immediate oper."
```
ALUx<-[B]
ALUy<-[MDR]
ALUr=[ALUx]+[ALUy]+[PSR(c)]
B<-[ALUr]
```

Opcode 12
Mnemonic "ADC addrword,A"
Description "Add with carry to reg. A from a direct addr"
```
MAR<-[MDR]
MDR<-[M[MAR]]
ALUy<-[MDR]
ALUx<-[A]
ALUr=[ALUx]+[ALUy]+[PSR(c)]
A<-[ALUr]
```

Opcode 13
Mnemonic "ADC addrword,B"
Description "Add with carry to reg. B from a direct addr"
```
MAR<-[MDR]
MDR<-[M[MAR]]
ALUy<-[MDR]
ALUx<-[B]
ALUr=[ALUx]+[ALUy]+[PSR(c)]
B<-[ALUr]
```

Opcode 14
Mnemonic "ADC (addrword),A"
Description "Add with carry to reg. A from an indirect addr"
```
MAR<-[MDR]
MDR<-[M[MAR]]
MAR<-[MDR]
```

```
MDR<-[M[MAR]]
ALUy<-[MDR]
ALUx<-[A]
ALUr=[ALUx]+[ALUy]+[PSR(c)]
A<-[ALUr]
```

```
Opcode 15
Mnemonic "ADC (addrword),B"
Description "Add with carry to reg. B from an indirect addr"
MAR<-[MDR]
MDR<-[M[MAR]]
MAR<-[MDR]
MDR<-[M[MAR]]
ALUy<-[MDR]
ALUx<-[B]
ALUr=[ALUx]+[ALUy]+[PSR(c)]
B<-[ALUr]
```

```
Opcode 16
Mnemonic "ADC B,A"
Description "Add with carry to A reg. from B reg."
ALUy<-[B]
ALUx<-[A]
ALUr=[ALUx]+[ALUy]+[PSR(c)]
A<-[ALUr]
```

```
Opcode 17
Mnemonic "ADC A,B"
Description "Add with carry to B reg. from A reg."
ALUy<-[A]
ALUx<-[B]
ALUr=[ALUx]+[ALUy]+[PSR(c)]
B<-[ALUr]
```

```
Opcode 18
Mnemonic "ADC (B),A"
Description "Add with carry to B reg. a reg. indirect oper."
MAR<-[B]
MDR<-[M[MAR]]
ALUy<-[MDR]
ALUx<-[A]
ALUr=[ALUx]+[ALUy]+[PSR(c)]
A<-[ALUr]
```

```
Opcode 19
Mnemonic "ADC (A),B"
Description "Add with carry to B reg. a reg. indirect oper."
MAR<-[A]
MDR<-[M[MAR]]
```

```
ALUy<-[MDR]
ALUx<-[B]
ALUr=[ALUx]+[ALUy]+[PSR(c)]
B<-[ALUr]
```

```
Opcode 1a
Mnemonic "ADC B+addrword,A"
Description "Add with carry to reg. A an indexed oper. (index in B)"
ALUy<-[MDR]
ALUx<-[B]
ALUr=[ALUx]+[ALUy]
MAR<-[ALUr]
MDR<-[M[MAR]]
ALUy<-[MDR]
ALUx<-[A]
ALUr=[ALUx]+[ALUy]+[PSR(c)]
A<-[ALUr]
```

```
Opcode 1b
Mnemonic "ADC A+addrword,B"
Description "Add with carry to reg. B an indexed oper. (index in A)"
ALUy<-[MDR]
ALUx<-[A]
ALUr=[ALUx]+[ALUy]
MAR<-[ALUr]
MDR<-[M[MAR]]
ALUy<-[MDR]
ALUx<-[B]
ALUr=[ALUx]+[ALUy]+[PSR(c)]
B<-[ALUr]
```

```
Opcode 20
Mnemonic "SUB #dataword,A"
Description "Subtract an immediate oper. from A reg"
ALUx<-[A]
ALUy<-[MDR]
ALUr=[ALUx]-[ALUy]
A<-[ALUr]
```

```
Opcode 21
Mnemonic "SUB #dataword,B"
Description "Subtract an immediate oper. from B reg"
ALUx<-[B]
ALUy<-[MDR]
ALUr=[ALUx]-[ALUy]
B<-[ALUr]
```

```
Opcode 22
Mnemonic "SUB addrword,A"
```

```
Description "Subtract from reg. A a direct oper."
MAR<-[MDR]
MDR<-[M[MAR]]
ALUx<-[A]
ALUy<-[MDR]
ALUr=[ALUx]-[ALUy]
A<-[ALUr]


Opcode 23
Mnemonic "SUB addrword,B"
Description "Subtract from reg. B a direct oper."
MAR<-[MDR]
MDR<-[M[MAR]]
ALUx<-[B]
ALUy<-[MDR]
ALUr=[ALUx]-[ALUy]
B<-[ALUr]


Opcode 24
Mnemonic "SUB (addrword),A"
Description "Subtract from reg. A an indirect oper."
MAR<-[MDR]
MDR<-[M[MAR]]
MAR<-[MDR]
MDR<-[M[MAR]]
ALUx<-[A]
ALUy<-[MDR]
ALUr=[ALUx]-[ALUy]
A<-[ALUr]


Opcode 25
Mnemonic "SUB (addrword),B"
Description "Subtract from reg. B an indirect oper."
MAR<-[MDR]
MDR<-[M[MAR]]
MAR<-[MDR]
MDR<-[M[MAR]]
ALUx<-[B]
ALUy<-[MDR]
ALUr=[ALUx]-[ALUy]
B<-[ALUr]


Opcode 26
Mnemonic "SUB B,A"
Description "Subtract from reg. A the contents of reg. B"
ALUx<-[A]
ALUy<-[B]
ALUr=[ALUx]-[ALUy]
A<-[ALUr]
```

```
Opcode 27
Mnemonic "SUB A,B"
Description "Subtract from reg. B the contents of reg. A"
ALUx<-[B]
ALUy<-[A]
ALUr=[ALUx]-[ALUy]
B<-[ALUr]


Opcode 28
Mnemonic "SUB (B),A"
Description "Subtract from reg. A a reg. indirect oper."
MAR<-[B]
MDR<-[M[MAR]]
ALUx<-[A]
ALUy<-[MDR]
ALUr=[ALUx]-[ALUy]
A<-[ALUr]


Opcode 29
Mnemonic "SUB (A),B"
Description "Subtract from reg. B a reg. indirect oper."
MAR<-[A]
MDR<-[M[MAR]]
ALUx<-[B]
ALUy<-[MDR]
ALUr=[ALUx]-[ALUy]
B<-[ALUr]


Opcode 2a
Mnemonic "SUB B+addrword,A"
Description "Subtract an indexed oper. from the reg. A (index in B)"
ALUy<-[MDR]
ALUx<-[B]
ALUr=[ALUx]+[ALUy]
MAR<-[ALUr]
MDR<-[M[MAR]]
ALUy<-[MDR]
ALUx<-[A]
ALUr=[ALUx]-[ALUy]
A<-[ALUr]


Opcode 2b
Mnemonic "SUB A+addrword,B"
Description "Subtract an indexed oper. from the reg. B (index in A)"
ALUy<-[MDR]
ALUx<-[A]
ALUr=[ALUx]+[ALUy]
MAR<-[ALUr]
```

```
MDR<-[M[MAR]]
ALUy<-[MDR]
ALUx<-[B]
ALUr=[ALUx]-[ALUy]
B<-[ALUr]


Opcode 32
Mnemonic "SHL addrword"
Description "Shift left a memory direct oper."
MAR<-[MDR]
MDR<-[M[MAR]]
ALUx<-[MDR]
ALUr=[ALUx]<<1
MDR<-[ALUr]
M[MAR]<-[MDR]


Opcode 34
Mnemonic "SHL (addrword)"
Description "Shift left a memory indirect oper."
MAR<-[MDR]
MDR<-[M[MAR]]
MAR<-[MDR]
MDR<-[M[MAR]]
ALUx<-[MDR]
ALUr=[ALUx]<<1
MDR<-[ALUr]
M[MAR]<-[MDR]


Opcode 36
Mnemonic "SHL A"
Description "Shift left reg. A"
ALUx<-[A]
ALUr=[ALUx]<<1
A<-[ALUr]


Opcode 37
Mnemonic "SHL B"
Description "Shift left reg. B"
ALUx<-[B]
ALUr=[ALUx]<<1
B<-[ALUr]


Opcode 38
Mnemonic "SHL (A)"
Description "Shift left a reg. indirect oper., addr in A"
MAR<-[A]
MDR<-[M[MAR]]
ALUx<-[MDR]
ALUr=[ALUx]<<1
```

```
MDR<-[ALUr]
M[MAR]<-[MDR]


Opcode 39
Mnemonic "SHL (B)"
Description "Shift left a reg. indirect oper., addr in B"
MAR<-[B]
MDR<-[M[MAR]]
ALUx<-[MDR]
ALUr=[ALUx]<<1
MDR<-[ALUr]
M[MAR]<-[MDR]


Opcode 3a
Mnemonic "SHL A+addrword"
Description "Shift left an indexed oper. (index in A)"
ALUy<-[MDR]
ALUx<-[A]
ALUr=[ALUx]+[ALUy]
MAR<-[ALUr]
MDR<-[M[MAR]]
ALUx<-[MDR]
ALUr=[ALUx]<<1
MDR<-[ALUr]
M[MAR]<-[MDR]


Opcode 3b
Mnemonic "SHL B+addrword"
Description "Shift left an indexed oper. (index in B)"
ALUy<-[MDR]
ALUx<-[B]
ALUr=[ALUx]+[ALUy]
MAR<-[ALUr]
MDR<-[M[MAR]]
ALUx<-[MDR]
ALUr=[ALUx]<<1
MDR<-[ALUr]
M[MAR]<-[MDR]


Opcode 42
Mnemonic "SHR addrword"
Description "Shift right a direct oper."
MAR<-[MDR]
MDR<-[M[MAR]]
ALUx<-[MDR]
ALUr=[ALUx]>>1
MDR<-[ALUr]
M[MAR]<-[MDR]
```

```
Opcode 44
Mnemonic "SHR (addrword)"
Description "Shift right a memory indirect oper."
MAR<-[MDR]
MDR<-[M[MAR]]
MAR<-[MDR]
MDR<-[M[MAR]]
ALUx<-[MDR]
ALUr=[ALUx]>>1
MDR<-[ALUr]
M[MAR]<-[MDR]

Opcode 46
Mnemonic "SHR A"
Description "Shift right the contents of reg. A"
ALUx<-[A]
ALUr=[ALUx]>>1
A<-[ALUr]

Opcode 47
Mnemonic "SHR B"
Description "Shift right the contents of reg. B"
ALUx<-[B]
ALUr=[ALUx]>>1
B<-[ALUr]

Opcode 48
Mnemonic "SHR (A)"
Description "Shift right a reg. indirect oper."
MAR<-[A]
MDR<-[M[MAR]]
ALUx<-[MDR]
ALUr=[ALUx]>>1
MDR<-[ALUr]
M[MAR]<-[MDR]

Opcode 49
Mnemonic "SHR (B)"
Description "Shift right a reg. indirect oper."
MAR<-[B]
MDR<-[M[MAR]]
ALUx<-[MDR]
ALUr=[ALUx]>>1
MDR<-[ALUr]
M[MAR]<-[MDR]

Opcode 4a
Mnemonic "SHR A+addrword"
Description "Shift right a memory indexed oper. (index in A)"
```

```
ALUy<-[MDR]
ALUx<-[A]
ALUr=[ALUx]+[ALUy]
MAR<-[ALUr]
MDR<-[M[MAR]]
ALUx<-[MDR]
ALUr=[ALUx]>>1
MDR<-[ALUr]
M[MAR]<-[MDR]
```

```
Opcode 4b
Mnemonic "SHR B+addrword"
Description "Shift right a memory indexed oper. (Index in B)"
ALUy<-[MDR]
ALUx<-[B]
ALUr=[ALUx]+[ALUy]
MAR<-[ALUr]
MDR<-[M[MAR]]
ALUx<-[MDR]
ALUr=[ALUx]>>1
MDR<-[ALUr]
M[MAR]<-[MDR]
```

```
Opcode 50
Mnemonic "AND #dataword,A"
Description "AND operation on A reg and an immediate oper."
ALUy<-[MDR]
ALUx<-[A]
ALUr=[ALUx]&[ALUy]
A<-[ALUr]
```

```
Opcode 51
Mnemonic "AND #dataword,B"
Description "AND operation on B reg and an immediate oper."
ALUy<-[MDR]
ALUx<-[B]
ALUr=[ALUx]&[ALUy]
B<-[ALUr]
```

```
Opcode 52
Mnemonic "AND addrword,A"
Description "AND operation on A and a direct oper."
MAR<-[MDR]
MDR<-[M[MAR]]
ALUy<-[MDR]
ALUx<-[A]
ALUr=[ALUx]&[ALUy]
A<-[ALUr]
```

```
Opcode 53
Mnemonic "AND addrword,B"
Description "AND operation on B and a direct oper."
MAR<-[MDR]
MDR<-[M[MAR]]
ALUy<-[MDR]
ALUx<-[B]
ALUr=[ALUx]&[ALUy]
B<-[ALUr]

Opcode 54
Mnemonic "AND (addrword),A"
Description "AND operation on A and an indirect oper."
MAR<-[MDR]
MDR<-[M[MAR]]
MAR<-[MDR]
MDR<-[M[MAR]]
ALUy<-[MDR]
ALUx<-[A]
ALUr=[ALUx]&[ALUy]
A<-[ALUr]

Opcode 55
Mnemonic "AND (addrword),B"
Description "AND operation on B and an indirect oper."
MAR<-[MDR]
MDR<-[M[MAR]]
MAR<-[MDR]
MDR<-[M[MAR]]
ALUy<-[MDR]
ALUx<-[B]
ALUr=[ALUx]&[ALUy]
B<-[ALUr]

Opcode 56
Mnemonic "AND B,A"
Description "AND on A and B, result in A"
ALUy<-[B]
ALUx<-[A]
ALUr=[ALUx]&[ALUy]
A<-[ALUr]

Opcode 57
Mnemonic "AND A,B"
Description "AND on B and A, result in B"
ALUy<-[A]
ALUx<-[B]
ALUr=[ALUx]&[ALUy]
B<-[ALUr]
```

```
Opcode 58
Mnemonic "AND (B),A"
Description "AND on A and a reg. indirect oper."
MAR<-[B]
MDR<-[M[MAR]]
ALUx<-[MDR]
ALUy<-[A]
ALUr=[ALUx]&[ALUy]
A<-[ALUr]

Opcode 59
Mnemonic "AND (A),B"
Description "AND on B and a reg. indirect oper."
MAR<-[A]
MDR<-[M[MAR]]
ALUx<-[MDR]
ALUy<-[B]
ALUr=[ALUx]&[ALUy]
B<-[ALUr]

Opcode 5a
Mnemonic "AND B+addrword,A"
Description "AND operation on A and an indexed oper."
ALUy<-[MDR]
ALUx<-[B]
ALUr=[ALUx]+[ALUy]
MAR<-[ALUr]
MDR<-[M[MAR]]
ALUy<-[MDR]
ALUx<-[A]
ALUr=[ALUx]&[ALUy]
A<-[ALUr]

Opcode 5b
Mnemonic "AND A+addrword,B"
Description "AND operation on B and an indexed oper."
ALUy<-[MDR]
ALUx<-[A]
ALUr=[ALUx]+[ALUy]
MAR<-[ALUr]
MDR<-[M[MAR]]
ALUy<-[MDR]
ALUx<-[B]
ALUr=[ALUx]&[ALUy]
B<-[ALUr]

Opcode 60
Mnemonic "OR #dataword,A"
```

```
Description "OR operation on A reg and an immediate oper."
ALUy<-[MDR]
ALUx<-[A]
ALUr=[ALUx]|[ALUy]
A<-[ALUr]


Opcode 61
Mnemonic "OR #dataword,B"
Description "OR operation on B reg and an immediate oper."
ALUy<-[MDR]
ALUx<-[B]
ALUr=[ALUx]|[ALUy]
B<-[ALUr]


Opcode 62
Mnemonic "OR addrword,A"
Description "OR operation on A and a direct oper."
MAR<-[MDR]
MDR<-[M[MAR]]
ALUy<-[MDR]
ALUx<-[A]
ALUr=[ALUx]|[ALUy]
A<-[ALUr]


Opcode 63
Mnemonic "OR addrword,B"
Description "OR operation on B and a direct oper."
MAR<-[MDR]
MDR<-[M[MAR]]
ALUy<-[MDR]
ALUx<-[B]
ALUr=[ALUx]|[ALUy]
B<-[ALUr]


Opcode 64
Mnemonic "OR (addrword),A"
Description "OR operation on A and an indirect oper."
MAR<-[MDR]
MDR<-[M[MAR]]
MAR<-[MDR]
MDR<-[M[MAR]]
ALUy<-[MDR]
ALUx<-[A]
ALUr=[ALUx]|[ALUy]
A<-[ALUr]


Opcode 65
Mnemonic "OR (addrword),B"
Description "OR operation on B and an indirect oper."
```

```
MAR<-[MDR]
MDR<-[M[MAR]]
MAR<-[MDR]
MDR<-[M[MAR]]
ALUy<-[MDR]
ALUx<-[B]
ALUr=[ALUx]|[ALUy]
B<-[ALUr]
```

```
Opcode 66
Mnemonic "OR B,A"
Description "OR on A and B, result in A"
ALUy<-[B]
ALUx<-[A]
ALUr=[ALUx]|[ALUy]
A<-[ALUr]
```

```
Opcode 67
Mnemonic "OR A,B"
Description "OR on B and A, result in B"
ALUy<-[A]
ALUx<-[B]
ALUr=[ALUx]|[ALUy]
B<-[ALUr]
```

```
Opcode 68
Mnemonic "OR (B),A"
Description "OR on A and a reg. indirect oper."
MAR<-[B]
MDR<-[M[MAR]]
ALUx<-[MDR]
ALUy<-[A]
ALUr=[ALUx]|[ALUy]
A<-[ALUr]
```

```
Opcode 69
Mnemonic "OR (A),B"
Description "OR on B and a reg. indirect oper."
MAR<-[A]
MDR<-[M[MAR]]
ALUx<-[MDR]
ALUy<-[B]
ALUr=[ALUx]|[ALUy]
B<-[ALUr]
```

```
Opcode 6a
Mnemonic "OR B+addrword,A"
Description "OR operation on A and an indexed oper."
ALUy<-[MDR]
```

```
ALUx<-[B]
ALUr=[ALUx]+[ALUy]
MAR<-[ALUr]
MDR<-[M[MAR]]
ALUy<-[MDR]
ALUx<-[A]
ALUr=[ALUx]|[ALUy]
A<-[ALUr]
```

```
Opcode 6b
Mnemonic "OR A+addrword,B"
Description "OR operation on B and an indexed oper."
ALUy<-[MDR]
ALUx<-[A]
ALUr=[ALUx]+[ALUy]
MAR<-[ALUr]
MDR<-[M[MAR]]
ALUy<-[MDR]
ALUx<-[B]
ALUr=[ALUx]|[ALUy]
B<-[ALUr]
```

```
Opcode 72
Mnemonic "NOT addrword"
Description "NOT operation on a direct oper."
MAR<-[MDR]
MDR<-[M[MAR]]
ALUx<-[MDR]
ALUr=~[ALUx]
MDR<-[ALUr]
M[MAR]<-[MDR]
```

```
Opcode 74
Mnemonic "NOT (addrword)"
Description "NOT operation on an indirect oper."
MAR<-[MDR]
MDR<-[M[MAR]]
MAR<-[MDR]
MDR<-[M[MAR]]
ALUx<-[MDR]
ALUr=~[ALUx]
MDR<-[ALUr]
M[MAR]<-[MDR]
```

```
Opcode 76
Mnemonic "NOT A"
Description "NOT operation on A reg."
ALUx<-[A]
ALUr=~[ALUx]
```

```
A<-[ALUr]


Opcode 77
Mnemonic "NOT B"
Description "NOT operation on B reg."
ALUx<-[B]
ALUr=~[ALUx]
B<-[ALUr]


Opcode 78
Mnemonic "NOT (A)"
Description "NOT on a reg. indirect oper. (addr in A)"
MAR<-[A]
MDR<-[M[MAR]]
ALUx<-[MDR]
ALUr=~[ALUx]
MDR<-[ALUr]
M[MAR]<-[MDR]


Opcode 79
Mnemonic "NOT (B)"
Description "NOT on a reg. indirect oper. (addr in B)"
MAR<-[B]
MDR<-[M[MAR]]
ALUx<-[MDR]
ALUr=~[ALUx]
MDR<-[ALUr]
M[MAR]<-[MDR]


Opcode 7a
Mnemonic "NOT A+addrword"
Description "NOT on an indexed oper. (index in A)"
ALUx<-[A]
ALUy<-[MDR]
ALUr=[ALUx]+[ALUy]
MAR<-[ALUr]
MDR<-[M[MAR]]
ALUx<-[MDR]
ALUr=~[ALUx]
MDR<-[ALUr]
M[MAR]<-[MDR]


Opcode 7b
Mnemonic "NOT B+addrword"
Description "NOT on an indexed oper. (index in B)"
ALUx<-[B]
ALUy<-[MDR]
ALUr=[ALUx]+[ALUy]
MAR<-[ALUr]
```

```
MDR<-[M[MAR]]
ALUx<-[MDR]
ALUr=~[ALUx]
MDR<-[ALUr]
M[MAR]<-[MDR]


Opcode 7c
Mnemonic "SWAP A"
Description "Swap A register lo and hi bytes"
ALUx<-[A]
ALUr(7:0)=[ALUx(15:8)];ALUr(15:8)=[ALUx(7:0)]
A<-[ALUr]


Opcode 7d
Mnemonic "SWAP B"
Description "Swap B register lo and hi bytes"
ALUx<-[B]
ALUr(7:0)=[ALUx(15:8)];ALUr(15:8)=[ALUx(7:0)]
B<-[ALUr]


Opcode 80
Mnemonic "CMP #dataword,A"
Description "Compare an immediate oper. with A reg"
ALUx<-[A]
ALUy<-[MDR]
ALUr=[ALUx]-[ALUy]


Opcode 81
Mnemonic "CMP #dataword,B"
Description "Compare an immediate oper. with B reg"
ALUx<-[B]
ALUy<-[MDR]
ALUr=[ALUx]-[ALUy]


Opcode 82
Mnemonic "CMP addrword,A"
Description "Compare a direct oper. with A reg."
MAR<-[MDR]
MDR<-[M[MAR]]
ALUy<-[MDR]
ALUx<-[A]
ALUr=[ALUx]-[ALUy]


Opcode 83
Mnemonic "CMP addrword,B"
Description "Compare a direct oper. with B reg."
MAR<-[MDR]
MDR<-[M[MAR]]
ALUy<-[MDR]
```

```
ALUx<-[B]
ALUr=[ALUx]-[ALUy]


Opcode 84
Mnemonic "CMP (addrword),A"
Description "Compare an indirect oper. with A reg."
MAR<-[MDR]
MDR<-[M[MAR]]
MAR<-[MDR]
MDR<-[M[MAR]]
ALUy<-[MDR]
ALUx<-[A]
ALUr=[ALUx]-[ALUy]


Opcode 85
Mnemonic "CMP (addrword),B"
Description "Compare an indirect oper. with B reg."
MAR<-[MDR]
MDR<-[M[MAR]]
MAR<-[MDR]
MDR<-[M[MAR]]
ALUy<-[MDR]
ALUx<-[B]
ALUr=[ALUx]-[ALUy]


Opcode 86
Mnemonic "CMP B,A"
Description "Compare A and B reg."
ALUx<-[A]
ALUy<-[B]
ALUr=[ALUx]-[ALUy]


Opcode 87
Mnemonic "CMP A,B"
Description "Compare B and A reg."
ALUx<-[B]
ALUy<-[A]
ALUr=[ALUx]-[ALUy]


Opcode 88
Mnemonic "CMP (B),A"
Description "Compare A with a reg. indirect oper."
MAR<-[B]
MDR<-[M[MAR]]
ALUx<-[A]
ALUy<-[MDR]
ALUr=[ALUx]-[ALUy]


Opcode 89
```

```
Mnemonic "CMP (A),B"
Description "Compare B with a reg. indirect oper."
MAR<-[A]
MDR<-[M[MAR]]
ALUx<-[B]
ALUy<-[MDR]
ALUr=[ALUx]-[ALUy]

Opcode 8a
Mnemonic "CMP B+addrword,A"
Description "Compare with A an indexed oper."
ALUx<-[B]
ALUy<-[MDR]
ALUr=[ALUx]+[ALUy]
MAR<-[ALUr]
MDR<-[M[MAR]]
ALUx<-[A]
ALUy<-[MDR]
ALUr=[ALUx]-[ALUy]

Opcode 8b
Mnemonic "CMP A+addrword,B"
Description "Compare with B an indexed oper."
ALUx<-[A]
ALUy<-[MDR]
ALUr=[ALUx]+[ALUy]
MAR<-[ALUr]
MDR<-[M[MAR]]
ALUx<-[B]
ALUy<-[MDR]
ALUr=[ALUx]-[ALUy]

Opcode 8c
Mnemonic "PUSH A"
Description "Push A onto the stack"
MAR<-[SP]
MDR<-[A]
M[MAR]<-[MDR]
ALUx<-[SP]
ALUr=[ALUx]-1
SP<-[ALUr]

Opcode 8d
Mnemonic "PUSH B"
Description "Push B onto the stack"
MAR<-[SP]
MDR<-[B]
M[MAR]<-[MDR]
ALUx<-[SP]
```

```
ALUr=[ALUx]-1
SP<-[ALUr]


Opcode 8e
Mnemonic "POP A"
Description "Pop A from the stack"
ALUx<-[SP]
ALUr=[ALUx]+1
SP<-[ALUr]
MAR<-[SP]
MDR<-[M[MAR]]
A<-[MDR]


Opcode 8f
Mnemonic "POP B"
Description "Pop B from the stack"
ALUx<-[SP]
ALUr=[ALUx]+1
SP<-[ALUr]
MAR<-[SP]
MDR<-[M[MAR]]
B<-[MDR]


Opcode 90
Mnemonic "MOVE #dataword,A"
Description "Move an immediate oper. into A"
A<-[MDR]


Opcode 91
Mnemonic "MOVE #dataword,B"
Description "Move an immediate oper. into B"
B<-[MDR]


Opcode 92
Mnemonic "MOVE addrword,A"
Description "Load reg. A from a direct addr"
MAR<-[MDR]
MDR<-[M[MAR]]
A<-[MDR]


Opcode 93
Mnemonic "MOVE addrword,B"
Description "Load reg. B from a direct addr"
MAR<-[MDR]
MDR<-[M[MAR]]
B<-[MDR]


Opcode 94
Mnemonic "MOVE (addrword),A"
```

```
Description "Load reg. A from an indirect addr"
MAR<-[MDR]
MDR<-[M[MAR]]
MAR<-[MDR]
MDR<-[M[MAR]]
A<-[MDR]


Opcode 95
Mnemonic "MOVE (addrword),B"
Description "Load reg. B from an indirect addr"
MAR<-[MDR]
MDR<-[M[MAR]]
MAR<-[MDR]
MDR<-[M[MAR]]
B<-[MDR]


Opcode 96
Mnemonic "MOVE B,A"
Description "Move B reg. to A reg."
MDR<-[B]
A<-[MDR]


Opcode 97
Mnemonic "MOVE A,B"
Description "Move A reg. to B reg."
MDR<-[A]
B<-[MDR]


Opcode 98
Mnemonic "MOVE (B),A"
Description "Load A reg. with a reg. indirect oper."
MAR<-[B]
MDR<-[M[MAR]]
A<-[MDR]


Opcode 99
Mnemonic "MOVE (A),B"
Description "Load B reg. with a reg. indirect oper."
MAR<-[A]
MDR<-[M[MAR]]
B<-[MDR]


Opcode 9a
Mnemonic "MOVE B+addrword,A"
Description "Load A reg from an indexed addr (index in B)"
ALUy<-[MDR]
ALUx<-[B]
ALUr=[ALUx]+[ALUy]
MAR<-[ALUr]
```

```
MDR<-[M[MAR]]
A<-[MDR]


Opcode 9b
Mnemonic "MOVE A+addrword,B"
Description "Load B reg from an indexed addr (index in A)"
ALUy<-[MDR]
ALUx<-[A]
ALUr=[ALUx]+[ALUy]
MAR<-[ALUr]
MDR<-[M[MAR]]
B<-[MDR]


Opcode a2
Mnemonic "MOVE A,addrword"
Description "Store the A reg. in memory at a direct addr"
MAR<-[MDR]
MDR<-[A]
M[MAR]<-[MDR]


Opcode a3
Mnemonic "MOVE B,addrword"
Description "Store the B reg. in memory at a direct addr"
MAR<-[MDR]
MDR<-[B]
M[MAR]<-[MDR]


Opcode a4
Mnemonic "MOVE A,(addrword)"
Description "Store reg. A at a mem. indirect addr"
MAR<-[MDR]
MDR<-[M[MAR]]
MAR<-[MDR]
MDR<-[A]
M[MAR]<-[MDR]


Opcode a5
Mnemonic "MOVE B,(addrword)"
Description "Store reg. B at a mem. indirect addr"
MAR<-[MDR]
MDR<-[M[MAR]]
MAR<-[MDR]
MDR<-[B]
M[MAR]<-[MDR]


Opcode a6
Mnemonic "MOVE #dataword,SP"
Description "Move an immediate oper. into SP"
SP<-[MDR]
```

```
Opcode a7
Mnemonic "MOVE addrword,SP"
Description "Load reg. SP from a direct addr"
MAR<-[MDR]
MDR<-[M[MAR]]
SP<-[MDR]


Opcode a8
Mnemonic "MOVE A,(B)"
Description "Store A reg. at an addr held in B"
MAR<-[B]
MDR<-[A]
M[MAR]<-[MDR]


Opcode a9
Mnemonic "MOVE B,(A)"
Description "Store B reg. at an addr held in A"
MAR<-[A]
MDR<-[B]
M[MAR]<-[MDR]


Opcode aa
Mnemonic "MOVE A,B+addrword"
Description "Store A reg. at an indexed addr (index in B)"
ALUy<-[MDR]
ALUx<-[B]
ALUr=[ALUx]+[ALUy]
MAR<-[ALUr]
MDR<-[A]
M[MAR]<-[MDR]


Opcode ab
Mnemonic "MOVE B,A+addrword"
Description "Store B reg. at an indexed addr (index in A)"
ALUy<-[MDR]
ALUx<-[A]
ALUr=[ALUx]+[ALUy]
MAR<-[ALUr]
MDR<-[B]
M[MAR]<-[MDR]


Opcode ac
Mnemonic "MOVE (addrword),SP"
Description "Load reg. SP from an indirect addr"
MAR<-[MDR]
MDR<-[M[MAR]]
MAR<-[MDR]
MDR<-[M[MAR]]
```

```
SP<-[MDR]


Opcode ad
Mnemonic "MOVE A,SP"
Description "Move A reg. to SP reg."
MDR<-[A]
SP<-[MDR]


Opcode ae
Mnemonic "MOVE B,SP"
Description "Move B reg. to SP reg."
MDR<-[B]
SP<-[MDR]


Opcode b0
Mnemonic "BCC #disword"
Description "Branch on carry clear to a PC relative addr"
if(PSR(c)==0)
ALUx<-[PC]
ALUy<-[MDR]
ALUr=[ALUx]+[ALUy]
PC<-[ALUr]


Opcode b1
Mnemonic "BCS #disword"
Description "Branch on carry set to a PC relative addr"
if(PSR(c)==1)
ALUx<-[PC]
ALUy<-[MDR]
ALUr=[ALUx]+[ALUy]
PC<-[ALUr]


Opcode b2
Mnemonic "BCC addrword"
Description "Branch to a direct addr if carry flag clear (C=0)"
if(PSR(c)==0)
PC<-[MDR]


Opcode b3
Mnemonic "BCS addrword"
Description "Branch to a direct addr if carry flag set (C=1)"
if(PSR(c)==1)
PC<-[MDR]


Opcode b4
Mnemonic "BCC (addrword)"
Description "Branch to an indirect addr if carry flag is clear"
if(PSR(c)==0)
MAR<-[MDR]
```

```
MDR<-[M[MAR]]
MAR<-[MDR]
MDR<-[M[MAR]]
PC<-[MDR]


Opcode b5
Mnemonic "BCS (addrword)"
Description "Branch to an indirect addr if carry flag is set"
if(PSR(c)==1)
MAR<-[MDR]
MDR<-[M[MAR]]
MAR<-[MDR]
MDR<-[M[MAR]]
PC<-[MDR]


Opcode b8
Mnemonic "BPL #disword"
Description "Branch on negative clear to a PC relative addr"
if(PSR(n)==0)
ALUx<-[PC]
ALUy<-[MDR]
ALUr=[ALUx]+[ALUy]
PC<-[ALUr]


Opcode b9
Mnemonic "BMI #disword"
Description "Branch on negative set to a PC relative addr"
if(PSR(n)==1)
ALUx<-[PC]
ALUy<-[MDR]
ALUr=[ALUx]+[ALUy]
PC<-[ALUr]


Opcode ba
Mnemonic "BPL addrword"
Description "Branch to a direct addr if negative flag clear (N=0)"
if(PSR(n)==0)
PC<-[MDR]


Opcode bb
Mnemonic "BMI addrword"
Description "Branch to a direct addr if negative flag set (N=1)"
if(PSR(n)==1)
PC<-[MDR]


Opcode bc
Mnemonic "BPL (addrword)"
Description "Branch to an indirect addr if negative flag is clear"
if(PSR(n)==0)
```

```
MAR<-[MDR]
MDR<-[M[MAR]]
MAR<-[MDR]
MDR<-[M[MAR]]
PC<-[MDR]


Opcode bd
Mnemonic "BMI (addrword)"
Description "Branch to an indirect addr if negative flag is set"
if(PSR(n)==1)
MAR<-[MDR]
MAR<-[MDR]
MDR<-[M[MAR]]
PC<-[MDR]


Opcode c0
Mnemonic "BNE #disword"
Description "Branch on zero clear to a PC relative addr"
if(PSR(z)==0)
ALUx<-[PC]
ALUy<-[MDR]
ALUr=[ALUx]+[ALUy]
PC<-[ALUr]


Opcode c1
Mnemonic "BEQ #disword"
Description "Branch on zero set to a PC relative addr"
if(PSR(z)==1)
ALUx<-[PC]
ALUy<-[MDR]
ALUr=[ALUx]+[ALUy]
PC<-[ALUr]


Opcode c2
Mnemonic "BNE addrword"
Description "Branch to a direct addr if zero flag clear (Z=0)"
if(PSR(z)==0)
PC<-[MDR]


Opcode c3
Mnemonic "BEQ addrword"
Description "Branch to a direct addr if zero flag set (Z=1)"
if(PSR(z)==1)
PC<-[MDR]


Opcode c4
Mnemonic "BNE (addrword)"
Description "Branch to an indirect addr if zero flag is clear"
if(PSR(z)==0)
```

```
MAR<-[MDR]
MDR<-[M[MAR]]
MAR<-[MDR]
MDR<-[M[MAR]]
PC<-[MDR]


Opcode c5
Mnemonic "BEQ (addrword)"
Description "Branch to an indirect addr if zero flag is set"
if(PSR(z)==1)
MAR<-[MDR]
MDR<-[M[MAR]]
MAR<-[MDR]
MDR<-[M[MAR]]
PC<-[MDR]


Opcode c8
Mnemonic "BVC #disword"
Description "Branch on no overflow to a PC relative addr"
if(PSR(v)==0)
ALUx<-[PC]
ALUy<-[MDR]
ALUr=[ALUx]+[ALUy]
PC<-[ALUr]


Opcode c9
Mnemonic "BVS #disword"
Description "Branch on overflow to a PC relative addr"
if(PSR(v)==1)
ALUx<-[PC]
ALUy<-[MDR]
ALUr=[ALUx]+[ALUy]
PC<-[ALUr]


Opcode ca
Mnemonic "BVC addrword"
Description "Branch to a direct addr if overflow flag clear (V=0)"
if(PSR(v)==0)
PC<-[MDR]


Opcode cb
Mnemonic "BVS addrword"
Description "Branch to a direct addr if overflow flag set (V=1)"
if(PSR(v)==1)
PC<-[MDR]


Opcode cc
Mnemonic "BVC (addrword)"
Description "Branch to an indirect addr if overflow flag is clear"
```

```
if(PSR(v)==0)
MAR<-[MDR]
MDR<-[M[MAR]]
MAR<-[MDR]
MDR<-[M[MAR]]
PC<-[MDR]


Opcode cd
Mnemonic "BVS (addrword)"
Description "Branch to an indirect addr if overflow flag is set"
if(PSR(v)==1)
MAR<-[MDR]
MDR<-[M[MAR]]
MAR<-[MDR]
MDR<-[M[MAR]]
PC<-[MDR]


Opcode d0
Mnemonic "JSR addrword"
Description "Jump to subroutine at a direct addr"
ALUx<-[PC]          }
MDR<-[ALUx]         }        write PC
MAR<-[SP]           }        to the stack
M[MAR]<-[MDR]       }
ALUx<-[SP]             }  decrement
ALUr=[ALUx]-1         }  SP
SP<-[ALUr]            }
ALUx<-[PC]          }
ALUr=[ALUx]-1       }
MAR<-[ALUr]         } go back for the operand
MDR<-[M[MAR]]       }
PC<-[MDR]           }


Opcode d1
Mnemonic "JSR (addrword)"
Description "Jump to subroutine at an indirect addr"
ALUx<-[PC]          }
MDR<-[ALUx]         }        write PC
MAR<-[SP]           }        to the stack
M[MAR]<-[MDR]       }
ALUx<-[SP]             }  decrement
ALUr=[ALUx]-1         }  SP
SP<-[ALUr]            }
ALUx<-[PC]          }
ALUr=[ALUx]-1       }
MAR<-[ALUr]         } go back for the operand
MDR<-[M[MAR]]       }
MAR<-[MDR]          }
MDR<-[M[MAR]]
```

```
MAR<-[MDR]
MDR<-[M[MAR]]
PC<-[MDR]


Opcode d2
Mnemonic "JSR A"
Description "Jump to subroutine at an addr held in the A reg."
ALUx<-[PC]              }
MDR<-[ALUx]            }      write PC
MAR<-[SP]             }      to the stack
M[MAR]<-[MDR]         }
ALUx<-[SP]                 } decrement
ALUr=[ALUx]-1              } SP
SP<-[ALUr]                 }
MDR<-[A]
PC<-[MDR]


Opcode d3
Mnemonic "JSR B"
Description "Jump to subroutine at an addr held in the B reg."
ALUx<-[PC]              }
MDR<-[ALUx]            }      write PC
MAR<-[SP]             }      to the stack
M[MAR]<-[MDR]         }
ALUx<-[SP]                 } decrement
ALUr=[ALUx]-1              } SP
SP<-[ALUr]                 }
PC<-[B]


Opcode d4
Mnemonic "JSR (A)"
Description "Jump to subroutine at an indirect addr held in the A reg."
ALUx<-[PC]              }
MDR<-[ALUx]            }      write PC
MAR<-[SP]             }      to the stack
M[MAR]<-[MDR]         }
ALUx<-[SP]                 } decrement
ALUr=[ALUx]-1              } SP
SP<-[ALUr]                 }
MAR<-[A]
MDR<-[M[MAR]]
PC<-[MDR]


Opcode d5
Mnemonic "JSR (B)"
Description "Jump to subroutine at an indirect addr held in the B reg."
ALUx<-[PC]              }
MDR<-[ALUx]            }      write PC
MAR<-[SP]             }      to the stack
```

```
M[MAR]<-[MDR]          }
ALUx<-[SP]             }  decrement
ALUr=[ALUx]-1          }  SP
SP<-[ALUr]             }
MAR<-[B]
MDR<-[M[MAR]]
PC<-[MDR]
```

```
Opcode d6
Mnemonic "JSR A+addrword"
Description "Jump to subroutine at an indexed addr (index in A)"
ALUx<-[PC]             }
MDR<-[ALUx]            }     write PC
MAR<-[SP]              }     to the stack
M[MAR]<-[MDR]          }
ALUx<-[SP]                }  decrement
ALUr=[ALUx]-1             }  SP
SP<-[ALUr]                }
ALUx<-[PC]             }
ALUr=[ALUx]-1          }
MAR<-[ALUr]            } go back for the operand
MDR<-[M[MAR]]          }
ALUy<-[MDR]            }
ALUx<-[A]
ALUr=[ALUx]+[ALUy]
MAR<-[ALUr]
MDR<-[M[MAR]]
PC<-[MDR]
```

```
Opcode d7
Mnemonic "JSR B+addrword"
Description "Jump to subroutine at an indexed addr (index in B)"
ALUx<-[PC]             }
MDR<-[ALUx]            }     write PC
MAR<-[SP]              }     to the stack
M[MAR]<-[MDR]          }
ALUx<-[SP]                }  decrement
ALUr=[ALUx]-1             }  SP
SP<-[ALUr]                }
ALUx<-[PC]             }
ALUr=[ALUx]-1          }
MAR<-[ALUr]            } go back for the operand
MDR<-[M[MAR]]          }
ALUy<-[MDR]            }
ALUx<-[B]
ALUr=[ALUx]+[ALUy]
MAR<-[ALUr]
MDR<-[M[MAR]]
PC<-[MDR]
```

```
Opcode d8
Mnemonic "JSR #disword"
Description "Jump to subroutine at a PC relative addr"
ALUx<-[PC]              }
MDR<-[ALUx]             }      write PC
MAR<-[SP]               }      to the stack
M[MAR]<-[MDR]           }
ALUx<-[SP]                 }  decrement
ALUr=[ALUx]-1              }  SP
SP<-[ALUr]                 }
ALUx<-[PC]              }
ALUr=[ALUx]-1           }
MAR<-[ALUr]             } go back for the operand
MDR<-[M[MAR]]           }
ALUr=[ALUx]+1           ALUx still contains PC
ALUx<-[ALUr]
ALUy<-[MDR]
ALUr=[ALUx]+[ALUy]
PC<-[ALUr]


Opcode e0
Mnemonic "JMP addrword"
Description "Jump to a direct addr"
PC<-[MDR]


Opcode e1
Mnemonic "JMP (addrword)"
Description "Jump to an indirect addr"
MAR<-[MDR]
MDR<-[M[MAR]]
MAR<-[MDR]
MDR<-[M[MAR]]
PC<-[MDR]


Opcode e2
Mnemonic "JMP A"
Description "Jump to an addr held in the A reg."
MDR<-[A]
PC<-[MDR]


Opcode e3
Mnemonic "JMP B"
Description "Jump to an addr held in the B reg."
PC<-[B]


Opcode e4
Mnemonic "JMP (A)"
Description "Jump to a reg. indirect addr."
```

```
MAR<-[A]
MDR<-[M[MAR]]
PC<-[MDR]


Opcode e5
Mnemonic "JMP (B)"
Description "Jump to a reg. indirect addr"
MAR<-[B]
MDR<-[M[MAR]]
PC<-[MDR]


Opcode e6
Mnemonic "JMP A+addrword"
Description "Jump to an indexed addr (index in A)"
ALUy<-[MDR]
ALUx<-[A]
ALUr=[ALUx]+[ALUy]
MAR<-[ALUr]
MDR<-[M[MAR]]
PC<-[MDR]


Opcode e7
Mnemonic "JMP B+addrword"
Description "Jump to an indexed addr (index in B)"
ALUy<-[MDR]
ALUx<-[B]
ALUr=[ALUx]+[ALUy]
MAR<-[ALUr]
MDR<-[M[MAR]]
PC<-[MDR]


Opcode e8
Mnemonic "JMP #disword"
Description "Jump to a PC relative addr"
ALUx<-[PC]
ALUy<-[MDR]
ALUr=[ALUx]+[ALUy]
PC<-[ALUr]


Opcode f0
Mnemonic "HALT"
Description "Halt processor"
HALT


Opcode f1
Mnemonic "RTS"
Description "Return from subroutine"
ALUx<-[SP]              }      increment
ALUr=[ALUx]+1          }      SP
```

```
SP<-[ALUr]              }
MAR<-[SP]               }  recover PC
MDR<-[M[MAR]]           }  from the stack
PC<-[MDR]               }


Opcode f2
Mnemonic "NOP"
Description "No operation"
NOP


Opcode ff
Mnemonic "RTI"
Description "Return from interrupt"
*
* Recover PC and PSR from the stack
*
ALUx<-[SP]              }     increment
ALUr=[ALUx]+1           }     SP
SP<-[ALUr]              }
MAR<-[SP]                  }  recover PC
MDR<-[M[MAR]]              }  from the stack
PC<-[MDR]                  }
ALUx<-[SP]              }     increment
ALUr=[ALUx]+1           }     SP
SP<-[ALUr]              }
MAR<-[SP]                  }  recover PSR
MDR<-[M[MAR]]              }  from the stack
PSR<-[MDR]                 }


Opcode f3
Mnemonic "INTE"
Description "Enable interrupts"
PSR(E)=1


Opcode f4
Mnemonic "INTD"
Description "disable interrupts"
PSR(E)=0


Opcode e9
Mnemonic "MUL B,A"
Description "Multiply A by B, result in A"
ALUx<-[A]
ALUy<-[B]
ALUr=[ALUx]*[ALUy]
A<-[ALUr]


Opcode ea
Mnemonic "DIV B,A"
```

```
Description "Divide A by B, result in A"
ALUx<-[A]
ALUy<-[B]
ALUr=[ALUx]/[ALUy]
A<-[ALUr]

Opcode eb
Mnemonic "MOD B,A"
Description "Mod of divide A by B, result in A"
ALUx<-[A]
ALUy<-[B]
ALUr=[ALUx]%[ALUy]
A<-[ALUr]

Opcode ec
Mnemonic "MOD B,#dataword"
Description "Mod of divide B by dataword, result in B"
ALUx<-[B]
ALUy<-[MDR]
ALUr=[ALUx]%[ALUy]
B<-[ALUr]

Opcode ed
Mnemonic "DIV B,#dataword"
Description "Divide B by dataword, result in B"
ALUx<-[B]
ALUy<-[MDR]
ALUr=[ALUx]/[ALUy]
B<-[ALUr]

Opcode ee
Mnemonic "DIV A,#dataword"
Description "Divide A by dataword, result in A"
ALUx<-[A]
ALUy<-[MDR]
ALUr=[ALUx]/[ALUy]
A<-[ALUr]
```

An Introduction to Digital Works

F.1 Introducing Digital Works

Digital Works is a tool that allows you to not only create digital circuitry, but to also test it in a simulation mode.

The aim of this brief introduction is to show how Digital Works can be used to understand the fundamental aspects of digital circuitry.

F.2 Obtaining Digital Works

The Digital Works package is copyright *Mechanique* and is distributed by Matrix Multimedia Ltd.

Their website is `http://www.matrixmultimedia.co.uk`

Additionally, a copy of Digital Works with a 30-day license is available on the accompanying CD.

F.3 Installing Digital Works

The Digital Works distribution is provided in the form of a standard self-extracting archive and installer for Microsoft Windows. Simply run the executable file and follow the on-screen menus - as part of this they will ask you for an installation directory.

F.4 Using Digital Works

On starting Digital Works for the first time you see the application as it is shown in figure F.1.

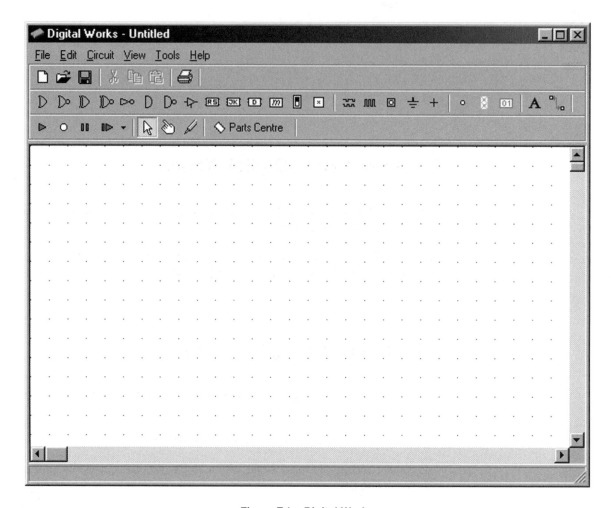

Figure F.1 *Digital Works*

As you can see, Digital Works has a menu bar and three button bars for the user to create and run digital circuits. Each of these bars are detailed below. You can also find out the use of each button by holding the mouse pointer over the button - a useful message pops over the button describing what it does. The main part of Digital Works is the drawing area, where circuits can be designed and run.

F.4.1 The Menu Bar

The menu bar is a standard Windows menu bar, and allows the user to create, open or save digital circuit files. It also gives access to features such as the logic history window, which is outside the scope of this brief introduction.

F.4.2 The File Button Bar

The top-most button bar provides functionality typical to most Windows programs, and will be recognizable to all those who have used other Windows programs.

These buttons provide the following functionality:

▶ Create a new circuit;
▶ Open a circuit;
▶ Save a circuit;
▶ Cut;
▶ Copy;
▶ Paste;
▶ Print a circuit.

F.4.3 The Objects And Devices Button Bar

The second button bar is a little more complex, and provides the main functionality to build digital electronic circuits. It is divided up into four sections, which are:

▶ Digital objects;
▶ Input devices;
▶ Output devices;
▶ Additional tools.

Each section is described below.

Digital Objects

The digital objects buttons allow the user to place components into the drawing area. To place a component into the drawing area you need to first click on the relevant button and then on the point in the drawing area where you wish the component to be placed. Each component needs to be selected individually, even if you wished to place multiple copies of the same component into the drawing area.

These buttons allow the user to select the following components:

▶ AND gate;
▶ OR gate;
▶ NOT gate;
▶ NAND gate;
▶ NOR gate;
▶ XOR gate;
▶ XNOR gate;
▶ Tri-state gate;
▶ D flip-flop;
▶ JK flip-flop;
▶ RS flip-flop;
▶ Memory device;
▶ Switch;
▶ Macro tag;

Input Devices

The input devices buttons allow the user to place input components into the drawing area.

These buttons allow the user to select the following components:

▶ Sequence generator;
▶ Clock;
▶ Interactive input;
▶ Ground;
▶ Power supply.

Output Devices

The output devices buttons allow the user to place output components into the drawing area.

These buttons allow the user to select the following components:

- ► LED;
- ► Seven segment LED;
- ► Numeric output device.

Additional

Finally, the additional buttons give the user the ability to add labels to components to describe their use, and provides the ability to wire up components to form a digital circuit.

F.4.4 The Control Button Bar

It is with the control button bar that users can then run their completed circuits.

These buttons are described here:

- ► Run the circuit;
- ► Stop the circuit;
- ► Pause the circuit;
- ► Step through the circuit;
- ► Object selector - the arrow pointer;
- ► Object interaction selector - the hand pointer;
- ► logic probe - to check the logic level on a particular wire;
- ► Access to the parts centre - a useful set of pre-created circuits that you can make use of.

F.5 Creating And Running Your Own Circuits

We will now look at how to use Digital Works to create and run a small circuit.

The circuit we wish to create is shown in figure F.2, which is the S output of a full-adder.

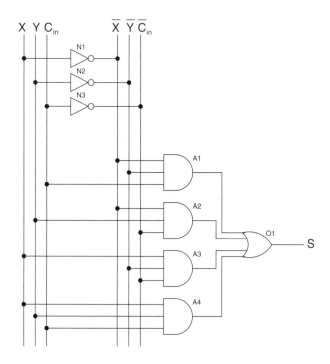

Figure F.2   *The circuit we wish to model*

We will create this circuit and test it in stages.

F.5.1 Creating The Circuit - Stage 1

The first thing we need to do is make use of the objects and devices buttons to place all the required components into the drawing area. This is shown in figure F.3.

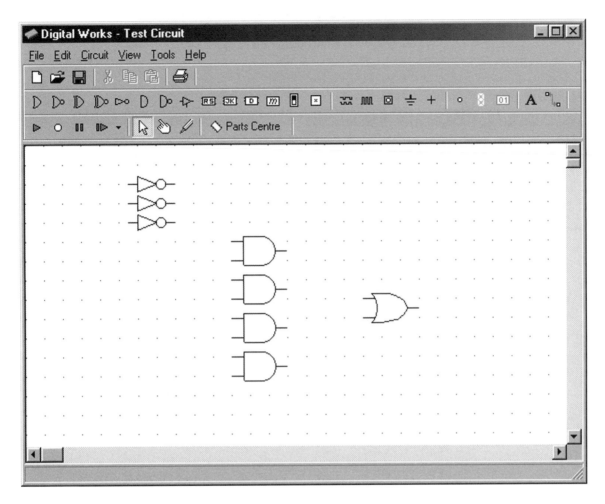

Figure F.3 *Stage 1*

At this stage the circuit has already been saved in a file called Test Circuit.dwm, as shown in the main application bar at the top of the application.

F.5.2 Creating The Circuit - Stage 2

Next we need to set all components to have the correct number of inputs - for example, the OR gate requires four inputs. These are changed by clicking on the components with the right mouse button and selecting the 'inputs' option.

Additionally, we need to add three interactive inputs, so we can change the values of the X, Y and C inputs. Also, we need to add tag devices to anchor the wire that do not have end points that are connected to components.

Lastly, a single LED is added to display the output.

We now have the circuit displayed in figure F.4.

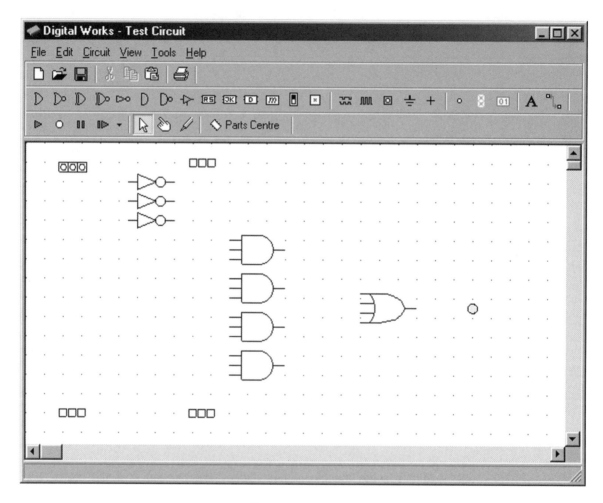

Figure F.4 *Stage 2*

F.5.3 Creating The Circuit - Stage 3

Next we use the wiring tool to wire the individual components together, starting with the lines that carry X, Y, C, $\bar{X}$, $\bar{Y}$ and $\bar{C}$. Once the wiring tools is selected, you can join up components - the message 'attach' appears when you place the wiring tool over a point that it can connect a wire. The wiring tools is a virtual soldering iron.

It is very easy to delete wires that you have wired incorrectly, you merely need to select them with the arrow pointer and then hit the delete button on your keyboard. You can either wire two components directly together, or with intermediate mouse clicks you can specify the route that the wire is to take - again, it is easy to move points just by selecting them with the arrow pointer and moving each point individually.

Once all wiring is completed we should now have the circuit displayed in figure F.5.

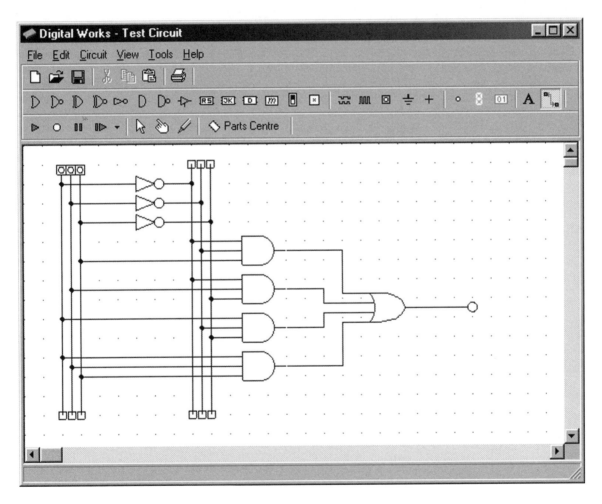

Figure F.5   *Stage 3*

F.5.4   Creating The Circuit - Stage 4

We can now complete the circuit design by adding labels, using the annotation button. The completed circuit is displayed in figure F.6. Of course, we haven't finished yet - we need to now run our circuit to see what it does.

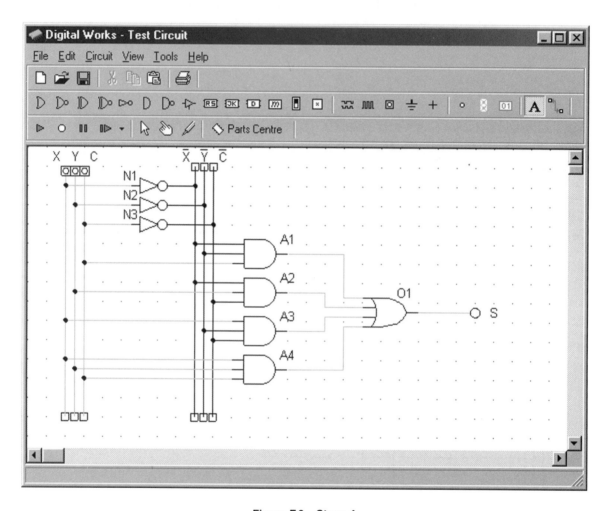

Figure F.6   *Stage 4*

F.5.5   Testing The Circuit

To run our circuit we first select the hand pointer and then we click on the run button. Once we do this our circuit is running - and we can see that with X, Y and C all set to zero, the output S is set to a logical zero because it is grey.

Later on, when we change the inputs to our circuit we will see the LED turn red, to indicate that the output is a logical one.

In fact, try clicking with the hand pointer on the interactive input for X. You should see the circuit as it is displayed in figure F.7.

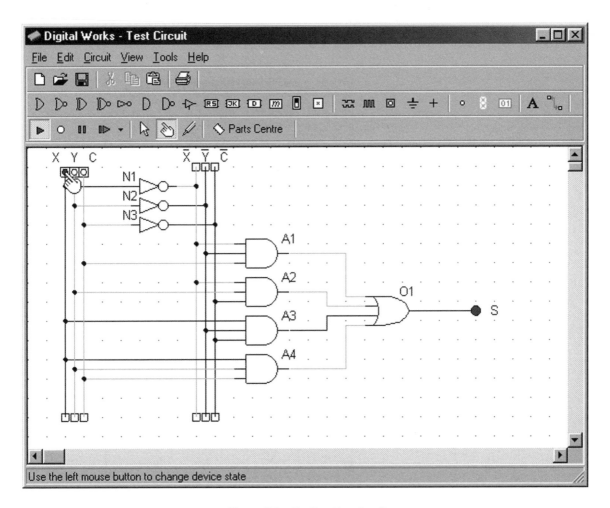

Figure F.7 *Testing the circuit*

As you can see, when a wire is carrying a logical zero, it appears grey, while any wire carrying a logical one appears in black - so just by looking at the circuit we can visibly see the state of all the inputs and outputs.

The creation and testing of all digital circuits within Digital Works would follow the same pattern as has been specified here.

F.5.6 The Parts Centre

In addition, Digital Works has a very powerful facility known as a *macro* facility. Within this facility it is possible to embed one circuit into another.

You can make use of the pre-created circuits by using the parts centre menu - as shown in figure F.8. To use any of the pre-created macros you click on the particular macro, and holding the left mouse button down, you drag the macro to the drawing area.

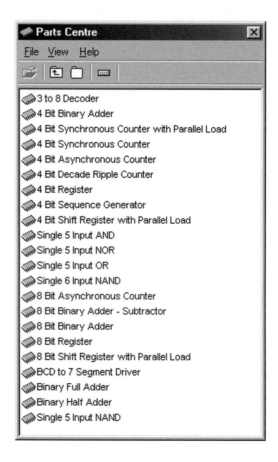

Figure F.8 *Macros available in the Digital Works part centre*

You can also build your own macro circuits, but the creation of new macros is beyond the scope of this brief introduction.

Answers To Self Test Exercises

G.1 Answers To Chapter 1

1 One possible program to make toast is:

- ▶ Acquire fresh loaf;
- ▶ Cut 2 slices, approximately 10mm wide, with cuts at a square angle to the longest axis of the complete loaf;
- ▶ Check toaster has electrical power;
- ▶ Turn on toaster;
- ▶ Place slices in toaster;
- ▶ Wait until toaster ejects hot toast;
- ▶ Spread butter on hot toast slices;
- ▶ Eat hot toast, one slice at a time.

   Please note that it is possible to be much more pedantic!

2 Obviously, your own program will be unique to you - it should contain information regarding the mode of transport (car, bus,etc) and details of the route itself.

G.2 Answers To Chapter 2

1 00101010_2

2 11_{10}

3 $4D_{16}$

4 1011111011101111_2

5 48879_{10}

6 $001C_{16}$

7 00000100_2

8 00100111_2

9 11000100_2 2's complement overflow has occurred - this is indicated because both initial values were positive and the result is negative

10 10001000_2 in hexadecimal is 88_{16}

11 In a 16-bit 2's complement representation, -12 is represented as $FFF4_{16}$, or 1111111111110100_2. In an 8-bit 2's complement representation, -12 is represented as $F4_{16}$, or 11110100_2

12 The ASCII representation of 'F' is 46_{16}

13 The ASCII representation of 'f' is 66_{16}

14 The ASCII representation of '5' is 35_{16}

G.3 Answers To Chapter 3

1 The circuit looks like this:

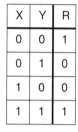 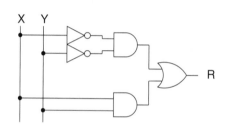

X	Y	R
0	0	1
0	1	0
1	0	0
1	1	1

This circuit is called an XNOR, because it outputs one only when both inputs are equal.

2 You will have seen that for every combination of inputs, both outputs are identical - proving that both parts of the circuit are functionally equal.

3 The truth table for this circuit is as follows:

X	Y	R
0	0	0
0	1	1
1	0	1
1	1	0

This circuit is an XOR circuit.

4 Your circuit should match the functionality of the circuit in

`\examples\chapter03\st3-4.dwm`

You will have seen that for every combination of inputs, both outputs are identical - proving that both parts of the circuit are functionally equal.

G.4 Answers To Chapter 4

1 $MAR \leftarrow [PC]$

2 Place the required input in D, then clock the register by setting C to one and then back to zero.

3 Place the required input in D, then clock the register by setting C to one and then back to zero.

4 The D flip-flop is edge triggered - Q is only updated at the edge of C being changed from 0 to 1. The D latch is triggered whenever C is set to one, if C is left at one then Q reflects the input D.

5 Set D3 to one, D2 to zero, D1 to one and D0 to zero. Clock the register by setting C to one and then back to zero. the register has now stored the bit pattern 1010_2.

6 Use the set pins on the D flip-flops of register one to store the bit pattern 1011_2, so D3 should contain 1, D2 should contain zero and both D1 and D0 should contain one. At this point register one has stored the bit pattern, so now we can enable the OE line of register one to place the bit pattern onto the bus. Next we clock the C line of register two and then set register one OE back to zero. We have now successfully transferred the bit pattern.

G.5 Answers To Chapter 5

1 4534_{16}

2 $BB34_{16}$. The N flag is set because the MSB of $BB34_{16}$ is one.

3 0000_{16}. Both the Z and C flags are set to one. The Z flag is set because all bits in the ALUr are set to zero, while the C flag is set because the addition generated a final carry.

4 0008_{16}. The shift left operation has effectively performed a multiplication by two.

5 0004_{16}

6 $003F_{16}$

7 Your circuit should match the functionality of the circuit in

```
\examples\chapter05\st5-7.dwm
```

You will have seen that for every combination of inputs, the outputs are identical to that of the full adder, and fully match the truth table that describes the full adder.

G.6 Answers To Chapter 6

1 The data bus is used to transfer bit patterns between registers and memory.

2 $B \leftarrow [ALUr]$

3 $MDR\leftarrow[A]$

4 The data bus is bi-directional, whereas individual lines of the control bus are uni-directional. The data bus is used as a single component, whereas the control lines that make up the control bus are used individually.

G.7 Answers To Chapter 7

1 The instructions required would be:

▶ $MAR\leftarrow0001_{16}$
▶ $MDR\leftarrow[B]$
▶ $M[MAR]\leftarrow[MDR]$

2 The instructions required would be:

▶ $MAR\leftarrow00E0_{16}$
▶ $MDR\leftarrow[M[MAR]]$
▶ $A\leftarrow[MDR]$

3 You would need to:

▶ Place $00FF in the MDR;
▶ Place $0003 in the MAR;
▶ Perform a memory write instruction, using either the menu or button options.

G.8 Answers To Chapter 8

1 By checking in appendix B you can see that opcode $90 is the instruction:
MOVE #data,A
and appendix C shows us that this consists of the following micro-instruction:

▶ $A\leftarrow[IR(operand)]$

2 By checking in appendix B you can see that opcode $C3 is the instruction:
BEQ addr
and appendix C shows us that this consists of the following micro-instructions:

▶ $if(PSR(z) == 1)$
▶ $PC\leftarrow[IR(operand)]$

3 The INC register is used to add 1 to the PC. It's use could be replaced by the use of the ALU, however this would mean that it would then be impossible to test the PSR flags after an ALU operation, as the PSR would also be updated as part of the fetch cycle.
The fetch cycle would have to be changed to:

▶ $MAR\leftarrow[PC]$

- $ALUx \leftarrow [PC]$
- $ALUr = ALUx + 1$
- $PC \leftarrow [ALUr]$
- $PC \leftarrow [INC]$
- $MDR \leftarrow [M[MAR]]$
- $IR \leftarrow [MDR]$
- $CU \leftarrow [IR(opcode)]$

4 The control unit decodes both the fetch and execute cycles.

G.9 Answers To Chapter 9

1 Here is one possible solution:

```
            # 0000 # * Self Test Question 9-1
            # 0000 # * Find the answer to 6 + 5
            # 0000 # *
ORG $0000   # 0000 #          ORG  0        * load program in memory starting
            # 0000 #                        *   at location 0
9006        # 0000 #          MOVE #$06,A   * A = 6
9105        # 0001 #          MOVE #$05,B   * B = 5
0600        # 0002 #          ADD  B,A      * A = A + B
F000        # 0003 #          HALT          * stop the program on completion
            # 0004 #                        *   result is in A
```

2 Here is one possible solution:

```
            # 0000 # * Self Test Question 9-2
            # 0000 # * Find the answer to 6 + 5 where the values
            # 0000 # * are stored in memory
            # 0000 # *
ORG $0000   # 0000 #          ORG  0        * load program in memory starting
            # 0000 #                        *   at location 0
9210        # 0000 #          MOVE num1,A   * A = num1
9311        # 0001 #          MOVE num2,B   * B = num2
0600        # 0002 #          ADD  B,A      * A = A + B
F000        # 0003 #          HALT          * stop the program on completion
            # 0004 #                        *   result is in A
ORG $0010   # 0010 #          ORG $10
```

```
0006        # 0010 # num1      DC.W $0006
0005        # 0011 # num2      DC.W $0005
```

3 Here is one possible solution:

```
              # 0000 # * Self Test Question 9-3
              # 0000 # * Compute the sum of the first ten integers
              # 0000 # *
              # 0000 # * In a high-level language:
              # 0000 # *
              # 0000 # * B = 0;
              # 0000 # * for (A=1; A < 11; A++) {
              # 0000 # *     // payload to run while the condition is true
              # 0000 # *      B = B + A;
              # 0000 # * } // end for
              # 0000 #
ORG $0000     # 0000 #              ORG  0         * load program in memory starting
              # 0000 #                             *    at location 0
              # 0000 #
9100          # 0000 #              MOVE #^00,B    * initialize B
9001          # 0001 # for          MOVE #^01,A    * initialize A
800B          # 0002 # loop         CMP  #^11,A    * check the condition
C307          # 0003 #              BEQ  end_for   * if the condition is false, branch
              # 0004 #                             *    to the end of the for construct
              # 0004 #                             *    otherwise run the PAYLOAD
0700          # 0004 #              ADD  A,B       * PAYLOAD : B = B + A
0001          # 0005 #              ADD  #^01,A    * increment A once the payload has
              # 0006 #                             * executed
E002          # 0006 #              JMP  loop      * run the loop again
F000          # 0007 # end_for      HALT           * halt the program
              # 0008 #                             *    the result is in B
```

4 Here is one possible solution:

```
              # 0000 # * Self Test Question 9-4
              # 0000 # * Sort the values held at $20 and $21 such that
              # 0000 # * the larger value is at the higher address.
```

```
                # 0000 # *
                # 0000 # * In a high-level language:
                # 0000 # *
                # 0000 # * A = num1;
                # 0000 # * B = num2;
                # 0000 # * if (num2 > num1) {
                # 0000 # *     num1 = B;
                # 0000 # *     num2 = A;
                # 0000 # * } // end if
                # 0000 #
ORG $0000       # 0000 #           ORG   0       * load program in memory starting
                # 0000 #                          *   at location 0
                # 0000 #
9220            # 0000 #           MOVE num1,A    * initialize B
9321            # 0001 #           MOVE num2,B    * initialize A
8600            # 0002 #           CMP  B,A       * check the condition
BB05            # 0003 #           BMI  true      * if the condition is true, branch
                # 0004 #                          *   to the payload
E007            # 0004 #           JMP  end_if    * if it isn't, go to the end of
                # 0005 #                          *   the 'if'
                # 0005 # true
A320            # 0005 #           MOVE B,num1    * } These lines
A221            # 0006 #           MOVE A,num2    * }   perform the swap
F000            # 0007 # end_if    HALT
                # 0008 #
ORG $0020       # 0020 #           ORG  $20
0045            # 0020 # num1      DC.W $0045
0088            # 0021 # num2      DC.W $0088
```

G.10 Answers To Chapter 10

1 Here is one possible solution:

```
                # 0000 # * Self Test Question 10-1
                # 0000 # * Sort the values held at $20 and $21 such that
                # 0000 # * the larger value is at the higher address.
                # 0000 # *
                # 0000 # * In a high-level language:
                # 0000 # *
                # 0000 # * A = num1;
```

```
                # 0000 # * B = num2;
                # 0000 # * if (num2 > num1) {
                # 0000 # *     swap();
                # 0000 # * } // end if
                # 0000 # *
                # 0000 # * subroutine swap() {
                # 0000 # *    num1 = B;
                # 0000 # *    num2 = A;
                # 0000 # * }
                # 0000 #
ORG $0000       # 0000 #           ORG  0        * load program in memory starting
                # 0000 #                         *   at location 0
                # 0000 #
9220            # 0000 #           MOVE num1,A    * initialize B
9321            # 0001 #           MOVE num2,B    * initialize A
8600            # 0002 #           CMP  B,A       * check the condition
BB05            # 0003 #           BMI  true      * if the condition is true, branch
                # 0004 #                          *   to the payload
E006            # 0004 #           JMP  end_if    * if it isn't, go to the end of
                # 0005 #                          *   the 'if'
D007            # 0005 # true      JSR  swap      * run the swap subroutine
F000            # 0006 # end_if    HALT
                # 0007 #
                # 0007 # swap
A320            # 0007 #           MOVE B,num1    * } These lines
A221            # 0008 #           MOVE A,num2    * }   perform the swap
F100            # 0009 #           RTS            * return from subroutine
                # 000A #
ORG $0020       # 0020 #           ORG  $20
0045            # 0020 # num1      DC.W $0045
0088            # 0021 # num2      DC.W $0088
```

2 All we have to do is update the list of values to be reversed - the program does not need to be changed in any way.

3 Here is one possible solution:

```
                # 0000 # * Self Test Question 10-3
                # 0000 # * Addition to subroutine.jas to
                # 0000 # * count the number of chars printed by putchar
                # 0000 #
                # 0000 # * Memory mapped I/O
                # 0000 # ODR       EQU $E2        * } definitions
```

```
             # 0000 # OSR        EQU $E3        * }
             # 0000 #
ORG $0000    # 0000 #            ORG 0          * load program in memory at addr 0
A6D0         # 0000 #            MOVE #$D0,SP   * initialize the stack pointer
             # 0001 #
9000         # 0001 #            MOVE #$00,A    * } set the putchar counter to 0
A21A         # 0002 #            MOVE A,count   * }
             # 0003 #
911B         # 0003 #            MOVE #data,B   * point at data
9800         # 0004 # next       MOVE (B),A     * get a character
8000         # 0005 #            CMP #$0,A      * is this the terminator?
C30A         # 0006 #            BEQ done       * yes - stop
D00C         # 0007 #            JSR putchar    * call the print sub-routine
0101         # 0008 #            ADD #$1,B      * increment data address
E004         # 0009 #            JMP next       * repeat loop
921A         # 000A # done       MOVE count,A   * finally, store count in A
F000         # 000B #            HALT           * halt the program
             # 000C #
             # 000C # *
             # 000C # * putchar routine (char in lo-byte of A)
             # 000C # *
8D00         # 000C # putchar    PUSH B         * save B on the stack
93E3         # 000D # _putch1    MOVE OSR,B     * move OSR to B
8100         # 000E #            CMP #$00,B     * can we print ?
C30D         # 000F #            BEQ _putch1    * if not, grab OSR again
A2E2         # 0010 #            MOVE A,ODR     * otherwise print lo-byte of A
D014         # 0011 #            JSR  counter   * increate the putchar count
8F00         # 0012 #            POP  B         * retrieve B from the stack
F100         # 0013 #            RTS            * return from subroutine
             # 0014 #
8C00         # 0014 # counter    PUSH A         * save A on the stack
921A         # 0015 #            MOVE count,A   * }
0001         # 0016 #            ADD #$01,A     * } count = count + 1
A21A         # 0017 #            MOVE A,count   * }
8E00         # 0018 #            POP  A         * restore A from the stack
F100         # 0019 #            RTS
             # 001A #
0000         # 001A # count      DS.W 1         * storage for the putchar count
             # 001B #
             # 001B # * data string
             # 001B # * (stored as unpacked ASCII)
0048         # 001B # data       DC.W 0048      * H
0065         # 001C #            DC.W 0065      * e
006C         # 001D #            DC.W 006C      * l
006C         # 001E #            DC.W 006C      * l
006F         # 001F #            DC.W 006F      * o
0020         # 0020 #            DC.W 0020      *
```

```
0057        # 0021 #        DC.W  0057      * W
006F        # 0022 #        DC.W  006F      * o
0072        # 0023 #        DC.W  0072      * r
006C        # 0024 #        DC.W  006C      * l
0064        # 0025 #        DC.W  0064      * d
0021        # 0026 #        DC.W  0021      * !
000D        # 0027 #        DC.W  000D      * <cr>
000A        # 0028 #        DC.W  000A      * <lf>
0000        # 0029 #        DC.W  0000      * Terminator
```

G.11 Answers To Chapter 11

1 Here is the revised program:

```
            # 0000 # * Self Test Question 11-1
            # 0000 # * This is a modification of reverse.jas to use
            # 0000 # * relative addressing with the JMP instructions
            # 0000 # *
ORG $0000   # 0000 #            ORG 0           * load program in memory at
            # 0000 #                            *   location 0
A6D0        # 0000 #            MOVE #$D0,SP    * initialize the stack pointer
            # 0001 #
9000        # 0001 #            MOVE #$00,A     * push 0 onto the stack, we can use
8C00        # 0002 #            PUSH A          *    this later to show us we've
            # 0003 #                            *    finished popping values
            # 0003 #
9012        # 0003 #            MOVE #list,A    * A contains the address of the 1st.
            # 0004 #                            *    list element
            # 0004 #
9900        # 0004 # pushloop   MOVE (A),B      * move the first element into B
8100        # 0005 #            CMP  #$0,B      * } if the number is 0 we have gone
            # 0006 #                            * } through the list
C30A        # 0006 #            BEQ  end_push   * }
8D00        # 0007 #            PUSH B          * otherwise push the value on to the
            # 0008 #                            *    stack
0001        # 0008 #            ADD #$01,A      * get next list element
E8FA        # 0009 #            JMP #pushloop   * and run the loop again
            # 000A #
9012        # 000A # end_push   MOVE #list,A    * A contains the address of the 1st.
            # 000B #                            *    list element
```

```
8F00        # 000B # poploop    POP   B         * get the element from the stack
8100        # 000C #            CMP   #$0,B     * if the number is 0 we have gone
            # 000D #                            *    through the list
C311        # 000D #            BEQ   end_pop   * so we need to end the loop
A900        # 000E #            MOVE  B,(A)     * otherwise, write the popped value
            # 000F #                            *    to memory
0001        # 000F #            ADD   #$01,A    * get to next list element
E8FA        # 0010 #            JMP   #poploop  * and run the loop again
F000        # 0011 # end_pop    HALT            * stop the program on completion
            # 0012 #
            # 0012 # * the list values
1234        # 0012 # list       DC.W  1234
2345        # 0013 #            DC.W  2345
3456        # 0014 #            DC.W  3456
4567        # 0015 #            DC.W  4567
5678        # 0016 #            DC.W  5678
0000        # 0017 #            DC.W  0000
```

2 Here is one possible solution:

```
            # 0000 # * Self Test Question 11-2
            # 0000 # * A program to add $12D5 to $073A
            # 0000 # *
            # 0000 # *
ORG $0000   # 0000 #            ORG   0         * load program in memory starting
            # 0000 #                            *    at location 0
9210        # 0000 #            MOVE  num1,A    * A = num1
9311        # 0001 #            MOVE  num2,B    * B = num2
0600        # 0002 #            ADD   B,A       * A = A + B
F000        # 0003 #            HALT            * stop the program on completion
            # 0004 #                            *    result is in A
ORG $0010   # 0010 #            ORG   $10
12D5        # 0010 # num1       DC.W  $12D5
073A        # 0011 # num2       DC.W  $073A
```

You can use memory direct addressing (as used above) to load the values into registers. You could also have used indirect addressing.

3 Here is one possible solution:

```
              # 0000 # * Self Test Question 11-3
              # 0000 # * A program to add a sequence of values, using
              # 0000 # * register indexed addressing to access the values.
              # 0000 # *
ORG $0000     # 0000 #            ORG  0          * load program in memory starting
              # 0000 #                            *    at location 0
A6D0          # 0000 #            MOVE #$D0,SP    * initialise the stack pointer
9000          # 0001 #            MOVE #$00,A     * } initialise storage
A215          # 0002 #            MOVE A,result   * }   for the result
              # 0003 #
9A0F          # 0003 # addlist    MOVE B+list,A   * access the list entry indexed
              # 0004 #                            *    by B
8000          # 0004 #            CMP  #$00,A     * check if the list entry is zero
C30D          # 0005 #            BEQ  done       *    and if it is terminate the
              # 0006 #                            *    program
              # 0006 #
8D00          # 0006 #            PUSH B          * save B on the stack
9315          # 0007 #            MOVE result,B   * }
0700          # 0008 #            ADD  A,B        * } result = result + A
A315          # 0009 #            MOVE B,result   * }
8F00          # 000A #            POP  B          * restore B from the stack
              # 000B #
0101          # 000B #            ADD  #$01,B     * increment the index
E003          # 000C #            JMP  addlist    * loop again
              # 000D #
9215          # 000D # done       MOVE result,A   * store the result in A
F000          # 000E #            HALT            * stop the program on completion
              # 000F #                            *    result is in A
              # 000F #
0023          # 000F # list       DC.W $0023      * the list of values to add
0045          # 0010 #            DC.W $0045
01D2          # 0011 #            DC.W $01D2
02F0          # 0012 #            DC.W $02F0
00D2          # 0013 #            DC.W $00D2
0000          # 0014 #            DC.W $0000      * terminator
              # 0015 #
0000          # 0015 # result     DS.W 1
```

G.12 Answers To Chapter 12

1 Here is one possible solution:

```
            # 0000 # * Self Test Question 12-1
            # 0000 # * This program reads 10 characters from the keyboard
            # 0000 # * and then prints them all out once they've been entered,
            # 0000 # * with a space character between between all characters.
            # 0000 # *
            # 0000 # OSR      EQU    $E3       * Output Status Register (OSR)
            # 0000 # ODR      EQU    $E2       * Output Data Register   (ODR)
            # 0000 # ISR      EQU    $E1       * Input Status Register  (ISR)
            # 0000 # IDR      EQU    $E0       * Input Data Register    (IDR)
            # 0000 #
ORG $0000   # 0000 #          ORG    0
9100        # 0000 #          MOVE   #$00,B    * count is storage for our
A324        # 0001 #          MOVE   B,count   *   counter value
            # 0002 #
92E1        # 0002 # loop     MOVE   ISR,A     * Get ISR
8000        # 0003 #          CMP    #$00,A    * is a char available?
C302        # 0004 #          BEQ    loop      * no - wait some more
92E0        # 0005 #          MOVE   IDR,A     * read the char
            # 0006 #
9324        # 0006 #          MOVE   count,B   * the address to write the
0125        # 0007 #          ADD    #data,B   * value to is count+data
A800        # 0008 #          MOVE   A,(B)     * write the char in there
            # 0009 #
9324        # 0009 #          MOVE   count,B   * add 1 to count
0101        # 000A #          ADD    #$01,B    *
810A        # 000B #          CMP    #$0A,B    * and see if we have reached 10
C30F        # 000C #          BEQ    gotchars  *   move to next section if we have
A324        # 000D #          MOVE   B,count   * otherwise write count back
E002        # 000E #          JMP    loop      * and get another char
9100        # 000F # gotchars MOVE   #$00,B    * count is storage for our
A324        # 0010 #          MOVE   B,count   *   counter value
            # 0011 #
92E3        # 0011 # write    MOVE   OSR,A     * get OSR
8000        # 0012 #          CMP    #$00,A    * OSR 1 can print, OSR 0 can't print
C311        # 0013 #          BEQ    write     * not yet, wait some more
            # 0014 #
9324        # 0014 #          MOVE   count,B   * the address to read the
0125        # 0015 #          ADD    #data,B   * value from is count+data
9800        # 0016 #          MOVE   (B),A     * get the char in there
A2E2        # 0017 #          MOVE   A,ODR     * print the char
            # 0018 #
92E3        # 0018 # writesp  MOVE   OSR,A     * get OSR
8000        # 0019 #          CMP    #$00,A    * OSR 1 can print, OSR 0 can't print
C318        # 001A #          BEQ    writesp   * not yet, wait some more
            # 001B #
```

```
9020        # 001B #        MOVE   #$20,A   * } print a space
A2E2        # 001C #        MOVE   A,ODR    * }   character
            # 001D #
9324        # 001D #        MOVE   count,B  * add 1 to count
0101        # 001E #        ADD    #$01,B   *
810A        # 001F #        CMP    #$0A,B   * and see if we have reached 10
C323        # 0020 #        BEQ    done     * and move to end if we have
A324        # 0021 #        MOVE   B,count  * otherwise write count back
E011        # 0022 #        JMP    write    * and write another char
F000        # 0023 # done   HALT            * done
            # 0024 #
0000        # 0024 # count  DS.W $01         * the counter
0000        # 0025 # data   DS.W $0A         * storage for our 10 characters
0000        #      #
0000        #      #
0000        #      #
0000        #      #
0000        #      #
0000        #      #
0000        #      #
0000        #      #
0000        #      #
```

2 Here is one possible solution, note that no checking is done to see if the input character is a lowercase character:

```
            # 0000 # * Self Test Question 12-2
            # 0000 # * This program reads lowercase characters from the
            # 0000 # * keyboard, and then converts them to uppercase prior
            # 0000 # * to printing them.  No checking is done on the input
            # 0000 # * characters.
            # 0000 # *
            # 0000 # OSR    EQU   $E3     * Output Status Register (OSR)
            # 0000 # ODR    EQU   $E2     * Output Data Register   (ODR)
            # 0000 # ISR    EQU   $E1     * Input Status Register  (ISR)
            # 0000 # IDR    EQU   $E0     * Input Data Register    (IDR)
            # 0000 #
ORG $0000   # 0000 #        ORG   0
92E1        # 0000 # loop   MOVE  ISR,A   * Get ISR
8000        # 0001 #        CMP   #$00,A  * is a char available?
C300        # 0002 #        BEQ   loop    * no - wait some more
93E0        # 0003 #        MOVE  IDR,B   * read the char into B
```

```
8120      # 0004 #          CMP    #$20,B    * was it a space character?
C30C      # 0005 #          BEQ    done      * yes, so finish
2120      # 0006 #          SUB    #$20,B    * convert the character
          # 0007 #
92E3      # 0007 # write    MOVE   OSR,A     * get OSR
8000      # 0008 #          CMP    #$00,A    * OSR 1 can print, OSR 0 can't print
C307      # 0009 #          BEQ    write     * not yet, wait some more
A3E2      # 000A #          MOVE   B,ODR     * print the char
E000      # 000B #          JMP    loop      * and get another char
F000      # 000C # done     HALT             * halt the program
```

3 Here is one possible solution:

```
            # 0000 # * Self Test Question 12-3
            # 0000 # * This program reads a characters from the
            # 0000 # * keyboard that should be a digit (no checking is done),
            # 0000 # * a corresponding number of asterisks is printed.
            # 0000 # *
            # 0000 # OSR    EQU    $E3       * Output Status Register (OSR)
            # 0000 # ODR    EQU    $E2       * Output Data Register   (ODR)
            # 0000 # ISR    EQU    $E1       * Input Status Register  (ISR)
            # 0000 # IDR    EQU    $E0       * Input Data Register    (IDR)
            # 0000 #
ORG $0000   # 0000 #        ORG    0
92E1        # 0000 # input   MOVE  ISR,A     * Get ISR
8000        # 0001 #         CMP   #$00,A    * is a char available?
C300        # 0002 #         BEQ   input     * no - wait some more
92E0        # 0003 #         MOVE  IDR,A     * read the char into A
2030        # 0004 #         SUB   #$30,A    * number of asterisks to print is
            # 0005 #                         *   now in A
8000        # 0005 # loop    CMP   #$00,A    * if the number is now 0
C310        # 0006 #         BEQ   done      *   then finish
2001        # 0007 #         SUB   #$01,A    * decrement the count
8C00        # 0008 #         PUSH  A         * save A on the stack
92E3        # 0009 # write   MOVE  OSR,A     * get OSR
8000        # 000A #         CMP   #$00,A    * OSR 1 can print, OSR 0 can't print
C309        # 000B #         BEQ   write     * not yet, wait some more
912A        # 000C #         MOVE  #$2A,B    * } print the * character
A3E2        # 000D #         MOVE  B,ODR     * }
8E00        # 000E #         POP   A         * restore A from the stack
E005        # 000F #         JMP   loop      * see if we want to print more
F000        # 0010 # done    HALT            * halt the program
```

G.13 Answers To Chapter 13

1 The program only prints dot characters, as an interrupt is never triggered and therefore the subroutine to display the time is never called.

2 Simply set the timer to trigger an interrupt every three seconds by updating the timer initialization to be like this:

```
9005        # 0002 #                MOVE #$05,A      *
A2EE        # 0003 #                MOVE A,TIMER     * initialize timer with 5 secs
```

3 Here is one possible solution:

```
             # 0000 # * Self Test Question 13-3
             # 0000 # * Uses a TRAP call to access the subroutine.
             # 0000 #
             # 0000 # ODR       EQU $E2      *
             # 0000 # OSR       EQU $E3      *
             # 0000 #
ORG $00F0    # 00F0 #           ORG $F0      * } set up vector table
0011         # 00F0 #           DC.W #handler * }
             # 00F1 #
ORG $0000    # 0000 #           ORG 0         * load program in memory at
             # 0000 #                         *    location 0
F300         # 0000 #           INTE          * enable interrupts
A6D0         # 0001 #           MOVE #$D0,SP  * initialize the stack pointer
             # 0002 #
9113         # 0002 #           MOVE #data,B  * point at data
9800         # 0003 # next      MOVE (B),A    * get a character
8000         # 0004 #           CMP #$0,A     * is this the terminator?
C309         # 0005 #           BEQ done      * yes - stop
FA00         # 0006 #           TRAP #$0      * trigger the level 0 interrupt
0101         # 0007 #           ADD #$1,B     * increment data address
E003         # 0008 #           JMP next      * repeat loop
F000         # 0009 # done      HALT          * halt the program
             # 000A #
             # 000A # *
             # 000A # * putchar routine (char in lo-byte of A)
             # 000A # *
8D00         # 000A # putchar   PUSH B        * save B on the stack
93E3         # 000B # _putch1   MOVE OSR,B    * move OSR to B
8100         # 000C #           CMP #$00,B    * can we print ?
C30B         # 000D #           BEQ _putch1   * if not, grab OSR again
A2E2         # 000E #           MOVE A,ODR    * otherwise print lo-byte of A
```

```
8F00        # 000F #           POP   B        * retrieve B from the stack
F100        # 0010 #           RTS            * return from subroutine
            # 0011 #
            # 0011 # * wrapper for trap 0
D00A        # 0011 # handler   JSR putchar * all we do is call the subroutine
FF00        # 0012 #           RTI            * return from interrupt
            # 0013 #
            # 0013 # * data string
            # 0013 # * (stored as unpacked ASCII)
0048        # 0013 # data      DC.W 0048      * H
0065        # 0014 #           DC.W 0065      * e
006C        # 0015 #           DC.W 006C      * l
006C        # 0016 #           DC.W 006C      * l
006F        # 0017 #           DC.W 006F      * o
0020        # 0018 #           DC.W 0020      *
0057        # 0019 #           DC.W 0057      * W
006F        # 001A #           DC.W 006F      * o
0072        # 001B #           DC.W 0072      * r
006C        # 001C #           DC.W 006C      * l
0064        # 001D #           DC.W 0064      * d
0021        # 001E #           DC.W 0021      * !
000D        # 001F #           DC.W 000D      * <cr>
000A        # 0020 #           DC.W 000A      * <lf>
0000        # 0021 #           DC.W 0000      * Terminator
```

G.14 Answers To Chapter 14

1 Once re-assembled to be loaded into memory from location $0010, all operands that refer to a memory location will have been updated. The program will run successfully from this new location.

2 Provided that you have successfully installed the JASP tools (see appendix A for details), then the following commands will create the machine code program that can then be executed in JASPer (use the advanced instruction set):

```
jcc < add.c-- > add.asm
jasm -a add.asm -o add.jas
```

3 Once the source program has been modified, you need to execute the same commands as listed above. On executing the program in JASPer (remember to use the advanced instruction set), you will see the new result displayed.

4 Here is the assembly language program of one possible solution:

```
* Self Test Question 14-4
* Displays the time in hexadecimal

SECS            EQU $E8
MINS            EQU $E9
HOURS           EQU $EA

                ORG $0

                MOVE #$D0,SP        * initialise stack pointer ($D0)

                MOVE #time,A        * move address of time string to A
                JSR  putstring      * jump to sub-routine putstring
                                    * (packed string)

                MOVE HOURS,A        * move hours value into A
                JSR  putbyte        * jump to sub-routine putbyte

                MOVE #$3a,B         * move a ':' into B
                JSR  putchar        * jump to sub-routine putchar

                MOVE MINS,A         * move mins value into A
                JSR  putbyte        * jump to sub-routine putbyte

                MOVE #complete,A * move address of complete string to A
                JSR  putstring      * jump to putstring routine
                HALT                * finished

                USE "basicio.lib"

time            DC.B 'The time is now ',0

complete        DC.B '\n',0
```

5 Here is the assembly language program of one possible solution:

```
* Self Test Question 14-5
* Takes a name from the user and prints it out.

SECS            EQU   $E8
```

```
MINS          EQU   $E9
HOURS         EQU   $EA

maxstring     EQU   $0A               * maximum string size is 10 chars

              ORG   $0                * set origin to 0
              MOVE  #$D0,SP           * initialize stack pointer ($D0)

              MOVE  #enter,A          * } print
              JSR   putstring         * }   'Enter your name : '


              MOVE  #namestore,A      * place address of namestore into A

              MOVE  #maxstring,B      * } initialize the char counter
              MOVE  B,count           * }    with maxstring
name_get
              PUSH  A                 * store A on the stack
              JSR   getchar           * get the char in A
              MOVE  A,B               * } move it to B
              JSR   putchar           * }   and print it
              POP   A                 * restore A from the stack
              CMP   #$0D,B            * see if is a CR
              BEQ   name_done         *   if it then the name is entered
              MOVE  B,(A)             * store the char
              ADD   #$01,A            * and index the storage
              MOVE  count,B           * }
              SUB   #$01,B            * } count = count - 1
              MOVE  B,count           * }
              CMP   #$00,B            * if we have hit the limit then
              BEQ   name_done         *   the name is entered
              JMP   name_get          * otherwise get more chars
name_done     MOVE  #cr,A             * } print '\n'
              JSR   putstring         * }
              MOVE  #$00,B            *   } add the terminator to the
              MOVE  B,(A)             *   }   name string

              MOVE  #hello,A          * } print 'Hello '
              JSR putstring           * }
              MOVE  #namestore,A      *   } print name
              JSR   putustring        *   }
              MOVE  #exclaim,A        * } print '!\n'
              JSR putstring           * }

              HALT                    * stop the program

* print unpacked string, assume start location in A
```

```
putustring   MOVE (A),B          * get a character
             CMP #$0,B           * is this the terminator?
             BEQ _pus_done       * yes - stop
             JSR  putchar        * otherwise print the character
             ADD #$1,A           * increment data address
             JMP putustring      * repeat
_pus_done    RTS                 * return from subroutine

             * include the basic library
             USE "basicio.lib"

count        DS.W 1              * keeps track of number of chars
namestore    DS.W $0B            * store for 10 chars + null terminator

enter        DC.B 'Enter your name : ',0
hello        DC.B 'Hello ',0
exclaim      DC.B '!\n',0
cr           DC.B '\n',0
```

G.15 Answers To Chapter 16

1 Here is the instruction definition:

```
Opcode f6
Mnemonic "MOVE -A,B"
Description "MOVE A to B, pre-decrement A"
ALUx<-[A]        *    }
ALUr=[ALUx]-1    *    } A = A-1
A<-[ALUr]        *    }
MDR<-[A]         * } B = A
B<-[MDR]         * }
```

2 Here is the test program:

```
# 0000 # * Self Test Question 16-2
```

```
              # 0000 # * A program to use our new instruction MOVE -A,B
              # 0000 #
ORG $0000     # 0000 #         ORG   0
9005          # 0000 #         MOVE  #$05,A      * initialize A with 5
9100          # 0001 #         MOVE  #$00,B      * initialize B with 0
F600          # 0002 #         MOVE  -A,B        * test our new instruction
F000          # 0003 #         HALT              * program complete
```

3 Here is the instruction definition:

```
Opcode f6
Mnemonic "MOVW #dataword,A"
Description "MOVW 16-bit word into A register"
MAR<-[PC]      * address of dataword now in MAR
INC<-[PC]      * } update PC for next fetch
PC<-[INC]      * }
MDR<-[M[MAR]]  * dataword now in MDR
A<-[MDR]       * dataword now in A
```

4 Here is the test program:

```
              # 0000 # * Self Test Question 16-4
              # 0000 # * A program to use our new instruction MOVE #dataword,B
              # 0000 #
ORG $0000     # 0000 #         ORG   0
F600          # 0000 #         MOVW  #$1234,A    * initialize A
1234          #      #
F000          # 0002 #         HALT              * program complete
```

G.16 Answers To Chapter 17

1 These are the micro-instructions executed by POP A:

▶ $ALUx \leftarrow [SP]$

- $ALUr = [ALUx] + 1$
- $SP \leftarrow [ALUr]$
- $MAR \leftarrow [SP]$
- $MDR \leftarrow [M[MAR]]$
- $A \leftarrow [MDR]$

Step	Register Output Enable											Register Clock													Memory	ALU Control Lines	ALU Data Bus Lines	Micro-instruction
	PC	INC	SP	IR	MAR	MDR	A	B	ALUx	ALUy	ALUr	PC	INC	SP	IR	MAR	MDR	A	B	ALUx	ALUy	ALUr	R/W	CS				
1	0	0	1	0	0	0	0	0	0	0	0	0	0	0	0	0	0	0	0	1	0	0	0	0	0	0	1	ALUx ← [SP]
2	0	0	0	0	0	0	0	0	0	0	0	0	0	0	0	0	0	0	0	0	0	1	0	0	0	1	0	ALUr = [ALUx]+1
3	0	0	0	0	0	0	0	0	0	0	1	0	0	1	0	0	0	0	0	0	0	0	0	0	0	0	1	SP ← [ALUr]
4	0	0	1	0	0	0	0	0	0	0	0	0	0	0	0	1	0	0	0	0	0	0	0	0	0	0	0	MAR ← [SP]
5	0	0	0	0	1	0	0	0	0	0	0	0	0	0	0	0	1	0	0	0	0	0	1	1	0	0	0	MDR ← [M[MAR]]
6	0	0	0	0	0	1	0	0	0	0	0	0	0	0	0	0	0	1	0	0	0	0	0	0	0	0	0	A ← [MDR]

Don't worry if you didn't fill in the fields for the ALU data bus lines - the definition of how these lines are used is in appendix A.

2 These are the micro-instructions executed by AND addr,A:

- $MAR \leftarrow [IR(operand)]$
- $MDR \leftarrow [M[MAR]]$
- $ALUy \leftarrow [MDR]$
- $ALUx \leftarrow [A]$
- $ALUr = [ALUx]\&[ALUy]$
- $A \leftarrow [ALUr]$

Step	Register Output Enable											Register Clock													Memory	ALU Control Lines	ALU Data Bus Lines	Micro-instruction
	PC	INC	SP	IR	MAR	MDR	A	B	ALUx	ALUy	ALUr	PC	INC	SP	IR	MAR	MDR	A	B	ALUx	ALUy	ALUr	R/W	CS				
1	0	0	0	1	0	0	0	0	0	0	0	0	0	0	0	1	0	0	0	0	0	0	0	0	0	0	0	MAR ← [IR(operand)]
2	0	0	0	0	1	0	0	0	0	0	0	0	0	0	0	0	1	0	0	0	0	0	1	1	0	0	0	MDR ← [M[MAR]]
3	0	0	0	0	0	1	0	0	0	0	0	0	0	0	0	0	0	0	0	0	1	0	0	0	0	0	1	ALUy ← [MDR]
4	0	0	0	0	0	0	1	0	0	0	0	0	0	0	0	0	0	0	0	1	0	0	0	0	0	0	1	ALUx ← [A]
5	0	0	0	0	0	0	0	0	0	0	0	0	0	0	0	0	0	0	0	0	0	1	0	0	0	1	0	ALUr = [ALUx]&[ALUy]
6	0	0	0	0	0	0	0	0	0	0	1	0	0	0	0	0	0	1	0	0	0	0	0	0	0	0	1	A ← [ALUr]

Bibliography

[Aga01] Jon Agar. *Turing And The Universal Machine*. Icon Books, 2001.

[BO03] Randal Bryant and David O'Halloran. *Computer Systems: A Programmer's Perspective*. Prentice Hall, 2003.

[CCW02] Sebastian Coope, John Cowley, and Neil Willis. *Computer Systems: Architecture, Networks And Communications*. McGraw Hill, 2002.

[Cha96] B. S. Chalk. *Computer Organisation And Architecture: An Introduction*. Palgrave, 1996.

[Cle00] Alan Clements. *The Principles of Computer Hardware*. Oxford University Press, 3rd edition, 2000.

[com02] *A Glossary Of Computing Terms*. Addison Wesley, 10th edition, 2002.

[Cri01] John Crisp. *Introduction To Microprocessors*. Newnes, 2001.

[Fey86] Richard Feynman. *Surely You're Joking, Mr. Feynman*. Unwin Paperbacks, 1986.

[Fey87] Richard Feynman. *What Do You Care What Other People Think?* Unwin Paperbacks, 1987.

[Fey99] Richard Feynman. *Lectures On Computation*. Penguin, 1999.

[Gib84] J. R. Gibson. *Electronic Logic Circuits*. Arnold, 2nd edition, 1984.

[Hod92] Andrew Hodges. *Alan Turing: The Enigma*. Vintage, 1992.

[HP02] John Hennessy and David Patterson. *Computer Architecture*. Morgan Kaufmann Publishers Inc, 3rd edition, 2002.

[HVZ02] Carl Hamacher, Zvonko Vranesic, and Safwat Zaky. *Computer Organization*. McGraw Hill, 5th edition, 2002.

[Kur92] Raymond Kurzweil. *The Age Of Intelligent Machines*. MIT Press, 1st edition, 1992.

[Lev94] Steven Levy. *Hackers: Heroes Of The Revolution*. Penguin, 1994.

[MH00] Miles Murdoca and Vincent Heuring. *Principles Of Computer Architecture*. Prentice Hall, 2000.

[NG99] Peter Norton and John Goodman. *Inside The PC*. SAMS, 8th edition, 1999.

[O'G00]   John O'Gorman. *Operating Systems*. MacMillan Press, 2000.

[PH98]   David Patterson and John Hennessy. *Computer Organization and Design*. Morgan Kaufmann Publishers Inc, 2nd edition, 1998.

[Pou92]   William Poundstone. *Prisoner's Dilemma*. Oxford University Press, 1992.

[RH00]   Raúl Rojas and Ulf Hashagen, editors. *The First Computers: History and Architectures*. The MIT Press, 2000.

[SACR91] Ian Sayers, Alan Adams, Graeme Chester, and Adrian Robson. *Principles of Microprocessors*. CRC Press Inc, 1991.

[SFK97]   Dezsö Sima, Terence Fountain, and Péter Kacsuk. *Advanced Computer Architectures: A Design Space Approach*. Addison-Wesley, 1997.

[SOC97]   Randal L. Schwartz, Erik Olson, and Tom Christiansen. *Learning PERL on Win32 Systems*. O Reilly, 1997.

[Sta03]   William Stallings. *Computer Organization And Architecture*. Prentice Hall, 6th edition, 2003.

[Tan99]   Andrew Tanenbaum. *Structured Computer Organization*. Prentice Hall, 4th edition, 1999.

[Tan01]   Andrew Tanenbaum. *Modern Operating Systems*. Prentice Hall, 2nd edition, 2001.

[TT00]   Robert Bruce Thompson and Barbara Fritchman Thompson. *PC Hardware In A Nutshell*. O'Reilly, 1st edition, 2000.

[Tur36]   Alan M. Turing. On computable numbers, with an application to the entscheidungsproblem. *Proceedings Of The London Mathematical Society*, pages 230–265, November 1936.

[vN00]   John von Neumann. *The Computer And The Brain*. Yale University Press, 2000.

[Wil01]   Rob Williams. *Computer Systems Architecture: A Networking Approach*. Addison-Wesley, 2001.